The Essential Guide to the Business & Law of Esports & Professional Video Gaming

7/14/22

THANKS FOR THE SUPPORT!

YOUR FRIEND,

The Essential Guide to the Business & Law of Esports & Professional Video Gaming

Justin M. Jacobson, Esq.

CRC Press is an imprint of the
Taylor & Francis Group, an informa business

First edition published 2021
by CRC Press
6000 Broken Sound Parkway NW, Suite 300, Boca Raton, FL 33487-2742

and by CRC Press
2 Park Square, Milton Park, Abingdon, Oxon, OX14 4RN

© 2021 Justin M. Jacobson, Esq.

The right of Justin M. Jacobson, Esq. to be identified as the author[/s] of the editorial material, and of the authors for their individual chapters, has been asserted in accordance with sections 77 and 78 of the Copyright, Designs and Patents Act 1988.

Reasonable efforts have been made to publish reliable data and information, but the author and publisher cannot assume responsibility for the validity of all materials or the consequences of their use. The authors and publishers have attempted to trace the copyright holders of all material reproduced in this publication and apologize to copyright holders if permission to publish in this form has not been obtained. If any copyright material has not been acknowledged please write and let us know so we may rectify in any future reprint.

Except as permitted under U.S. Copyright Law, no part of this book may be reprinted, reproduced, transmitted, or utilized in any form by any electronic, mechanical, or other means, now known or hereafter invented, including photocopying, microfilming, and recording, or in any information storage or retrieval system, without written permission from the publishers.

For permission to photocopy or use material electronically from this work, access www.copyright.com or contact the Copyright Clearance Center, Inc. (CCC), 222 Rosewood Drive, Danvers, MA 01923, 978-750-8400. For works that are not available on CCC please contact mpkbookspermissions@tandf.co.uk.

Trademark notice: Product or corporate names may be trademarks or registered trademarks and are used only for identification and explanation without intent to infringe.

ISBN: 978-0-367-69945-1 (hbk)
ISBN: 978-0-367-67512-7 (pbk)
ISBN: 978-1-003-14396-3 (ebk)

Typeset in Garamond
by Deanta Global Publishing Services, Chennai, India

To my Perri.

Contents

Preface

Coming from the traditional entertainment and sports world and being a life-long gamer (I still "game" in some form each day); I saw a natural fit within the esports and professional gaming space which complemented my experience, expertise and knowledge. When I began working with professional gaming talent and negotiating their player contracts with professional organizations about five years ago, I noticed many similarities between the legal and business needs of the individuals within the gaming world and those within the music and sports worlds that I was already working in. Starting on the talent side of esports, I worked directly and indirectly with many established esports talent agencies. This is where I developed my own repertoire and familiarity with professional gamers, streamers, coaches, and team owners and their contracts. Since my initial start, I have successfully negotiated many professional gamer and coach contracts for five- and six-figure yearly salaries. This included player contracts for professionals in franchise leagues such as the *Overwatch League*, *Overwatch Contenders*, and *Call of Duty League* with teams such as New York, Chicago, and Seattle as well as securing professional player deals with many of the world's top esports organizations and teams (both existing and now defunct) in almost every existing competitive titles, such as *Fortnite*, *CS:GO*, *Halo*, *Gears of War*, *Rainbow Six*, *PUBG*, *Madden*, and *League of Legends*. Some of these organizations include Counter Logic Gaming, Luminosity Gaming, Cloud9, FaZe Clan, Rogue, Immortals, Optic Gaming, NRG Esports, XSET, and many others. I have also acted as in-house counsel for several esports small and established organizations, including preparing a multi-million dollar franchise bid as well as successfully negotiated sponsorship deals for both established endemic and non-endemic brands with organizations within the space. In creating this work, I wanted to give a special thank-you to some pioneers in the esports legal and business space, colleagues of mine who formulated a working body, including Bryce Blum, Harris Peskin, Krista Hiner, Roger Quiles, ESG Law, the Esports Bar Association, and the rest of the budding professional community. I would also like to thank my mom, dad, and sister Sari for their endless support. With this experience, I present a glimpse into some important matters that a professional in the esports world should be aware of. This is by no means exhaustive and with the ever-evolving state of the industry, updates will be frequent; rather, this book is intended to provide a framework of what a person should know. This book is intended to be read from start to finish as each section progresses and builds on prior literature. Also, the negotiation tactics are meant to provide a little insight into some potential reasonable requests that may be presented from both parties in the deal. They are by no means legal advice as every situation is different and requires its own specific analysis. Without further ado, I present "the" guide.

About the Author

Justin M. Jacobson, Esq. is an entertainment and esports attorney located in New York City. For the last decade, he has worked with professional athletes, musicians, and fashion designers, as well as professional gamers, streamers, coaches, on-air talent, and esports organizations. He assists these individuals with their contract, copyright, trademark, immigration, tax, and other related business, marketing, and legal issues. He has been featured on a variety of entertainment, music, and esports publications and podcasts, including *Business Insider*, *The Esports Observer*, *Esports Insider*, *Tunecore*, and *Sport Techie*. He works with gaming talent in a variety of franchise leagues including the Overwatch League, and Call of Duty Pro League, as well as in many popular titles such as *Fortnite*, *Counter-Strike: Global Offensive*, *Gears of War*, *Halo*, *PlayerUnknown's Battlegrounds*, and *Madden*.

1

Introduction to Esports & Professional Video Gaming Law

With the advent of innovative technologies, today's global entertainment market continues to evolve creating new forms of entertainment. This includes the development and world-wide growth of competitive video gaming or "esports." In the last few years, "electronic sports" or "esports" have transitioned to the mainstream with professional video gamers competing in a variety of console, mobile and computer games against other professionals for substantial sums of money on a world-wide basis.

This book explores the various intricacies of esports and professional video game law as well as the associated business matters surrounding this new entertainment field. It will focus on the main "players" in the esports business landscape, including the event organizers, game developers, professional gamers, coaches, analysts, gaming content creators, streamers and shoutcasters. Professional esports teams and organizations as well as other matters related to the legal and business side of esports and professional competitive video gaming will be explored.

This book also highlights some of the recent legal and business developments that have emerged due to the continued international expansion and viewership growth of professional gaming. It is meant to ensure the reader receives a full understanding of the trends that are dominating today's competitive gaming landscape and how to best navigate as well as tackle them both legally and properly.

1.1 A Brief History of Esports and Competitive Gaming

While there is no "official" history of esports and the competitive videogame world, the following is meant to be a compilation highlighting a selection of monumental events throughout the history of competitive gaming. These series of events have molded today's professional competitive gaming scene and shaped the growing business world surrounding it. Many sources agree that the first video game competition occurred on October 19, 1972, at *Stanford University.*[1] This first competition was for the computer game *Spacewar.*[2] The event provided the eventual winner, Bruce Baumgart, with a year's subscription to *Rolling Stone* magazine.[3] The next large gaming event occurred in 1980 with Atari's *Space Invaders* Championship.[4] The event attracted over 10,000 players with Rebecca Heineman emerging victorious and was an early glimpse into what the competitive scene could be.[5]

Following the previous year's success, the 1981 Atari World Championship occurred featuring a $50,000 total prize pool with $20,000 of it being provided to the event winner.[6] In a common occurrence within the early days of the esports industry, the report was that the actual "tournament is a disaster" with the "prize-money cheque bounc[ing]" causing Atari to sue the event organizer.[7] Around the same time, the iconic Twin Galaxies was created by Walter Day.[8] Twin Galaxies was an organization that recorded and tracked the "world records" for video games.[9] This included verifying and compiling the "official" list of the "highest scores" for various arcade games, such as *Pac-Man* and *Donkey Kong.*[10] The chase and competition for "top scores" caused the creation of the first wave of television shows, including "*Starcade* in the United States and *First Class* in the United Kingdom."[11] These television programs "pitted players against each other in competitive gaming to battle for [the] high[er] score."[12] For example, *Starcade* provided each contestant with "30– or 50 seconds of time" to try to beat their opponent's score in a particular game.[13]

The budding interest from the mainstream media and entertainment worlds as well as the vast collection of "high score" records curated by Twin Galaxies led businessman Jim Riley to create the Electronic Circus tour.[14] The Electronic Circus was intended to be what many of today's music festivals actually are, a large attraction that included live musical performances, a giant video-game "arcade with 500 cabinets" and a "Superstar Pro Tour" featuring some of the country's best video gamers.[15] While, the overall production was not as successful as intended, the event was important as it marked the first time in history that an individual was paid a "wage to play a video game at a high level."[16]

From there, the competition for "high scores" continued to rage on with certain gamers setting themselves apart from the rest. This led to another momentous event in the development of professional gaming, the creation of the *U.S. National Video Game Team* (*USNVGT*).[17] In July 1983, Walter Day gathered some of the nation's top gamers to form the aforementioned *USNVGT* in an effort to monetize the mounting interest in competitive gaming.[18] Some of the initial team members were Ben Gold, Billy Mitchell (the *Donkey Kong* legend)[19], Jay Kim, Steve Harris and Tim McVey.[20] The team began by going city to city to raise "money to fight cystic fibrosis" as well as operating their own Video Game Masters Tournament intended to "uncover future stars" for their gaming team.[21]

A few years later, in 1987, Walter Day had left the *USNVGT* and, in the same year, the new team captain, Donn Nauert secured a rare paid promotional opportunity for the "*Atari 7800* console."[22] The marketing campaign included "a series of [television] commercials" featuring Nauert.[23] Nauert's sponsorship opportunity was important in the growth of the esports business "ecosystem" as it set a precedent of utilizing notable gamers in a company's product marketing campaign. Also, in an effort to further expand their reach and impact upon the gaming world, the *USNVGT* formed the *Electronic Gaming Monthly*, a publication that was eventually acquired by Ziff Davis.[24]

As gaming continued to grow in notoriety, the notion of large competitive video game tournaments for substantial prize money was cultivated along with it. Eventually, in 1988, the television show *That's Incredible!* featured a segment with *USNVGT* members acting as the judges for three teenage gamers competing against each other in a series of various Nintendo games.[25] The winner of this competition, Jason Reynolds, was later put on "cereal boxes" and potentially inspired the motion picture *The Wizard*.[26] The movie starred Fred Savage and featured a "$50,000 gaming tournament" that the actor intended to compete in.[27] The motion picture ended up being a significant "marketing tool for Nintendo."[28] Additionally, the movie's premise may have also laid the foundation for the next big moment in the evolution of professional gaming, the 1990 Nintendo World Championship.[29]

In 1990, the Nintendo World Championship tour visited "29 U.S. cities" with more than "8,000 players competing each weekend."[30] The tournament featured the gamers competing against each other in a few Nintendo games to see who could achieve the highest scores, including playing "*Super*

Mario Brothers 3, Rad Racer and *Tetris.*"[31] The event was an early example of the large gaming tournament concept expressed in the motion picture and laid a blueprint for future esports event organizers to follow. Later, in 1994, building off the previous tournament's success, Nintendo held another world championship, the Nintendo PowerFest '94, known as "Nintendo World Champions II," to promote the release of their new gaming console, Super N.E.S.[32] During the competition, the various top gamers battled in a variety of titles, including *Super Mario Brothers: The Lost Levels, Super Mario Kart* and *Ken Griffey Jr. Home Run Derby.*[33]

While Nintendo was leading the way with gaming consoles, new gaming genres began to steal the show and helped move the professional scene forward. For instance, in 1991, another monumental change in the competitive digital gaming scene occurred with the release of *Super Street Fighter II.*[34] *Street Fighter II* was significant as it became one of the first "player versus player" (PVP) competitive titles.[35] Previously, all competitive gaming tournaments and events were focused on beating an opponent's "high score" in a specific game. However, the newly created genre of "fighting games" actually positioned one competitor directly against another one to determine a winner.[36] This was a perfect set-up to captivate fans and begin to allow the competitor to focus on beating their direct opponent while showcasing their "incredible reaction speeds, frame-perfect timing [and] deep, calculated strategy."[37] Eventually, in 1996, the first major *Street Fighter* tournament, the *Battle by the Bay* took place in California; and, eventually grew into an annual "fighting game" competition.[38] This annual "fighting game" event later evolved into the aptly named, Evolution Championship Series (Evo).[39]

Additionally, another emerging gaming genre was brought to the competitive scene due to the development and advancement of personal computers (PCs), the "first-person shooter" (FPS). This new game type first arrived on the scene in 1991 with the game publisher, id Software's *Quake.*[40] *Quake* was the first time that the "idea of [in-game] maps being designed specifically for online multiplayer" became popular, which was a driving force in shaping the FPS esports community and its fan base.[41] *Quake* was followed by more advanced FPS titles from id Software, including *Wolfstein 3D* in 1992, *Doom 1* in 1993 and *Doom 2* in 1994.[42] The emergence of this new game genre continued to focus on the exciting "one versus one battling" featured in various fighting games and it helped further move esports toward what it is today.

In 1997, another seismic shift in the competitive gaming landscape occurred with the iconic *Quake* match coined the "Red Annihilation."[43] This memorable *Quake* match pitted Dennis "Thresh" Fong against Tom

"Entropy" Kimze.[44] Due to the advancement of internet speed, over 2000 gamers entered the competition and faced each other in one-on-one *Quake* battles until the field was narrowed down to the final 16 players.[45] These finalists were then all flown into Atlanta, Georgia to compete against each other at the Electronic Entertainment Expo (E3).[46] Dennis "Thresh" Fong eventually won the tournament by "pick[ing] apart Entropy" in the finals to earn *Quake* programmer John D. Carmack's *Ferarri 328 GTS*.[47] This event was important in the development of esports as it demonstrated the potential mainstream interest and excitement that a live gaming event could create as it was viewed by in-person spectators as well as received online, newspaper and television network coverage.[48]

As the interest in competitive gaming continued to develop, a series of organized professional leagues were created hoping to capitalize on the growing interest in live gaming events. One such organized league was the *Cyberathlete Professional League* (*CPL*).[49] In 1997, the *CPL* was created by Angel Munoz and the league "consider[ed] itself the N.F.L. of head-to-head computer gaming."[50] The league operated for many years and was the breeding ground for many esports professionals, including Johnathan "Fatal1ty" Wendel.[51] In the same year, another league, the *Professional Gamers League* (*PGL*) was created by Total Entertainment Network.[52] The *PGL* was initially sponsored by computer processor developer, AMD, electronics company, Logitech and modem maker, U.S. Robotics.[53] Meanwhile, at the same time in Germany, the *Deutsche Clanliga* (DeCL) was formed.[54] In 2000, this "clan" eventually became the event organizer Electronic Sports League (ESL).[55] The esports event organizer ESL was originally owned by Turtle Entertainment but it was more recently sold to the Modern Times Group (MTG).[56]

In 1998, a year after the "Red Annihilation," one of the largest catalysts in international esports development occurred. This was the release of Blizzard Entertainment's "real time strategy" (RTS) game *StarCraft* and its later expansion edition, *StarCraft: Brood War*.[57] This new competitive title led to the development of an enormous competitive gaming scene in South Korea.[58] The level of interest was so high that the South Korean government even formed the Korean e-Sports Association (KeSPA) to regulate the esports industry.[59] *KeSPA* was formed for a variety of reasons.[60] Some of these included to regulate professional gamers' salaries; to negotiate fees "with broadcasters;" as well as to issue professional "licenses" to competitive players through its "ladder" system.[61] The explosion of esports in South Korea due to the release of *StarCraft* brought many firsts for professional gamers desiring to embark on a competitive gaming career.[62] For instance,

StarCraft superstar, Lim "BoXeR" Yo-hwan was the earliest gamer to negotiate a sizable six-figure salary (and later salary increases to "well over $250,000 a year").[63] He was also the first individual to establish his own competitive team, which was later purchased by the telecommunications company SK Telecom.[64]

In 1999, the competitive gaming world was further sculpted with the emergence of additional FPS titles such as *Unreal Tournament* and *Counter-Strike*.[65] These new games, in particular *Counter-Strike*, continued to shape the entire esports landscape by capitalizing on the growing third-party interest in organized video-game competitions. In fact, entire fan "communities" began to develop and modify existing games to increase the "skill ceiling" involved in playing a particular game.[66] One title that underwent a fan-modified birth was *Counter-Strike*.[67] *Counter-Strike* is a modification or "mod" of Valve Software's existing *Half Life* game and it took gaming communities by storm.[68] In particular, the *Counter-Strike* mod helped create "esports' first megahit" by establishing a new game sub-genre that had not previously existed, the "team multiplayer FPS."[69] Previously, most competitive FPS games were only "one on one" contests like *Quake* but *Counter-Strike* created a FPS title that consisted of two multi-member teams battling each other.[70] Due to the widespread online success of the mod, the developer Valve Software purchased the rights to it from its creators and hired them to continue creating and developing the game.[71]

In April 2000, another step in the monetization of a professional gamer's career transpired. Specifically, the 2000 Razer CPL occurred and featured *Quake 3*'s "Arena" mode that was designed explicitly for multiplayer combat.[72] This event was significant as it had a total prize pool of over "$100,000" with "$40,000" going to the eventual winner, Johnathan "Fatal1ty" Wendel.[73] Wendel then used his prize winnings to begin building his own personal brand, including creating "mouse mats, headsets, motherboards and shoes" featuring his name and likeness.[74] This was a milestone in the development of esports business as it was the first instance where a professional gamer began utilizing his own funds to monetize and profit off his own name and likeness.[75] In addition, as a result of his growing notoriety, Wendel received substantial mainstream U.S. media coverage.[76] This included being featured in *MTV's True Life* series "I'm A Gamer," appearing on the iconic U.S. television show *60 Minutes* as well as being highlighted in the *New York Times*.[77]

In the same year, the esports world continued its international expansion with the first World Cyber Games (WCG).[78] This event was important in the development of the esports business ecosystem because it was considered by many to be "the first real international eSports tournament" and it helped to lay the foundation for subsequent esports events to follow.[79] The Games attempted to "fashion itself as an Olympics of e-sports."[80] The first WCG consisted of "430 players from 37 nations" competing in six different games, including in *StarCraft: Brood War, Counter-Strike, Quake 3, Unreal Tournament, Ages of Empire II* and *FIFA 2000*.[81]

In the following year, the growing *CPL* hosted its 2001 World Championship with a total prize pool of "$150,000" sponsored by the technology company *Intel*.[82] In this year, due to its growing fan base, *Counter-Strike* had risen to a "premier event" when it had previously only been incorporated into just one of the prior "*CPL* Events."[83] The overall success of the event caused more expansion into the competitive side of *Counter-Strike*, including the creation of an online league, the *Domain of Games* that eventually became part of the *CPL* operating as the Cyberathlete Amateur League (CAL).[84] In 2002, another key player, Major League Gaming (MLG) was created to operate competitive gaming events within the United States for console games such as *Halo* and *Super Smash Brothers Melee*.[85]

After the launch of *Super Smash Brothers* on Nintendo 64 in 1999, two years later in 2001, the next installment, *Super Smash Brothers Melee* was released on Nintendo's GameCube.[86] This updated game created a new competitive title within the "fighting gaming" community, *Super Smash Brother Melee*, which had a lasting effect on its scene.[87] The *Smash Brothers* competitive gaming scene had its ups and downs throughout the different reiterations of the title on Nintendo's subsequent platforms, including *Super Smash Brothers Brawl* on Nintendo Wii and the latest title, *Super Smash Brothers Ultimate* on Nintendo Switch but its emergence created a new gaming circuit with familiar characters such as Mario and Luigi.[88] However, a turning point in establishing this fighting game's competitive scene happened in 2004 when the game was added to MLG for its New York final.[89] While MLG eventually dropped *Melee* from its tournaments in 2007, the event producer, Evo, quickly added the game to its event roster to keep the *Smash Brothers Melee* competitive scene alive.[90] Eventually, the 2013 Evo event drew a substantial competitor pool becoming one of the largest *Melee* tournaments ever.[91] Finally, in 2019, Evo officially dropped *Smash Brothers Melee* from its competitive circuit in favor of Nintendo's newer version, *Super Smash Brothers Ultimate* on its Nintendo Switch console.[92] The history of *Smash Brothers'* competitive scene is so compelling that it sparked the 2013 documentary *The Smash Brothers* and is an example of how a passionate community can keep a competitive title profitable many years beyond its initial release.[93] Also, *The*

Smash Brothers documentary is considered to be "one of the greatest esports documentaries of all time" as it highlights the voyage that the title has taken to spotlight its unique place within esports and demonstrates another way in which young gaming entrepreneurs are attempting to monetize the gaming world around them.[94]

At the same time as competition organizers were being established, some savvy business owners within the esports ecosystem began ensuring that their business was handled properly due to the rapidly growing total prize pools and the expanding worldwide competitive circuit. For instance, in 2003, the German *Quake* team *SK Gaming* became the first "non-Korean organization" to execute written agreements with its gamers.[95] A year later, another unique business transaction occurred with the first "real transfer" of a professional gamer with *Counter-Strike* player Ola "Element" Moum being sent from *SK Gaming* to *Team NoA*.[96] Furthermore, the growing *Counter-Strike* competitive scene helped esports take another crucial step in professionalization and building a workable business ecosystem with many competitive *Counter-Strike* teams beginning to pay their "players a salary" for competing on behalf of them.[97]

In addition, during these years, the total global esports business space continued to expand with a sudden increase in frequency of large "international" competitions for more sizable prize pools in a variety of gaming titles. For example, in 2003, the first Electronic Sports World Cup (ESWC) occurred in France.[98] The ESWC provided a "$156,000" total prize pool and featured "358 players from 37 different countries" competing in several games including *Warcraft 3*, *Quake 3* and *Counter-Strike*.[99] The following year, another pivotal event in the competitive gaming industry occurred, the 2004 World Cyber Games (WCG) in San Francisco.[100] The event showcased the magnitude that professional gaming had reached as it featured over "600 gamers from 62 different countries" competing in "eight different games" with American team "*Team 3D*" winning the *Counter-Strike* event.[101] Four years later in 2008, the World Cyber Games in Germany continued its growth with over "800 players from 78 countries" competing "in 14 official events."[102] These were a few examples of the growing global marketplace for competitive gaming as the professional esports business world continued to flourish with the addition of more professional gamers competing for more frequent and significant prize money as well as for international glory and prestige.

The next few years saw a growth in the esports business ecosystem with an increase in event exposure as well as in the prize money with the amounts "almost tripling between 2004 and 2007."[103] During this same time period there were some notable milestones, including some mainstream television coverage as well as a seven-figure prize pool. One of these memorable events is known as the "*Evo Moment 37*," which occurred at the 2004 Evolution Championship Series for the title, *Street Fighter III: 3rd Strike*.[104] That match is considered by some as "esports' most thrilling moment."[105] It featured competitive gamer Justin Wong facing off against Daigo "The Beast" Umehara.[106] Umehara ultimately won the match by defeating Wong by parrying "15 hits" from his opponent while having almost no "health" left on his in-game character.[107] This moment received substantial online notoriety and coverage, including receiving more than "20 million views worldwide."[108] It also provided another look into the skill and the intensity level that competitive gaming can create in addition to the substantial exposure that brands and players involved in these events could garner.[109]

In addition, the 2005 *Cyberathlete Professional League (CPL) World Tour* marked another milestone in the growth of the professional gaming business.[110] The 2005 *CPL World Tour* was for the FPS gaming title, *Painkiller*.[111] The tour spanned "eight months and four continents," had a $1 million total prize pool and the finals were even live on television network MTV (with Fatal1ty winning the $150,000 grand prize).[112] The $1 million total prize pool proved just how far competitive gaming events had come from its origins and further substantiated the validity of a potential career in esports. A year later in 2006, another esports event organizer, the World Series of Video Games (WSVG) was created by Matt Ringel to act as a competitor to the *CPL*.[113] The WSVG initially succeeded as the *CPL* began to "struggle" and the organization was even able to attract prominent sponsors such as Intel and Nestle for its event, including for its 2006 Intel Summer Championship.[114]

Due to the rising popularity in esports, some event producers in the space began looking for television broadcast deals to increase their potential earning power.[115] For instance, the operator of ESL, Turtle Entertainment acquired rights for "NBC GIGA," a television network focused "on video games."[116] Similarly, in July 2006, event organizer MLG started to televise its events for the FPS title *Halo* on the USA Network television station.[117] Building off of MLG's foray into television as well as the success of a few "one-off specials" featuring the WSVG on *MTV* and *CBS*, DirecTV began the first true venture into creating and televising an organized league with established city-based franchises (similar to what Activision-Blizzard has created for the *Overwatch League*).[118] The television series was called *The Championship Gaming Series* (*CGS*) and it included "seventy-five competitors and four teams" competing for "$50,000."[119] In addition, as a further example of how far the professional side of the competitive gaming industry had come, DirecTV was also "pay[ing all] the players" a salary, flying them across the country to compete, "put[ting] them up in hotels;" and, even, providing them with "spending money."[120] To say that this experiment was a failure is an understatement, as the *CGS* attempt at a "big twist" was to "make the competition multi-title" instead of just one game.[121] However, after spending the reportedly "$50 million [budget] for the project," the league eventually folded for a variety of reasons.[122] Some of these included the fact that many of the games they picked "lacked a [supportive fan] community behind them."[123] Another fatal mistake was the widespread fan resistance to the changing of the "rules for *Counter-Strike*," which some fans claimed "wrecked the game's strategy."[124]

During this time, there were other attempts by game publishers and event organizers to capitalize on the increased potential television audience. This included in 2007 when television broadcaster CBS aired the "the World Series of Video Games tournament."[125] Similarly, from 2005 until 2008 the U.S. sports television network ESPN, in partnership with game publisher Electronic Arts (EA) broadcasted *Madden Nation*.[126] This was a televised series of competitive *Madden* football games on their ESPN2 cable network.[127] These examples were in addition to other U.S. cable networks such as "*Spike*, *ESPN* and *USA*" that had "occasionally shown game coverage" as well as other smaller television networks such as "*G4* and *Gameplay HD*" that had solely focused on "gaming culture."[128]

In April 2006, the professionalization of the esports world continued with the creation of additional esports associations intended to govern competitive play. While *KeSPA* has been functioning in South Korea for several years, the first non-Korean esports association focusing on professionalizing the gaming space was formed, the *G7 Federation*.[129] The association was formed by seven top *Counter-Strike: Global Offensive (CS:GO)* teams, including *Fnatic*, *Made in Brazil (MIB)*, *Mousesports*, *Ninjas In Pyjamas* (NiP) and *SK Gaming* in an effort to improve events, "promote cooperation" between its members and to impose sanctions on any event organizers that failed to pay out prize money.[130] The association eventually folded but it helped lead the way for later esports associations and other governing bodies to form.[131] Similarly in August of 2008, the international eSports Federation (ieSF) was founded by "nine-member nations from Europe and Asia" in an effort to "work with commercial and governmental partners toward steady growth" in esports.[132] Esports professional associations and organizations are discussed in Chapter 6.

In 2010, the entire competitive gaming landscape experienced yet another monumental change and continued its voyage toward becoming an entertainment business force with the release of the real-time strategy (RTS) game *StarCraft II*.[133] The new game was Activision-Blizzard's follow-up title to the extremely successful predecessor titles, *StarCraft* and *StarCraft: Brood War*.[134] *StarCraft II* (*SC2*) took the competitive gaming world by storm and elevated many facets of the existing esports business ecosystem.[135] Initially, many competitive *StarCraft* players received the new game with "a lot of skepticism;" so, it took a little while for *StarCraft II* to catch on within the professional circuit.[136] However, once legendary *StarCraft* player Lim "BoXeR" Yo-hwan "crosses the floor" and starts playing *StarCraft II*, the floodgates open and the rest is history.[137] The huge interest caused its publisher Activision-Blizzard to negotiate an exclusive "online broadcast deal with *GOMTV*" for all of the *StarCraft II* competitions in South Korea as the title's competitive play was "predominantly shown online" as opposed to on traditional broadcast television.[138] The title marks another milestone in the growing business of professional gaming as the events were highly successful and lucrative for the game publisher as well as for the other parties involved.[139] In addition, the title boosted an ever growing prize pool that at first in 2010 was "around $280,000" and, eventually, grew to "$3.2 million" the following year.[140] This substantial prize money included winnings from the newly organized *Global StarCraft II League* (*GSL*).[141] The *GSL* was televised in South Korea and provided over $500,000 in total prize money to its competitors.[142] *StarCraft II* also brought the "highest-earning female esports athlete of all time" to the scene, Sasha "Scarlett" Hostyn.[143] Scarlett's success and demeanor helped further re-shape the "esports stereotype" and opened new lanes for future female gamers to follow her path toward a competitive gaming career.[144]

While many event, league and tournament organizers were initially solely focused on distributing esports competitions on television, another electronic medium appeared and ended up becoming a colossal catalyst in bringing the competitive gaming business ecosystem forward toward establishing a more stable business model. In 2011, at the same time that the competitive *StarCraft* II scene was gaining international traction, the live streaming website *Justin.tv* was founded.[145] In 2013, Justin.tv launched the "Twitch" gaming division paving the way for esports' exponential growth and, as they say, the rest is history.[146] Twitch was instrumental in the growth of esports as the platform provided easy, stable and inexpensive access to livestreaming so that "anybody could stream" and everybody did.[147] As a result, professional gamers as well as tournament organizers (including ESL and Evo) began utilizing Twitch to "broadcast their training" sessions and, eventually, to webcast their actual live gaming competitions.[148] The company even acquired the exclusive globe rights to "broadcast *GOMTV's GSL*."[149] In addition to a stable presentation, the Twitch platform provided in-depth viewership analytics.[150] This made the platform instrumental in securing sponsorships and brand partnerships, which is one of today's largest and most dominant streams of income across all of the various stakeholders in the esports business world.[151] Twitch was eventually purchased by Amazon in 2014 for "$970 million" and is still one of the most important driving forces in the esports business industry.[152]

In addition to providing a steady outlet for fans to watch competitive gaming, the use of Twitch by professional gamers such as *StarCraft II* player Sean "Day9" Plott, helped create a new revenue stream for gamers, the Twitch "subscription" (which is still a substantial stream for many Twitch streamers).[153] In fact, Plott initially received "droves" of fans donating funds to him "via *Paypal*" for the great content that he was producing on Twitch.[154] In response to these fans' actions, he reportedly "suggest[ed]" to Twitch to include "some sort of subscription model for fans to connect with streamers" that "unlock[ed] extra perks."[155] This led to Twitch*'s* eventual inclusion of this suggested "subscription" system that has now become an essential income stream for most professionals within the esports and gaming space.[156] Plott is noted as becoming the "first Twitch partner to receive a subscription button" as his insight helped grow the professional side of gaming.[157]

The previous era that was dominated by RTS games, such as *StarCraft* and *WarCraft 3*, was drawing to a close with the rise of a new genre, the "multi-player online battle arena" (MOBA).[158] In particular, in 2009, game developer Riot Games catapulted esports forward with the release of its free-to-play (F2P) game, *League of Legends* (*LOL*).[159] *League of Legends* was an instant hit with "11.5 million monthly players" by 2011 and by 2014, it had over "67 million" active gamers (and currently has over "100 million").[160] At the same time, another similar MOBA game *Dota* and its eventual successor *Dota 2* joined *LOL* at the forefront of competitive gaming.[161] Both games were important in the fostering and stabilizing of the esports ecosystem, including through the creation of a professional franchise league in *LoL*[162] and with the substantial "crowd-funded" multi-million dollar prize pools offered in *Dota 2*.[163] Both titles continued elevating the entire professional gaming world and, eventually, in 2008, the ESWC featured the first competitive *Dota* tournament showcasing the potential viability of the title.[164]

In later years, both MOBA titles continued to grow with Valve's The International annual competition for *Dota 2*[165] and with Riot Games' World Championships for *League of Legends*.[166]

These games helped create stable sizable income streams for professionals involved in the various aspects of esports business. This included esports organizations earning larger prize money and having more constancy in their operations as well as the competitive players who began earning larger salaries and more tournament winnings.[167] For instance, the 2011 *International* for *Dota 2* had the "astronomical prize pool of $1.6 million," which has grown every year since.[168] Competitive *League of Legends* was first added to the *Intel Extreme Masters*, operated by Turtle Entertainment (the owners of ESL).[169] A year later, building off their previous success, publisher Riot Games created its own franchise league, the *League of Legends* Championship Series (LCS).[170] The new publisher-operated league was directly supported and administered by the game developer.[171] It was created to attempt to bring "stability to the eSports scene" while incorporating a "more spectator friendly" gameplay.[172] The LCS continued to grow in the following years; and, from that point forward, the title was involved in some of the largest milestones in the development of the global professional gaming business. For instance, in 2013, the *League of Legends* World Championship for Season 3 was held at a sold-out Staples Center in Los Angeles, California.[173] The following year saw an even larger growth in the scale of esports live events with the 2014 *League of Legends* World Championship in Seoul, South Korea.[174] That event had over 40,000 fans in attendance and featured a live performance by the band Imagine Dragons.[175] Another indicator of where the title had risen to was the viewership of 2018 *League of Legends*' World Finals, which had "nearly 100 million viewers."[176] Needless to say with the arrival of these two MOBA titles, the esports professional ecosystem was moving toward a more predictable and workable business model for all of its stakeholders.

In 2012, at the same time that MOBA games were making their mark in esports, Valve released their new FPS title, *Counter-Strike: Global Offensive*. This title was released as an attempt to bring together the opposing two scenes that had emerged within its previous *Counter-Strike* title.[177] In particular, there had been two notorious "mods" of *Counter-Strike*, *Counter-Strike 1.6*, and *Counter-Strike: Source*, whose fans both felt their "game was better."[178] The release of *CS:GO* was a success and it showed how a game publisher could succeed with active involvement in supporting and understanding their "community."[179] In fact, in 2015, a few years after its release, the game was the "second most played" game on *Twitch*.[180] The FPS title also had an evergrowing prize pool which was initially at "$250,000;" and, by 2016, had grown to its "first $1 million tournament" at MLG's Columbus event.[181]

In 2014, Microsoft launched the "*Halo Championship Series*" (*HCS*), which was an "organized esports league" for its FPS console series *Halo*.[182] This established another competitive console game circuit for professionals to compete in and for teams to generate revenues from. This was followed by another new FPS title from gaming publisher Blizzard-Activision, *Overwatch*.[183] In fact, at BlizzCon 2016, the developer revealed that they planned to implement a geographic-based franchise league system for its competitive *Overwatch* esports scene, which is explored in detail later.[184]

In addition to the development of various genres, there was also a budding competitive sports simulation game scene. This included popular titles such as *Madden* football, *FIFA* soccer, and *NBA 2K* basketball. Each of these titles created their own esports circuits, including the *FIFA* eWorld Cup,[185] the *Madden* Bowl, and *the Madden* Championship Series.[186] In addition, the basketball title from Take Two Interactive, *NBA 2K* had its own extensive competitive history. This scene initially grew through the grassroots efforts of its community members. The competitive or "comp" *NBA 2K* scene includes both the competitive five versus five "Pro-Am" game-mode with its corresponding tournaments that eventually paved the way for the formation of the *NBA 2K League* as well as the $250,000 annual "My Team" tournament for its "My Team" team-card building mode.[187]

As a result of widespread online gameplay, the *NBA 2K* community began establishing their own organized tournaments and leagues created and operated by passionate game users to unify its dedicated and top players. One such prominent third party-created league was the *My Player Basketball Association* (*MPBA*).[188] The *MPBA* was originally operated by current Net Gaming head coach, Ivan "OGKINGCURT" Curtiss and current Mavs Gaming head coach, Latoijuin "LT" Fairley.[189] Another similar event organizer created to service the competitive *NBA 2K* community was the "*W.R. League*."[190] This league is currently operated by Evens Mathurin and Brandon Luxe, who are also both player scouts and analysts for the Warriors Gaming Squad *NBA 2K League* franchise.[191] Specifically, both of these organizations provided a way for individual gamers to create their own five-man rosters and compete against other user-created teams for prize money.[192] In fact, many top draft picks from the past seasons of the *NBA 2K League* have participated in these community-created leagues.[193] These are seen by many as a potential "feeder" and scouting ground for top *NBA 2K League* talent.[194] These entities have also even acted as tournament operators and event hosts on behalf of select *NBA 2K League* franchises, including the Warrior Gaming Squad[195] (Golden State Warriors' NBA 2K League team) and the Celtics Crossover Gaming (Boston Celtics' NBA 2K League team).[196]

This growing competitive scene led game developer Take Two Interactive to create the *NBA 2K16* "Road To The Finals" Pro-Am competition.[197] This tournament featured online play between organized five-person teams with the finalists competing live for a quarter-million dollar prize.[198] This was followed by another five versus five event, the *NBA 2K17* "Road To The All Star Game."[199] This tournament featured another $250,000 prize pool for the winning Pro-Am team *Still Trill*.[200] The success of the previous two $250,000 *NBA 2K* "Pro-Am" tournaments influenced game publisher Take Two Interactive to establish the *NBA 2K League* in partnership with the NBA.[201]

The league was launched in 2018 with 17 NBA-affiliated 2K franchises competing live on the *NBA 2K18* title in Long Island City, New York.[202] The Season 1 new player draft was held at the Madison Square Garden in New York with the first pick, Arteyo "Dimez" Boyd being announced by NBA commissioner Adam Silver.[203] The Season 2 draft was held at Barclays Center in Brooklyn, New York and featured the addition of four new teams.[204] Other influential esports professionals have emerged from this scene including former number 4 overall pick, Mitchell "Mootyy" Franklin,[205] *NBA 2K League* Season 2 champion, Mihad "Feast" Feratovic,[206] as well as the winner of the first ESPN ESPY (Excellence in Sports Performance Yearly) award for "Esports Moment of the Year," Timothy "oLARRY" Anselimo.[207] The *NBA 2K League* continued its growth by adding two new franchises in Season 3, including its first international team operated by esports organization Gen. G, the Shanghai Dragons.[208] The league has grown to the level that ESPN 2 has televised many of its Season 3 games.[209] The future of the league is also interesting as many European and other international sports franchises have begun operating their own competitive *NBA 2K* "Pro-Am" teams in independently organized leagues and tournaments.[210] This includes soccer franchise F.C. Bayern's creation and operation of its "Bayern Baller" competitive *NBA 2K* team.[211] Furthermore, the global competitive *NBA 2K* scene continues to grow with the International Basketball Federation (FIBA) hosting its "FIBA Esports Open 2020" that featured "17 national teams" competing against each other in the title.[212] In fact, the *NBA 2K League*'s Managing Director Brendan Donohue has stated he is focusing on international expansion for the coming years, so this will be a potential lucrative development in the simulation sports esports scene.[213]

Overall, the future of the business esports seems to be trending toward more stable and structured leagues, as this is currently the case with many large competitive titles such as *Overwatch* (*OWL*), *Call of Duty* (*CDL*), and *League of Legends* (*LCS*) all adopting franchise league systems.[214] Today, in 2020, in light of the COVID-19 global pandemic, esports content and competitive gaming has taken front stage.[215] It has been a replacement on many U.S. television stations as most of the world's major entertainment channels are closed, including concert venues, movie theaters, and sports arenas.[216]

Now that we have briefly explored where esports and the competitive gaming scene has grown from, it is now time to explore how to successfully and legally operate within this complex and evolving business world.

1.2 Introduction to Today's Professional Esports Business Ecosystem

In the last few years, there has been an explosion of international exposure and interest in the world of competitive video gaming, better known as "esports."[217] The definition of whether a specific game title is an "esport" or not is a complex question but a good starting point is a video game with "regular publisher support and updates," "a massive fan base" who wants to watch competitive gameplay, and the existence of a "clear ranking or ladder system so that players know where they stand relative to other players."[218] While the debate on what actually constitutes an "esport" rages on, it is clear that it is a budding global entertainment sector that is ripe for growth in the coming years with a projected total global esports market that will reportedly "top $1 billion" by the end of 2020.[219] In fact, the Entertainment Software Association (ESA) reports that "over 164 million adults in the United States play video games" and "three-quarters of all Americans have at least one gamer in their household."[220] As a result of the widespread interest in video and computer games, individuals have begun competing in international competitions against other top competitors for significant prize money. This includes both competitive online tournaments as well as live competitions referred to as "local area networks," known as "LANs."[221] For example, 2018's *Dota 2* championship competition, "The International" featured a prize pool of almost $25 million, which surpassed the prior year's record- breaking prize pool of $24.6 million.[222] There are also live esports events viewed by hundreds of thousands or even several million times, such the over 3.9 million "peak viewers" of the *League of Legends* 2019 World Championship.[223] Additionally, the emergences of new competitive games, such as *Fortnite*, have also begun increasing the allocated sums of money for participant prize pools. For example, the July 2019 "Fortnite World Cup" boasted a $30 million prize pool with each participating gamer "guaranteed [to earn] at least $50,000 in winnings."[224] Furthermore, there are millions of people currently watching gaming content on live streaming platforms at any moment, including Twitch (owned by Amazon) and YouTube (owned by Google).[225] Esports fans also enjoy the gaming competitions live in person at arenas and stadiums across the globe.[226] In fact, the 2018 *Overwatch League* "Grand Finals" were held at the Barclays Center in New York and had over 20,000 tickets sold for the event. [227] Finally, professional gaming is even displayed on live network television in the United States and in other countries. For instance, Activision-Blizzard's *Overwatch League* is televised on U.S. sports network ESPN as well as on Disney's Disney XD channel.[228] It is clear that esports has infiltrated all areas of the traditional entertainment world.[229]

1.3 About Today's "Competitive" Gaming Circuit

Some Popular Game Genres & Titles

Shooter Games	Strategy Games	Fighting Games	Sports Games
FPS - Solo & Squads	Real-Time Strategy		
- Overwatch - CS:Go - Call of Duty - Valorant	- StarCraft II - WarCraft III	- Super Smash Bros. - Street Fighter - Mortal Kombat - Tekken	- Madden - NBA 2k - FIFA - NHL - Rocket League
Battle Royale	MOBA		
- Fortnite - PUBG - Apex Legends	- League of Legends - Dota 2 - Heroes of the Storm		

There are also many other game titles in many genres and sub-genres.

To begin, it is important to understand the types of game genres that exist within the competitive gaming circuit as well as to identify the specific games that have stood out from the crowd to develop their own extensive competitive scene. Generally, most esports games fall into one of a few select genres; however, there are many other competitive genres and sub-genres within each of these.[230] These popular game genres include "shooter" games, "strategy" games," "sports" games, "role playing games" ("RPG"), and "fighting" games.[231]

Under each of these genres, there are a variety of different types of games. For instance, there are various types of "first-person shooter" games.[232] One popular genre is the "class-based" or "hero" shooters ones, such as *Overwatch*.[233] First-person shooter games are unique in that the gamer's in-game "view" is in the "first person" so that they "can only see [their] hands" and any items that the player "holds in [their] hands."[234] In addition, another sub-genre is the "squad-based" or team multiplayer first-person shooter games, such as *Counter-Strike Global Offensive* and *Call of Duty ("COD")*.[235] These involve multiple players each trying to eliminate each other in the iconic "first-person" view.[236] There are also "battle royale" shooter titles, such as *Fortnite* and *PlayerUnknown's Battlegrounds* ("*PUBG*").[237] These games are "third-person online multiplayer shooter" games that consist of many competitors "battl[ing each other] until only one [player or team of gamers] survives."[238]

There are also various types of "strategy" games.[239] One of the largest sub-genres in the esports world is the "real time strategy" games, such as *StarCraft II* and *Warcraft III*.[240] These games "consist of maps" where each competitor must protect a "base" and "gather resources and build units" to "destroy any other players' bases."[241] There are also "multiplayer online battle arena" games.[242] In simplest terms, a typical MOBA game is a "team-versus-versus team competition" where each team tries to "destroy the opponent's base" by using different unique "player characters"— who each has a specific role and ability.[243] Two of the most popular esports are MOBA titles, including *Defense of the Ancients 2* ("*Dota 2*") and *League of Legends*.[244] This is in addition to "card and deck building" strategy games also known as "collectible card" games (CCGS), such as *Hearthstone* and *Magic The Gathering Arena* (MTGA).[245]

A whole genre of traditional "sports" video games also exists. These include "traditional sports simulators," such as *Madden* football,[246] *NBA 2K* basketball,[247] *NHL* hockey,[248] and *FIFA* soccer.[249] Other "sports" genre games include "racing games," such as *Formula One* and its budding esports community.[250] In addition, another popular sub-genre are the "non-simulation" or "other sports simulators," such as *Rocket League* and its organized competitive circuit.[251] Similarly, there are a variety of "player versus player" (PVP) "fighting" games.[252] Some of popular competitive titles include *Street Fighter*, *Mortal Kombat*, *Super Smash Brothers*, and *Tekken*.[253] Finally, another prominent game genre is "role playing games."[254] This category includes popular titles such as *Farming Simulator* and *World of Warcraft*.[255]

These different titles can be played on either a personal computer (a "PC"), a gaming console (i.e., *Xbox* or *Playstation*), or on a mobile device (i.e., a smartphone or tablet). While there are hundreds of existing gaming titles, a few select ones in these different genres have emerged and secured positions as prominent ones within the international competitive tournament circuit. Some of these larger competitive gaming titles include: *Overwatch*; *Fortnite*; *Defense of the Ancients 2*; *Call of Duty*; *League of Legends*; *Counter-Strike Global Offensive*; *Rocket League*; *StarCraft II*; *Rainbow Six* ("R6"); *Halo*; *Hearthstone*; *Street Fighter*; and, the newly emerging game, *VALORANT*.[256] Additionally, there are more competitive titles continuing to emerge, including a variety of "sports" esports titles, such as *Madden* football, *NBA 2K* basketball, and *FIFA* soccer. There has also been a recent expansion and growth in competitive mobile esports, including games such as *Arena of Valor*; *Clash Royale*; and *Brawl Stars*, to name a few [257] as well as the development of a competitive gaming scene for the title *Farming Simulator*.[258] Some of these competitive titles have full teams playing together against other organized competitive teams, including teams of four or five individual players on a single team. Alternatively, other titles, such as *Street Fighter* or *StarCraft II*, are merely a one versus one competition whereby one professional gamer battles against another to emerge victorious.

Speaking of *VALORANT*, this new FPS is from game publisher Riot Games and is taking the gaming world by storm.[259] It has become a new trending competitive title with many top esports organizations signing streamers and professional players[260] to compete on behalf of them in the various new competitions and tournaments.[261] Additionally, there has also been a shift of prominent esports professionals in other competitive titlesmoving to this game for new competitive opportunities, including former professional *Overwatch* gamers.[262] Furthermore, there are current reports of fairly large payouts by top esports organizations to top competitive *VALORANT* teams and players who are currently just competing and streaming the game.[263] Finally, there is widespread industry speculation that this game title may become a new franchise league, similar to Riot Games' other franchise league, the *League of Legends'* Championship Series.[264]

Overall, esports and competitive gaming exixts in many genres and subgenres, including within the above listed game classifications. While there are hundreds, if not thousands, of unique game titles available for play, the above are a list of a few that have stood out thus far.

1.4 Exploring the Professional Esports Business Ecosystem

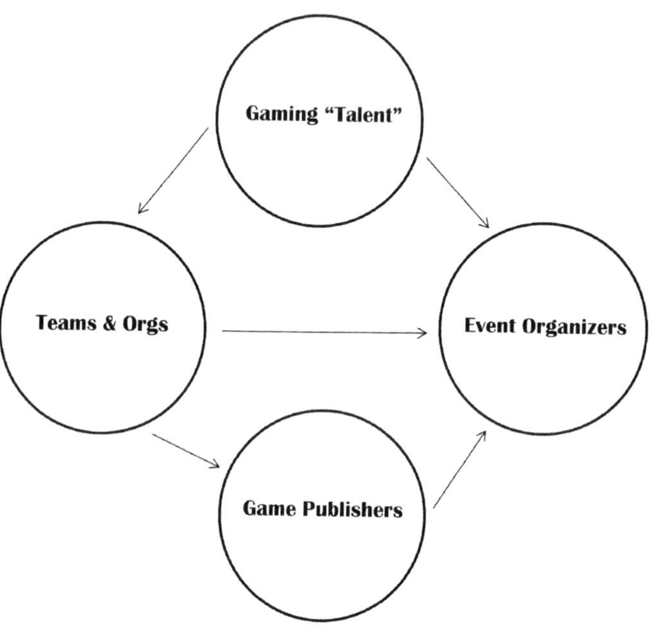

Now that the history of the competitive video-game landscape and its many unique gaming genres have been explained, some thoughts on the business side of the professional video-game world come next. The professional esports industry is composed of a variety of independent stakeholders working together to create a functioning business ecosystem. In particular, the various interested individuals and companies' successes and failures hinge on the other parties' contribution. The main contributors in the traditional esports business system include (1) the professional gamers and content creators, including streamers, competitive players, coaches, analysts, and shoutcasters; (2) the professional organizations and teams; (3) the game developers; and (4) the event, tournament, and league organizers. These distinct parties work together to participate in, host, coordinate, and license the content needed to present a competitive gaming event. To best understand how they operate and where they fit into the global esports business ecosystem, each individual component is described below.

1.4.1 Gaming "Talent" in the Esports Business Ecosystem

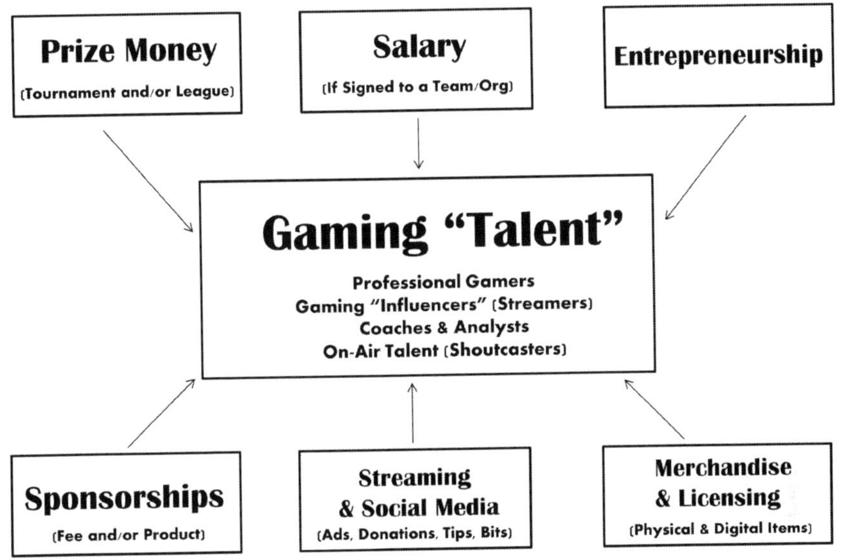

1.4.1.1 "Competitive" Gamers and Gaming "Influencers": Gamers, Coaches, Analysts, Shoutcasters, Content Creators, and Streamers The most abundant piece in the esports ecosystem is the individual "gamers" or the gaming "talent." This includes professional competitive players, gaming content creators and streamers, professional gaming coaches and analysts, as well as announcers and shoutcasters. All of these individuals are involved in some aspect of esports, whether they are actually playing and participating in a competition or match, acting as an announcer for live gameplay, or engaging in the creation of or streaming of gaming-related content.

1.4.1.1.1 Professional Competitive Gamers Professional gamers are individuals who compete against other professionals for prizes. The gamer could participate as part of a team against another team or individually against a single competitor. There are a variety of revenue streams available to a professional esports player.[265] Some of these include a player's salary if they are "signed" to an organization or team, their tournament and competitive play winnings, any independent endorsement or sponsorship earnings, any streaming revenues, as well as those monies received through the sale of player merchandise and other licensing opportunities.[266]

If a professional gamer is signed to a competitive esports team or organization, one of the most common income streams that a gamer earns is a salary.[267] The salary earned by a professional gamer varies substantially based on the player's competitive performance and history, the title that they are competing in, as well as the player's level of notoriety. In most instances, professional gamers signed to an esports organization receive either a weekly, monthly, or yearly salary in exchange for performing exclusively for that team and agreeing to a list of other obligations (typically enumerated in an executed contract).[268] Some player salaries range from as low as several hundred dollars ($250–$500) up to $1,000–or $2,000 a month for competitive titles with small viewership and small prize pools. However, some gamer salaries might earn several thousand dollars or more per month or a year for larger competitive games.[269] For example, in 2018, the reported average yearly salary of a professional *League of Legends* gamer competing in the organized franchise league, *League Championship Series* (LCS) was "over $300,000" and has continuously grew in the following years to "approximately $410,000."[270] In the previous year, top *Counter-Strike* players were earning yearly salaries of around "$200,000."[271] Additionally, professionals who have achieved individual success may command a much higher salary than other comparable players.[272] One such instance is former *Overwatch League* player, Jay "sinatraa" Won, who in 2017 signed a "$150,000 per year contract" with NRG Esport's *Overwatch* franchise team, *San Francisco Shock*.[273] At the time of that deal, the player salary was triple the then current minimum salary paid to other *Overwatch League* professionals.[274] Finally, in addition to earning a salary, some top players, such as Lee "Faker" Sang-hyeok[275] and Søren "Bjergsen" Bjerg,[276] have begun receiving an actual ownership interest in their team entitling them to a share of the entire organization's profits.

In addition to a professional's salary, a gamer also may earn revenues from any tournaments or organized leagues that they participate in, either individually or on behalf of their team.[277] A gamer's total earnings from tournament play differs based on the number and frequency of tournaments that they compete in as well as their placement and the total amount of the prize pools associated with those competitions. Total tournament prize pools and the shares allocated for each competitor for major tournaments can range anywhere from several thousand or hundreds of thousands of dollars all the way up to multi-million dollar prize pools. In instances where a gamer is part of a team competing with other professional gamers, any prize money or tournament earnings are usually split among the team members. In some cases, the organization as well as a team's coach and/or analyst may also be entitled to a portion of a gamer's tournament prize money. A listing of the "top 100 highest overall" esports earners includes multiple professional gamers who have each earned several million dollars through professional esports competitions and tournaments.[278]

Another potentially large stream of income for a pro gamer is independent sponsorship or endorsement monies.[279] A sponsored arrangement can differ significantly based on the notoriety of the player, the reputation of the sponsoring brand, and the length and extent of the relationship.[280] An endorsement can range anywhere, including from a small, one-off activation such as a "sponsorship in kind." That is a situation where the third-party sponsor only provides equipment or other free product to an individual in exchange for some form of marketing or promotion by the gamer. Sponsorship arrangements can also be for more elaborate, paid campaigns that last several months or even years. Sponsorship deals in esports vary from player to player as some endorsements are for several thousand dollars for a few months or a year and others are longer deals for much larger sums that last many years. Currently, there exist many more team-focused sponsorships than individual gamer ones; however, as more individuals continue to separate themselves from other gamers and establish their own large, active fan bases, the opportunities for individual gamer sponsorships should increase. For example, gaming peripheral company Matrix Keyboards secured a licensing deal with professional *Fortnite* player Cody "Clix" Conrod to create his own "Clix"-branded keyboards and keycaps.[281] Sponsorships are discussed in more detail later in this book.

Another important avenue of revenue for professional gamers is the income generated from utilizing a streaming content platform such as Twitch, YouTube, Facebook Gaming, or Caffeine.[282] In particular, these streaming platforms typically display paid advertisements prior to as well as during a live stream and, based on the number of viewers, the stream's owner earns revenue when an initial viewership threshold is reached. These platforms also provide the gamer with the opportunity to directly connect with their fans online. In particular, some content streaming systems, such as Twitch and YouTube, have a live chatting feature that permits live viewers to comment on what they see and to interact with other concurrent viewers. These steaming sites also allow fans to interact with the streamer themselves.

The live communications between the viewers and the streamer have caused some of these streaming platforms to create additional avenues for a user to earn income during their broadcasts and for the viewers to further engage in addition to supporting the individuals that they enjoy watching. For example, Twitch provides the spectator with the opportunity to use "bits" and "emoticons," also known as "emotes," specific to a particular streamer to support the streamer.[283] "Bits" are animated cheering "emotes" that a viewer can use in the streamer's chat to support them. "Bits" are a virtual good and a form of in-stream currency that can be purchased online through Twitch.[284] "Bits" can also be earned by the viewer over time through observing free online advertisements displayed by Twitch.[285] A viewer can use and submit these "bits" to cheer on a streamer while watching their live streams. Twitch currently pays their "Affiliates" and "Partners" level content creators one ($0.01) cent for every "bit" that a fan uses on their channel.[286]

Additionally, many streaming platforms also have different tiers of account membership, which may be based on the user's viewership metrics. For instance, in addition to a basic streaming account with Twitch, there are additional higher account levels of "Affiliates" and "Partners." A streaming account can achieve these higher levels by satisfying specified criteria.[287] Some of these criteria are based on reaching a set number of followers or "subscribers," the frequency and length of the user's streams, as well as the average viewership of the streamed content. As a content streamer's metrics increase due to additional viewers and as they engage in longer and more frequent streams, the streamer may begin earning these advanced account levels.[288] Specifically, each level-up helps the streamer potentially earn additional income by entitling the account owner to a larger portion of revenue for the advertisements displayed during their stream at higher account levels.[289]

Platforms, such as Twitch, also provide paid "subscription" opportunities that a viewer can purchase in order to gain access to private or other unreleased or unavailable content from the content creator.[290] These "subscriptions" (known as "subs") allow viewers to support a specific broadcaster.[291] A subscription also permits the subscriber to use a special streamer specific "emotes" images that are only accessible to a particular channel's subscriber.[292] The existence of subscribers may also enable a content creator to produce unique content that is paywall protected and requires a paid subscription in order to view. For example, a service, such as Twitch, provides a multi-tiered subscription service that permits a viewer to subscribe to a particular broadcaster's channel by paying a recurring monthly charge of $4.99, $9.99, or $24.99, depending on which "tier" they subscribe to.[293] Each tier usually corresponds to a different level of access and content. Generally, any income earned from "standard subscriber rate of $4.99/month" is allocated in a "50/50 split between Twitch and the streamer."[294] Additionally, this split can "scale" depending on the particular influencer's "viewership," with the streamer earning "up to a 60/40 [split or] about $3.00 per [standard] subscriber."[295] In some cases, a streamer can earn on average "about $250 per [every] 100 subscribers," which can add up quickly as the individual continues to grow their following.[296] For instance, if a streamer has "200 subscribers" they could potentially make around "$60,000 per year" by streaming full time.[297]

Furthermore, since Twitch is owned by Amazon, Amazon Prime members can use the "tokens" that are earned from their Prime membership to subscribe to a Twitch channel.[298] In these situations, since the "tokens" renew every month, a Prime member can re-subscribe to a broadcaster's channel solely using their Prime "tokens." Generally, Twitch and the streamer equally split all of the income from subscriptions, "bits," and Prime "tokens." [299]

There has also been the development of ancillary services, such as Streamlabs, which provides additional avenues of income for content streamers.[300] This company permits a viewer to "donate" or "tip" funds to the streamer. This means that a stream viewer can contribute money directly to a broadcaster through these third-party services without buying "bits" or purchasing a monthly subscription through Twitch. Goldman Sachs has estimated that the total U.S. "tipping" market is "roughly $129 million, and as of 2017 was growing 26%" year on year.[301] This fact further reinforces the large sums that a successful individual can earn through streaming.[302]

Finally, in rare cases, a player may act as an entrepreneur and develop their own separate business as well as create and sell their own individual merchandise featuring their likeness, picture, and/or unique gamer-tag or player logo.[303] For example, former professional *Call of Duty* gamer Skyler "FoRePLayy" Johnson was an original founder of *Team EnvyUs* (later renamed *Team Envy*) as well as more recently establishing the *CTRL* meal replacement brand (who then secured investment from *FaZe Clan*).[304] While any professional gamer can design and make available merchandise containing any image that they legally own, unless the player is well known and has a very established fan base, it may be difficult for a professional esports gamer to earn significant, or any, income through selling their own merchandise. For instance, legendary gamer Johnathan "Fatal1ty" Wendel has successfully created and distributed his own branded "gaming products" in partnership with *Monster* for decades.[305] In some instances, a player may create t-shirts, hats, sandals, pins, patches, bandanas, or anything else that they can brand with their unique imagery and logo. Any income generated from these types of sales would generally be solely for the gamer without any other party earning a portion of it.

Overall, as a result of the growing player salaries, the expanding prize pools (more than $211 million provided the previous year), and the sponsorship opportunities, many professional gamers are earning several million dollars a year.[306] Specifically, in 2019, "15 players became millionaires [...], 288 [gamers] made $100K or more, and 196 [players] made over $60K in prize money alone."[307]

1.4.1.1.2 Professional Esports Coaches and Analysts In addition to professional gamers, many esports organizations and teams hire team coaches, analysts, and scouts to assist their professional gamers.[308] These team personnel members work with the players to help refine and enhance their skills as well as assist with the day-to-day operations and logistics of the team.[309] Generally, these individuals provide in-depth statistical analysis and feedback on a player's strengths and weaknesses and identify areas for improvement.[310] Some coaches are former professional gamers and some others are aspiring professionals who did not turn "pro."[311]

In many cases, an esports team's coach or analyst simply earns a salary. For instance, it was reported that *Team Liquid* was paying "$32,000 per annum" for a *League of Legends* head coach.[312] Payment frequency for these individuals can be an hourly, a monthly, or an annual rate depending on the time commitment on behalf of the club. The amounts paid vary greatly based on the title that they are coaching, the coach's previous experience, as well as the anticipated time commitments of the job. In addition to a salary, some teams may also offer the coach housing, including potentially living in the "gaming house" with the players as well as other traditional employee benefits, such as health insurance.[313] In some occasions, the coaches or analyst of a specific team may also be entitled to a portion of the team's tournament winnings. In rare circumstances, especially when a team's coach was also a former professional gamer, independent sponsorship or endorsement opportunities may also be available to them. However, most of the time, the coach represents their organization's sponsors and is generally prohibited from any additional endorsement or other sponsorship arrangements with a competitor of the coach's team.

Overall, many professional coaches and analysts earn income in many of the same ways that professional gamers do. As the profession continues to evolve, it is fair to assume that coaches' salaries will continue to increase. There may also be additional new areas of potential business development for coaches, analysts, and even former professional gamers to begin establishing and operating their own esports competitive "training camps" to help train the next generation of esports competitors.[314]

1.4.1.1.3 Gaming "Influencers"—Streamers and Content Creators Other prominent persons within the esports realm are the "streamers" and content creators. These individuals engage in the public streaming of gaming content to live viewers and in the creation of gaming content for viewing. This is generally accomplished by the person's use of a third-party streaming platform, such as Twitch, YouTube, Facebook, and Caffeine (co-owned by 21st Century Fox). While these two parties seem fairly similar, in addition to streaming their gameplay, a content curator also produces unique gaming content that incorporates actual gameplay. This could be in the form of "how to" and other gameplay user tutorials, strategy guides, and other related content; while a streamer only engages in live streams of gameplay without creating and distributing custom-created assets.

Most of these influencers' income is generated by actually creating content and through the live streaming on their respective platform.[315] For example, there are several YouTube content creators that are currently earning several million dollars a year.[316] In 2019, *Forbes* reported that the ten highest-paid gamers made "more than $120 Million."[317] In fact, some streamers have obtained a level of success that permits them to determine which streaming platform to use and, in some cases, receive some type of fee from the streaming platform owner to exclusively utilize their streaming platform instead of another.[318] For example, one of the largest *Fortnite* streamers, Tyler "Ninja" Blevins left Twitch to begin streaming exclusively on Microsoft's former Mixer platform for what was presumed to be a "big check" (later reported to be around "$30 million.)"[319] In 2019, Blevins reportedly earned a total of "$17 million dollars" from his various income streams.[320] This move by Ninja was followed by another large streamer, Michael "shroud" Grzesiek (who reportedly earned "$12.5 million" in 2019)[321] leaving Twitch to also exclusively stream on Microsoft's Mixer steaming service (which has eventually closed down and merged into Facebook Gaming).[322] Building on this trend, *Hearthstone* streamer, Jeremy "Disguised Toast" Wang inked an exclusive streaming deal with Facebook Gaming.[323] Continuing this pattern, "popular

Instagram model, digital influencer and '*Fortnite*' Twitch streamer," Corinna Kopf and her "millions of followers," entered into a similar exclusive deal with Facebook Gaming.[324] While the amounts for these deals have not been publicly reported, since many of these streamers are leaving a platform where they already have an established income stream, including a substantial amount of followers, views, and subscribers, there has to be some additional monetary incentive to formalize such an arrangement.[325]

In addition to the earnings that they generate from their stream as described above, there are several other additional avenues of revenue available to content creators and streamers.[326] Some of these ancillary sources of income include individual sponsorship and appearance fees.[327] Also, if the streamer is signed to an esports organization, then they may also earn a monthly salary in exchange for the individual streaming exclusively on behalf of the team and representing the organization and its sponsors on their social media and streaming platforms. There are also some opportunities for the gaming influencer to earn an appearance fee or other payment for attending a conference or for speaking as part of an informative panel.[328]

Similar to a professional gamer, individual sponsorship of a content streamer is very rare; however, in recent years, many more streamers have achieved enormous success, in part to their large, consistent viewership.[329] This recent notoriety has translated into new sponsorship and endorsement opportunities.[330] For example, *Fortnite* streamer, Tyler "Ninja" Blevins is reportedly earning "$500,000 a month" [331] and has signed endorsement deals with companies such as Redbull[332] and Uber Eats.[333] Other large gaming content streamers have also inked their own individual endorsement deals. For instance, former professional gamer turned streamer, Michael "shroud" Grzesiek has a deal with food delivery service Postmates[334] and *Fortnite* streamer Benjamin "DrLupo" Lupo is sponsored by insurance giant, State Farm.[335]

As with professional gamers, selling a streamer's own merchandise can generate additional income. In fact, the entire streamer merchandise industry is over a billion dollars with revenues potentially hitting "$4 billion" in 2020.[336] Similar to gamers, it takes a streamer achieving substantial fame and notoriety to earn funds through "branded" merchandise. However, when an individual does achieve such stardom, they may engage in the sale of merchandise. For example, British *Minecraft* streamer, Daniel Robert "DanTDM" Middleton sells his own merchandise which includes his own branded "backpacks, baseball caps and hoodies."[337] In 2018, *Forbes* reported Daniel's earnings at $18.5 million[338] and in 2019, he earned a reported "$12 million."[339] In addition, content streamer, Michael "shroud" Grzesiek has a variety of different "branded" items, such as sunglasses, t-shirts, pins, and hats, all available for purchase through the company "J!NX."[340]

Furthermore, some prominent streamers have entered into partnerships with game publishers in order to license and sell custom-created "in-game" items incorporating the streamer's likeness, such as character "skins." For example, the creators of *PlayerUnknown's Battlegrounds* partnered with several top Twitch streamers to enable them to each create their own "custom skin" that was purchasable by the game's players through Twitch.[341] The developer then provided a portion of the earned revenues directly to "the streamer that contributed to the [in-game item's] design."[342] Similarly, the developer for *Fortnite*, Epic Games created its "Icon Series" where "top creators" receive their own custom in-game branded items.[343] In particular, the series was launched with custom items for *Fortnite* streamer, Tyler "Ninja" Blevins, including a purchasable "Ninja Outfit, Ninja's Edge Back Bling, Ninja Style Emote and Dual Katanas Pickaxe."[344]

Overall, gaming "influencers" earn income in many of the same ways that professional gamers do. However, a gaming influencer or streamer may be able to more easily obtain independent sponsorship as well as exclusive streaming and content distribution deals due to their generally more widespread notoriety and the fact that they interact and engage directly with their fans.

1.4.1.1.4 On-Air Talent: Esports Hosts, Shoutcasters, and Announcers One last part of the traditional talent side of the esports industry is made up of the on-air talent, which includes event hosts, announcers, and "shoutcasters."[345] As the name alludes to, these are the individuals who act as traditional casters and color commentators during a competitive gaming broadcast.[346] In esports, they are sometimes referred to as "shoutcasters" as they "shout" on the stream broadcast as they deliver an entertaining narrative about the game.[347]

In many cases, these individuals are former competitive gamers or coaches, while some are just gaming enthusiasts or other broadcast professionals.[348] There has also been the development of formal classes to assist the development of "shoutcasters." For example, the University of Oklahoma created a "Shoutcasting Program" at its university to "develop announcers for real-time play by play announcing with heavy analytic breakdown, color casting, and after action review emphasis."[349] In addition to announcers, a broadcast team might also consist of a host or other gameplay analysts.[350] The host may interview the players and interact with the crowd while the analyst may provide unique gameplay insight into a team's strategies and help breakdown the match for the viewers.[351]

Most esports on-air talent, such as a shoutcaster, generally only earn a salary for their services. The amount that they receive varies on the talent's notoriety, their social media influence, their previous track record, the estimated event viewership, and the time commitments and obligations of the job.[352] Besides an announcer earning a fee for their on-air services, some larger individuals are able to secure independent sponsors and brand endorsements. Others may also stream their own gaming content whereby they can earn income through advertisements, subscriptions, and donations in the same ways that a traditional streamer does. An announcer may also try to curate and interact with their own fans in an effort to create an active fan base for "branded" merchandise sales.

Overall, most of the individuals who engage in professional gaming as well as those who stream and create gaming content all earn revenues in similar ways. The ancillary professions, including coaches and on-air talent, such as event hosts and shoutcasters, also generate income in some of the same ways that traditional gamers and streamers do.

1.4.2 Professional Esports Organizations and Teams

Other key players in the esports ecosystem are the professional organizations and teams. There are a variety of competitive gaming organizations and teams that operate in various countries around the globe. Generally, an

esports "team" consists of a group of individuals playing together under a unified banner or team. In contrast, an esports "organization" is larger than a team and consists of a variety of distinct teams (groups of gamers) fielded in different games all under one organizational banner. Some major esports organizations include Cloud9, Fnatic, Dignitas, Team Liquid, FaZe Clan, Immortals Gaming Club, and Gen.G. Each of these organizations has different gaming squads competing in various competitive events against other esports organizations and teams.

The primary function of esports teams and organizations is to field lineups that compete in tournaments and organized leagues against other competitive teams.[353] However, some of these companies also sign individual content streamers to broadcast under the organization. A streamer signed to a particular organization is generally required to stream for a specific number of hours per month and to display the team's logo on their social media accounts as well as to advertise the organization's sponsors and partners during their broadcasts.

Many esports teams typically have an entire internal infrastructure of employees and other independent contractors assisting in the day-to-day operations of the team. This includes professional coaches and analysts who help train the competitive players. There are also social media managers and content creators who engage in photography, videography, as well as associated video and photo editing on behalf of the organization.[354] These individuals create and distribute the team's announcements, score updates, as well as any created content, such as photographs and audiovisual works, on the team's social media networks, such as Twitter, Instagram, Facebook, and Tik Tok.[355] Generally, most of the works created by any team operations personnel as well as any individuals are owned exclusively by the organization.

In most cases, organizations and teams enter into written agreements with gamers and streamers for their services. In exchange for these obligations, the organization pays the player a salary and may also help the talent with their associated expenses.[356] For example, the organization may pay for the gamer's travel and lodging for tournaments, scrimmages, and "boot camps" as well as paying for the player's living amenities, such as rent, food, and other living expenses.[357] Some teams may also provide the gamers with professional coaches and analysts to improve their game.[358] Other organizations may offer their players physical and mental trainers to assist their growth and development as well as potentially supplying them with gaming peripherals and equipment necessary to compete and stream.[359] This assistance could include providing their signed players with computers, keyboards, headsets, gaming chairs, and other computer hardware. "Boot camps" are what the industry refers to as gaming training "camps" where the players on a team undertake an intensive practice schedule regime over a short span of time meant to get the team ready for an upcoming tournament or other competition.[360]

Similar to professional gamers and streamers, esports organizations and teams earn revenue in a variety of ways.[361] These could include a percentage of their competing team's tournament winnings, funds from third-party investors, sponsorship and brand partnership revenues, physical and digital merchandise income, as well as streaming revenues.

Some Notable Esports Team/Org Investors

Esports Team/Org	Investors
FaZe Clan [367]	- Pitbull - Offset - Josh Hart - Ben Simmons
NRG Esports [366]	- Jennifer Lopez - Alex Rodriguez - Shaquille O' Neal - Michael Strahan - Marshawn Lynch
Team Liquid [362]	- Michael Jordan - Magic Johnson
Team SoloMid [362]	- Stephen Curry - Steve Young - Andre Iguodala
Gen. G Esports [363]	- Will Smith
Rogue Gaming [367]	- Steve Aoki - Imagine Dragons - Landon Collins

One of the most lucrative income streams for an organization is outside third-party investment into the team. In recent years, there has been a series of multi-million dollar investments by prominent sports, entertainment, and technology figures infusing esports organizations with substantial funds.[362] These funds are generally invested to be used to recruit new talent, pay league franchise "buy-in" fees, as well as to finance and develop an organization's current competitive rosters. For example, esports organization Gen.G received a "$46 million investment" from several individuals, including actor Will Smith.[363] Additionally, a former esports organization Echo Fox was originally founded by former NBA player Rick Fox and later received investments from the *New York Yankees*[364] as well as from athletes, Kevin Durant and Odell Beckham, Jr.[365] Another large, celebrity-driven investment was a $15 million raise for NRG Esports, which included musician Jennifer Lopez and athletes Alex Rodriguez, Michael Strahan, and Marshawn Lynch.[366] However, it is important to understand that these third-party investments are not being considered "revenues" of the organization. This is because these funds are merely intended to help the organizations comply with their current and prospective financial obligations as well as to accelerate the organization's growth.[367] The third-party investment is also typically provided by these individuals in exchange for "equity," which is an ownership interest in the organization.

In addition to outside investment funds that an organization receives, professional esports teams may also earn a set percentage of their signed team and individual gamer's tournament money. The percentage that the team reserves ranges from as little as 5% or 10% of the total prize winnings to larger amounts such as 20% or 25%. Since an organization usually pays for the player's living, travel, and gaming related expenses, this allows the team to attempt to recoup some of these personnel expenditures. The amounts earned by teams have increased greatly in the last few years due to the increased frequency of competitions as well as growing total tournament prize pools. For example in 2019, at least ten esports organizations earned several million dollars in total prize money.[368] This includes the largest earner, "*OG*," who earned $15.84 million in total prize money (including winning the 2019 *DOTA 2* The International championship), followed by Team Liquid, who won $9.40 million (including second place in *DOTA 2* The International), then, NRG Esports, who earned $5.28 million in total tournament winnings (including the 2019 *Overwatch League* title).[369] Some of these other high-grossing teams include organizations such as Lazarus ($4.22 million), Gen.G ($3.45 million), Team Secret ($3.31 million), and FaZe Clan ($3.166 million).[370]

Sale of both physical and digital team merchandise has also become an additional source of income for esports organizations. Teams have begun selling their own merchandise containing the team's imagery as well as individual player merchandise on their own websites.[371] Some organizations contract directly with a merchandise distributor who sources and dispenses the items and some teams actually produce and distribute their own inventory. Additionally, some other teams have instead partnered with existing peripheral companies, such as keyboard and mouse pad companies, to license their imagery. This enables these companies to create team "branded" items in exchange for a royalty paid to the team for any sold items. For example, esports organization Fnatic has created an extensive internal merchandise distribution operation.[372] The team currently offers a variety of "branded" gaming peripherals as well as traditional merchandise, including t-shirts, hats, water bottles, backpacks, and mouse pads.[373]

In addition, some teams have begun establishing "fan clubs" or other activations designed solely to interact with their fans. For example, esports organization Rogue, founded by electro dance music (EDM) producer and DJ Steve Aoki, created the "Rogue Nation" fan club.[374] This club provides both free and premium subscription options for its fans. Options include the "free" subscription tier, as well as several other tiers, including a "$4.97 per month," a "$9.97/month," and a "$19.97/month" tier.[375] Those fans who subscribe to the highest tier (Legendary) "are eligible for live online group coaching, early access to pre-orders and team announcements, and a Rogue jersey once 10 consecutive monthly payments are made" as well as "opportunities for members to compete with and against Rogue players."[376]

Some esports teams have even acted as property owners in addition to fielding competitive teams. For example, esports organization Simplicity Esports, owned by Jed Kaplan, the minority owner of the NBA team *Memphis Grizzlies* owns an extensive national network of gaming centers.[377] The team has also recently purchased the Brazilian-based esports organization Flamengos, which includes access and ownership in their Brazilian gaming facility locations.[378] Other esports organizations are also partnering with event space developers to help establish and develop "gaming venues."[379]

In conjunction with the game publishers, esports teams also may earn proceeds from the sale of digital in-game products bearing their team name or logo. This could include the selling of "stickers" or "skins" for characters that represent an individual team. For example, competitive gaming title *Rocket League* provided each of the 11 organizations in its *Rocket League* Championship Series (RLCS) with the ability to earn "30% of the revenue from the sale of their respective branded [in-game] item."[380] These items include "branded [car] decals," team-specific player "banners," and custom "wheel options" that a fan may purchase, equip, and use on their own console.[381] Additionally, the developers for *Rainbow Six*, Ubisoft has created a similar revenue-sharing program.[382] Under this program, each of the league's 14 participating teams earned "30% of the revenue [for] its own respective item sales" consisting of a team-branded "bundle that includes branded headgear, a uniform, and [a] weapon skin" as well as an equal share of "30% of the revenue" earned from the sale of any "*Rainbow Six* Pro League-branded items."[383] Another example is in *Gears of War* where "four of the *Gears 5 Pro League* teams," including NRG Esports and Rise Nation, are currently entitled to earn a percentage of any in-game revenues for the sale of "weapon skins and other in-game items" purchased by the game's users.[384] Finally, the *National PUBG League* also provided its 16 participating teams with a portion of the profit earned from specific in-game items.[385] In 2019, it was reported that a "total of $21,498.01 was raised through [the sale of] a branded in-game jacket" with "25 percent of the figure, $5,[375].50, [split] between the 16 teams in the league." [386] This meant that "each team received $335.91 in revenue" from the sale of this in-game item.[387] In addition, PUBG Corp. followed this in-game item with a new item, "an NPL-branded baseball bat."[388] This second item provided "the same 25 percent split for the teams," which totaled "$2775.84" with each team earning "$173.49."[389] While the actual amounts an organization earns from the sale of in-game items might not be substantial, it is an important income stream that has the potential to grow in the future, especially as teams continue to prosper and as more fans continue purchasing these digital products.[390]

While the team has other available avenues of revenue, the primary source of income for most organizations is from sponsorships and brand partnerships.[391] For instance, this income stream accounts for "nearly 60% of the [organization's] revenue."[392] In fact, sponsorship and brand activation have become so essential to major team that new leagues have been established, including the implementation of geo-location franchising to provide some stability and long-term predictability for sponsors when entering into long-term deals with esports teams.[393] Brand marketing in the gaming space is particularly valuable because the target demographic for esports are males aged 17–25.[394] This demographic is a highly sought after and is typically difficult to reach through traditional marketing avenues.[395] This fact has caused many major endemic and non-endemic brands in the last few years to enter into brand partnerships with esports organizations, including Nike, Coca-Cola, Red Bull, Audi, Kia, Mountain Dew, AT&T,[396] T-Mobile, and Mercedes Benz.[397] "Endemic" brands are those that are naturally a part of esports and gaming, such as computer processors and hardware, gaming monitors, gaming controllers, gaming chairs, keyboards, and joysticks.[398] In comparison, "non-endemic" brands account for everything else that is not "endemic."[399] For instance, "non-endemic" brands could include soft drinks, energy and alcoholic beverages, financial institutions such as banks, clothing and apparel companies, motor vehicle brands, food and snacks sponsors, as well as beauty care and hygiene products.[400] For example, Miller Lite, a non-endemic alcoholic beverage, entered into a sponsorship arrangement with esports team Complexity, which is owned by *Dallas Cowboys*' owner Jerry Jones.[401] Other recent large organizational sponsorships include a partnership between fast food dining restaurant chain Chipotle and esports organization TeamSoloMid,[402] as well as TeamSoloMid's extensive brand partnership with soft drink Dr. Pepper.[403] Finally, Korean esports organization T1 received a sponsorship from apparel company Nike.[404] In addition, new peripheral brands such as Matrix Keyboards became the official "keyboard" and "keycap" sponsor for organization Misfits and its *Overwatch League* and *Call of Duty League* franchise teams.[405] Professional esports team sponsorship is discussed in more detail later in Chapter 5.

Finally, similar to content streamers, an organization may earn revenues through the live streaming of gaming content by those individuals signed to their organization on social media platforms such as Twitch and YouTube. Organizations may contract directly with these streaming platforms for a portion of advertisement and subscription revenues received while a player is streaming under their team. While the funds earned from streaming are not as large as some of the other avenues available to esports organizations, teams with a large and active following are able to earn some revenue while also providing opportunities for live fan engagement. Streaming also provides additional opportunities to present the team's sponsors on stream to a live audience. In recent years, it is becoming the norm for professional organizations to enter into exclusive streaming partnerships with one specific platform. For example, a few esports organizations, including Fnatic, TeamSoloMid, and Cloud9, had all inked exclusive streaming deals withTwitch. For instance, the Fnatic deal required that "each and every one of Fnatic's roster of professional players, spanning multiple esports titles, stream live exclusively on Twitch."[406] This is similar to parameters contained in Cloud9 and TeamSoloMid's deal, whereby both teams selected "Twitch [as] the exclusive streaming platform for [all of the] players and personalities signed to their respective organizations."[407] Furthermore, content-streaming platform Caffeine, which received a substantial investment from 21st Century Fox[408] entered into a content streaming and production deal with esports organization Dignitas.[409] Caffeine acted as the team's "exclusive broadcaster for team-related content and streams" and permits the team to "produce original series based on" the organization's existing competitive teams.[410] In addition to exclusive streaming arrangements for an organization's United States streams, some teams have also secured additional stream licensing distribution deals in other international markets. For instance, Team Liquid and Team Secret[411] both secured streaming partnerships with Chinese livestreaming platform Huya,[412] which includes the streaming of "select Team Liquid competitive esports content" where some streams are actually "translated [in]to Mandarin in 'real-time' for Huya's audience."[413]

Besides the advertising revenues earned during a live stream, organizations have the opportunity to receive additional income from any created content or other saved media they produce. For example, a team may upload created content to a social media platform such as YouTube, Tik Tok, or Twitch. The organization could then receive advertising revenues for any advertisements displayed during a viewing session of the content. Again, while this might not be a substantial sum, as more viewers watch the content and as more original content is posted, more opportunities are created for the team to derive income in this fashion.

Furthermore, similar to game publishers, several successful esports teams have actually formed and "funded" their own professional league, *Flashpoint*.[414] The league will operate a new *CS:GO* "tournament series" and it will be the first organized league "fully owned and operated by team organizations."[415] It is also not "tied to specific cities" in the same way that the *Overwatch League* and *Call of Duty League* are.[416] The league will have "two seasons a year of about six weeks in length" and a total prize pool of "$2 million."[417] This new league will presumptively permit the participating teams to earn a portion of income through any league "sponsors," "broadcast/webcast," and any merchandise or other ancillary revenue streams that the venture creates.[418] It will be interesting to see if other esports organizations that compete in other competitive titles will follow this trend and establish their own leagues, especially in games with little to no game developer support of its competitive scene.

Overall, professional esports organizations and teams earn income in many of the similar ways that professional gamers and streamers generate revenue; however, one chief difference between them is the ability for some organizations to receive large outside investments which is generally unavailable to most professional gamers, streamers, coaches, and shoutcasters. These companies also usually have the capital to invest in other potential lucrative ventures, such as property investments.

1.4.3 Game Developers and Publishers

Another dominant force within the esports business is the game developer. These are the companies who actually create, sell, develop, and publish the video game.[419] They earn a substantial amount of their income through the

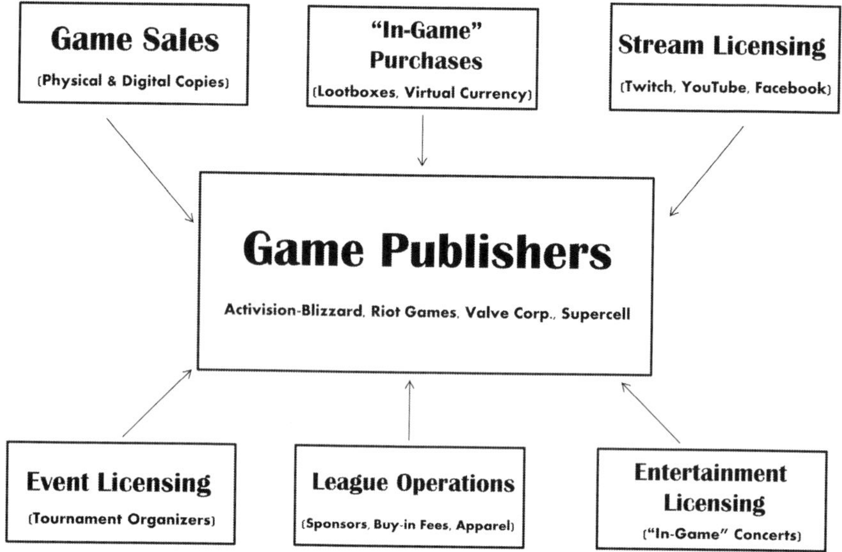

sale of the actual game.[420] However, some popular games, such as *League of Legends*, are actually F2P.[421] These F2P titles provide a basic game experience for free with many available in-game purchase options for additional game characters, game maps, items known as "micro-transactions."[422] In-game micro-transactions are any unique in-game item, any game-mode "pack" as well as any character "skin" available for purchase within the title.[423] A skin is an in-game file that alters the appearance of a character or of an item.[424] Thus, a game publisher may make available a special or "upgraded" weapon purchasable through the system to upgrade a weapon's firing capabilities. For example, Epic Games' *Fortnite* title offers many unique character skins from various pop culture series that are available for purchase by its user base.[425] In these cases, the game publisher earns additional income from a user's in-game purchases in their digital stores.[426] These transactions might include the purchase of a "loot box" for a special in-game item or utilizing other forms of virtual currency, such as "VC" in *NBA 2K* to purchase "MyTeam" card packs for specific players to use within the game or using "VBucks" in *Fortnite* to obtain a unique playable item.[427] These in-game currencies are either purchased with real funds or earned in-game through playing the actual game.[428] Game publishers earn large revenue from these micro-transactions, including the title *Team Fortress 2*, which has an established in-game economy worth over "$50 million within [its first] year."[429] Additionally, game publisher Electronic Arts reportedly previously earned "$993 million from [its] live services," which includes revenue from all of its in-game "microtransaction[s]."[430] While the legalities-related to the odds of earning a particularly advertised item and the potential legislation applicable to these in-game micro-transactions, such as "loot boxes" and other in-game purchases, are outside the scope of this text, it is clear that game publishers generate millions (if not "billions") of dollars through these payment mechanisms and the amounts will continue to grow as mobile and other forms of gaming prospers globally.[431]

Some of the major game publishers involved in esports include Activision-Blizzard (creators of *Overwatch*, *Call of Duty*, *StarCraft 2*, *Heroes of the Storm*, and *Hearthstone*); Valve Corporation (creators of *Dota 2* and *Counter-Strike: Global Offensive*); Riot Games (creators of *League of Legends* and *VALORANT*); Microsoft Studios (creators of *Halo* and *Gears of War*); Nintendo Company (creators of the *Super Smash Brothers* series); Supercell (creators of *Brawl Stars*, *Clash of Clans*, and *Clash Royale*); Take Two Interactive (creators of the *NBA 2K* series); Capcom (creators of the *Street Fighter* series); Electronic Arts (creators of the *FIFA* soccer, *Madden* football, and *NHL* hockey series); and Epic Games (creators of *Fortnite*) and who have also recently purchased Psyonix Inc. (creators of *Rocket League*).[432] In fact, in 2018, these companies had grossed over "$107.3 billion," with revenues continuing to grow in the following years.[433]

The game publishers are central players within the esports ecosystem due to these companies owning the exclusive intellectual property rights to the game's underlying software. This is because video and computer games are protected by copyright law as both an audiovisual work for the game and the graphic images as well as a literary work for the underlying software code. In particular, proper licensing or permission from the rights holder, the developer, is required to utilize the protected work for any purpose.[434] This means that the publisher possesses the absolute ability to control and dictate the terms for any third-party usages of their game, including controlling "everything regarding the eSports title."[435] In practice, the game developer has the right to charge a licensing fee and to determine how a video game is exploited by others, including when and how the game is used. Furthermore, they can dictate how the gameplay is displayed in online videos, on streams, and at in-person tournaments and other competitions. It is important to understand that any individual engaging in these actions without the appropriate permission or license from the game publisher may be subjected to liability for copyright infringement. Copyright in video games as well as game developer licensing are explored in more detail later in the text.

In this respect, esports is extremely different from other traditional professional sports since any individual can participate or stream themselves playing basketball as well as start their own professional basketball league (e.g., *ABA*,

BIG3) or host their own tournament without the requirement of a license or other permission from an organizing body, such as the NBA. In contrast, if an individual wants to publicly stream *League of Legends* or host their own *League of Legends* competition, they are generally required to secure a license from the game developer (Riot Games) in order to utilize its copyrighted content (the game) for commercial purpose, such as a competitive tournament or a monetized live stream or content piece. Generally, the licensing fees paid by third parties, including streaming platforms and tournament organizers, differs based on the length of the license and the anticipated uses of the licensed material. For instance, a large international competition that is broadcasted live to thousands of people on a social streaming platform may have a larger licensing fee associated with it than a local in-person tournament hosted at a gaming store which is not streamed. The amount paid for a license by a third party can be for as little as a few hundred dollars to several thousand or hundreds of thousands of dollars or more. Esports licensing is discussed in additional detail later.

There has been a new trend whereby certain game developers have begun acting as a league organizer in addition to their traditional role as a game developer and have started formulating their own organized "franchise" leagues.[436] These new leagues provide esports organizations with exclusive rights to a specific geographic territory or guaranteed league "spot" in exchange for a substantial "franchise fee" paid to the game publisher.[437] As part of the franchise fee that an organization pays to the company, the developer handles the logistics and operations of the league, including establishing uniform rules and practices as well as selling these individual geo-location "spots." For example, Activision-Blizzard launched the *Overwatch League*, with reported franchise buy-in fees initially starting at "$20 or $25 million for Season 1."[438] The publisher also created another franchise league the *Call of Duty League*, which has similar franchise fees associated with the purchase of exclusive rights to a specific geographic territory.[439]

These new developer-established leagues have attempted to create some new benefits and stability within the esports economy.[440] One of the greatest purported benefits of these franchise leagues is that participating teams are guaranteed a permanent league spot, while, in the past, underperforming teams were subject to potential "relegation," demotion, or removal from a league.[441] Also, participating franchises now have local, in-market sponsorship revenue opportunities that were not available prior to the establishment of these city-based franchises.[442] Therefore, as a result of the development of franchised leagues, gaming companies are now able to earn new revenues in ways similar to how professional gamers, esports organizations, and league organizers do. This includes league-wide product sponsorships and brand partnerships as well as the sale of television and streaming broadcast and media rights.[443] These new leagues, formed by game developers, can also collect admission and entrance ticket fees for the events that they host as well as earn additional revenues through advertising displayed during a league broadcast.[444] Needless to say, the development of these new franchise leagues has become a large income generator for these game publishing companies.[445]

With developers getting involved in new areas of esports, these entities have begun to exert additional control over other components of the esports business ecosystem. For example, some have imposed restrictions on the licensee (the party licensing the gaming content from them) related to their newly developed franchise league. One such restriction is limiting and determining which sponsors a team can and cannot work with in an effort to prevent an organization from conducting business with a particular brand that competes with the developer's current sponsors; or, at a minimum, refraining from publicly displaying a competitor to a league sponsor during league gameplay.[446]

In addition to the substantial sums that the publishing companies earn from third-party license fees to use their title, another unique monetization opportunity for them is incorporating more traditional entertainment, media, and music into their gameplay. For instance, EDM producer Marshmello held "a concert in *Fortnite* [...] which brought in 10 million players as in-game concert attendees."[447] This successful event led *Fortnite* to continue with additional live in-game entertainment activations.[448] This paved the way for the highly successful digital performance of rap artist Travis Scott that featured the "premiere [of] his music video" for "12.3 million concurrent players" and totaled "a staggering 27.7 million unique players from around the globe."[449] Epic Games have also begun incorporating other forms of traditional entertainment in its *Fortnite Party Royale*, including presenting live motion pictures within the game for the players to congregate and enjoy together including showing "*Inception*, *Batman Begins*, and *The Prestige*."[450] Other game developers have followed this model including musical artist Charli XCX performing "live" within the game *Minecraft*[451] as well as the iconic rock band The Offspring playing a live "gig" within the game *World of Tanks* and even receiving their own branded in-game vehicle.[452] This is possible because the developers own the exclusive rights to the game so any in-game activation flows through them. Therefore, any esports organizations as well as any third-party entertainment company, such as a recording label or motion picture studio, wishing to earn any in-game revenues or otherwise operate within an existing video game is required to work with and contract directly with the game publishers.

Currently, video game developers are earning substantial revenues from the sales of the actual game as well as from third-party license fees to utilize its copyrighted material. They are also generating large income from the monetization of in-game digital content through micro-transactions as well as by the incorporation and licensing of other third-party protected works. Lately, these companies have also begun acting as league organizers, thereby creating new streams of income, such as league franchise "buy-in" fees, sponsorship revenues for league-wide partnerships, as well as the income from the broadcast and streaming licensing fees for rights to the league's gameplay.

1.4.4 Event, Tournament, and League Organizers

The final party in the esports business ecosystem is made up of the event, tournament, and league organizers. These are the entities that arrange, manage, and operate the competitive gaming matches that professional gamers and esports organization compete in. Some are international companies that run competitive gaming events throughout the globe, and some are merely regional or national-based organizations that only produce competitions within their home territory.

In particular, these companies establish competitive gaming tournaments and handle all of the logistics associated with presenting and producing the contest. This includes the creation of rules and participant regulations that list all the guidelines for the competition.[453] Since the game publisher owns the rights to the game title, the organizer must also obtain proper licenses to use the game for a commercial purpose from the game developer.[454] However, in some cases, the game publisher might actually support the organizer and instead of receiving a licensing fee from the organizer, the developer may actually pay a fee to the organizer to prepare an event on behalf of the publisher. This may occur in instances where the game publishing company might not have the necessary infrastructure or may not want to spend the funds needed to undertake these endeavors themselves but the publisher still wants to provide a way for them to receive "good-will" from its customers and from its competitive community by hosting events that spotlight its game.

The tournament and league operators also handle the logistics for the competition participants, such as scheduling their flights and lodging accommodations as well as handling any technical or gameplay matters associated with actually competing in the matches.[455] In most cases, the organizer provides the tournament participants with all of the hardware and other gaming equipment required to play, such as a monitor, a gaming chair, and a gaming "rig" (custom gaming computer) or console. As explored later, most of these gaming peripherals are provided by the league or tournament sponsors and are traditionally part of a brand partnership between a sponsoring company and the competition organizer. In addition to handling the operations of the league or tournament, these entities also plan and produce the coverage around the events. This includes handling the event marketing and promotions, hiring the talent necessary to present the competition, including sideline announcers, analysts, reporters, and shoutcasters. The organizer will also assist with any mechanical issues that arise during the match, including providing on-site gaming technicians to remedy any problems.

There are a variety of both small and large local, national, and international tournament and league organizers around the world. Some of these include Major League Gaming (owned by Activision- Blizzard); ESL; RFRSH Entertainment; Ultimate Gaming Championship (UGC); OGN, and, DreamHack.[456] There are also several organized competitive gaming leagues around the globe. Some of these include *ELEAGUE*, which is a gaming league that is televised on the North American television channel TBS; the *NBA2K League*, which is a partnership between the National Basketball Association (NBA) and the game developer Take Two Interactive for their *NBA 2K* basketball title, and eMLS, which is a partnership between *Major*

League Soccer (*MLS*) and EA for its *FIFA* soccer game. Additionally, as explored above, companies such as Activision-Blizzard and Riot Games, in addition to acting as game developers, have also begun operating as league organizers and created their own franchise leagues centered on their competitive esports titles. In particular, Activision-Blizzard has established the *Overwatch League* and the *Call of Duty League* and Riot Games operates its own regional *League of Legends* Championship Series for its *League of Legends* title. As previously explored, the development of new franchise leagues operated by traditional game publishers provides these entities with additional opportunities for monetization typically only reserved for the competition organizers, including broadcasting, streaming, and other media rights.

An event, league, or tournament arranger earns income in a variety of ways. The major source of income for most organizers is from securing broadcast and media rights deals for the distribution of their live tournament gameplay.[457] Since most esports competitions are currently not locked behind a "subscription" fee or other "pay wall" system, the matches can usually be watched for free both live and later "on-demand" through content platforms. However, the rights to the initial live broadcasts are generally sold to streaming platforms and the fees paid by these broadcasters vary substantially. Two of the major factors in determining the licensing fee paid to disseminate a gaming tournament are whether the streaming rights are exclusive or non-exclusive and what the anticipated number of viewers is. In addition, there has been a recent industry shift whereby "the success of any live [esports] broadcast" is "measured by Nielsen's average minute audience (AMA)."[458] This is opposed to solely focusing on different statistics such as "unique viewers, peak concurrent viewers, or total hours watched."[459] The "average minute audience" is defined by Nielsen as the "average number of individuals or (homes or target group) viewing a TV channel, which is calculated per minute during a specified period of time over the program duration" and has been adopted by the *Overwatch League* for presenting its viewership data.[460]

In situations where a broadcaster contracts for the exclusive live streaming rights for an event, there is usually a large licensing fee paid to the league organizer, potentially several thousand or more dollars.[461] However, non-exclusive arrangements may be substantially cheaper than exclusive rights. This is because the organizer has the ability for other broadcasters to transmit the same content by entering into multiple non-exclusive deals with a variety of broadcasters in different geographic territories or regions. Generally, each competition organizer selects the most appropriate arrangement for them, as some platforms have smaller viewership numbers than others. For instance, Twitch has "more than 15 million daily active users" with over "355 billion minutes [of gaming content] watched" on its platform.[462] As a result of these substantial viewership numbers, the platform has entered into several exclusive streaming rights arrangements with tournament organizers. For example, this includes an exclusive partnership between Twitch and tournament organizer DreamHack[463] as well as a previous two-year exclusive deal with the *Overwatch League* costing Twitch "at least $90 million."[464] At the end of the Twitch streaming deal, Activision-Blizzard on behalf of its *Overwatch League* and *Call of Duty League* entered into a new streaming partnership agreement with YouTube Gaming for a reported "$160 Million over three years."[465] In contrast, other rival streaming platforms, such as Facebook Gaming, have begun entering into both exclusive and non-exclusive streaming contracts in an attempt to grow their gaming platforms. For example, Facebook Gaming entered into an exclusive broadcast partnership with ESL for its *ESL Pro League*.[466] Facebook Gaming also created a non-exclusive arrangement with the *Capcom Pro Tour*, whose broadcast partners include both Facebook and YouTube content-streaming platforms.[467] Similarly, competition organizers are able to enter into individual streaming deals for specific foreign territories. For instance, Chinese streaming platform DouYu entered an agreement to "be the exclusive Chinese streaming partner of the *World Electronic Sports Games* (WESG)." [468] This deal permits the WESG to negotiate with other platforms to stream its competitions in other countries.[469] Similarly, Chinese broadcaster Bilibili reportedly pay $113 Million for "a three-year exclusive live streaming deal for the *League of Legends World Championships* in China," which further exemplifies the substantial revenue a league organizer could earn from licensing its event coverage.[470] Furthermore, Chinese live streaming platform Huya signed a one-year exclusive deal for the platform to act as its "exclusive digital media partner for Chinese-language broadcasts of the *ESL Pro Tour* and *Dota 2* competitions."[471]

While typically providing smaller metrics than most streaming viewership numbers, there has been a rising number of television broadcast deals for esports in the United States as well as in other countries, which continue to rise today. For example, the virtual race on Fox Sports 1 (FS1) television network for the "inaugural *eNASCAR iRacing Pro Invitational Series* drew 903,000 viewers [,…] making it the highest-rated esports TV program to date."[472] Similar to streaming deals, these broadcast arrangements can be worldwide or apply to a select number of countries or geographic areas. For example, American broadcaster ESPN provides live television coverage of the *Madden* Championship Series[473] as well as presents *Overwatch League* matches on Disney XD and the ESPN networks.[474] Other U.S. television networks have also begun telecasting esports content, including TBS televising both[475] *Counter-Strike: Global Offensive* and *Rocket League*[476] as well as *NBC Sports* displaying *Rocket League*.[477]

There has also been a growth in international esports television broadcasts. For example, Germany's Sport1 created its own eSport1 television channel to provide "24/7 esports coverage including live coverage and highlights of tournaments."[478] Similarly, the United Kingdom's Ginx TV is a 24/7 esports television network that was purchased by UK broadcasters, ITV and Rupert Murdoch's Sky TV.[479] In addition, the Danish television company TV 2 Denmark acquired telecast rights for the *ESL Pro Tour*.[480] Similarly, Canadian company Blake Broadcasting reached an agreement with tournament organizers, "ESL and DreamHack to broadcast their tournaments in the United States, Canada and Asia, with the exception of China," including the *"Intel Extreme Masters, ESL One*, and the *ESL Pro League*, as well as the DreamHack Masters and DreamHack Open tournaments" through its "regional distribution network of cable, free-to-air satellite, and OTT streaming" services.[481] Most television broadcast distribution deals usually provide the tournament organizer with a licensing fee and other potential revenues from the broadcaster in exchange for the right to broadcast the organizer's competition. As with most broadcast and media rights in the traditional entertainment and sports worlds, the larger the viewership is, the more likely that large license fees will be charged.

On top of the broadcast fees that these networks pay to the competition organizers, some of these league creators also generate revenues from any advertisements displayed on stream during the live broadcasts. Likewise, these companies may earn income through online banner sales and advertisements. This is because they possess the ability to monetize their recorded content after the broadcast originally airs. This is achieved by the tournament organizer uploading the event media to a social media platform, such as YouTube or Twitch, which is then used to monetize the content. Some of this content could include recorded matches, player interviews, and "behind the scenes" footage, as well as tournament recap shows or other media coverage focused on the competition.

Similar to esports organizations, one of the largest income streams available to event organizers are sponsorship and brand partnerships.[482] In this context, a variety of brands are enlisted by an organizer and they each pay a sponsorship fee to act as an official event sponsor or partner in exchange for a set list of deliverables from the organizer to the brand.[483] There has been a number of successful league- and tournament-specific brand partnerships, including the *ELEAGUE* partnering with AXE as the league's "official personal care partner"[484] as well as tournament organizer DreamHack partnering with a variety of brands, including Doritos,[485] Chipotle,[486] Turtle Beach headsets,[487] and Samsung.[488]

In addition to a sponsorship fee paid by a brand, event organizers may also offer to provide sponsoring companies with designated space for an exhibition or product stand at the event as part of the organizer's deliverables to the brand.[489] This opportunity could include a brand having an on-site, physical stand where the sponsor's logos and banners appear or some other sort of "branded" area. For example, as part of DreamHack's activation with Doritos, the organizer provided the snack brand with "a booth at the event that allowed attendees to challenge pro *Counter-Strike: Global Offensive* and *Fortnite* players." [490]

In most of these situations, the partnering brand contracts for category exclusivity, meaning that no other similar or competing products will be permitted to be an event sponsor for that product category. This exclusivity may also extend to prohibit any professional participating in the competition from displaying or otherwise promoting a rival sponsor during the event. The monetary fees paid as well as other compensation differs based on a variety of factors. Some of these include the number of sponsored events, the amount of product that is provided to the organizer, the cost of the product, and the anticipated viewership or "impressions" that the brand will receive as a result of the particular promotional campaign. In the case of more expensive products, such as computer processors and laptops, the partnering company may simply provide the necessary hardware; however, in other cases, the brand will provide both product and currency to the organizer.

Another revenue stream available to league and tournament creators is event operation income, including entrance fees, ticket sales, concession stands, and any "VIP" or fan "experiences."[491] The amounts earned by these entities vary substantially, in particular, the larger the venue, the more opportunity that the organizer has to earn ticket sales.[492] Some events are inexpensive to attend and others, such as the 2018 *Overwatch League* finals at Barclays Center in Brooklyn, New York, feature higher ticket prices (reported $152 for the final day).[493] Ultimately, it is clear that fans do purchase live event tickets for both large and small events, as the 20,000 tickets allotted for the 2018 *Overwatch League* finals "sold out in two weeks."[494]

In addition, the 2017 *League of Legends'* World Championships held at the 80,000-person capacity Beijing National Stadium in China "sold out in less than a minute."[495] Some tournament organizers have begun further branching out into ancillary areas. This includes into original content production, online tournament hosting, as well as new talent development.[496] For example, UGC has created a series of original esports content which provides commentary on a variety of gaming titles hosted by both established and upcoming personalities.[497]

One final stream of revenue available to competition organizers is the income earned from event-specific merchandise. This includes tournament and league-specific items such as t-shirts, hats, jerseys, socks, pins, patches, and more. For example, tournament organizer ESL sells its own custom "ESL" branded merchandise as well as markets individual products for some of its larger individual competitions.[498] This includes selling specific custom items for the Intel Extreme Masters and ESL One.[499] This is similar to event production company DreamHack, who also sells its own custom merchandise, including backpacks, mugs, and clothing with its imagery on them.[500] Similarly, many league organizers have created specific merchandise featuring the various franchise logos on a variety of items. This includes the *Overwatch League*[501] as well as the *NBA 2K League*,[502] who both have merchandise deals with clothing manufacturer Champion Apparel. Building on this revenue stream, a few companies, including UGC, are also providing opportunities for individuals to design and purchase customized merchandise, including t-shirts, jerseys, backpacks, and mouse pads.[503]

Overall, esports event organizers generate income in many similar ways that other components within the ecosystem do; however, one substantial stream of revenue solely available to competition creators is the licensing of the content for streaming and television broadcasts, which is generally unavailable to most other parties in the competitive gaming scene as well as ticket sales and other event day sales for the events they host.

1.4.4.1 Some Esports Event Operation, Production, and Management Tips

Tournament and event organizers that are establishing and operating events must be aware of some potential legal protections as well as many beneficial business practices that might be adopted by an individual or a business presenting an esports competition. This applies to events produced by established event organizers such as ESL and DreamHack as well as those hosted by smaller independent companies who create and plan their own live esports

10 Tips for Esports Event Production

When Planning An Esports Event...

- **Select the Appropriate Venue**
  (Examination of availability and status of Technical and Internet Connectivity)
- **Protect the Tournament or Event Series Name**
- **Obtain Applicable License from Game Publisher**
- **Obtain Public Performance License**
  (If contains a live musical performance)
- **Create Competition Rules, Participant, Technical Guidelines**
- **Obtain Sponsors, Set Prize Pools and Entrance Fee (if any)**
- **Market and Promote Event & Hire Event Talent**
  (Social Media & Print Ads, Security, Door Staff, Casters, Event Hosts)
- **Obtain Streaming and/or Television Distribution Deal**
- **Provide "On-Site" Technical Equipment and/or Assistance**
- **Handle Competitor & Fan Logistics, including "day of"**
  (Travel, Lodging, Accommodations, Food, Beverage, Merchandise)

competitions. One such practice is selecting the appropriate game title or titles for the competition.[504] When an organizer determines this, they may account for the potential fan and participant interest in the particular game (i.e., are a lot of people playing the game or is it an old title), the current viewership of the title (i.e., looking at past similar event viewership and the current Twitch viewership numbers for the title), and the time constraints of the event (i.e., hours or days). For instance, a *StarCraft II* match might take 30 minutes while a fighting game like *Super Smash Brothers Melee* may finish in a few minutes.[505] The selection of a particular game might hinge on the time and budgetary restrictions of an event operator. This is because the event planner must also be aware of any potential licensing fees that the operator must pay to the game's publisher to actually operate the event. Additionally, typically the longer that the event organizer needs a particular location, the more costly the overall event becomes due to the added staff costs, rental fees, and other associated operational expenses.

Another important consideration is the specific location of the gaming event and how the actual venue is designed. In particular, different titles require different event set-ups and configurations as a FPS tournament might involve "multiple computers" that are "all connected to the internet" and other games may require other arrangements.[506] For instance, the CEO of 1337 Facilities Robert D. Jordan suggests that when selecting an event space, an ideal place has "black walls, black ceiling, [and] lighting," "a lot of programmable video," and possesses easy internet "connectivity."[507] The ease of technology usage and the existence of a "strong technical infrastructure" are also particularly important, especially if the event is streamed online.[508] This is because the chosen venue must have "sufficient bandwidth to handle the throughput" from the stream, which might require at least an upload rate of "35 Mbps."[509] In addition to potential "internet costs" for hosting or streaming the event online, the venue's "electric capacity" and the associated electrical fees can also be a factor in selecting a location.[510] This fact is very important, especially when a tournament is hosted at a non-"high-power ready facility," because the venue might need to purchase additional power in order to fuel all of the competitors' consoles, monitors, computers, and any other technical equipment utilized at the event.[511]

Additionally, when operating an event at a large arena or stadium, the *Overwatch League*'s Senior Director of Marketing Kristin Connelly advised that it was important to ensure that the large esports venue "feel[s] communal and authentic."[512] Another initial consideration is whether the event is a "bring your own" equipment or "bring your own computer" (BYOC) event or if the tournament organizer provides the participants with the required hardware.[513] This is because the overall event set- up differs greatly based on who is providing the equipment, the competitor or the event production entity.[514] For example, if an organizer is hosting a competitive game on a console such as Playstation 4, the operator may need to "rent" the consoles and the selected games for the competitors to play on; or the organizer may "purchase" the equipment and games outright in order that they own these resources for their future events (or they receive the required items from an event sponsor).[515] In situations where an event producer rents audio, video, or other technical equipment, it is advantageous to create a written contract listing the parameters and conditions of the transaction. This is particularly important when dealing with these types of expensive and fragile materials.

When choosing a potential venue, an organizer has a variety of options.[516] For instance, the tournament can be hosted solely online or it may occur live at a local "game store," at a "bar," or even at a "public event space," such as a "hotel" or "convention center."[517] There has been a development of dedicated gaming centers and "esports venues" specifically equipped for such gaming events, including the HyperX Esports Arena located at the Luxor Hotel & Casino in Las Vegas, Nevada.[518] When choosing a venue, especially for larger events, it is ideal to select a place with "more room" to ensure that there is space for the hundreds or even thousands of competitors and spectators to congregate and participate in the competition.[519] This consideration is particularly important if the event company has a live "broadcast" team presenting the competition that requires ample room to operate.[520] It is also important for an organizer to be aware of any local "lodging" options for any media members, the event participants, as well as for any spectators who may travel to view the match.[521] As part of selecting an event location, an organizer should be aware of their "equipment transportation" needs as well as ensuring proper event security plans for the equipment and competitors.[522]

In addition to securing the venue, an organizer has the crucial role of creating "the rules and tournament specifications."[523] This might include the event provider imposing "age restrictions" on the participants, especially if a title is a graphic or violent one, as well as listing any other participant or "passport requirements."[524] When establishing a tournament or event rulebook, there should also be written "guidelines regarding team size," any "player substitution[s]," as well as established "equipment guidelines for players" who bring their own gear.[525]An organizer should also agree on the "technical specifications for tournament," pre-determine all of the "time issues," such as match duration and rules for "disconnections," as well as establish the applicable "game settings," such as the "difficulty level, character selection, [and the] speed of play."[526] Generally, in most established competitive communities, it is ideal to not change any of the settings unless the organizer "informs everyone" participating in the event of the "changes *well* in advance."[527]

When creating an event, it is important to utilize proper trademark protection for the event or series name.[528] This might include conducting a trademark screening search to determine the availability of an event name as well as to evaluate any ones that might block the tournament or league organizer's use of a selected mark. Once a search is conducted and it is clear, the organizer may file a federal trademark application in the United States with the United States Patent and Trademark Office (U.S.P.T.O.) for event operators in the United States as well as in any other countries that they may host events in to secure exclusive rights to the event or series name in those territories.[529] This consideration is especially important if the organizer intends to create a series of similarly named gaming competitions that reoccur each year. In fact, it is beneficial for an organizer to host "frequent" and "scheduled competitions" to "build a fan base."[530] For example, event organizer DreamHack has secured the exclusive trademark rights in its event name in a variety of classes for both its name[531] as well as for their unique logo design.[532]

There are also other business and financial considerations when operating a live esports competition.[533] This includes whether there are any independent or third-party investments to fund the event's operational costs.[534] This may factor into whether or not the tournament charges a participation fee for each player or for each competitive team.[535] If an entrance fee is charged, it is important to maintain a proper balance because if the cost is too high, then "lower skilled players won't show up" but if the "prize pool is too low," then professional and other top players may not participate in it.[536] While the topic is outside the scope of this text, different states and countries have different "gambling" laws applicable to any cash payouts of any offered prize "pots" for competitive gaming events.[537] In these cases, an organizer might instead use any allocated "prize funds" to "purchase something else, [such as] a gift card, store credit, a console" for the event winner.[538]

Additionally, as explored above, sponsorship and brand partners account for a substantial portion of the event's expenses as well as being generally used "toward [the] prize."[539] Therefore, these essential income streams require proper implementation of strategic planning and partnerships with the presenting brands to optimize the sponsor's return. To ensure each party receives the benefit of their bargain, it is beneficial to enter into a written event sponsorship agreement outlining all of the parameters and associated "deliverables" under the deal. These types of sponsorship arrangements are explored in detail later in this book.

Once an event is conceptualized, it is crucial to secure a venue or access to some other space to host the event. In this respect, it is advisable for the organizer to enter into a written agreement with the venue or premises owner. This agreement should include incorporating the essential terms related to the operation of the event, such as date and time as well as any refreshments or other catering options.[540] This document should also list who is responsible for providing and paying for any event security as well as any other operational staff.[541] It also best practice to include any cancellation terms as well as "force majeure" provisions.[542]

A force majeure clause provides one or both of the parties with the right to terminate, suspend, or otherwise "toll" (pause) an existing agreement as a result of the occurrence of a specific event. While this is not an exhaustive list, as every agreement can be edited by its parties, such events could include acts of God such as hurricanes or earthquakes, wars, riots, and "health" epidemics or pandemics, such as COVID-19.[543] This is especially relevant in light of today's COVID-19 situation where many businesses in the live event production spaces have cancelled or otherwise re-scheduled their existing events.[544] Thus, the use of these clauses in an event production agreement may assist in successfully navigating any unforeseen and potentially event-ending circumstances that could arise.

Once an event planner secures the rights to a location, there are a variety of other "licenses" or "permits" that might be required when producing the live event. Some of these might include a business license, a liquor license, or other health permit when serving any food to attendees. It is prudent that an organizer properly investigates and obtains all the required licenses and permits prior to hosting any match. Additionally, an event creator might acquire a variety of insurance policies to protect their event.[545] One obtained policy might be one that covers any potential injuries suffered by a tournament attendee. This protection might be in the form of general commercial liability or some other type of event liability insurance.[546] An event owner may also obtain business interruption coverage, which can cover a loss resulting from a business stoppage.[547] Additionally, a tournament organizer might also obtain force majeure insurance, which could provide remuneration for any financial losses resulting from a force majeure triggering event, such as those mentioned above.[548]

Finally, if the event has live music and the venue or location is unlicensed, the company might need to secure a public performance license from the applicable performing rights organization(s), such as the American Society of Composers, Authors, and Publishers (A.S.C.A.P.), Broadcast Music, Inc. (B.M.I.), or the Society of European Stage Authors and Composers (S.E.S.A.C.) (in the United States).[549] Additionally, as mentioned above, when hosting paid tournaments and other commercial events, the organizer might also need to secure licenses from the game developers.[550] This license would generally be obtained from the game publishers such as Riot Games or Activision-Blizzard. In particular, "each publisher's rules are different" so most game licensing agreements entered into between the developer and a tournament organizer list the various "stipulations" on how the particular "event can be monetized."[551] In general, the "licensing fee" for a particular tournament depends on the "scope and scale" of it.[552] For example, the licensing fee paid by an esports event producer can range from as "low as $2,000 to $10,000 for a single-day event."[553]

Once an event is ready, the organizer must begin marketing and promoting the competition. When it is live, the organizer may either "open up" the event registration for any individual that wants to compete in it or they may provide an "invite-only" tournament where the creator selects and invites the permitted teams and selected gamers.[554] When marketing an event, the organizer might secure a special guest host, a live performance, or a notable caster to create hype and exposure for the event through these selected influencers' networks.[555] In addition, the event promoter may utilize their company social media accounts and other digital marketing and public relations techniques to garner exposure for the competition. They may also create "media materials, such as pictures of [the] players [and] team presentation videos" for the event.[556] Furthermore, any created marketing communications, such as event flyers or promotional videos, could also include any "pictures or videos of any past events."[557] Also, when an event date is approaching, the organizer should be aware to announce what time the matches are scheduled for in advance as well as to use all of their social media accounts to promote and notify viewers of when the competition stream is "live."[558]

Finally, a tournament organizer may also focus their marketing efforts on further public outreach to any local event promoters, to any potential spectators, to any applicable host governments, as well as to various non-government organizations (NGOs). These outlets might also include a specific city-wide organization, such as a chamber of commerce as well as other community organizations, such as the Center for Educational Innovation (CEI) in New York.[559] In addition, there has been a rise in national NGOs "hosting video game and esports events," such as the Young Men's Christian Association (YMCA) and Young Women's Christian Association (YWCA).[560]

The success of an event hinges on a variety of factors; however, the common factor seems to be proper preparation and trying to prepare for the unforeseen. This might include preparing for "power outages," hacker attempts, competitor's disconnecting in the middle of a match, or for unpredictable global health pandemics.[561] Therefore, it is important that an esports event organizer is aware of some potential legal protections and beneficial business practices that might be adopted by a company that produces and hosts competitive gaming events.

Now that the stage is set, including having examined how each essential party in the professional video-game industry contributes, there are a few specific legal genres applicable to the esports world which are related to a developing new body of esports and professional video-game law.[562]

2

Intellectual Property Law and Its Impact on The Esports Business Ecosytem

This chapter explores some intellectual property matters related to video games and esports. In particular, it surveys two major intellectual property protections, copyright and trademarks. This section includes general information on copyright in video games as well as examining how each of these legal mechanisms protects professional gamers, gaming "influencers," and professional esports organizations and teams.

2.1 Copyright Law

One important legal protection available to secure and protect esports individuals and companies' creative assets is copyright law. Copyright law grants the owner of a protected work the exclusive right to it for a limited duration of time. To be eligible for copyright protection, a created work must be original and fixed in a tangible form, such as a sound recording fixed on a CD or a literary work printed (affixed to) on paper.[563] Many types of works are entitled to copyright protection, including original literary works, dramatic works, choreography, musical works, audiovisual works, and any other graphic or artistic work.[564] Some of these could be poetry, motion pictures, songs, computer software, dance choreography, photographs, and comics.[565] It is important to be aware that copyright law does not protect facts, ideas, systems, or methods of operation.[566]

In the United States, the Copyright Act provides the owner with five exclusive rights in their protected work.[567] These exclusive rights include (1) the right to reproduce the work; (2) the right to distribute the work; (3) the right to prepare derivative works based on the original one; (4) the right to publicly perform the work; and (5) the right to publicly display, including the exclusive right to do and to authorize third parties to create copies of the existing work.[568] This statutory language means that the copyright owner has the exclusive right to prepare and approve others to create a "derivative" work based on their original protected work. A derivative work could be a sequel or spin-off of the protected work, such as a motion picture existing as a derivative work of a particular literary publication. The owner is also provided with the exclusive right to publicly distribute copies of the work, including through sale, rental, or lease. This could include selling copies of a novel or a video game. Additionally, a copyright holder has the right to publicly perform and display the work. This right includes publicly playing a musical recording at a nightclub or other public space. For any works created on or after January 1, 1978, copyright protection lasts for the life of the author plus 70 years after the author's death.[569] This time period permits an owner's heirs to monetize the protected works after the original creator's death.

While it is widely established under international copyright treaties, such as the Berne Convention, that a copyright is automatically created when an original work of authorship is fixed in a tangible medium of expression, a formal registration of the creative materials with the United States Copyright Office within three months of publication provides valuable benefits to the copyright owner.[570] One of these benefits include that the work is a matter of public record, so it is available for search within the U.S. Copyright Office database. This makes it easy for any individual to search and to verify the exact ownership information of an existing copyrighted work. This also permits an individual to quickly ascertain a copyright owner's contact information in the event that the individual desires to use or otherwise license the copyrighted material. A valid registration certificate also constitutes prima facie evidence of valid copyright ownership of the work after five years.[571] It also permits the owner to easily license and catalog the various rights an owner possesses in their works, which is extremely beneficial when working with potential brand partners.

Additionally, prior to instituting a lawsuit for copyright infringement, which is a claim where an author believes that one of their copyrighted works has been infringed upon, the work must be registered with the U.S.

Copyright Office.[572] Furthermore, if the owner has filed for registration prior to the alleged infringement or within three months of initial publication of the work, the author may be entitled to recover actual damages incurred, statutory damages as well as the attorney's fees spent in pursuing the matter.[573] In some cases, these legal fees recovered can even exceed the actual damages suffered by the copyright owner.[574]

Registering a copyright is as easy as preparing and submitting an application to the United States Copyright Office with the appropriate filing fee. After the submission is filed, the applicant then uploads a "deposit" copy of the copyrighted material with the Office.[575] Once the work is registered and the registration certification is issued, the benefits of the registration begin immediately and are retroactive to the application's initial filing date.

A protected work can also exist in a "joint-work."[576] These are ones that are created by two or more individuals, where one of the creators, at time of conception of the work, intends to merge or otherwise mesh his or her work with another's creation.[577] This means that the joint-creation must be prepared by this author "with the intention" that the different creator's contributions will be merged together "into inseparable or interdependent parts of a unitary whole" with each author contributing separate material that "could have been independently copyrighted."[578] However, in these situations, each author's contributions to the final work do not have to be equal nor do the authors have to be physically located next to each other or even need to create the work at the same time.[579]

Generally, each co-author will own an equal ownership share in a joint-work unless otherwise agreed to in a signed writing. This is true even if one of the co-creators has contributed a greater quantity toward the completed work than the others. Additionally, since each co-author owns an "undivided" interest in the entire work, each co-owner is only permitted to grant non-exclusive licenses to third parties without the other owners' permission. This is subject to an accounting of any profits to the other co-owners earned through this license. However, in these situations, in order for an individual to issue an exclusive license, prior approval by all of the owners of the work is required. Each co-author can also fully assign his or her ownership share in the joint-work to a third party as well as bequeath his or her ownership share to his or her heirs.[580] Finally, each co-owner is entitled to equal authorship credit for the joint-work. The length of a copyright for a "joint-work" is 70 years after the last surviving author's death.[581] However, as with most arrangements, the parties can agree and negotiate any appropriate parameters or contractual terms that govern their ownership interests.

In conclusion, it is important to understand the applicability of copyright law as it relates to video and computer games, both of which are protectable assets that can be sold, licensed, and otherwise distributed by the game's owner.

2.1.1 Copyrights for Game Developers and Publishers

2.1.1.1 Copyrights in the "Game" in the United States Copyright protection for a video game and for computer software is a complex matter. This is because they are multifaceted works of authorship which require protection for both the underlying software code as a "literary" work as well as for the artwork and sound as an "audiovisual" work. Specifically, these works actually contain and combine multiple protectable art forms (music and video) with a computer program code that actually manages some of the audiovisual elements of the game. The interaction between the software language and the other components permit a user to interact and play the game. The fact that these types of works contain several individual elements provides that each element can be individually protected.[582] Some potential protectable elements include (1) any "audio elements," such as any "musical compositions, sound recordings, character voice-overs, and any imported or internal sound effects;" (2) any "video" or "visual" elements, such as "any photographic images, any digitally captured moving images, animations, or text;" and (3) the "actual computer code (including both the source code and object code)."[583] This means that a copyright can safeguard a variety of the creative elements contained in a finished game. For example, the protection may extend to the creator's specific in-game characters, any original music, the specific gameplay storylines, as well as the actual finished game. In most cases, the game designer or developer owns the copyright in the finished work. As explored later, this enables this party to license or otherwise regulate any and all third-party uses of their protected work.

2.1.1.2 The Copyright Dilemma for Game Publishers: User-Generated Content ("UGC") & "Modifications" ("Mods") In most cases, the game developer owns the exclusive intellectual property rights to the game's underlying software. However, there has been new copyright ownership discussion as a result of the recent rise in "user-generated" content, commonly referred to as UGC. In particular, video game players have started crafting their own unique content (or user "generated" works) based on existing, protected works. These include "mods" or "modifications" that are "fan-made hack or edit[s] of a game that changes its rules, layouts, or other features."[584] This means that a game's player designs their own game content that includes existing protected elements owned by the developer. A well-known mod that sparked its own competitive community was *Counter-Strike*.[585] A mod might consist of including the original protected game's characters, gameplay maps, as well as in-game items in a new user creation. This practice is potentially problematic as in almost every situation, in order to access or otherwise use the program, the new work's creator is required to agree to a game developer's "Terms of Service" (TOS) or "End-User License Agreement" (EULA). While the substance of these agreements changes, it is fairly common that they include language that prohibits, regulates, or otherwise curtails and limits the type of actions that a software user may undertake with the protected game.

However, with the rise of UGC and with the existence of these independent creations sometimes reaching their own separate level of success, gaming developers have begun adopting different philosophies and approaches on how they police third-party content that is created with or based upon their existing game.[586] In particular, the level of approval and participation on the part of game developers significantly varies. It ranges from those companies who take affirmative actions to support creators to those who do not permit them at all and may even try to stop them.[587]

As mentioned, some of these game development companies have adopted a "zero tolerance" policy against any UGC. These companies may attempt to block or otherwise prevent the creation or dissemination of any of these user-created works. While it may appear that this is just an owner merely enforcing their exclusive rights in their protected expression, many fans and gamers may not be pleased with such actions, and this could cause public backlash against the developer. This public perception has led to some game creators adopting less stringent policies toward UGC.[588]

In particular, a few companies have started to actively support and provide assistance for the development and expansion of UGC. One method occurs when the developer establishes in-game stores or other recognized marketplaces where these authors can sell or otherwise share their creations with others. For example, the developer for the title *Second Life* has recognized a creator's rights to the in-game content that they generate from their game.[589] This developer has gone even further "by granting themselves [the developer] the right to use and incorporate [...any] player-generated content into their game."[590] This is a unique formula as the company is able to incorporate and use any player-created content for their game without expending the resources to develop it themselves.

Another example of a game developer regulating the creation of UGC is Microsoft Studios. They develop titles for their gaming console, Xbox. Microsoft has enacted their own "Game Content Usage Rules" that apply to any UGC derived from their protected assets.[591] These rules provide the creators of a work with a limited right to use Microsoft's copyrighted content in their own creations "so long as the use is noncommercial."[592] This means that the newly created content cannot be made available for sale by its creator.[593] In addition, these creators must include a Microsoft copyright notice that explains that the content was created under the terms of Microsoft Studio's usage rules.[594] Similarly, Sony Entertainment has also established its own Player Studio for its gaming console, PlayStation.[595] This platform allows a user to create their own items for games like *EverQuest* and *EverQuest II*.[596] The creator is then able sell those items for "real-world money," as it is reported that the "first Player Studio user reach[ed] $100,000 in earnings to date from creating and selling in-game assets."[597] With the success of some of these unique UGC policies, other developers have begun following this model. For example, the creators of *Team Fortress 2* introduced an online store "for virtual item purchases and player-to-player trading."[598] In fact, as of October, 2011, the online store had "earned more than $2 million."[599] Finally, some game developers decline to take any position on UGC and passively allow its creation and publication without providing any additional support or assistance to the creators.

Overall, each company has adopted their own policy for policing these works. Some of these are more successful than others, so it is interesting to see whether software developers will follow others' examples and begin to monetize or otherwise incentivize the creation of UGC.

2.1.1.3 The UGC that Literally Changed The Game: Warcraft III and Dota One of the most well known and earliest examples of UGC is the evolution of the *Defense of the Ancients (Dota)* game mode from its original game *Warcraft III*.[600] *Warcraft III* was the latest installment in Blizzard Entertainment (Activision-Blizzard)'s *Warcraft* gaming series.[601] The game had initially sold over one million units and had shipped "more than 4.4 million units of the game" worldwide.[602] At the time of its release, the title was "the fastest-selling PC game ever."[603] This new computer game included a unique program called the "World Editor."[604] This program was included with each copy of the game and enabled the program's user "to create new [in-game] settings, characters, storylines, and rules [...] and then share them online with the gaming community."[605] In particular,

> [t]he World Editor enables members of the public to use *Warcraft III*'s underlying software and graphical art assets, including the character art, sounds and terrain models of the underlying game to create custom items, maps, characters, environments and campaigns (also known as a 'modification' or 'mod').[606]

The included editor also permitted the user to "'modify the strength or abilities of individual units.'"[607] The finished program file is called a mod, which "is a small computer file that can be shared with other players to permit them to play the mod using their own *Warcraft III* software."[608] However, this newly created mod "cannot be played without first installing and loading a copy of [the] game software."[609] In addition, an individual could utilize the "World Editor" to "take an existing mod and make further changes themselves;" thereby, creating a mod of an existing mod.[610]

While the editing software included with the title permitted a user to create a new mod or separate, stand-alone map and gameplay mode, these creators (and their mods) were still subject to "the terms of an End User License Agreement ('EULA') between Blizzard and users of *Warcraft III*."[611] In particular, the EULA specifically listed the "rights and responsibilities of the parties regarding their use of *Warcraft III* and the World Editor."[612] The EULA language applicable to the software "is displayed to users during the installation of *Warcraft III* and the World Editor."[613] It requires that "all users of *Warcraft III* and the World Editor consent to the EULA" or they are not permitted to utilize the game.[614]

At the time of the title's release, a potential issue emerged, as "Blizzard did not ensure that *Warcraft III*'s End User License Agreements assigned [the] intellectual property [to the works] created using the World Editor back to the company."[615] However, the EULA did state

> that players could not "use or allow third parties to use the [World Editor or the mods] created thereby for commercial purposes including, but not limited to, distribution of [the mods] on a stand-alone basis or packaged with other software or hardware through any and all distribution channels, including, but not limited to, retail sales and on-line electronic distribution without the express written consent of Blizzard."[616]

This meant that "[t]he EULA prohibits the use of *Warcraft III* or the World Editor for any commercial purpose without Blizzard's prior written consent."[617] This license also "restrict[ed] any [third-party] distribution of 'New Materials' [defined as modifications of Warcraft III created using the World Editor] on a stand-alone basis [...] through any and all distribution channels [...] without the express written consent of Blizzard."[618]

As a result of the title's new content creation capabilities, the game was highly successful, leading to a myriad of mods being created and circulated among the game's users.[619] One particular user was named Kyle Sommer, who created the original "'Defense of the Ancients' a/k/a '*Dota*'" mod.[620] This mod "pitted two teams of heroes against one another, [with] each [team] trying to destroy the other's 'central structure' while defending one's own."[621] Specifically, it was widely accepted that *Dota* was a mod from *Warcraft III*.[622] In fact, Mr. Sommer was said to have "conceived of *Dota's* setting, heroes, rules, and name—and then built them using the World Editor in late 2002."[623] After several years of success, Mr. Sommer stopped working on updates to the *Dota* mod.[624] He then made a public post on "a gaming community web forum" where he declared that "from this point forward, *Dota* is now open source. Whoever wishes to release a version of *Dota* may without my consent, I just ask for a nod in the credits to your map."[625]

After this announcement, several other individuals created their own mod variations of the original *Dota* mod by modifying Mr. Sommer's initial mod file.[626] As a result of these widely circulated and successful mods, game developer Valve Corporation became interested in creating and selling its own stand-alone, *Defense of the Ancients* game.[627] Valve then began working to commercially release its own *Dota 2* based on the mod created with *Warcraft III*'s World Editor.[628] This led to a dispute between Valve Corporation and the owner of *Warcraft III*, Blizzard (now Activision- Blizzard).[629] This ownership disagreement was ultimately settled out of court but the situation highlights the potential issues that could arise due to user-generated and fan-modified content.[630] Furthermore, as a result of the mod's worldwide success, this particular type of game mode continues to increase in popularity. In fact, it has "spawn[ed] a number of spin offs including *League of Legends*, *Heroes of Newerth* and, most recently, *Dota 2*."[631]

Even though the *Warcraft/Dota* dispute had both contract and other intellectual property matters involved in it, one argument at the heart of the dispute was whether the derivative work (the *Dota* mod) was sufficiently "original" as to distinguish itself from the original protected work (*Warcraft III*). If this was the case, then this fact could provide the creator of the derivative work with distinct and separate rights in the mod from those owned by the rights holder of the original game.[632] While the specific legalities related to the protection of a derivative work are outside the scope of this text, some guidance can be gleamed. For example, it is important to "focus on whether the new[ly] [created] content is sufficient[ly] 'original' from [the] original" work.[633] This is because "player-generated content is less likely to be [considered] original if the creator's choices are tightly constrained by the mechanics of the games [that] they play."[634] When examining whether a newly created virtual work made from an existing game is sufficiently original, it is beneficial to determine whether the creator has a "large amount of creative freedom" or not.[635] For example, if the user is provided with the option to utilize "hundreds of building materials with billions of possible configurations," then this fact could be beneficial in recognizing the derivative work as being sufficiently original.[636] This is because the newly fashioned work "is more a function of the player's creativity than of [a] game-imposed limitation."[637] This seems to be true of *Warcraft III*'s World Editor, which included many different options to create the user's own new "world." Essentially, this could mean that a derivative work created under these conditions might then be eligible to be separately copyrighted by the UGC creator. This is in contrast to a situation that only permits the author to "choose [from] one of two genders and [from] one of five classes."[638] This fact may result in the UGC being seen as "not 'original'" due to the game only presenting "10 possible combinations of gender and class."[639] While this is a very superficial analysis of this topic, it is important for any creative individual to be aware of the need to create a sufficiently original work in order to potentially achieve separate, stand-alone rights in any user-created work.

Common Copyrights For Gaming "Talent" & Esports Teams/Orgs

Gaming "Talent"	Teams/Orgs
Logo Design	**Logo Design**
Merchandise Design	**Merchandise Design**
Original Content - Social Media Headers - Stream Overlays - Emotes - Thumbnails - Cover Images - Photographs - Videos	**Original Content** - Social Media Headers - Stream Overlays - Emotes - Thumbnails - Cover Images - Photographs - Videos

2.1.2 Copyrights for Gaming "Talent": "Competitive" Gamers, and Gaming Influencers

In addition to copyright protection for the underlying software, professional gamers and content creators can also utilize copyright law to protect a few of the gaming talent's creative assets. For example, an individual can obtain copyright protection for a player logo or any custom-designed merchandise. In addition, the gaming influencer can copyright their individual website as well as any created social media banners or other "headers" that they utilize. A gaming influencer can also receive protection for any Twitch or other streaming platform "overlays" designs, any custom "emotes," as well as for any photographs or audiovisual works produced by a videographer or photographer for the gamer. However, in instances where the gamer is utilizing a third party to create any of the aforementioned creative assets, it is important that the individual and the third party enter into a written agreement. This includes entering into a contract that provides the gamer with the necessary rights to any created work by a photographer, videographer, "thumbnail," video, or audio editor or designer. This agreement generally includes providing the individual owner with the exclusive rights to reproduce, to distribute, and to otherwise use the created asset for any commercial and promotional purpose. Copyright law can also provide protection for any original created content that is shared on social media, including on Instagram, Facebook, Tik Tok, and YouTube.

2.1.3 Copyright for Professional Esports Organizations and Teams

Similar to individual gamers, professional esports organizations and teams should be aware of how copyright law is used to protect some of their valuable creative materials. For example, similar to a gamer, an organization can obtain copyright protection for their team logo as well as any merchandise or other graphic designs that are created for them. In addition, analogous to gaming 'influencers, the team can also copyright their team website as well as any social media banners or other headers created for any signed talent or for their team pages. An esports organization may also protect any Twitch or other streaming platforms overlays made for any signed gamers as well as for official team pages. Protection could also extend to any custom-created 'emotes' utilized by the team or its players as well as any photographs or audiovisual works produced for the organization. This could also include protecting any created content, such as a YouTube or Tik Tok video. However, such protection must only be applicable to the original footage contained in the video, without applying to the actual gameplay. This is because the game developer typically owns the exclusive rights to the gameplay. Again, similar to individuals involved in the gaming world, esports organizations utilizing third parties to create any of their assets must ensure that appropriate documentation is in place with this individual. The created document should specifically provide the team with all the rights to the work. It is also prudent to ensure that any agreement includes a transfer of exclusive ownership from the creator to the organization, including providing the esports company with the right to sell or otherwise license the created asset.

As a result of the increased value in a team's logo and associated creative assets, proper copyright protection has become even more important for proper monetization. This is especially true as the professional esports spaces continue to expand and as enterpreneurs continue to rely on building a gamer or a team's unique brand and "image," proper protection of their associated imagery becomes of central importance.

2.2 Trademark Law

A party wishing to properly exploit and monetize their brand must focus on proper brand management techniques. Thus, in addition to copyright law, another intellectual property protection available to professionals and individuals in the esports space is a trademark.[640] Trademark law grants the owner of a mark the exclusive right to use a mark or brand to differentiate the goods or services provided by that individual or business from those provided by another. This protection can apply to a word, a phrase, a slogan, a logo, a design, a smell, a sound, or a combination of these, that is used in relation to a particular good or service.[641] It can even apply to a "hashtag" that is used for marketing or as an indicator of a good or service.[642] Trademark protection also includes a party utilizing a name as a "service" mark, which is obtained for providing a particular service (e.g., participation in professional video game competitions). Essentially, trademarks and service marks exist to identify and distinguish the source of a particular good or service to the consuming public from another product or company. Trademark protection exists at both the federal and state level as well as internationally in many countries across the world.

In the United States, trademark rights are established through "actual use." This means that the party must actually be utilizing the mark in commerce for the selected goods or services in order to acquire rights in the brand name. In addition to an actual use trademark application, a U.S. application can be filed for a mark that the owner intends to use. This is called an "intent-to-use" application and is filed prior to the actual use of a mark in United States commerce to "reserve" the brand name for a specific good or service. The name must then actually be used in U.S. commerce within six months after a Notice of Allowance is issued by the United States Patent and Trademark Office (U.S.P.T.O.). If the mark is not currently in use, an extension of time to submit the Notice of Allowance must be filed. This prolongs the deadline to use the mark so that the applicant can continue to reserve the name until they successfully use it in commerce. A failure by the applicant to file a Notice of Allowance or an applicable extension could forfeit the application as it is seen as "abandoning" it.

Generally, a mark can only be registered if it is distinctive and is not generic for the goods or services provided. A distinctive trademark is one that is able to differentiate the goods or services provided by one individual or company from the goods or services provided by others. Under trademark law, a mark can either be fanciful, arbitrary, suggestive, descriptive, or generic. Fanciful marks are those that have no other meaning other than existing as an indicator of the source of a particular good or service, such as "Exxon" for gasoline or "Kodak" for cameras. An arbitrary mark is one that has no relation to the goods or services being provided, such as "Apple" for computers. A suggestive mark suggests a quality or particular characteristic of the goods or services provided, such as "L'eggs" for pantyhose. A descriptive mark is one that merely describes the goods or services provided without requiring any additional imagination or thought on part of the consumer, such as "Sharp" for television. A descriptive mark generally cannot be registered; however, in some cases, it can be registered if the name has acquired secondary meaning. "Secondary meaning" is typically substantiated by proving that the relevant consumer marketplace associates this particular mark with the goods provided by the owner.[643] If a party uses a mark in commerce for over five years, this fact can assist in creating a presumption of secondary meaning which the owner may use to their advantage.[644] Finally, a trademark that is generic cannot be registered as such a mark is inherently incapable of acting as a trademark. This is because the term is or has become a common word that identifies the products and services without specifying a particular source for the goods or services. For example, the former Toronto-based esports teams, whose fairly generic name, *Toronto Esports Club* was involved in a name usage dispute, which led the aforementioned organization to ultimately fold as a result of it.[645] This trademark dispute highlights the potential downfall an esports business could face without proper brand management and strategic planning.

Due to the large, worldwide audience for competitive gaming, it is prudent to ensure that any intellectual property works are properly protected. Some countries have individual offices or agencies that administer trademarks. Other nations, such as the United States, are also signatories to international treaties, such as the Madrid Protocol. This means that the Madrid Protocol permits a U.S. trademark applicant or owner to apply for protection in many other signatory countries around the world based on an existing American application or registration without applying for protection in each country individually directly through that country's intellectual property office.[646] Further discussions of international trademarks are outside the scope of this work.

2.3 Trademarks in Esports

Common Trademarks & International Classes For Gaming "Talent" & Esports Teams/Orgs

Gaming "Talent"	Teams/Orgs
Gamer-Tag	Team Name
Logo	Logo
Slogans & Hashtags	Slogans & Hashtags
U.S.P.T.O. International Classes - Computer Hardware (009) - Clothing & Apparel (025) - Gaming Equipment (026) - Endorsement Services (035) - Entertainment Services (041)	U.S.P.T.O. International Classes - Computer Hardware (009) - Clothing & Apparel (025) - Gaming Equipment (026) - Endorsement Services (035) - Entertainment Services (041)

2.3.1 Trademarks for Gaming "Talent": Competitive Gamers and Gaming Influencers

In the esports context, competitive gamers, gaming influencers, as well as esports organizations may desire to obtain protection for their brand name through trademark law.[647] Generally, a competitive gamer or gaming influencer may attempt to protect their in-game name known as a "gamer-tag" as well as the gamer's unique logo design. For esports organizations and teams, the entity might protect the team name as well as the organization's logo. It is important to be aware that a logo design and a team or gamer names are two distinct trademarks that may each be protected. Thus, in order to protect both a logo and the team name or gamer-tag, two separate trademark applications must be filed. This means that one application must be filed for the competitor's gamer-tag or the organization's team name as well as the filing of an additional trademark application to protect the gamer or team's unique logo design. This is true, even if the logo design already includes the player's gamer-tag or the team's name in it.

Prior to attempting to protect a specific mark, similar to an esports event organizer, it is prudent for a party to conduct a trademark screening search to determine the availability of the selected name. The search can be beneficial in evaluating the existence of any other confusingly similar ones that may block the gamer or team's registration. Additionally, since official player and team websites, merchandise, and social media platforms are essential streams of income for most prominent esports parties, a screening search may also be beneficial by identifying any potential barriers to a name's usage in these areas prior to establishing and developing these platforms under that name. Once a search is conducted and a name is cleared, federal or state trademark applications can then be filed with the appropriate state department for a specific state's protection and/or with the U.S.P.T.O. for national coverage.

A valid trademark registration provides the owner with valuable rights in the name and any protected logo designs. In particular, a registration provides the owner with the ability to prevent other individuals from "stealing" or otherwise impersonating the protected gamer or esports organization name or logo. This includes preventing a non-owner from utilizing a protected gamer-tag or team name in another gaming title. A registration could also assist in protecting against or prosecuting any imposter user who slightly modifies an established name, such as by adding a number or letter, and then uses it. For example, if "WorldWideJust" is a protected gamer-tag owned by a legendary *Overwatch* gamer and an imposter "WorldWideJust1" creates a YouTube account, there could be potential confusion if the imposter account begins transmitting *Overwatch*-related content on this platform. If "WorldWideJust" was a registered mark, this registration may permit the mark owner to file an infringement claim with the social media platforms, in attempt to retrieve or block the infringing account, including with Facebook, Twitter, Instagram, YouTube, and Twitch.[648] A valid registration also permits the owner to contact the United States Customs and Border Patrol to prevent the importation of any infringing or counterfeit goods bearing the protected mark or any goods containing marks that are confusingly similar to the mark.[649]

Furthermore, when a player or team desires to enter into a sponsorship or other licensing arrangement, the existence of a registered trademark may be useful. This is because in order for the brand to enter into the partnership with the player or organization, the potential brand partner may require rights to some identifiable asset, such as a team name, team logo, player logo, or gamer-tag. A registered mark may also be compulsory for licensed products developed by a third party, such as any officially licensed player or team-branded merchandise or gaming peripherals. This is because without documented proof of exclusive ownership of a particular mark or phrase that the registration provides, it may be difficult to ensure that the sponsor or other licensor has exclusive rights to the use the name or logo for the licensed item. Therefore, since a trademark registration provides clear information on who owns what mark and for what type of goods or services, the lack thereof can become problematic and may create a barrier to business dealings with some third parties.

In addition, the failure of a player or esports organization to register a trademark in their team name, gamer-tag, or logo may cause confusion or potential legal disputes over who actually owns the name. For instance, if a gamer is signed to a professional esports team or organization, the team may claim that they own rights to a player's gamer-tag as a result of the competitor competing on behalf of the team. This may be true, as in many cases, the organization's right to utilize the signed gamer's name, trademarks, and other likeness language is included in the standard player agreements (which are explored later). However, in these situations, a player can potentially protect themselves by first registering their gamer-tag prior to utilizing it in a competition and prior to signing an agreement with the organization that grants the team the rights to the gamer's name. This would be because the gamer would be the only party allowed to use the name for the particular good or service. This fact can also be a useful bargaining chip in negotiations. For example, an individual could provide the team with a license to use the name instead of a full assignment of the rights to utilize the protected name in commerce. A gamer can also attempt to potentially exclude assigning the rights to utilize the name to the team the player signs with unless certain conditions are met. Furthermore, the lack of a registration could also act as a stumbling block in prosecuting a potential infringer. For instance, if a party utilizes a gamer-tag or team name first in another game and if the original mark is not protected, the original user will have little to no recourse against them. They could even potentially end up losing the right to use the name entirely.

Finally, the ownership of a valid trademark registration could potentially be utilized by a gamer or a team to pursue a sponsor or a tournament organizer for failure to pay them. In these instances, the mark owner could argue that they only permitted and provided a limited license to use their protected mark to the sponsors or the competition organizer solely for the commercial advertising and promoting of the organization or sponsor. Therefore, the failure by the entities to provide the negotiated for compensation could be tantamount to a breach of this license and may even permit the owner to recover any damages that they incur as a result of this breach. While this may seem far- fetched, with the rise of organizations and tournaments defaulting on owed payment,[650] the existence of a trademark registration may act as a weapon in a player or team's arsenal when pursuing owed compensation, such as tournament winnings and sponsorship monies.[651]

There are a variety of classes of goods that a team or gamer might apply for protection in. Some of these potential classes include International Class 041 for "organizing and conducting competitive and non-competitive games in the field of video games" as well as "entertainment services, namely, participation in video game competitions." Additionally, protection might also be applied for in International Class 009 for different types of computer equipment, such as "computer hardware; computer keyboards; computers; computer monitors; computer mice; mouse pads." A trademark might also be registered in International Class 025. This class is for various clothing and other merchandise items, such as t-shirts, sweatshirts, pants, and hats. Another potentially applicable classification might be International Class 035. This particular class is for the provision of "endorsement and advertising services, namely, promoting the goods and services of others." In addition, a professional gamer might protect their name in Class 028 for "gaming mice," gaming keyboards, and "gaming headsets." These select international classes are in addition to any of the other trademark classes that an applicant can choose from and that may be applicable to their brand.[652]

While most professional gaming individuals are still not securing a registration in their trade name (their gamer-tag) or in their logo design, there has been a recent trend of top gaming professionals beginning to secure registrations. For example, iconic competitive gamer, Johnathan "Fatal1ty" Wendel has received protection for his gamer-tag, "FATAL1TY."[653] Additionally, competitive gamer, Matthew "Nadeshot" Haag has protected his gamer-tag, "NADESHOT" in a variety of classes, including for "dietary and nutritional supplements;" for "video game controllers;" and, for "live performances by e-athletes and competitive gamers.[654] Another gaming influencer, *100 Thieves* content creator Jack "CourageJD" Dunlop has received protection for his gamer-tag for entertainment services.[655] *Fortnite* streamer Tyler "Ninja" Blevins has also applied for trademark protection in many different classes for both his gamer- tag as well as his unique "Ninja" logo.[656] In addition, *Fortnite* streamer Benjamin "DrLupo" Lupo received trademark protection for his gamer-tag, "DRLUPO" in a variety of classes as well as for his unique "D" logo.[657] Furthermore, *Fortnite* streamer Turner "TFUE" Tenney is also attempting to register his gamer- tag "TFUE" for clothing and entertainment services.[658] Also, another prominent streamer, Timothy "TimTheTatman" Betar has applied for protection in his gamer-tag in several categories, including "books" and "entertainment services."[659] Finally, YouTube streamer Felix Arvid Ulf Kjellberg has protected his gamer-tag, "PewDiePie" for "posters," "clothing," and for entertainment services, including "live performances featuring video game playing with player commentary and narration."[660]

2.3.2 Trademarks for Professional Esports Organizations and Teams

In addition to gaming talent protecting their gamer-tag, many professional esports teams have also engaged in the protection of their team name and other associated imagery and logos. Some of these organizations include Team Liquid, who owns a variety of registrations in several classes.[661] In addition, other teams such as esports organization FNATIC,[662] Evil Geniuses,[663] Splyce,[664] OpTic Gaming,[665] Cloud9,[666] Counter Logic Gaming,[667] Complexity,[668] and Flyquest[669] all have trademark registrations protecting their team name. Additionally, after its rebrand, Immortals Gaming Club (IGC) has applied to protect its team name and logo[670]as well as for its "IGC" mark.[671]

Overall, any party involved in the gaming world should be aware of how they protect their brand. This includes being knowledgeable about what mechanisms exist to provide such protection. For instance, this might be in the form and use of trademark and copyright registrations to reinforce owners' rights to their protected assets.

3

Business and Tax Law and Its Impact on the Esports Business Ecosytem

3.1 Business Entities in Esports

As esports revenues continue to increase, the need to ensure that every individual involved is maximizing their earned funds becomes even more pressing. This applies to any talent involved in professional gaming, including "competitive" gamers and gaming "influencers" as well as any professional esports teams and organizations. Consequently, in many cases within the United States, it is advisable and most convenient for a gamer or team to form their own business organization entity, such as a corporation or a limited liability company (LLC). Whether the party ultimately forms a C-Corporation, S-Corporation, LLC, or some other type of business entity typically will depend on which state the entity will be formed in as well as other issues including taxation and control. An examination of the anticipated business structure that the business owners envision creating is also of interest. The operating location of the company may also be a factor in this decision. For instance, a corporation in New York does not have the same costly publication requirement that a New York LLC has.[672] However, the fact that each entity has its own unique ownership restrictions is important to explore prior to selecting one of these business entity types. Additionally, each state provides different tax treatment for the business entities established within its state as well as imposing different statutory limitations on ownership of a particular entity. Therefore, in most cases, it is prudent to consult with a qualified professional, such as an attorney or accountant, when deciding which type of business entity to form as well as when selecting which state is appropriate for a particular gamer or team to form the entity in. Once the company is established, the entity acts as the foundation for all of the team and player's business endeavors.

One of the most important benefits of many formal business organizations is that the entity may protect the business entity organizer's personal assets. This means that these limited liability entities may shield the owners from personal liability for any claims arising from any contracts or other arrangements entered into on behalf of the individual through its entity. This includes protecting any residential and personal property as well as any financial investment and bank accounts personally owned by the gamer or team owners. These companies can protect their assets such as cars, stocks, bonds, jewelry, securities, and bank accounts which are established in the individual gamer or team owner's name. Again, an individual should always consult an experienced attorney or other tax professional for assistance in forming any of these business organizations as well as to understand the intricacies and specific entity requirements.

Generally, to receive this protection, the created business entity is the party that should enter into an agreement with a third party on behalf of the entity's owner (the gamer or the team owner). If this occurs, then if a sponsor, a league organizer, or some other third-party creditor has an existing claim against a team or individual gamer (who had properly entered into the original agreement using their created entity), the only recourse for that creditor would be against the business entity, not the individual owner and their personal assets. This means that creditors generally cannot recover against the individual owner's personal assets. For example, this may be beneficial if you are an owner of an esports team and during a tournament one of the team members spills a drink on a computer and destroys it. If the agreement with the tournament organizer is solely entered into with the limited liability company entity (which it should be), then the entity and their assets will be the only party contractually responsible for the damaged property while the team owner and its individual team members are not held personally liable for the damage. Therefore, the tournament organizer's only option is to attempt to recover the funds required to fix or replace the broken equipment from the entity (which may not have sufficient assets to cover this amount). However, if this did not occur, then the organizer might be able to recover any suffered damages or losses directly from the team owner or gamer personally.

The existence of these companies also provides easy management over any tangible property owned by the organization or the gamer. This could include ownership of any streaming equipment, gaming peripherals, consoles, or computers as well as any commercial or residential property. The created entity also provides its owner with the ability to easily manage all of their intellectual property for licensing and distribution purposes. This includes managing any trademarks, copyrights, audiovisual works, photographs, logos, or web sites owned by them. The created entity is also perfect for organizing and utilizing traditional "work-for-hire" arrangements and other rights assignment documentation. These documents are useful to ensure that all the rights that any ancillary parties may possess in a created work are properly owned by the company. This would then permit the company to use the work for whatever purpose they require. Such agreements could be with any third parties utilized by the gamer or esports organization, such as any graphic designers, photographers, videographers, and any other independent individual.

Additionally, some of the third parties that the team or gamer works with could require that any payment to them is made with the entity's Employer Identification Number (E.I.N.) (also referred to as a Tax-ID number), as opposed to paying them personally. This could include payments from a streaming platform such as Twitch or a merchandise website that processes orders on their behalf. In these cases, an entity must be created as an E.I.N., which is analogous to the company's social security number, can only be obtained by an existing business entity.

As with any business, more than one individual or even another entity can possess an interest or a share of the created business and be an owner of it. This could include ownership by any potential third-party investors or any other industry professionals such as a talent manager or an agent (if the gaming talent has one). In the situations where there are multiple parties involved in an entity's ownership, it is prudent to execute a written agreement that outlines each party's ownerships rights, how the company is managed, and any other powers of each interest holder. Therefore, in most cases, a business entity is typically governed by a written contract that outlines how the entity will operate. For example, an operating agreement is created for an LLC and a shareholder agreement is drafted for a corporation. These documents typically include an outline of the split of any profits and losses among owners. They may also specify how any management decisions shall be addressed and how additional owners and members can be added to or removed from the entity. Without these established outlined contractual procedures, it may be very difficult to determine certain business decisions, especially when more than one individual is involved in these important choices.

While these business entities provide numerous benefits to their owners, there are potential ways a third party can "pierce the corporate veil." Piercing the corporate veil is an attempt by a third party to disregard an existing business entity's protection of its owners and attach an individual's personal assets.[673] To combat this action, it is essential that a company follows any and all mandated statutory procedures and guidelines, which are different in each state. One of these formalities includes the preparation of annual corporate minutes to ensure that a corporation is a real functioning entity. Other requirements might be the filing of an annual Statement of Information or other yearly documents. Also, careful usage of the company's bank accounts is essential to ensure the separation of business revenue from any personal accounts. This is meant to ensure that the entity is utilized for a proper business purpose and not just merely as a "shield" for the owner from personal liability. Further explanation of this topic is out of the scope of our discussion but is a factor that a business owner must be aware of.

It is clear that the use of a business entity provides unique protections and benefits for its owners.[674] Thus, an individual should explore the need for the entity and how the existence of it may factor into the party's long-term business goals.

3.1.1 "Loan-Out" Companies for Gaming "Talent": Competitive Gamers and Gaming Influencers

As with many other participants in the entertainment and sports world, a U.S. business entity created by an individual competitive gamer or gaming influencer is referred to as a loan-out company. For example, "WorldWideJust, Inc." could be a corporate entity that conveys the right to the owner's competitive gaming performances. The loan-out company created by the gamer then provides the individual's services as an "employee" of the loan-out entity to a third party, such as an esports organization or a sponsoring brand. As the name indicates the entity "loans out" the services of the employee (the gamer) by contracting with another party (the esports team) instead of this party (the team) contracting directly with the gamer. This means that the loan-out company executes the agreement with the third party and then "hires" the gamer to perform the work that they are contracted for. However, before the loan-out company is able to enter into agreements on behalf of the professional gamer or content creator with other parties, the individual must first sign themselves to this created entity. This means, in a sense, that the gamer will actually be signing themselves to an agreement with the entity that they also are an owner of.

If an agreement is structured as such, ultimately, the corporate entity (the loan-out company), not the individual owner of it, is liable for any debts and contractual obligations of the entity. This means that the loan-out company will be the only party contractually responsible for any damage suffered by a third party so any creditors of the owner generally cannot recover against the individual's personal assets. Therefore, it is prudent to ensure that any agreement is solely entered into with the gamer's holding company so that the gamer will not be personally liable for any damage. In these situations, the damaged party's only opportunity is to attempt to recover the funds from the loan-out entity (which may not have sufficient assets) without being able to recover its losses from the individual.

3.1.2 Business Investments and Transfers for Professional Esports Organizations and Teams

The existence of a corporate entity provides unique benefits for professional esports organizations. In particular, it enables a team to more easily structure the transfer of any of its assets. This includes transactions with any third-party investments in the organization, the sale or purchase of any professional gamer's contracts, as well as the acquisition or transfer of an organization's rights to a specific tournament or league "spot" or "slot."[675]

With the rapid and constant changes to competitive team rosters, the ability for a team to seamlessly sign, release, trade, or otherwise transfer an existing contractual obligation is accomplished easily through an entity.[676] In this respect, the business entity acts as a "house" that holds all of the various rights that the organization has to any players as well as to any competitive tournament or league spots. The ownership of a spot or slot in an organized league or tournament enables its owner to field a team and compete in specific events.[677] This is in contrast to the lack thereof, which prevents a competitive team from participating in a closed-field tournament (which is an invite-only situation which is not open to the public). It is also important for a team owner to be aware that for a player or competitive slot or spot transfer to be enforceable, the organization must follow any established league or tournament regulations governing how such actions can be enacted. In many cases, the failure of a team to adhere to any existing established transfer rules could cause any transaction to be deemed invalid and not be processed.

Furthermore, with the rise in esports investments by third parties, the proper business structuring of a team provides for a much easier and seamless fundraising process. In fact, in 2018, there was a total of "over $4.5B USD in disclosed investment" spent on esports.[678] This figure is up from the previous year's total of "$490M" in esports-related investments.[679] Of that total amount, "$258M USD" was invested directly into esports teams and organizations in the last few years.[680] There has also been talk and hope for even larger organization valuations in the future.[681] In particular, the amounts contributed to an esports organization have come from a variety of investment sources. These include investments from venture capital (VC) firms, private equity companies, as well as from "family offices."[682] For example, "39" different venture capitalist firms invested, including Hersh Interactive Group (invested in Team EnvyUS), Bessemer Venture Partners (invested in TeamSoloMid), WISE Ventures (purchased *Minnesota Røkkr* franchise in the *Call of Duty League*),[683] and The Kraft Group (invested in *Andbox*, owners of *New York Subliners* franchise in the *Call of Duty League* and the *New York Excelsior* franchise in the *Overwatch League*).[684] In addition, some private equity firms have begun investing in the professional gaming space.[685] For example, the Artist Capital Management, a firm that raised "$100 million" has acquired ownership stakes in esports team 100 Thieves and *Overwatch League* franchise, *Washington Justice*)[686] Similar to traditional sports teams, some private family offices are investing in esports franchises.[687] One such transaction was when The Jones Family (the financial vehicle for *Dallas Cowboys* owner Jerry Jones) and Goff Capital (the family office for the real estate investor John Goff) purchased a majority ownership in Jason Lake's Complexity Gaming.[688]

Venture capital firms are the type of entities that invest in "early-stage" companies, usually those which are in a "pre-revenue" state.[689] These types of investments are usually considered "riskier" due to the "lack of historical performance/financials" of the business, including many esports organizations.[690] This is because many esports teams do not have several years or decades of financial records and analytics to substantiate its potential value. In general, private equity companies are usually much more "risk adverse" than venture capitalists.[691] Thus, most private equity institutions primarily invest in a company to own either a "minority" or "majority" interest.[692] However, in many of these cases, prior to any investment by these entities, "strong historical financials" in the potential investment property must be substantiated.[693] Due to this fact, there have not been many private equity firms investing in esports organizations. This is because these type of financial companies are very risk-averse, so the "unpredictable cash flows" associated with esports has created barriers to investments from these institutions.[694] Finally, a family office investment is another common type of third party investing capital in esports teams.[695] These investment vehicles are owned by "wealthy individuals," who have established "private wealth advisory firms" in an effort to "preserve [the family's] capital as opposed to [focusing solely on] generat[ing] significant" returns on the funds.[696]

There are many aspects that a potential investor may scrutinize when conducting their due diligence prior to investing in an esports team. These factors are relevant in determining whether the third party will invest their funds in an esports organization or not. One important consideration by an outside investor could be the existence of a "dedicated team training facility or gaming house."[697] This is because the existence of such a facility provides the esports organization with unique opportunities for "naming rights, on-site activations and content curation opportunities" at the premises that would be unavailable without it.[698]

Another factor could be whether any "consistent future revenue streams" exist.[699] For instance, if an existing team is unable to currently show this, they can instead demonstrate "that there are future plans to develop consistent revenue streams."[700] This could be accomplished by providing evidence that the team intends to begin selling "merchandise" or some other new product.[701] In addition, the existence of "a consistent sponsor [... even], if the dollar contribution is low, [...] could help in building a strong case for an investment" from a third party.[702] Consequently, the terms and the existence of organizational "partnerships [...] may offer [... another] consistent revenue stream outside of merchandise sales" which might appeal to a prospective investor.[703]

In addition, other relevant factors that might assist in validating the potential "growth prospects" of a particular esports team include if the organization has a "large following on gaming and/or social media platforms"[704] as well as if the organization has signed any "[m]ajor [gaming] influencers" to it.[705] Potential investors may also examine "the company's historical financials" in an effort to "verify and confirm the accuracy of the financials provided" to them.[706] Furthermore, an examination of the amount of the team's "working capital" can also be an important determining factor.[707] "Working capital" is the "current operating assets less current operating liabilities" available to the organization.[708]

Finally, the existence of a "strong management team" that has "prior experience," extensive industry connections, and an outlined plan for "future growth" is beneficial.[709] Furthermore, another factor that third-party investors may look at and value is if the current "[m]anagement's willingness to remain" with the team to "help minimize any potential disruptions in the business' daily operations."[710]

Overall, there are many considerations that a potential investor might take into account when determining whether or not to finance or otherwise invest in an esports team. All of these must be examined and may factor into the ultimate determination on whether a party invests.

3.2 Tax Matters in Esports

Some Example Business "Write-offs" for Gaming "Talent" or Esports Teams/Orgs
• **Streaming & Video Recording Equipment Costs** (Microphones, Webcams, Pop Filters, Stands, Camera)
• **Streaming, Audio, and Video Editing Software Costs**
• **Internet & Data Storage Costs & Actual Game & Console Costs** (Xbox Game, Playstation Console, P.C. Game, Computer Components)
• **Social Media & Physical Marketing Costs** ("Ad Buys," Facebook "Boosts," IG and Twitter "Ads," Promotional Giveaways & "Branded" Items – T-Shirts, Stickers, VC, V-Bucks, Game Codes)
• **Travel and Meal Expenses**
• **Photographer & Videographer Fees**
• **Website, Graphic and Video Design and Editing Costs** (Websites, Logos, Overlays, Emotes, YouTube videos)
• **Accounting, Business, & Legal Fees** (including Trademark and Copyright Filing Fees)
• **Personnel Salary & Associated Costs** (Gamers, Managers, Coaches) (Travel, Housing, Bootcamp, Equipment, Team Merchandise)

3.2.1 Personal Income Tax Matters for Gaming "Talent": Competitive Gamers and Gaming Influencers

As with most occupations, United States residents are subject to personal income tax on any income they earn. This includes any professional gamers, gaming content curators, as well as streamers.[711] In particular, these individuals must pay federal income tax to the Internal Revenue Service (I.R.S.) on their worldwide income.[712] They may also be responsible for potentially paying personal income tax in every country, state, and, sometimes, the city that they "work" in and earn revenues from.[713]

In most cases, in addition to federal income taxes, an individual just pays their personal state income tax to their state of residency; however, in recent years, there has been a rise in new state legislation intended to tax the personal income earned in a state by a non-resident.[714] The tax created by these new statutes is commonly referred to as a "jock tax."[715] This tax applies to any income "earned" in a particular state by a non-resident. For instance, New York imposed a non-resident income tax on visiting professionals who have earned income within the state.[716] In these situations, New York taxes the income earned by the non-resident in state, including any salary. The taxable income payable to the state is based upon the percentage of total "duty days" that the individual spends and earns income within the state.[717] A "duty day" is defined as any day that the professional provides some form of work on behalf of their employer within the state.[718] This could include a media or sponsorship appearance, a team practice or scrimmage, or participation in a tournament or a league match. This concept is exemplified by the professional gamers who participate in the *NBA 2K League*.[719] These individuals are subject to the traditional federal income tax on their personal earnings, such as their salary and tournament winnings. Additionally, these gamers are also subject to state income tax payable to the state that the franchise is located in. For example, if the gamer plays for the Los Angeles Lakers' *NBA 2K League* affiliate franchise, Lakers Gaming, then they are subject to federal income tax as well as state income tax in all of the states that they compete in. This would include California as well as New York. This is because the *NBA 2K League* studio is located in New York and that is where all the competitions were held. This means a professional *NBA 2K League* player on Lakers Gaming is subject to federal income tax (payable to I.R.S.), California state income tax (payable to California Tax Department), as well as New York state income tax (payable to the New York Tax Department).

As discussed above, a professional video gamer or content curator must pay taxes to all of the states and countries that they earn income from.[720] In the United States, this means that any individual who is paid over six hundred ($600.00) dollars should receive a "1099-Misc" form from the payor detailing the received income.[721] This reporting requirement applies to one of the largest avenues of a gamer's income, their content streaming and advertising revenue. This means that streaming services submit a "1099" form so that a streamer can document the monies that they earned through its platform. This applies to the entities that operate Twitch[722] and YouTube.[723] In particular, each streaming platform has its own individual requirements and tax information that should be reviewed prior to signing up and beginning to earn income through these third-party services.[724]

Additionally, a streamer is also subject to personal income taxes on all of the funds that are earned through their stream. This includes any funds earned through the advertisements embedded in the cast as well as any "donations" or "tips" that they received from their viewers. While these payments may be characterized as donations to the consuming public, this does not reflect their true tax characteristics. In fact, these payments are more akin to "income" than charitable donations.[725] This means that these payments camouflaged as donations qualify as ordinary taxable income and cannot be claimed as a charitable donation potentially eligible for a tax deduction.[726]

Furthermore, the geographic location of a specific tournament dictates which tax laws are applicable to the tournament prize pool monies.[727] This means that a gamer's tournament winnings over $600 earned in the United States are taxed similarly to the streaming revenues earned by an individual. For example, the 2014 *Dota 2* "The International" competition was located in the United States and boasted a $10.9 million prize pool.[728] In this case, the gamers that won a portion of this prize pool were subject to U.S. federal income tax on their respective tournament winnings due to the tournament's geographic location within America.[729] This tax was even applicable to those non-U.S. citizen gamers.[730]

Consequently, most tournament organizers typically list the applicable tax law for the disbursement of prize monies. This information may be noted in the competition's rules and regulations in a section labeled as "prize money" policies. For instance, any prize money earned from a DreamHack-produced event requires that a "private individual [...] receive [this prize] money as salary, [...] according to Swedish Tax Law."[731] This means that the competition organizer first "deduct[s] both a general payroll tax and [an] employment tax from the [...] prize amount, before [any] money is paid out to [the] individual" gamer.[732] Another example is tournament organizer PGL, who organizes several *Dota 2* and *CS:GO* competitions, including the 2017 "The Kiev Major" and 2016 "The Boston Major."[733] In particular, two of these PGL-run competitions, the "Open – Bucharest" and the "*Legends of The Rift—Season 1*" required that all "private individuals [...] receive the prize money in their own bank account."[734] The payout rules continued by stating that "a 16% tax will automatically be deducted [from the prize money], in accordance with Article 77 of the *Romanian Fiscal Code*."[735] However, the rules further stated that "no tax will be deducted if the prize value is lower than 600 RON, in accordance with Article 77 of the Romanian Fiscal

Code."[736] With the different ways that tournament organizers approach prize payout, it is prudent for a gamer to evaluate and understand each tournament organizer's prize pool disbursement policies as well as how these winnings are taxed prior to participating in them. This is because the taxation rules could have a significant effect on the final amounts that the gamer actually earns from the competition.

In addition to a gamer's tournament winnings and streaming revenues, many professional gamers are also signed to player contracts with esports organizations or professional teams.[737] As explored earlier, these organizations typically pay the player a weekly or a monthly salary. The payment differs greatly, ranging from several hundred to several thousand dollars a month, or more, depending on the caliber of the player and the title being played. In these situations, whether the gamer is classified as an "independent contractor" or employee of the team has significance. For example, this classification determines which party is responsible for paying any associated employment taxes. These taxes could include any unemployment, disability, or federal and state withholding taxes. If the gamer is considered an employee of the employer esports organization, then this imposes a myriad of withholding obligations on the employer, including requiring the team to withhold and pay federal and state employment taxes on behalf of the player from the salary that they pay the player. Conversely, if the individual is classified as an independent contractor, then the actual gamer, not their employer, is responsible for paying any and all applicable taxes to the appropriate administrative bodies. This distinction is explored further later in this text.

In addition to the other available revenue streams, most professional gamers may have either an organizational or a personal sponsorship or both.[738] These deals might include monthly payments, yearly fees, and/or "trade in kind" provided to the gamer in exchange for a set of listed "deliverables" or requirements. Generally, any sponsorship money received by a gamer is taxed similar to the other player's streams of income.[739]

On top of a fee paid to the gamer, a sponsoring company could also provide a player with free equipment or other related "fringe" benefits. For example, an influencer could receive free food as part of an endorsement deal with a restaurant. Similar to any other type of income, these fringe benefits are subject to applicable income tax laws. For tax purposes, the amount that is taxed is based upon the fair market value (F.M.V.) of the benefit received. For example, if a gamer is provided free food as part of a brand partnership, they will be taxed on the F.M.V. of those free meals. Therefore, it is prudent that a player is aware that any "free" or other promotional goods that they receive from a brand partner are also subject to appropriate income taxes and are taxed similar to the funds earned from a fee paid within the sponsorship deal. Sponsorship in esports is explored in detail later in this text.

Likewise, it is also important that a gaming influencer is aware of potential business "write-offs" or "deductions" available to them in an effort to decrease their personal "net" taxable income (amount of income subject to taxes).[740] This is especially important in light of the large sums that a gamer may earn, which may subject them to fairly large taxable obligations. For example, *Dota 2* player, Topias Miikka "Topson" Taavitsainen reportedly "paid nearly €1M ($1.1M) in taxes in 2018" on his "over €1.7M ($1.87M)" total earnings.[741] In particular, most of his taxable income was as a result of his substantial "prize winnings."[742] This fact leads to another inherent advantage of forming a separate business entity. Specifically, the existence of an entity permits the owner to open a company bank account in an assumed name. This is valuable because the bank account can be used to easily track the gamer's various revenues and expenses. In particular, a separate company bank account enables the owner to utilize the account to pay for any relevant business expenses as well as to track all of their potential business transactions. This makes it easier to identify and substantiate any potential tax deductions or write-offs.

In order for an entity to be eligible for appropriate tax deductions, the company must be considered a "for-profit" business. When determining whether or not a company is a for-profit one, the I.R.S. has presented a non-exhaustive list of factors that may be considered.[743] For instance, when evaluating a business entity's eligibility for these deductions and to not have the I.R.S. categorize your gaming career as "a hobby" (which disallows the deducting of your losses), the entity must substantiate that they are actually carrying on the business activity (gaming career) for profit or that the owner is attempting to make a profit. Since many gamers do not typically earn a profit initially and they may end up incurring losses for great spans of time, the individual is permitted to document their incurred losses on their tax returns.[744] In evaluating these situations, the government examines how the business is operated, such as whether the gamer carries on the activity in a business-like manner, and the amount of time and effort that they put into the activity indicating the intent to make it profitable. An examination might also focus on whether the gamer depends on income from the activity for their sole livelihood. In addition, a decision-maker might evaluate whether the individual's losses are due to circumstances beyond their control and whether the talent changed any of their prior methods of operation in an attempt to improve profitability of the venture. Furthermore, it might be relevant to inquire into whether the gamer was successful in making a profit in similar activities in the past, whether the business activity actually made a profit in some years, as well as the amount of profit that it made previously [745]

While every taxpayer must consider their own facts and circumstances, these individuals may have the ability to deduct a variety of related business expenses. Some deductions could include the cost to purchase a game that the individual streams as well as any equipment necessary to record and livestream the content.[746] Additionally, an individual may be permitted to recover the cost of any marketing or promotional services used to promote their streaming channel or content (i.e., Facebook paid "boosts" or Twitter advertisements, promotional items created for giveaways and contests), any website and graphic design costs, and video recording and editing software costs.[747] An influencer might also be able to recoup the costs associated with data storage or broadcasting of the stream, such as internet costs.[748] Additional write-offs could include the costs for filing any copyrights and trademarks for the gamers' protected assets, any travel and meal expenses (hotel, airfare, on-site travel, fuel costs) associated with producing any gaming content, any equipment rental costs as well as any related depreciation of these assets (streaming equipment, gaming equipment). It is also important that the gamer organizes and documents all of these expenses by maintaining contemporaneous business records. For example, this could mean keeping copies of receipts in case any tax authority is interested in a more detailed examination of them. Additionally, some countries, such as Finland, have begun providing specific tax benefits and write-offs to professional video game competitors.[749] A few more typical business deductions available for gaming talent are also listed above.

On a final note, every U.S. citizen must file their own personal federal income tax. Also, most individuals may be responsible for the filing of state tax returns for the state that they reside in as well as submitting separate personal state tax payments for each state that they earn income from pursuant to the jock tax explained above. If a player fails to properly file or otherwise misfiles their personal federal or state income taxes, then they may be subject to a tax investigation called an "audit." The failure to timely pay appropriate tax liabilities can cause serious problems for an individual, ranging from interest and penalties on owed taxes to potential imprisonment for serious cases. While the specifics of an audit are outside the scope of this text, a gamer must be aware of and be extremely careful about what they say, if anything, in any response to a governing body (e.g., the I.R.S.) if a player is presented with this type of audit inquiry. Specifically, an individual should be aware that anything the player responds with will be used as a statement of fact in the matter.

While the above is a brief synopsis, it is advisable for a gamer to have an independent tax advisor or other competent professional advising them on their taxable business decisions. The above information is also fairly applicable to professional esports coaches and other gaming talent who earn income from professional gaming. Even if a third-party professional assists them, a gaming influencer should still be aware of the potential income streams subject to federal, state, and city taxes as well as the potential available write-offs.

3.2.2 Some Tax Matters for Professional Esports Organizations and Teams

Esports teams and organizations earn income from many of the same sources as professional gamers and content creators. However, if a team business entity exists (in most cases, they do), then that entity is subject to corporate income tax in the state that they were formed in. The entity is also subject to federal corporate income taxes that are payable to the I.R.S. In addition, some cities and counties impose taxes on businesses operating or otherwise earning income in their territories.

Additionally, esports teams have many similar potential write-offs as those possessed by professional gamers and content creators. For example, professional esports organizations are able to claim taxable deductions for any marketing or other advertisement expenses incurred promoting the team, its players, its sponsors, and any of the team's created assets, including any expense related to paid social media ads or other "ad buys." It could also include any free promotional giveaways that the organization hosts for game codes, gaming consoles, or other "virtual currency" purchased for marketing purposes. There is also potential to write-off for any player or personnel expenses, including salary (if any), travel costs for participation in any tournaments or other industry relate events, as well as the costs associated with any of the gamer's other obligations on behalf of the team. These could include any housing costs (gaming house, apartment), any training costs (i.e., "boot camps," physical and mental trainers), lodging costs during tournaments or league matches as well as those expenses associated with any of the team's other obligations (i.e., a sponsorship appearance).[750] The potential write-offs available for an organization may also apply to any photographers, videographers, content editors, or other individuals hired to create or design any imagery or visual works on behalf of the organization, such as a team logo, any player social media assets, and the team's website. Similar to content creators, a variety of other items could potentially be deductible, including any equipment purchased by the team, such as any recording and content editing equipment, any gaming consoles or peripherals (i.e., keyboards, monitors, gaming chairs, stream "deck" software) as well as any required software, such as content editing, stream broadcasting, or other content management software. Another related cost that could potentially be recouped is any cost related to data storage or the broadcasting of the stream, such as internet coverage and "cloud" storage or other file-hosting system.

Furthermore, any costs associated with continued education and research in the field may be claimed. These instances could include a team representative attending or speaking at a seminar, on a webinar, or as part of an informative panel. In these cases, the costs related to the educational experience may be recoupable, such as travel and lodging fees. Finally, some other documented business costs may also be recoverable, such as the fees to form a business entity, equipment rental costs, the costs for the filing of any copyrights and trademarks, as well as the fees paid to any third- party professionals (e.g.., attorney, accountant).

In conclusion, proper business management can have a profound effect on gaming influencers and professional organization "bottom-lines." In particular, the better equipped these parties are to navigate and properly structure their business, the better the chance they have to earn a sizable amount of the monies they generate.

4

Immigration and Employment Law and Its Impact on the Esports Business Ecosystem

4.1 Immigration Law in Esports

4.1.1 Work Authorization for Gaming "Talent"

Some Common Evidence For P1 Visas for Gaming "Talent"
• **Biographical Information on the Talent** (Player or Team Ranking, Total Prize Pool, Career Achievements)
• **Press on the Event and on the Talent** (From Reputable Outlets – Forbes, The Esports Observer, Esports Insider, Dot Esports)
• **Copy of Executed Personnel Contract** (Player Contract, Coach, Caster or other Employment Contract)
• **Itinerary for the Visit** (Event Location, Lodging and the Type of Event (CS:GO Tournament, OWL Season)
• **Recommendation & Participation Letters from Game Publisher** (Activision-Blizzard, Riot Games, Valve Corp., Ubisoft)
• **Recommendation & Participation Letters From Event, Tournament or League Organizer** (Dreamhack, ESL, MLG, OGN)
• **Reference Letter from Notable Industry Press and Members**

4.1.1.1 O1 and P-1A Visas for "Competitive" Gamers and Coaches As the global esports market continues to grow, foreign professional gamers from around the world are attempting to come to the United States to participate in tournaments and organized leagues hosted within the country. There are also coaches and other team gameplay analysts who require visas to coach and to earn an income from an esports organization.[751] However, in order for any foreign citizen to enter the United States and earn any type of income, such as a salary or tournament winnings, the individual must first acquire the proper work authorization or "visa."[752] In the United States, there are two government agencies involved in this procedure, the United States Citizenship and Immigration Services (USCIS) and the U.S. Department of State.[753]

Since competing as a professional video gamer in a tournament or organized league is a "for-profit" venture, proper work authorization is required.[754] A non-U.S. citizen must obtain this authorization prior to participating and earning a wage in the United States. There is no minimum or maximum age requirement when applying for a visa; so, as long as the other qualifications for the visa are met, a minor (an individual under 18 years old) may apply for one. The two types of visas most likely to be available for a competitive gamer is either the O-1 or the P-1A visa.[755] In fact, in 2013, professional *League of Legends* player, Danny "Shiphtur" Le became "the first pro gamer to receive a [U.S.] visa acknowledging him as an 'internationally recognized' athlete."[756] Soon after, professional *StarCraft II* gamer Kim Dong-hwan received a visa permitting him to enter the country to compete in American-based gaming competitions for prize money.[757] In particular, these two individuals both received "P-1A" visas, which have become the norm for most professional esports competitors to apply for.[758] Additionally, Germany has gone even further than the United States by creating "a dedicated visa that accommodates esports athletes from outside of the European Union."[759] This was reportedly undertaken in an effort "to allow eas[ier] access to tournaments and leagues [held in Germany] for esports athletes [from] all over the world."[760]

Some esports professionals have also applied for and successfully received "*EB-1A* green cards."[761] These are rare, only available for "esports players seeking permanency resident in the U.S." and are outside the scope of this text.[762] However, in the United States, the two most commonly applied for work authorizations in the non-permanent residency professional talent sector are the O-1 and the P-1A visa.[763] The key difference between the O-1 and the P-1A is the applicant's personal notoriety. In the United States, the O-1 visa is only for an individual who possesses "extraordinary ability" in a particular field and "have been recognized nationally or internationally for those achievements."[764] This type of visa is typically only appropriate for a professional who made a substantial mark in the particular field. This means that the applicant possesses sufficient industry-wide name recognition to justify the visa's issuance on this basis alone without any other evidence. In esports, this is extremely rare, as an O-1 work authorization requires substantial evidence to corroborate the individual's high level of notoriety. Specifically, most professional gamers have not achieved enough individual fame to justify the issuing of this type of work authorization. However, in the coming years, this may change, as esports continues to expand and as more superstars emerge that transcend the gaming world.

In order to obtain an O-1 visa in situations where a professional competitor has achieved a high level of notoriety, the individual must present evidence that displays their "extraordinary talent." This means that the applicant must provide sufficient and appropriate documentation to support this assertion. If the foreign talent has been recognized nationally or internationally by being nominated for or being a recipient of an industry award, then, the gamer should be immediately qualified for an O-1 visa.[765] For example, in the music world, this could be satisfied by the applicant musician winning a *Grammy* for their musical works.

However, in instances where an individual cannot provide such evidence (which is in most cases), the applicant can instead substantiate their achievement level by documenting at least three of the following selected criteria. This means that an O-1 petitioner could present evidence that establishes them as "a lead or starring participant in productions or events which have a distinguished reputation."[766] This fact could be substantiated through the use of "critical reviews, advertisements, publicity releases, publications, [testimonials] or endorsements" on the production.[767] The applicant can also provide evidence of "national or international recognition" of their "achievements."[768] This criterion may be satisfied through the use of "critical reviews or other published materials by or about the [applicant] in major newspapers, trade journals, magazines, or other publications."[769] Alternatively, a petitioner may also present evidence that they have "[p]erformed and will perform in a lead, starring, or critical role for organizations [...] that have a distinguished reputation."[770] Again, this fact can be substantiated through "articles in newspapers, trade journals, publications, or testimonials."[771]

The petitioner's relevant notoriety may be substantiated by showing a previous record of "major commercial or critically acclaimed successes."[772] This may be proven by the individual earning a high "rating or [...] other occupational achievements reported in trade journals, major newspapers or other publications."[773] An individual can also present evidence that they "[r]eceived significant recognition for achievements from organizations [...] or other recognized experts in the field."[774] This fact may be demonstrated with written "testimonials [...] indicating the author's authority, expertise and knowledge" of the petitioner's achievements.[775] Finally, proving that the applicant's salary is high "in relation to others in the field" can be submitted as long as this fact is "shown by contracts or other reliable evidence."[776] When submitting this type of evidence, it is important to ensure that any evidentiary or other recommendation letter submitted in a visa application is properly addressed to the USCIS.

As mentioned, in most cases, the P-1A is the appropriate visa for most gamers or coaches to apply for.[777] This work authorization is only available for an individual that has been internationally recognized as a person who has demonstrated a "degree of skill and recognition substantially above that ordinarily encountered."[778] Similar to an O-1 visa, a gaming talent applying for a P-1A must provide documentation to substantiate their claim that they possess the level of skill required for the issuance of this type of work authorization.[779] Some of the mandatory information required in this submission include a letter from "an appropriate labor organization" stating that the applicant is a member of a team or an individual competitor and that he or she has been recognized as a professional in the area.[780] In the esports space, this could be satisfied through a letter from the game developer (i.e., Valve Corporation or Riot Games) and/or from the event, tournament or league organizer (i.e., DreamHack or Major League Gaming). A P-1A applicant must also present a copy of any "written contracts or summaries of the terms [...] of [their] employment."[781] This requirement could be satisfied through the submission of the professional gamer or the coach's contract with an esports team (if one exists) or a "letter of intent" listing material employment terms.[782] The gamer must also submit an "explanation of the nature of the events or activities" that they intend to undertake if the visa is issued.[783] This can be accomplished by presenting an itinerary listing where the visa applicant will be performing the work (i.e., the location of a tournament or event) and what type of work will be performed by the applicant (i.e., competing in an *Overwatch* tournament for prize money).[784]

Furthermore, any individual (such as a professional esports competitor) submitting evidence for a P- 1A application on the basis of being an "internationally recognized individual" must provide documentation of at least two of the following evidentiary requirements.[785] The applicant must provide proof "of having participated to a significant extent in a prior season with a major United States sports league" or they may demonstrate that they have "participated to a significant extent in international competition with a national team or individually in recognized competitions and/or leagues."[786] This requirement can be substantiated through presenting a player or other official contract with a team, letters of reference from notable industry practitioners as well as any relevant press on the event or league. This standard could also be satisfied by listing any league results for the visa applicant, including how well the gamer did in a competition, how much money they earned from it and what place they finished in as well as any other relevant highlights regarding the gaming "talent." The individual can also submit a "written statement from a member of the sports media or a recognized expert in the sport which details how [the individual …] is internationally recognized."[787] This could be in the form of a recommendation letter addressed to USCIS from an esports league or tournament organizer or from some other official governing body for the league.[788] Evidence that the petitioner or their esports "team is ranked" or has "received a significant honor or award" can also be submitted.[789] This criterion can be substantiated by presenting press coverage and articles reporting on the event or by presenting some official international ranking system (if one exists) that proves the gamer's high level of achievements.[790] While the above information is not an exhaustive list of the requirements for a visa, it serves to highlight a few important requirements that a professional gamer should be aware of when applying for a foreign work authorization.[791] Ultimately, the more substantive evidence demonstrating the gamer's exceptional skill, the more likely that a visa will be issued to a professional gamer.

An O-1 visa is valid for up to three years and can be extended for additional one-year increments. In contrast, the P-1A visa is valid for a limited amount of time, which is usually only for the length of time required by the gamer to compete in the specific tournament or competition.[792] Furthermore, generally, a P-1A will not be issued for longer than five years. However, the petitioner can extend this visa for additional increments of time "up to 5 years in order to continue to or complete the event, competition, or performance."[793] Under this visa classification, an applicant's "total stay [is] limited to 10 years."[794]

In order to ensure that the gamer receives the visa approval in sufficient time to permit them to participate in a tournament or league match, it is prudent for an individual who foresees the need for a foreign work visa to begin the process as early as possible.[795] In addition, when filing with the immigration department in an effort to avoid being subject to the several-month application backlog for either the O-1 or P-1A visa, it is prudent for a professional gamer to strongly consider using the Premium Processing option available from the USCIS.[796] This option is beneficial as it assists in eliciting a response on a pending visa application within two weeks of the application's filing date.[797] While this option may be more costly than not using it, in situations where time is of the essence because the individual requires the visa approval immediately or in a short time frame, this may be the appropriate decision. In some cases, this processing option might be the only way to ensure a timely response from the USCIS.

Another factor to consider when preparing a visa application is the specific wait time at the local consulate. Specifically, after an applicant receives the notice of the approval of their visa documentation, they must then appear at their local country consulate to finalize the matter.[798] Since each consulate has its own workload, it is prudent for an applicant to factor in at least an additional seven to ten business days (if not more) to visit the appropriate consulate and receive the approved visa paperwork from the appropriate consulate.[799] In light of the COVID-19 global pandemic, worldwide travel and immigration has been shut down and has only recently started to slowly re-open.[800] This is certain to cause further delays in the issuance of visas for professional gamers so careful and prudent planning is even more essential.

In addition, the lack of proper work authorization can and has already caused issues for the gamer and their competitive team (if they are signed to one). Some of these issues include preventing the individual from competing in or attending a specific tournament as well as prohibiting the gamer from earning a salary from a professional organization.[801] In particular, there have already been several instances of visa issues impacting esports professionals.[802] For example, "visa issues" delayed several gamers on the *Overwatch League* franchise *Shanghai Dragons* from participating in the start of the season.[803] Immigration issues also prevented Russian *Overwatch* player, Denis "Tonic" Rulyov from participating in the Season 1 *Overwatch* Contenders Playoffs.[804] In addition, esports organizations, 100 Thieves[805] and Gambit Esports[806] were both prevented from competing in major tournaments because they were unable to obtain visas for their gamers in time. Finally, the *Overwatch League* team *Philadelphia Fusion* had to withdraw from their Season 1 pre-season matches due to "player logistic issues."[807] Therefore, as evident by these unfortunate examples, it is important that a professional gamer applies for the proper visa in a timely matter in an effort to avoid some of the same pitfalls encountered by their peers.

Overall, obtaining a proper and timely work authorization is essential to being able to compete in an esports competition in the United States. In most cases, due to the complex nature of the visa application, it may be advisable for a gamer to have an attorney or other competent professional advising them on these matters. However, even if a third-party professional assists them, a professional gamer should still be aware of the process as well as the type of documentation required for the visa application procedure.

4.2 Employment Law in Esports

4.2.1 Employment Matters for Esports Organizations and Teams

4.2.1.1 A Look at "Employee" vs. "Independent Contractors" One central consideration for esports organizations and teams that field competitive teams or sign individual gamers and streamers is how the signed person is classified.[808] In particular, it is crucial to determine whether the signed player is an "employee" or an "independent contractor."[809] While this may not seem like an important distinction, the categorization as one or the other imposes several obligations upon the employer (the team).[810] For example, if the gaming talent is classified as an "independent contractor," then the individual gamer is responsible for certain tasks. This could include paying any and all applicable employment taxes to the appropriate governing body. In contrast, if a player is considered an "employee" of the employer, the esports organization; then, this imposes a myriad of withholding obligations on the employer.[811] Some of these could include the provision of employment benefits (401K/retirement plans), the payment of social security and Medicare taxes, the payment of unemployment compensation insurance as well as expenditures related to worker's compensation insurance on behalf of the gamer.[812] Therefore, in most cases, it is generally less costly for the team to classify a signed gaming talent as an "independent contractor" as opposed to an "employee."[813]

Additionally, parties classified as "independent contractors" do not receive many of the same federal and state law protections available to "employees." For example, it is much easier to terminate an independent contractor's employment than it is for an "employee." Also, in certain circumstances, a business can be found liable for the wrongful actions or other torts of their employees; however, since independent contractors are not employees, the business is usually not liable for any of their actions. In fact, the hiring company may actually be shielded from any liability for any damage caused by the independent contractor's actions.

While the application to each specific esports organization is beyond the scope of this book, many arguments for each classification can be made. Ultimately, there are no specific criteria that determine whether an individual is acting as an "employee" or "independent contractor;" however, many Courts, State Labor Departments, and the I.R.S. have all articulated several factors that can be examined when making this determination.[814] It is important to be aware that no one factor is controlling as any fact-finder will examine all of the relevant facts to determine whether the individual is properly characterized as an "employee" or an "independent contractor." In particular, the improper designation or otherwise misclassification of a person could subject the employing company to fines and other penalties.[815] Additionally, some states have begun passing extensive legislation regulating these worker classifications, including most recently California.[816] This new legislation is explained in more detail later in this chapter.

One relevant criterion that is examined in these situations is which party "has the right to direct and control the work performed by the worker."[817] When evaluating this factor, it is important to examine the "types of instructions given" to the individual, including if they included information about "when and where to work, what tools [or equipment] to use or where to purchase supplies and services" to perform the requested job.[818] An individual that receives extensive "instructions" may indicate that the worker is considered an "employee" and not an "independent contractor."[819] Additionally, another relevant examination is the "degree of instruction" provided to the worker.[820] In particular, in situations where "more detailed instructions" are provided by an owner to the worker, then this fact may indicate that the person is an "employee" and not an "independent contractor." In contrast, a party receiving "less detailed instructions" from a hiring party may exemplify "less control [over the individual], indicating that the worker is more likely an 'independent contractor' than an "employee."[821] This might exist in situations where the esports organization has full and exclusive creative and editorial control over a piece of content created by a team's influencer or by any other creative talent paid by the organization.

Furthermore, another factor that may point to the talent being classified as an "employee" and not as an "independent contractor" is if an "evaluation system" is in place that quantifies and "measure[s] the details of how the work is done."[822] Anther strong indicator that substantiates the gaming talent is an "employee" and not an "independent contractor" is whether the hired individual is provided with "training [...] on how to do the job."[823] This could include receiving a training manual or procedure guide from the employer as well as undergoing "periodic or on-going training about procedures and methods" of the business.[824]

Another criterion utilized to analyze whether an individual is properly classified as an "employee" or "independent contractor" is who has the "right to direct or control the financial and business aspects of the worker's job."[825] In examining this, it is important to consider who has invested funds to obtain "the equipment [that] the worker uses in working."[826] If the individual has made significant investment to purchase the equipment or machinery required to perform the work, this fact might signify that they are an "independent contractor" and not an "employee" of the business owner.[827] However, if the employing party provides the equipment required for the job, then this fact might indicate that the person is an "employee."[828]

It is also relevant to examine whether or not "some or all business expenses" are reimbursed.[829] This is because an "independent contractor" is "more likely to incur unreimbursed expenses than [an] employee" would.[830] Specifically, this means that the employee will more likely be reimbursed by their employer for any business-related expenses. Also, an additional indicator that the person is an "independent contractor" and not an "employee" is if there is an "opportunity for profit or loss" to the individual.[831] This is because an "employee" usually does not have an opportunity for any profit or losses as a result of fulfilling their job responsibilities.

In addition, another factor that favors classification of the individual as an "independent contractor" and not as an "employee" is if the person's business "services [are] available to the market," such that the party is "free to seek out [other] business opportunities."[832] Also, an inspection into how the worker is paid can shed additional light on whether the gaming talent is classified as an "employee" or an "independent contractor."[833] For example, if the professional is paid a "guaranteed regular wage amount for an hourly, weekly, or other period of time even when supplemented by a commission," this will most likely favor the individual being classified as an "employee" and not an "independent contractor."[834] This is because "independent contractors are most often paid for [a] job [on] a flat fee" basis and not an hourly or a yearly rate.[835] It is also important to examine whether or not the services provided by the gamer are a "key activity or aspect of the regular business of the company."[836] This is because if the work performed by the influencer is an aspect of the company's regular business, this may signify that the individual should be classified as an "employee" and not as an "independent contractor."[837] In contrast, if the provided work is not part of the entity's everyday business, this might indicate that the individual performing the work is an "independent contractor" and not an "employee" of the company. This might include whether the individual acts as the team's social media or player manager or merely a photographer or videographer that is hired on a project by project basis.[838]

Furthermore, a decision-maker will also look at the "type of relationship" and "how the worker and business perceive their interaction with one another."[839] This includes an analysis of any existing "written contracts which describe the relationship the parties intend to create."[840] While "a contract stating the worker is an employee or an independent contractor is not sufficient to determine the worker's status," it might demonstrate what the individuals intended for the situation to be.[841] A strong indication of the individual being an "employee" and not an "independent contractor" is if the business provides employee-type benefits to the hired person, such as "insurance, a pension plan, vacation pay, paid leave, or sick pay."[842] This is because "businesses generally do not grant these benefits to independent contractors." [843]

Finally, another relevant inquiry is the "permanency of the relationship."[844] This is because if there is an "expectation that the relationship will continue indefinitely, rather than for a specific project or period" exists, then, this fact "is generally seen as evidence that the intent was to create an employer-employee relationship" and not an "independent contractor" one.[845] As mentioned initially, no single factor is controlling, so a company attempting to classify a worker as an "independent contractor" needs to be aware of how they operate to ensure that the relationship is actually performed correctly to maintain the desired classification.

Since many esports organizations and teams as well as some game developers are all located in California, including Riot Games, Activision-Blizzard, and Ubisoft, it is important to understand the unique employment laws applicable to workers in that state. Recently, the state of California has enacted its own unique system for governing employment and labor issues within their state.[846] This new system provides additional guidance on how to determine whether an individual is an "employee" or an "independent contractor."[847] In particular, California has established law that creates the presumption that the worker is an "employee."[848] This is a "rebuttable presumption," which requires an arbiter to conduct an investigation to determine whether a worker is an "employee" or "independent contractor."[849] This judicial inquiry is based "upon a number of factors, all of which must be considered, and none of which is controlling by itself."[850]

As a result of this new legislation, most employment cases before California's Division of Labor Standards Enforcement (DLSE) apply the "'multi-factor' or the 'economic realities' test" established by the California Supreme Court in *S. G. Borello & Sons, Inc. v Dept. of Industrial Relations.*[851] When applying this test to a particular situation, one of the

> most significant factor to be considered is whether the person to whom service is rendered (the employer or principal) has control or the right to control the worker both as to the work done and the manner and means in which it is performed.[852]

Furthermore, California's Department of Industrial Relations has articulated some other factors that may be considered in a determination of the proper classification for an individual and are similar to the ones explored above, including:

> [w]hether the person performing services is engaged in an occupation or business distinct from that of the principal (employer); [w]hether or not the work is a part of the regular business of the principal or alleged employer; [w]hether the principal or the worker supplies the instrumentalities, tools, and the place for the person doing the work; [t]he alleged employee's investment in the equipment or materials required by his or her task or his or her employment of helpers; [w]hether the service rendered requires a special skill; [whether t]he kind of [...] work is usually done under the direction of the principal or by a specialist without supervision; [t]he alleged employee's opportunity for [a] profit or loss depending on his or her managerial skill; [t]he length of time for which the services are to be performed; [t]he degree of permanence of the working relationship; [t]he method of payment, whether by time or by the job; and, [w]hether or not the parties believe they are creating an employer-employee relationship.[853]

In addition, in cases where the business does not exercise "control over work details," an employer- employee relationship can still be found if "the principal retains pervasive control over the operation as a whole."[854] This means that "the worker's duties are an integral part of the operation, and the nature of the work makes detailed control unnecessary."[855]

Most recently, the California Supreme Court provided additional interpretation of these factors in *Dynamex.*[856] In this case, the Court stated that there is a "burden on the hiring entity to establish that the worker is an independent contractor who was not intended to be included within the wage order's coverage."[857] In order for a company to satisfy this burden, they must prove "three factors," including that

> the worker is free from the control and direction of the hiring entity in connection with the performance of the work, both under the contract for the performance of the work and in fact; that the worker performs work that is outside the usual course of the hiring entity's business; and, that the worker is customarily engaged in an independently established trade, occupation, or business of the same nature as the work performed.[858]

In conclusion, it is very important for every business to be aware of how they utilize and classify any third parties that work for them. This is especially true in the professional gaming business where teams' house and train players across the globe, including many of these premises being located in California.[859] This fact is important for esports team operators because each classification creates legal obligations that must be adhered to or the company may be subject to civil liability or other penalties. In particular, those companies that operate and employee individuals in California must be aware of their responsibilities and potential repercussions for misclassification of an employee.[860] Some of these consequences could include the issuance of "[s]top orders and penalty assessments" against the employer as well as them being liable for "overtime premium" payments, "[e]xposure for unfair business practices, "[t]ax liability and penalties" as well as potential "[c]riminal liability."[861]

4.2.2 Employer Law Matters for "Competitive" Gamers

4.2.2.1 "Collective Bargaining" and Esports Player Unions and Associations Another related employment law concept is the idea of "collective bargaining" and its potential application to esports.[862] While no existing "esports"-wide players union or any organized labor body collectively representing the players exist, some individual competitive titles have developed such organizations to govern the contractual and workplace conditions for pro gamers.[863] Specifically, as the esports business continues to grow, an emerging issue is the issue of players' rights.[864] This includes both rights that are included as well as those rights that are not included within a contract that they sign with a professional esports team. As a result of the industry's growth and the rising salaries of professional gamers, discussions have begun regarding the creation of recognized player unions and associations, similar to those that exist in traditional sports such as the NBA, NFL, NHL, and MLB.[865] However, one unique and crucial difference between the traditional "bat and ball" sports such as baseball and football and esports is the existing labor dynamic. In most major sports, there are only two distinct parties who are involved in these types of labor-related negotiations: the team owners and the players. In contrast, in addition to the team owners and the players (the gamers), esports has an additional interested stakeholder, the game developer. As explored earlier, the developers hold all the rights to the underlying game, so they determine how a game may be utilized, including how it can be licensed and monetized. The existence of this additional party in the labor discussion has caused individuals who wish to advocate for greater gamer protections to look for other workable models that take into account this additional interest holder and address their potential concerns.[866]

While the details of the collective bargaining process, the National Labor Relations Board (NLRB)[867] and the formation of formal unions are outside the scope of the text, to date, there are no recognized or existing labor unions that can collectively bargain on behalf of professional gamers or any other group of esports competitors.[868] Even though no formal esports unions have been established yet, there has been the formation of player associations in different games intended to protect the rights of individual gamers competing in that game title.[869] In particular, there have been three well-known esports player associations that have publicly declared their existence and who have begun advocating on behalf of their member players.[870]

One of these associations and the only one that was actually funded and established by a game developer is the NALCS Players' Association (NALCSPA).[871] This organization represents any professional gamer involved in the *North American League of Legends* Championship Series (NALCS), which is part of Riot Games' *League of Legends* Championship Series (LCS).[872] The NALCSPA was initially created by the title developer and league organizer, Riot Games to ensure that "the players have a voice at that table and [they] are able to have someone in those discussions whose sole responsibility is to answer to the players and look out for their interests."[873] While it is hard to imagine an unbiased labor association funded by an employer, the Associations' Executive Director, Hal Biagas maintains that "the organization is able to operate independently."[874] In this respect, the association began making strides to protect its professionals by working to enact a rule that permitted "players released from a team within 48 hours of the league's roster deadline to have an additional three days to sign with another organization."[875] This was done in an effort to provide these released gamers with the "chance to sign with another team" so that they are not prevented "from competing in the rest of the split" (season).[876]

In contrast to the game developer-founded NALCSPA, the *Counter-Strike* Professional Players' Association (CSPPA)[877] and the *Fortnite* Professional Players' Association (FNPPA)[878] were instead established by the professional gamers themselves without any financial assistance or other involvement with either title's developer. The CSPPA was created to act as "worldwide representative association for professional *CS:GO* players."[879] It exists to "safeguard, protect and promote professional *Counter-Strike* players' interests both during and after their active career."[880] Membership is available to any "player who is contracted or actively seeking a contract as a professional *Counter-Strike* player and who competes at an elite level."[881] Similarly, the *Fortnite* Professional Players' Association was "established by 16 pro [*Fortnite*] players [in] North America and Europe," including the "Fortnite World Cup Solo competition winner Kyle 'Bugha' Giersdorf."[882] This association was founded in order to provide a platform for members to "voice [their] opinions on the future of the competitive scene of *Fortnite*, so that [the players] may have the most productive dialogue possible with the developers."[883] In this respect, the CSPPA actually successfully worked toward the creation of accepted "framework" with tournament organizers "ESL and DreamHack" that is intended to create a workable revenue model, delineate each "players' rights and obligations at events, as well as attempting to [... establish standard] tournament conditions."[884] It will be interesting to see what other strides these associations make on behalf of their members, including focusing on player-specific issues such as "mental health."[885] There is also potential "conflict of interests" that might begin to emerge with certain interested parties allegedly "advocating" on behalf of its association members while also acting in potentially other professional capacities.[886]

Ultimately, in light of the volatile nature of the competitive gaming and the amounts of money at stake and as the need for independent labor protections for professional gamers becomes more apparent, it is fair to assume some other large game developers may follow Riot Games' example and begin to establish their own developer-funded player protection associations. Notwithstanding, there may also be the development of gamer rights' associations in other titles that follow *Fortnite* and *CS:Go* players' example and create their own independent labor associations without any developer involvement or financing. This reportedly might include professional *Overwatch League* players[887] and potentially *Rainbow Six*.[888]

5

Contract Law and Its Impact on the Esports Business Ecosytem

5.1 Gaming "Talent" Agreements

One of the unique facets of the esports business ecosystem is the way in which each component interacts and "contracts" with each other. While there are too many different contractual relationships to highlight, there are a few prominent ones that are explored below. These arrangements include ones where the professional gamers, coaches, and other gaming "influencers" sign a deal with a professional esports team or organization. In addition, there is information on the contractual agreements between on-air talent, including shoutcasters, and the hiring event, tournament, or league organizers. Many other types of written agreements also exist in today's professional gaming business, including a sponsorship agreement between a brand partner and a gaming "talent," such as a professional gamer or streamer, as well as those similarly structured deals entered into between a sponsor and an esports organization. Furthermore, there are a variety of "licenses" and other written authorizations for a gaming talent's "likeness" rights that are acquired by an esports team, a tournament organizer, as well as a sponsoring brand. Additionally, all commercial gaming event organizers must acquire gaming licenses from the game publisher to present their competitive gaming contests, including any third-party tournament hosts. Finally, there is an exploration of some of the licensing arrangements between game publishers and event organizers with various broadcast outlets, including streaming and television deals.

5.1.1 A Look at Professional Gamer Contracts with an Esports Team

Some Common Professional Gamer Contract Provisions
• **Term** (Length of Agreement & Any Options, Extension or Renewals)
• **Roster Management, Transfer & Retirement** (Starting Spot and Bench, No Trade Clause, Transfer Bonus)
• **Gamer Compensation & Contract Buy-Out** (Salary, Signing Bonus, Streaming Income, Prize Money Split)
• **Gamer Obligations** (Number of Streaming Hours, Personal Appearances, Media Appearances)
• **Physical & Digital Merchandise Income & I.P & "Likeness" Rights** (Right of Publicity, Player-branded Merchandise Split, "Likeness" Usage Rights)
• **Team Covered Expenses** (Lodging, Event Travel, Daily Stipend, Equipment, Boot Camps)
• **Gamer Restrictions** (No Poaching, No Defamation, Wear Team Jersey, Use & Display Team Sponsors)
• **Right of First Refusal and Matching Right**

In order for the esports ecosystem to function properly and to best protect all of the individuals involved in it; it is prudent to use formalized written contracts between a team and any personnel member that they hire.[889] This includes agreements between the team and any gamers, coaches, assistants, analysts, graphic designers, or any other third parties that they employ.[890] While there is no esports-wide established "standard" professional gamer or talent contract such as those that exist in major sports,[891] many professional teams have begun utilizing similar agreements that only contain slight variations in their language and structure.[892] Predominantly, these often-used agreements typically outline the player's salary, the frequency of salary payment, and any other compensation due to the person as well as include information on the individual's obligations to the team.[893] The document could also include information on the number of streaming hours that a player must adhere to, a set number of tournaments or events that a coach must attend, or any other listed job requirements that the organization wants to ensure are properly adhered to by its personnel. In a few cases, some organized esports leagues have begun implementing and mandating the use of minimum player salaries and guaranteed benefits.[894]

In particular, Activision-Blizzard's *Overwatch League* mandated that every league participant sign the same standard written contract that included a set contract term of "one guaranteed year and [...] a second-year option" as well as establishing a minimum set salary for all competitors (the gamer can get paid more than the minimum amount, but not less).[895] In addition, Activision-Blizzard's *Call of Duty League* also created a required minimum yearly salary of $50,000 and mandated other traditional health benefits for its participating gamers.[896] While the actual agreements used by many teams are not available publicly, some of the most important provisions that are usually included are explored below.[897] It is important to be aware that the following clauses are not as detailed as typical agreement language is.[898] Furthermore, the information below is meant to be a guide of the potential clauses and matters discussed within these types of contracts and should not be viewed or used as sample language for drafting a professional gaming contract. In fact, these were all abstracted from existing esports player contracts with prominent esports organizations, including those competing in franchise leagues.

> **Term**—(a.) The ORGANIZATION agrees to retain the GAMER as a skilled esports professional beginning on January 1, 2021 (the "Effective Date") and ending one (1) year thereafter (the "Term"), unless the Agreement is earlier terminated pursuant to this Agreement or the Term is extended pursuant to this Agreement.
>
> (b.) Upon written notice to the GAMER, on a minimum of fifteen (15) days prior to the expiration of the Term, the ORGANIZATION, at its sole discretion, may extend the Term of this Agreement for an additional one (1) year period ("Option"), pursuant to the same terms and conditions contained herein.

One of the most important provisions included in a contract is the term. This is how long the agreement lasts for. The term of an agreement can be structured as a monthly, yearly, or any other timeframe that the parties select.[899] As described in the provision above, it is also common for the term of an agreement to contain an option or several option periods.[900] An option in a contract is the right to extend and renew the agreement's term for an additional period of time. For example, the above language contains a one-year contract term with the option for an additional one year, meaning the total term for the agreement could be a maximum of two years.

When reviewing and negotiating the term of an agreement, a player may desire flexibility in the length of the term as well as in any included options or other contract extensions.[901] This is especially true in cases where the gamer achieves a high level of recognition and individual success that did not previously exist and now the individual may desire or command a revised contract on terms different than those initially entered into.[902] Conversely, an organization may desire that the term of a player agreement continues for as long as possible or as long as they desire.[903] This includes the organization possessing the potential option to renew the agreement for additional time to try to ensure that the organization has the exclusive rights to the professional.[904] In an effort to resolve these differences, a player may attempt to shorten the length of the term or try to reduce the number of renewal options that the team has. A gamer could possibly include specific "milestones" or other listed obligations or achievements that can either extend the term of the agreement or not. In addition, these milestones could provide the gamer with the option to terminate or re-negotiate the existing agreement if they achieve a listed milestone. For example, a milestone could include the gamer winning a major tournament, reaching a certain social media "follower" threshold, or earning a certain amount of total prize money for the team during a given time period. In these cases, if the gamer does fulfill the criteria, the language could then provide the gamer with the right to re-negotiate the contract or even with the right to terminate their existing agreement with the organization. This would be in hopes of the player obtaining a more lucrative or more favorable agreement due to achieving the agreed-upon event. Termination for the breach of the agreement might also be beneficial for a professional gamer to incorporate in a case where the team fails to make its owed payments to them or if it does not fulfill any of their other agreed-upon duties under an agreement.[905]

> **Roster Management**—The ORGANIZATION's active roster shall consist of a minimum of five (5) gamers, including the GAMER. Each GAMER shall compete in esports competitions and/or tournaments on behalf of the ORGANIZATION (the "Starting Roster"). The Company may contract with more than five (5) gamers, in which case some Gamers will be members of the ORGANIZATION but shall not actively compete in competitions and/or tournaments (the "Replacement Roster"). The GAMER is not guaranteed a spot on the Starting Roster and can be moved from the Starting Roster to the

Replacement Roster in the ORGANIZATION's sole and absolute discretion.

When a gamer is part of a team of other competitors, another typical clause in most standard professional gamer contracts is one that addresses how the team can add and remove players from their existing roster. This includes language focused on the procedure utilized to move a gamer from a starting role to a "substitute" or "bench" spot.[906] In most situations, the organization will want (and have) sole control over which gamer is a "starter" and which one is not.[907] However, in an effort to curtail some of the organization's power, a player may try to include language that requires the organization to first consult with them and discuss their plans with the gamer prior to moving them to or from the starting lineup.[908] This could include language requiring written discussions between the team and the gamer in addition to mandating formal conversations with the other teammates and the team's coaches and analysts when making this determination.[909] Another protection that a gamer may try to implement on their behalf is to ensure that their monthly salary is not reduced if they are benched and are no longer on the starting roster. In some cases, the team may provide language that the organization may lower the player's salary if they are no longer competing on behalf of them. Therefore, if possible, a gamer may try to combat this and negotiate for language that still guarantees them the same compensation whether or not they are on the starting team. While the organization may not be amenable to paying the bench player the same rate as if they were a starter, the parties may try to compromise and work out a reasonable reduced salary if such an occasion arises.

The GAMER's Obligations to the ORGANIZATION—(a.) The GAMER agrees to wear the ORGANIZATION's clothing, uniform, hat, and/or any other ORGANIZATION apparel as well as to utilize, and/or otherwise display any and all hardware, equipment, peripherals, food items, beverage items, and any other goods and services specified by the ORGANIZATION at any and all competitions and/or tournaments while competing on behalf of the ORGANIZATION as well as during any and all Promotional Activities on behalf of the ORGANIZATION and/or the ORGANIZATION's Sponsors. The GAMER also further agrees to wear the ORGANIZATION's apparel and to promote the goods and services specified by the ORGANIZATION during and while streaming on behalf of the ORGANIZATION.

(b.) The GAMER agrees to use any custom stream "overlay" or other custom graphics provided by and created by the ORGANIZATION.
(c.) The GAMER agrees to exclusively stream on any streaming service provider that the ORGANIZATION selects, at its sole discretion, including but not limited to: Twitch, Facebook Gaming, and/or YouTube. The GAMER agrees that the GAMER shall stream on behalf of the ORGANIZATION for approximately forty (40) hours per month.
(d.) At the ORGANIZATION's request, the GAMER agrees to participate in a reasonable number of marketing, advertising, content production, and/or promotional activities on behalf of the ORGANIZATION and/or the ORGANIZATION's Sponsors ("Promotional Activity"). The Promotional Activity shall take place at such dates, times, and locations as determined by the ORGANIZATION at its sole discretion. The GAMER shall undertake any and all actions during said Promotional Activity in a first-class and professional manner and shall adhere to and shall be subject to the written and/or verbal instructions and directions of the ORGANIZATION and/or the ORGANIZATION's Sponsors' representatives, employees, and/or agents.
(e.) During the Term, the GAMER agrees to be available for up to two (2) personal appearances ("Appearance Days") per month, at a time and place as selected by the ORGANIZATION. During the Term, the ORGANIZATION has the option to request and the GAMER agrees to be available for additional Appearance Days. In the event the ORGANIZATION requests additional Appearance Days by the GAMER, the ORGANIZATION and/or the ORGANIZATION's Sponsors agrees to pay the GAMER the additional compensation in the amount of two hundred ($200.00) U.S. dollars per day for each additional Appearance Day requested by the ORGANIZATION and/or the ORGANIZATION's Sponsors.
(f.) The GAMER warrants that the GAMER's Services set forth in this Agreement shall not be in violation of any immigration or other relevant work authorization laws; the GAMER agrees that the GAMER will not engage in any dangerous activities or other hazardous acts that may expose the GAMER to physical risks during the Term of this Agreement, including but not limited to motorcycle racing, car racing, bungee jumping, boxing, kickboxing, MMA (mixed martial arts), sky diving, wrestling, and/or hang gliding; and, that the GAMER

> will present themself to the public in a professional fashion, and the GAMER's conduct will always confirm to the highest standards of honesty, morality, fair play, and good sportsmanship.

In exchange for the compensation that a gamer receives (salary) from an organization, the team usually requires a certain set of "obligations" or duties that the individual must fulfill in order for the player to receive the agreed-upon compensation such as those listed above. While the exact obligations on behalf of an organization differs in every case, most major esports organizations generally require that their signed gamers wear their team uniforms during all competitions as well as to support and utilize all of its sponsors' products.[910] Many organizations also require that the gamer display the team's logo as well as any brand partners on their social media platforms.[911] While streaming, a gamer may also be obligated to utilize or promote a team's sponsors on-screen through product placement and on-air "shout-outs."[912]

In addition to competing on behalf of the organization, a team may require that the talent participate in promotional and other marketing and content creation activities on behalf of them as well as in support of their partners and sponsoring brands.[913] Some of these activities could include fan "meet and greets" at a competition or tournament.[914] Other promotional events could be attending an industry convention where the gamer participates or otherwise appears on behalf of the organization or its sponsors. For example, a sponsored "activation" could be a product demonstration on behalf of a gaming peripheral company or a new product "tasting" or "sampling" on behalf of a sponsoring beverage.[915]

Since a player is required to comply with all of a contract's duties, it is beneficial for a gamer to ensure that any of their organizational obligations are clearly defined in writing.[916] In particular, it could be prudent to address and list the number of required sponsorship appearances as well as describe which party covers any costs associated with the gamer's participation in these events.[917] A player might also try to negotiate for additional compensation if they are requested to exceed a specified minimum promotional appearance amount. Similar to the provision above, a gamer may attempt to negotiate for additional compensation for the player's participation beyond the set number of appearances. This insertion could be seen as a way to further incentivize the gamer's participation in additional marketing activities that further the organization and their sponsoring brand's marketing initiatives.

A typical player agreement might also include certain restrictions on the professional gamer's actions. Some of these might include a limitation on which streaming platform a gamer can use when streaming as well as list a set number of streaming hours that they are required to fulfill on behalf of the organization.[918] As with most agreement provisions, each party may attempt to reduce or increase the minimum required hours as well as attempt to provide additional incentives for the player to exceed the listed minimum. This could be in the form of a bonus or other additional forms of compensation to incentivize the player to stream for longer. A gamer may also try to negotiate for some flexibility in their streaming hour requirements, especially in light of their other team commitments.[919] For instance, an individual may request language that provides them with "reasonable" or other fair reductions in the monthly streaming requirement for any travel time as well as for any time spent participating in competitions, tournaments, and other organization-related activities.[920] This type of limitation could help ensure that the gamer does not fail to fulfill or otherwise breach their contractual obligations due to the daily time restrictions imposed by travel to and from competitions, sponsored events, as well as for any other team-related events.[921]

In many cases, a professional gamer agreement with an organization may also proscribe the type of equipment that the competitor must utilize.[922] This includes listing what equipment the gamer uses during their stream as well as potentially during any organized tournaments or matches.[923] Generally, the talent is permitted to only use gaming peripherals and equipment from their organization's sponsors. These relationships could include ones with established brands for all or some of the gamer's equipment, such as a keyboard, a computer monitor, a headset, or a gaming chair. However, situations may arise where a gamer is so familiar with their current equipment, especially with their keyboard or mouse that they may not perform at the same level while utilizing different technology.[924] In such a case, the player may attempt to include language that accommodates or otherwise permits the gamer to use their desired equipment. This concession is rare because the team may be contractually prohibited from displaying a sponsor's competitor during any team-affiliated or sanctioned activities. This may also be true in cases where a sponsoring brand provides all of the equipment for a "gaming house" or other training facilities that the players consistently work, live, and/or train in.[925] This is because all of the provided equipment at the premises would usually be supplied by the same sponsor, such as Team Liquid's fully-sponsored, "Alienware Training Facility."[926]

Additionally, similar to the contracts signed by many professional athletes, provisions exist which forbid the gamers from participating in or engaging in any "dangerous or other hazardous" activities.[927] Some of these prohibitions could be preventing the gamer from boxing, motorcycle racing, bungee jumping, or sky diving. This is important to the organization because if a player does partake in any "dangerous" or other "hazardous act" and they sustain an injury as a result of it, the injury may provide the esports team with grounds to terminate (i.e., for material breach of the provision) or otherwise rescind the agreement.[928] The contract might also provide the team with the option to "toll" (put the contract on hold) the term of the contract until the gamer is healed. While this is the extreme case, with the rise of action sports and other high-risk activities, there is a need for a team to ensure that a signed professional takes care of themselves and is prevented from engaging in actions that could seriously jeopardize their ability to perform to the level that they are expected to.

The GAMER's Compensation

(a.) **Salary**—For the duration of the Term, the GAMER shall receive a salary of five thousand ($5,000.00) U.S. Dollars (the "Monthly Compensation") per month. The Monthly Compensation shall be paid on the first day of each month by the ORGANIZATION. Notwithstanding, if the Monthly Compensation payable to the GAMER listed in this Agreement ever fails to comply with any and all rules or regulations of any and all competitions, tournaments, and/or third-party esports leagues in which the ORGANIZATION competes in or participates in, then the ORGANIZATION agrees to adjust the Monthly Compensation payable to the GAMER hereunder in order to comply with the applicable rules and regulations regarding player compensation.

(b.) **Sponsorship Guarantee**—The ORGANIZATION shall provide the GAMER with a minimum guaranteed annual sponsorship payment in the amount of ten ($10,000.00) dollars per year (the "Sponsorship Guarantee") in addition to the above Monthly Compensation. In the event at the end of the applicable calendar year, the GAMER has not earned the amount listed in Sponsorship Guarantee, the ORGANIZATION shall pay the difference to the GAMER.

As with most contract negotiations, one of the important and potentially contentious points involves the compensation from the organization to the gamer.[929] This is largely due to the wide range in compensation paid to these individuals.[930] In particular, there is no established maximum amount that an organization or team may pay a professional.[931] Therefore, in some cases, the team may only pay a small salary or just simply cover the gamer's competition-related expenses, such as their travel and lodging for a tournament. In other circumstances, a player may earn several hundred or thousand dollars a month depending on their notoriety and the gaming title that they compete in.[932] Some listed salaries may increase over time, especially as the viewership and other avenues of monetization for a specific game increase.[933] For example, the average salary for a professional *League of Legends* player has steadily risen. An article from January 2017 stated that the average base salary in North America was "$105,385;" and, in Europe, it was "$80,816."[934] By February 2018, the average salaries for North American competitors in *League of Legends* reportedly grew to "over $320,000."[935] Finally, there has been a trend of certain teams, especially those with existing brand partnerships to "guarantee" or otherwise promise that a certain amount of additional compensation shall be paid to the gamer in exchange for the promotional services that they provide for the organization's sponsors.

While no maximum salary exists, some organized franchise leagues have established a minimum annual salary payable to a competitor.[936] For example, both the *Overwatch League*[937] and the *Call of Duty Pro League*[938] have mandated minimum player salaries. These leagues provide each player with a minimum yearly salary of $50,000; however, this is just a minimum, as the individual gamer still has the right to negotiate for a higher salary.[939] For example, former professional *Overwatch League* competitor, Jay "sinatraa" Won negotiated a salary three times ($150,000) the minimum amount.[940] This means that he earned "$100,000 more than the league minimum" for his participation.[941] However, in subsequent years, the average salary for an *Overwatch League* professional was "somewhere between $80,000 and $120,000."[942]

Additionally, once a salary is agreed upon between the parties, it is prudent to incorporate language that permits the gamer to earn a pro-rata or other reduced amounts if they are terminated (dropped) or otherwise released prior to finishing an entire month or term of the agreement.[943] For instance, if a gamer is dropped by the team halfway through a month or a contract, it is beneficial to include language providing the individual with a pro-rata payment of their salary for the accrued time to provide the player with some form of compensation for this employment period. Furthermore, some agreements may include language that permits the team to adjust the monthly compensation paid to the individual if the current salary fails to comply with any organized league or tournament. For instance, if a gamer is currently signed to an organization as a professional *Call of Duty* player and their team now obtains a franchise spot in the *Call of Duty League*, then the organization may now need to raise or otherwise re-negotiate the talent's current salary level to adhere to the newly imposed league minimum amount so that they can comply with the league's rules.[944] Therefore, it is prudent for a gamer to request the insertion of similar language to permit the required compensation adjustment, especially when competing in non-franchise league game titles.

> **Prize Money**—Any and all tournament, league, and/or event ("Competition(s)") total prize pool money earned by the GAMER shall be paid directly to the ORGANIZATION and shall not be paid directly to the GAMER. However, if the GAMER does receive payment from Competition, the GAMER will immediately direct the payment of the funds to the ORGANIZATION. The ORGANIZATION then agrees to pay the TEAM eighty (80%) percent of all such Competition winnings received by the ORGANIZATION, with each Gamer on the Starting Roster of the TEAM receiving an equal share ("Team Prize Money"). For example, if there are four (4) members of the TEAM, then each Gamer shall receive twenty (20%) percent of the total Team Prize Money. The remaining twenty (20%) percent of total Team Prize Money shall be retained by the ORGANIZATION ("Company Prize Money"). All Team Prize Money payments to the GAMER shall be calculated after any and all applicable state, federal, and/or city taxes have been deducted from the total Team Prize Money.

Another common provision is displayed above and is included in most competitive gaming contracts. This clause may also be another point of serious contention depending on the size of the available prize pools. This is because it addresses how any competition winnings are divided between the gamer and the team.[945] Specifically, how the funds earned from a tournament are split is of particular importance and should be discussed and negotiated between the gamer and the organization, as some takes may take as little as 5% to 10% or more, including up to "20% percent."[946] This is especially true in larger competitive titles which may provide substantial tournament or league prize winnings.[947] In fact, in the last few years the total prize money available and the amounts allocated for each competitor or team has steadily risen. For instance, one of the largest annual tournament prize pools is for *Dota 2*'s "The International" competition.[948] This tournament has been one of the longest running professional competitions and has boosted some of esports' largest prize pools ever.

For example, the 2019 competition had a total prize pool that eclipsed "$30.2 million"[949] and eventually "finished at $34million."[950] Of this $34 million total prize pool, the winning team earned a total of "$15,620,181."[951] This provided each competitor with "about $3.1 million" as there were five members on the winning competitive team.[952] The 2019 total prize pool amount was larger than the 2018 The International, which had provided the winning team with a total of "$11,234,158"[953] of a then "record [total prize pool] of $25.5M."[954] In fact, total prize pool available in The International in *Dota 2* is still continuing to grow each year, including "break[ing] $30 million" again for the upcoming, The International 10.[955] Other competitive titles have also begun providing substantial prize money, including Epic Games' *Fortnite* World Cup.[956] This competition provided a total of $30 million in prizes for gamers with the winner of the "singles" and "duos" matches each receiving $3 million.[957] In addition, the prize pools available for competitors in Activision-Blizzard's *Overwatch League* have also increased annually.[958] The organized league "has upped its prize pool from $3.5 million in 2018 to $5 million for the 2019 season."[959] Specifically, the 2019 overall season winning team earned "$1.1 million [dollars] with the runner-up team walking away with $600,000, [and additional] decreasing amounts for [the other] lower-ranked teams."[960] It is apparent from these large prize pools that the percentage that a player or team is entitled to should be determined and agreed upon in advance as this negotiation could be the difference between hundreds or even thousands of dollars.

> **"In-Game" Content**—Any and all Gross Revenue generated from any in-game digital assets, including but not limited to any promotional items, stickers, and/or skins ("In- Game Content") related to the ORGANIZATION shall be divided as follows: the ORGANIZATION agrees to pay the TEAM forty (40%) percent of all such income ("Team Game Content"). The Team Game Content will be divided equally among each Gamer on the Starting Roster with each Gamer receiving an equal share of the Team Game Content revenues. The remaining sixty (60%) percent of the In-Game Content revenue shall be solely retained by the ORGANIZATION.

With the rise in additional opportunities for professional gamers and for organizations to earn income from in-game transactions, it is essential for these parties to discuss how these revenues are distributed. This includes a determination on how any monies generated from the sale of a team or a player-branded in-game item is split. Some of these in-game items could be in the form of a specific weapon "skin" or armor featuring the organization's colors or logo or an item that includes a particular gamer's gamer-tag, image, or other likeness. For example, Ubisoft's *Rainbow Six Siege Pro League* provides any participating team with "30% of the revenue [earned from] its own respective item sales."[961] Consequently, the 30% of these sales earned by the esports organization is then dispersed between the players and the team based upon their agreed-upon split for in-game item sales.[962] As exemplified above, the competitive team players under this agreement would be entitled to split 40% of the total earned by the team from this source. Similarly, many other established competitive leagues have introduced revenue-sharing options for its participating teams including *Rainbow Six*,[963] *PUBG*,[964] *League of Legends*,[965] and *Overwatch*.[966]

In addition to negotiating the split of this revenue stream, a gamer might also try to carve out an exception. Specifically, the player may try to negotiate language that provides them with the full amount allocated for the "gamer side" of in-game revenue that the organization earns if their name, image, or gamer-tag is solely used for the in-game item instead of the monies being subject to "split" provisions.[967] This could be in the form of a character skin only containing the player's name or gamer-tag. While this might not always be possible, if a particular player has achieved a high level of notoriety that such in-game assets might be created solely utilizing their likeness, it would be beneficial for the gamer to try to receive additional compensation for this use. Ultimately, this is a point that the organization might accept in light of the bargaining power of the particular gamer and whether or not they intend to create or otherwise license gamer-specific content.

Merchandise—(a.) **"Gamer-Branded" Merchandise**—The ORGANIZATION shall receive sixty (60%) percent of the Net Profits earned from "Gamer-Branded Merchandise" sales. The GAMER and the rest of the TEAM shall divide the remaining forty (40%) percent (the "Gamers' Share") equally between them. "Gamer-Branded Merchandise" includes any and all items that utilize and/or otherwise display the GAMER's name, image, gamer-tag, and/or likeness, and/or contains all or some of the Gamers of the ORGANIZATION.

(b.) **"Team-Branded" Merchandise**—The ORGANIZATION shall receive eighty (80%) percent of the Net Profits earned from "Team-Branded Merchandise" sales. The GAMER and the rest of the TEAM shall equally divide the remaining twenty (20%) Percent of the Net Profits earned from "Team-Branded Merchandise" sales. "Team-Branded Merchandise" includes any and all items that utilize or display

> the ORGANIZATION's name and/or logo and that does not specifically list, utilize, and/or use the GAMER's individual name, image, gamer-tag, and/or likeness and/or any use the name, image, gamer-tag, and/or likeness of any of the other players of the TEAM.

With the escalating importance of team merchandise sales, a gamer contract may address which merchandise the player generates income from (if any) and specifies how much the professional gamer earns from these sales (if anything).[968] Generally, the merchandise sold by an organization falls into one of two categories, either it is team-branded or it is gamer-branded merchandise.[969] Team-branded merchandise are any items created that contain the organization's name or logo.[970] In contrast, gamer-branded goods are those that possess an individual's name, gamer-tag, photograph, or other uses of the player's likeness.[971] Similar to in-game items, in instances where only one player is featured on the gamer-branded merchandise, the gamer may try to include language that ensures that only that particular individual is entitled to the full "gamers' share" allotment for any income generated from the sale of the specific gamer-branded merchandise.[972]

In addition to a specified percentage of merchandise sales, some organizations may also provide a signed player with an affiliate or other "check-out" discount code or link that is specific to the gamer.[973] This player-specific code or URL can then be used by a customer at the time of purchase of any team-branded merchandise in order to receive a discount or other benefit, such as a free gift.[974] In this context, the player could negotiate that the use of this specific affiliate code or URL link when purchasing any team-branded items provides the gamer with a set percentage of that purchase. This could be a technique utilized by an esports organization to incentivize their individual players to encourage their fans to purchase the team's merchandise. As with most points, the actual discount percentage and the amount that the player earns from such a sale are also subject to negotiation and should be ironed out in advance in the agreement.

> **Streaming Revenue**—For the duration of the Term, the GAMER is entitled to one hundred (100%) percent of any and all streaming revenue earned by the GAMER, including but not limited to any advertising revenues, subscription(s), tips, bits, and/or donation(s) revenues.

As discussed earlier, one of the most prevalent forms of income within the esports business ecosystem is live streaming. In fact, many professional gamers, content creators, and professional esports organizations earn substantial and, sometimes, a majority of their revenues through this avenue. Similarly, most major player deals outline how much the streaming party is entitled to from their streaming earnings. While each agreement is different, many professional organizations permit their signed gamer to keep all of their streaming income.[975] This includes any money generated from any advertisements displayed during their broadcast as well as funds earned from any commercials played on their saved content. A gamer might also be able to retain all of the money earned from any viewer "donations," "tips," and subscription fees. However, in some cases, the team may insist on receiving a percentage of the person's streaming income in exchange for a set salary that the team pays them or for any other benefits that the organization provides to the streamer. This may be common in situations where the individual is only a streamer or content creator for the team and does not compete in tournaments or leagues. The benefits provided by the team to the streamer could be in the form of additional exposure and promotion of the talent as well as introductions to sponsors or other potential brand partners for the streamer. As with most points within a contract, the exact percentages are generally subject to negotiation between the parties.

GAMER Housing—At the ORGANIZATION's sole discretion, for the duration of the Agreement, the ORGANIZATION shall provide the GAMER with reasonable, fully-furnished lodging accommodations or other housing options, including providing the GAMER with all necessary computers, gaming gear, and network/internet connections, at the ORGANIZATION's sole cost. These lodging accommodations may vary based upon the country in which the GAMER resides, and may include a separate apartment for the Gamer and/or a single gaming house for the GAMER to live in with the rest of the ORGANIZATION's TEAM.

In addition to offering a professional gamer a salary, some teams may also provide the individual with housing accommodations. This is particularly true of organizations that require their players to move from their home market to live and train elsewhere. The actual provided accommodation may differ greatly based on the number of gamers who require housing as well as the city or geographic area that the housing is located in.[976] In some cases, the team may provide a gaming house where all of the teammates live and practice together.[977] This type of living arrangement may provide unique benefits and opportunities for the organization. For example, not only are all of the players able to live and practice together in the same room without much interruption but it also provides the organization with opportunity to create content within the residence as well as to provide product placement opportunities for its brand partners.[978] For instance, esports organization Cloud9 had a gaming house in California for its *CS:GO* team.[979] The premises was equipped with a gaming room, a dining room, and a full kitchen as well as having individual rooms for each gamer.[980] In other situations, the team may just provide the gamers with their own apartments or other shared living quarters.[981] Furthermore, some teams may not provide any housing accommodations for its signed talent. This is especially true when the gamer is not part of a larger competitive team, such as a fighting game participant, or in instances where the costs outweigh the benefits of having the team living together. While each organization determines whether to provide housing to the gamer as well as what type of housing will be provided, in instances where no housing is provided, a player may still be required to move away from his home market. If this is the case, the gamer might attempt to negotiate for some type of "stipend" or other payment from the team that can be applied toward their housing and living arrangements. While this may not be possible in many situations, as with most things, it is beneficial to attempt to negotiate for it, especially in light of the costs associated with moving into a new market.

> **Boot Camp Housing**—At the ORGANIZATION's sole discretion and cost, the ORGANIZATION may provide the GAMER with reasonable, fully-furnished lodging accommodations during a "boot camp." These lodging accommodations may vary based upon the country in which the ORGANIZATION resides, and may consist of a separate apartment for the GAMER, hotel room(s) for the GAMER, and/or a single gaming house for the GAMER to live in with the rest of the ORGANIZATION's TEAM.

As indicated earlier, a "boot camp" is the name for the intense training sessions that a competitive player or team of gamers undertakes in order to prepare for an upcoming tournament or league season.[982] The language above expresses that the team will cover all of the costs of the gamer's participation in any boot camps. Since such camps have become very common occurrences among major organizations, it is fairly common for a team to cover these expenses. In particular, these programs provide the team with the ability to simply "play games [and practice] for up to 16 hours a day [, ...] seven days a week [to refine] their strategy."[983] For example, the pro players on esports teams Virtus.pro and Natus Vincere participated in a "joint" boot camp where each team "train[ed] for multiple hours a day over the course of four days [including ...] playing, planning out strategies, and analyzing footage from competitors."[984] In addition to playing and studying the game, the camp provided each member of both "team[s] [with] an opportunity to train under the care of both [organization's] trainers [as well as with] a special psychologist."[985] Due to the unique benefits that many professional teams have found through these types of activities, it is fair to assume that such boot camps will continue to be part of a professional gamer's training regimen.[986]

> **Travel and Per Diem Expenses**—In the event that the GAMER is required to travel to a location more than twenty (20) miles from the GAMER's residence or if the GAMER is housed at the ORGANIZATION's residence, from the ORGANIZATION's house, the GAMER shall receive first-class travel accommodations to and from the residence to the event and/or competition, at the ORGANIZATION's sole cost. The GAMER shall receive a per diem expense allowance of fifty ($50.00) U.S. dollars per day during the Term of this Agreement when traveling as well as three (3) meals per day while traveling to an event and/or competition, all at the ORGANIZATION's sole cost.

While a professional organization may cover the living and training expenses of a signed player, some teams also provide their team members with funds to cover other living expenditures. For instance, a team may reimburse a gamer for the travel costs to and from a competition or other team mandated event.[987] An esports organization might also offer their signed talent a "per diem." This is a "daily allowance" that the company pays to the player to help cover their daily costs such as food.[988] These additional funds are not necessarily provided in every esports player contract; however, it could be beneficial for a player to try to negotiate with the team to attempt to have the organization cover some of their other related expenses. Again, this is another point of contention that must be agreed to between the parties; otherwise, if no language is to the contrary, then the gamer will be solely responsible to pay for anything that the team does not explicitly agree in writing to pay for.

The GAMER's Assumption of Risk—The GAMER understands, warrants, and agrees that there are inherent risks involved with participation in professional gaming, including but not limited to, any and all eye and/or retina damage, carpal tunnel syndrome, and/or other arm and wrist injuries, repetitive stress injuries, and/or other damage associated with extended periods of computer-based work. The GAMER hereby expressly assumes any and all such risks and results of participation in professional video gaming on behalf of the ORGANIZATION. The GAMER hereby releases the ORGANIZATION and the ORGANIZATION's representatives, employees, officers, directors, and shareholders from and against any and all claims, suits, judgments, costs and/or fees, relating to and/or arising out of activities performed by the GAMER in connection with any and all injuries associated with participation in professional gaming on behalf of the ORGANIZATION.

It is important for a competitive gamer to be aware of the potential risks and hazards that they could encounter as a result of participating in esports.[989] Similar to many other professional sports, an esports competitor generally "assumes the risk" of any foreseeable injury or bodily harm that they may suffer as a result of their participation.[990] In the gaming world and similar to the language above, the individual usually accepts and removes any legal liability upon the organization for any of the listed injuries that manifest as a result of the player's gaming.[991] Therefore, the inclusion of such language in a player's contract may absolve the organization from any potential liability for any injuries a gamer sustained while playing on behalf of them, including any eye or wrist injuries as well as any other "repetitive stress injuries."[992] Since incorporating this type of language is a fairly common practice among companies, a professional gamer should be aware that even if they do suffer such foreseeable injuries, they most likely have already "assumed" this risk. This then means that the organization will be held harmless from any liability and not be legally responsible for any of the gamer's injuries.[993]

GAMER Restrictions—(a.) **Non-Solicit**—The GAMER agrees to not solicit or otherwise induce any other professional gamer and/or employee to terminate and/or reduce their relationship with the ORGANIZATION.

(b.) **No Poaching**—The GAMER agrees that the GAMER will not solicit, lure, poach, and/or otherwise make any offer of or attempt to offer employment to any currently contracted player competing in any game, whether the GAMER competes in that game or not. The GAMER agrees not to encourage any other player to breach or otherwise terminate an existing contract with any other third party, including but not limited to an existing esports organization and/or team.

(c.) **Non-Disparagement and Liquidated Damages**—The GAMER agrees that they will not, at any time, publicly disparage, or make any derogatory, slander, or offensive remarks about the ORGANIZATION, the ORGANIZATION's employees, officers, directors, shareholders, agents, sponsors, other gamers or streamers, or affiliates. The GAMER also shall not, at any time, make, post, publish, or communicate to any person or entity in any public forum any false, defamatory, libelous, and/or otherwise slanderous remarks or make public communications intending to cause injury to the ORGANIZATION's business interest, including but not limited to making public statements questioning the integrity and/or competence of the ORGANIZATION, the ORGANIZATION's Sponsors, and/or the administrators of any tournament and/or a league organizer that the ORGANIZATION participates in. In the event that Gamer breaches this clause, GAMER shall pay to ORGANIZATION liquidated damages in the amount equal to one ($1.00) dollar per Impression of the Disparagement. "Impression" shall be defined as "a single instance of the display or provision of the Disparagement directly or indirectly to any person, regardless of whether such Disparagement was viewed, heard, or otherwise experienced."

(d.) **Objectionable Posts**—While GAMER has the sole and absolute discretion over their Social Media posts, the ORGANIZATION may request in writing that GAMER remove and/or delete any Social Media post that ORGANIZATION reasonably believes violates or otherwise breaches any of the provisions of this Agreement; and the GAMER agrees to promptly within twenty-four (24) hours of said request from the ORGANIZATION remove or delete any such Social Media post.

(e.) **Fines, Suspensions, and Disciplinary Action**—During the Term of this Agreement, the GAMER agrees and acknowledges that the GAMER may be subject to fines, suspensions, and/or disqualifications imposed by the ORGANIZATION and/or any competition, tournament, and/or league organizer, and that these fines, suspensions, and/or disqualifications are reasonable and necessary in order to maintain the integrity of competitive esports. The GAMER further acknowledges

> that the ORGANIZATION has the power to levy fines on the GAMER for conduct that is detrimental to the ORGANIZATION, including but not limited to the repeated failure to attend training, practice, and/or Sponsorship Appearances by the GAMER (without prior authorization or written permission from the ORGANIZATION) and/or any unsportsmanlike or other public disruptive behavior directed at the ORGANIZATION and/or the ORGANIZATION's other gamers, coaches, analysts, and/or managers as well as any and all opposing players and coaches, fans, announcers, casters, streamers, referees, and/or tournament, league, and/or competition organizer officials or referees. Unless challenged by the GAMER pursuant to the Official Rules and/or Regulations, the GAMER agrees to immediately pay any and all such fines as requested by the ORGANIZATION and/or any competition, tournament, and/or league organizer or host. Notwithstanding, after prior written notice to the GAMER, the ORGANIZATION shall have the right to deduct all reasonably incurred fines from the GAMER's Monthly Compensation and/or from any other compensation owed to the GAMER pursuant to this Agreement.

Most businesses, including those involved in professional sport, generally provide a list of limitations and obligations that a professional under their banner must adhere to. Esports is no different, as most competitive team agreements contain several prohibitions. These restrictions could include anti-poaching, anti-disparagement, as well as non-solicitation provisions intended to safeguard competitive integrity as well as to ensure that all public communications made about the team or the league by a gamer are positive.[994] Other restrictions could include preventing the player from attempting to solicit or otherwise "poach" another gamer or other employee signed to another team.[995] Such actions could be undertaken in an effort to convince the player to leave their current organization to join the gamer's team.[996] Provisions related to these concepts can also be fashioned to protect the organization's current employees from leaving the entity to work for a competitor, such as through a non-compete clause.[997]

Furthermore, similar to many traditional companies, especially those in the public light whose business may be influenced by public perception, esports organizations generally impose regulations on what a signed gamer can say publicly.[998] These could include restricting the substance of the gamer's statements on social media as well as during any on-air interviews or in any articles or other press pieces.[999] In particular, the team may incorporate language to attempt to ensure that the player does not publicly disparage or otherwise defame the organization, any of the team's sponsors, their opponents, as well as the tournament or league organizers and their brand partners.[1000] Some organizations have even gone further by including a potential "liquidated damages" clause that provides a specific amount to the team for any defamatory remarks made by a gamer, either online or otherwise.[1001]

Analogous to many other professional sports, a competitive esports organization might impose a fine or other penalty for a violation of any of these types of constraints.[1002] In addition, most organized tournaments and leagues enact their own code of conduct or other regulations that a gamer must adhere to in order to compete.[1003] In fact, many tournament and competitive league rulebooks may also provide the organizer with the option to impose penalties, fines, or other sanctions (suspension, expulsion) for any infractions and other violations of any of the competition's rules.[1004] In these cases and similar to the language above, it is important that a gamer is aware of the potential penalties that exist for a rules infraction.[1005] This is because many agreements generally permit the organization to impose penalties and fines upon the gamer for violations.[1006] An agreement might also provide the team with the right to deduct any fined amounts directly from any compensation payable to the gamer.

In addition to the above provisions, there are several other important ones incorporated in many professional gaming contracts that affect the contract's term. In fact, there are various ways for a professional player's contract to end earlier than the natural expiration of the contract's term. Some of these methods could include the team dropping or releasing a player by terminating the contract or through a buyout payment made by the player, by the signed team or by another team.[1007] A professional player could also formally retire from competitive gaming or they could be subject to "loan out" or other transfer of the professional to another team, such as being sold or traded to another organization.[1008]

> **Buyout**—This Agreement may be sold and/or assigned to another esports team or organization, without the prior consent of the GAMER, at the ORGANIZATION's sole discretion, for an amount no less than twenty thousand ($20,000.00) U.S. dollars ("Buyout Amount") payable to the ORGANIZATION. The GAMER shall also have the option to provide the Buyout Amount to the ORGANIZATION in order to be released from this Agreement.

An example of a "buyout" provision is exemplified above. This clause enables the parties to prematurely end their contractual relationship in exchange for a payment. A buyout is the monetary amount that must be paid to the organization in order to purchase or otherwise assign an existing contract to another party.[1009] This sum can be paid to the original team by the individual gamer themselves or by another team who wishes to acquire the rights to the player. In many circumstances, the negotiation of the buyout amount in a contract is extremely vital. This is because the listed amount can act as a barrier to a player's transfer or other movements within their professional gaming career. This is especially true when the listed figure is for a large amount and the original team is not willing to modify or alter the required amount. In those cases, such a large buyout could actually prevent another team from proceeding with the gamer due to the buyout amount being cost prohibitive. This could be because the new team does not feel that the significant expenditure could be recouped by them. In fact, some teams, such as esports organization G2 Esports, allegedly applied large buyout prices for several of its players.[1010] Specifically, the organization is said to have applied a "$800,000 price tag per player."[1011] This reported buyout amount might act as a barrier to another team purchasing their contracts, thereby preventing them from playing for another team (or at all).[1012]

In addition to agreeing to a specific buyout amount, a player can also try to negotiate for additional compensation as a result of a third party exercising the provision. For instance, the gamer could try to negotiate for a "transfer bonus." This could be in the form of a set percent of the buyout amount earned by the team being paid to the gamer. The inclusion of this language could be beneficial to both parties in the transaction. This is because a team may agree to a larger buyout with a "transfer bonus" in their contract in an attempt to incentivize the gamer to focus on performing well so that another organization desires to purchase the gamer for the large sum listed. If this occurs, then the player would also receive some compensation from the buyout. This is especially true in minor leagues such as *Overwatch Contenders*, whereby franchises competing in the *Overwatch League* look to the *Contenders'* teams for replacement gamers.[1013] In most of these cases, the teams are required to pay the original organization the listed buyout amount to facilitate this transaction.[1014] In fact, existing organizations do sign successful competitive *Overwatch League Contenders'* teams.[1015] For example, esports organization Team Envy signed an entire *Contenders* team that finished within the top four of Season 1 of *Overwatch League Contenders*.[1016]

Retirement Clause—In the event that the GAMER chooses to terminate this Agreement and to discontinue any and all competitive esports play for at least the next two (2) years, the GAMER shall have the right to terminate this Agreement by paying the ORGANIZATION a buyout fee of five thousand ($5,000.000) U.S. dollars ("Retirement Buyout"). "Competitive play" is defined as any and all participation in any and all competitions or tournaments offering a collective tournament and/or competition prize pool of more than two thousand ($2,000) U.S. dollars. Notwithstanding, in the event that the GAMER exercises this "Retirement Clause" and pays the required Retirement Buyout and then later returns to competitive play within three (3) years after the Retirement Buyout is paid, this Agreement shall resume and remain in full force and effect on all of its terms.

Another way for an agreement to end before the term expires is if the gamer retires from competitive gaming.[1017] Similar to a professional athlete's retirement, an individual may indicate to their team that they want to discontinue all competitive gaming for a set period of time or indefinitely.[1018] In fact, this has become a common trend due to the fact that "[m]ost esports players retire by their late 20s or early 30s."[1019] In these cases, similar to the above, a player's contract may have language that permits the player to terminate the agreement early and retire by paying the team a retirement buyout or they may just retire without any financial requirement.[1020] If the player refuses or cannot pay this amount, he may potentially just stop competing and effectively "retire" from competitive play. While this player might not be playing competitively anymore, they might still be in breach of his existing player agreement for failing to perform its services (being a competitive gamer for the team). The retiring gamer's lack of performance may not be excused or otherwise waived by the team because the gamer failed to utilize the proper protocols to correctly effectuate their retirement (i.e., paying the retirement buyout). If the player is in breach for failing to compete and for not paying the required retirement buyout, the team may be permitted to toll or otherwise stop the agreement while still retaining their exclusive rights to the individual's gaming career. In contrast, if the gamer fulfills the agreement criteria and retires properly, they would be released from their exclusive obligation to the team as long as they comply with the listed requirements.[1021] In negotiating this type of provision, a gamer may try to either reduce or completely eliminate the need to pay any type of fee or buyout when retiring before the expiration of their contract. However, the team may counter this point by arguing that they have already paid the player compensation as well as other covered expenditures on behalf of the player so that they can compete for the team and intended to receive reimbursement throughout the entire contractual time period. Ultimately, this point of contention comes down to leverage and bargaining power. In particular, in many cases, the more funds expended on behalf of a gamer, the more likely that the organization will want to ensure that they have every possible opportunity to recover these disbursements and expenditures.

> **Trades and Movement**—For the duration of the Term, the ORGANIZATION shall have the sole right to trade or otherwise assign the ORGANIZATION's existing rights to the GAMER under this Agreement to another esports organization or team, without the prior consent of the GAMER. The ORGANIZATION shall have the sole right to license or otherwise "loan out" the ORGANIZATION's existing rights in the GAMER under this Agreement to another esports organization or team for a specific period of time and/or the remainder of the Term, without the prior consent of the GAMER.

Similar to other sports, a professional gamer signed to an esports organization can be traded or loaned out to another team.[1022] In most instances, the team will have full and unlimited discretion on whether to assign an existing player contract to another organization as well as approval over which team the gamer is traded to.[1023] The player transfer provisions can be for a specified period of time, such as a "loan-out." In other cases, the transaction could be for the remaining period of the gamer's contract. This is more akin to a trade or a "full assignment" of the rights that the original team had to the competitor.[1024] While the organization generally has the sole right to trade or transfer a player, a gamer may try to negotiate for some limitations on the team's power. One such restriction could be the inclusion of a "no trade clause."[1025] This type of a provision provides the gamer with the right to approve or reject a proposed trade to another team. This means that the gamer can say "no" to a potential trade offer presented to them. A no trade clause can be tailored to require a player's prior approval for any loan-out or for the full trade of the gamer. This provision can be tailored to be applicable to every transaction involving the professional. Alternatively, if a full no trade clause is unavailable, a gamer may try to impose a geographic restriction to prevent the team from trading or otherwise transferring the gamer to a specified country or countries (e.g., no European-based teams). A player could also try to negotiate for a provision that includes an organizational restriction. This could prevent an assignment of the gamer to a specific team or list of teams (e.g., no trade to Gen.G). If such a limitation is accepted, it is essential that the parties list the country or countries that a transfer is prohibited to as well as include the names of any team or organizations that the player will not accept a trade to. Analogous to these transfer restrictions in other traditional sports, the more a team desires to sign and appease the gamer, the more likely that they will accept such player transactional limitations.

> **Change In Management**—At the GAMER's sole option, this Agreement may be terminated by GAMER upon prior written notice to ORGANIZATION in the event that ORGANIZATION undergoes a transfer or sale of all or substantially all of the business of the ORGANIZATION which this Agreement relates to, whether by merger, sale of stock, sale of assets, or otherwise, whether voluntary or involuntary, and by operation of law or otherwise, to any third party.

Another method a professional gamer can utilize to prematurely terminate a player agreement is the inclusion of a "change in management" clause. Similar to the one exhibited above, the language can be written to provide the player with the right to opt-out of their existing contract for any change in the team's management or executive structure. For example, this could include if a team owner or CEO resigns or is otherwise replaced.[1026] The clause can also be fashioned to operate during any change in the actual personnel of the signing team, such as the hiring of a new coach or analyst or if a current coach or player is released. This might also operate as the result of any other transfer of ownership of the team, such as new ownership buying the organization. However, in today's esports business, this might be a point of strong contention with the signing team, because many teams look for outside investment in order to fund their organization. In these cases, the new investors or ownership group might desire to bring in their own management or other new personnel to run the acquired esports team. Therefore, in these situations, it may be tough to incorporate language that contractually provides a signed gamer with the ability to leave the team if such a transfer occurs as it may limit the organization's growth. Again, depending on the notoriety and leverage the gamer has, the individual may be able to require these types of restrictions be included in their player contract.

Right of First Refusal and First Negotiation—If at any time during the Term, GAMER receives a bona fide offer from a third party (the "Third-Party Offer") from any esports team or organization for the GAMER's services and the GAMER desires to accept such Third-Party Offer, the GAMER agrees to first offer in writing to the ORGANIZATION the opportunity on the same terms and conditions contained in the Third-Party Offer (the "First Offer"). The First Offer must specify all of the terms and conditions of the Third- Party Offer. If the ORGANIZATION does not agree to match the First Offer within fifteen (15) days after the ORGANIZATION's receipt thereof, then the GAMER will have the right to accept the Third-Party Offer. However, any agreement with such third party must be effectuated within fifteen (15) days after the rejection of the First Offer by the ORGANIZATION and the agreement with the third party may only be effectuated upon terms and conditions no less favorable to the GAMER as those contained in the First Offer from the ORGANIZATION. If such a sale is not so effectuated, the GAMER will not sign to another esports team or organization without again first offering the GAMER's services to the ORGANIZATION as provided hereinabove. After the end of the Term of this Agreement, the GAMER hereby agrees to negotiate exclusively and in good faith utilizing its best efforts with the ORGANIZATION, for a period of thirty (30) days, to reach an agreement with the ORGANIZATION for the GAMER to continue the GAMER's Services listed herein on behalf of the ORGANIZATION. If the ORGANIZATION and the GAMER fail to finalize the material terms of such agreement by the end of such thirty (30) day period, then the GAMER shall thereafter be free to negotiate with any other third party for the GAMER's services as a esports player, but only on terms and conditions that are no less favorable to the GAMER than those last offered by the ORGANIZATION to the GAMER.

In situations where an agreement ends naturally, which means that it did not terminate early and the player was not bought out, released, or otherwise transferred to another team, then the above provision may be applicable. The displayed clause includes both a "right of first negotiation" sometimes referred to as the "right of first offer."[1027] It also might contain a "right of first refusal" also known as a "matching right." This above language may be included in situations where a team only signs a gamer for a few years but they would like the opportunity to discuss extending their relationship upon its expiration.

A "right of first negotiation" provides the party, usually the esports organization, with the initial right to decide whether they want to extend and enter into another agreement with the gamer. This language generally requires that contract renewal discussions occur with the existing team before any other organization has the opportunity to weigh in on this decision. This means that the player is first required to negotiate or attempt to negotiate a new contract with the original organization prior to exploring any other options. These clauses typically include a stated period of time, such as the 30-day time limit illustrated above, that the parties must exclusively negotiate with each other in an attempt to finalize a new deal. A proscribed time limit is included in most instances in an effort to prevent the negotiations from carrying on for an unlimited period of time. In some cases, there is also included language which ensures that the parties will attempt to engage in "good faith" negotiation. This generally means that the parties will refrain from offering an extremely unfair or "low ball" offer that is completely different from anything else that was agreed to previously. If the negotiation time period expires and the parties have not entered into a new agreement, then the gamer may be permitted to start discussions with other teams to compete elsewhere.

Additionally, many agreements that include a "right of first negotiation" may also contain a right of first refusal or a matching right. In most cases, a right of first refusal provides one party, usually the esports team, with the right to "match" any proposal from another organization made to the gamer on the same terms and conditions as those offered by the other organization. If the original team does not match the third party's offer, then the gamer is free to enter into the agreement with the other organization on the same terms presented to the original team. However, it is important to be aware that an esports organization may include contractual language that prevents the team from being obligated to accept any offer terms which cannot be filled by any other major esports team or organization. For example, if an esports organization's owner also owns a professional football team and offers a gamer season tickets and an ownership interest in the NFL franchise to join them, this would not be a condition that the original team would be required to match if such language was incorporated. This would be because providing an "NFL ownership interest or season tickets" is not something traditionally offered by esports organizations. In some cases, this clause could require that if the gamer's contract negotiations with another team fail, then the player is contractually obligated to re-offer their services to their original organization prior to beginning negotiations with a different team. While the structure of this contractual mechanism may differ, it is important that a professional gamer is aware of their obligations to their prior team before signing with a new one.

> **The GAMER's "Likeness" Rights**—The GAMER grants to the ORGANIZATION the non-exclusive, licensable right throughout the world to use the GAMER's name, likeness, image, voice, gamer-tag, nickname, persona, voice, or any other personal indicia, and/or biographical information that the GAMER has provided to the ORGANIZATION, as well as any and all photographs, audio, and/or audiovisual footage taken of the GAMER and/or featuring the GAMER (collectively, the "GAMER Content") in connection with any and all advertising, sponsorships, sponsorship materials, or other exploitation of the GAMER in any manner in connection with the GAMER's Services hereunder, without additional compensation to the GAMER. During the Term, the GAMER agrees to allow the ORGANIZATION to film, record, and photograph the GAMER, either alone or together with others, for still photographs, motion pictures, television, and/or digital media, at such times and places as the ORGANIZATION requests. The rights in all of the GAMER Content shall belong to the ORGANIZATION and the GAMER shall be not entitled to any royalties or any other additional compensation for the ORGANIZATION's exercise of such rights.

The above is an example of a "right of publicity" clause and is explored in further detail in a later section of this chapter. As an introduction, this right is included in most standard talent agreements, including in professional gamer contracts.[1028] The negotiation and proper understanding of this particular provision is extremely important to a gamer.[1029] The right of publicity is an individual's right to "control and profit from the value of his or her name, image, likeness, and other indicia of [the individual's] identity."[1030] This means that a person "has a right in the publicity value of his photograph, i.e., the right to grant the exclusive privilege of publishing his picture" or other likeness.[1031] Therefore, a third party must receive prior permission before they may utilize another individual's likeness for any commercial purpose, which extends to the right to use a gamer's voice, signature, or gamer-tag on a product.[1032]

In particular, the language listed above outlines the various likeness rights that the organization receives from the gamer. For instance, the team receives the right to utilize the player's likeness for any commercial purpose that it requires. This includes the option to utilize their gamer's real name, gamer-tag, any photographs, or any audio files of them as well as any using any biographical information on the player as they desire. This also means that the team can incorporate the player's likeness, such as the player's name, logo, or voice, on any merchandise, in any team advertisements, as well as in any sponsored content distributed by the organization.

Since the typical rights granted under most right of publicity provisions are very broad and encompass most avenues of an individual's likeness, it is crucial that a professional gamer understands the scope of the rights that they negotiate away as well as comprehend both the short-term and long-term ramifications of such actions. If possible, it may be beneficial for a gamer to negotiate a limitation on the length of time that the organization holds these publicity rights solely to the contract's duration. In this case, the esports team will only have the exclusive right to the gamer's likeness for commercial purposes for the term of the agreement. While this is the rare case, a prominent professional gamer may be able to negotiate for such a limitation so that they can fully monetize their likeness after they depart from the team.

If this option is unavailable, a gamer may try to negotiate for some proscribed limit on the time that the team can use the player's likeness when they are no longer signed to the organization. For example, a player might try to provide the organization with a stated time period, such as six months, after the expiration of the contract that the team can continue to license and monetize the gamer's likeness. This clause could be fashioned to require that after this time period expires, the organization must pay a negotiated fee to the player in order to continue utilizing the individual's persona for commercial uses. However, if this fee is not paid by the organization, then the team's rights to the former gamer's likeness completely expires. Another potential negotiated imitation might be that after the contract's expiration, the team may only utilize the former player's likeness for non-commercial, promotional, or "archival" purposes as opposed to any new or continued commercial ones. This way the team can still use any prior photographs and the gamer's name as well as the gamer-tag and the professional gamer is still able to limit the for-profit avenues available to the team so the player can potentially license their likeness to other parties to earn additional income. This is particularly important as a gamer's independent notoriety grows, which may lead to additional paid opportunities to license their likeness.

> **The GAMER's Intellectual Property Rights**—The GAMER acknowledges and agrees that the results and proceeds of the GAMER's services on behalf of the ORGANIZATION shall, from the inception of creation, constitute a "work made for hire" for the ORGANIZATION within the meaning of the United States Copyright Act of 1976. If for any reason any of the Services provided by the GAMER pursuant to this Agreement do not qualify as a "work made for hire," then the GAMER hereby irrevocably transfers and assigns to the ORGANIZATION any and all of the GAMER's rights, titles, and interests in and to all of the GAMER's Services rendered pursuant to this Agreement, together with all rights therein. Without limiting the generality of the foregoing, the ORGANIZATION shall have the exclusive, unrestricted, worldwide, and perpetual right to use, distribute, and sell any and all of the results and proceeds of the GAMER's Services performed under this Agreement in any and all media now known or hereafter invented. Any assignment to the ORGANIZATION hereunder includes all rights of attribution, integrity, modification, and any other rights throughout the world that may be known as or referred to as "moral rights," or "droit moral" (collectively "Moral Rights"). To the extent that Moral Rights cannot be assigned under applicable law, the GAMER hereby waives and agrees not to enforce any and all Moral Rights, including, without limitation, any limitation on subsequent modification, to the extent permitted under applicable law.

As illustrated above, all of the gamer's services on behalf of the team are considered "works for hire." This means that the individual gamer is commissioned by a third party (the team) to create a specific work for them (i.e., a YouTube or Tik Tok video).[1033] This party (the esports organization) is then the owner of the work created by the other party.[1034] Generally, for a work to be considered a "work for hire," it must be prepared by an employee within the scope of his or her employment for their employer.[1035] While this may seem straightforward, an analysis of who is considered an "employee" and whether the work was created "within the scope" of the employee's employment, are determined on a case by case basis. Specifically, this distinction is adjudicated based on similar factors as those explored earlier in Chapter 4 of this text. In addition, a work may also be considered a "work for hire" if a

> work [is] specifically ordered or commission for use as a contribution to a collective work, as a part of a motion picture or other audiovisual

> work, as a translation, as a supplementary work, as a compilation, as an instructional text, as a test, as answer material for a test, or as an atlas

as long as "the parties agree in writing that the work is a work made for hire."[1036] This is particularly important to esports as the standard language provides the team with exclusive ownership over anything that the gamer creates or provides to them during their entire contract. Typical contractual language also grants the organization with the right to utilize any recorded content created by the gamer for any purpose it desires. In these cases, a player may try to negotiate an exemption for any content that they create during the agreement term on their own personal social media platform, such as on YouTube, from the works that the team has rights to. This would mean that the gamer, not the organization, owns rights to the exempted content. Furthermore, the above language includes a "catch-all" provision that states if any of the work provided under the agreement to the team is not considered a work for hire under the law, then the player assigns and transfers any and all rights that they may have in the works to the team.[1037] This is a typical clause inserted in most entertainment and talent industry contracts in an effort to ensure that anything that the individual creates under an agreement is owned by the party paying for the individual's services.

Additionally, the agreement's language also addresses a party's droit moral or moral rights in a created work. Moral rights refer to the ability of the original author to control their work.[1038] While this right is much broader in scope in other countries, such as France, than in the U.S., this specifically "refers to the right of an author to prevent revision, alteration, or distortion of their work, regardless of who owns the work."[1039] While a more in-depth explanation of this concept is outside the scope of this text, it is important that a gamer is aware that if their country of citizenship acknowledges such a right, they may be waiving it as a result of the above language.

As explored in depth, there are a variety of important factors that a professional gamer must be aware of when signing to a professional esports team. Without too much elaboration, the type of agreement that a gaming influencer, such as a content creator or streamer, enters into an agreement with an esports organization is similar in many respects; however, most of these individuals do not earn tournament winnings.[1040] In all of these cases, it is vital that a party understands how much leverage or desire the other party has to enter into a deal with them. This is especially crucial when considering which points to strongly negotiate and which to consent to. Overall, many of the considerations for a professional gamer are similar to those of other personnel members within the esports ecosystem; however, professional coaches as well as shoutcasters and announcers have some specific issues only relevant to their careers.

5.1.2 A Look at Esports Coach Contracts with a Team

As explored earlier, another important individual within the professional esports world is a team coach. Coaches are generally hired by an existing esports organization to help prepare and strategize with the organization's gamers.[1041] They usually live with or near the signed players and act on behalf of the organization and may work with one or more of their gaming teams.[1042] Similar to professional gamers, a coach being hired by an organization will usually sign an agreement that outlines each parties' obligations. An agreement for a professional coach includes many of the same prohibitions on the types of gaming peripherals and equipment the coach may use as well as the type of apparel that they must wear during team-related activities. Many esports team coaches also provide promotional services and other social media and streaming on behalf of their organization.[1043] A few exemplary clauses are exhibited and discussed below.

I. **The COACH's Services**—(a.) For a period commencing on the Effective Date until such date on which this Agreement is terminated in accordance with the terms of this Agreement or December 31, 2022, whichever is earlier (the "Term"), the ORGANIZATION shall retain the COACH as coach of the ORGANIZATION's team, performing such duties and services as may be assigned to the COACH by the ORGANIZATION.

(b.) During the Term, the COACH shall devote the necessary time, attention, and skill to perform the services set forth in this Agreement, to the best of the COACH's ability exclusively for the ORGANIZATION. The COACH shall perform all duties in a diligent, competent, professional, and skillful manner and in accordance with any and all applicable laws. All Services provided by the COACH during the Term shall be provided on an exclusive basis, and the COACH shall only compete for the ORGANIZATION and shall not provide any form of services for, or on behalf of, another esports team during the Term.

(c.) The COACH shall wear the clothing, uniforms, hats, patches, and other materials designated by and provided by the ORGANIZATION while performing the Services.

(d.) The COACH shall use, test, display, and feature any and all hardware, equipment, peripherals, food items, beverage items, and other goods and services specified by and provided by the ORGANIZATION when performing the Services.

(e.) During the Term, the COACH shall participate in all of the following on behalf of the ORGANIZATION, including but not limited to: live event appearances/engagements; social media content/programming appearances; and social media activities and publicity services, including using reasonable efforts to actively grow, retain, and engage with the fan bases of the ORGANIZATION through social media, including active use of all major social media platforms (Twitter, Instagram, Facebook).

II. **The COACH's Compensation**—(a.) Salary—During the Term, the ORGANIZATION shall pay the COACH Two Thousand ($2,000.00) U.S. Dollars (the "Monthly Compensation") per month. The Monthly Compensation shall be paid on the first day of each month by the ORGANIZATION.

(b.) Signing Bonus—The COACH shall receive said amount as a one-time, flat fee of five thousand ($5,000.00) dollars upon the COACH's execution of this Agreement.

(c.) Prize/Tournament Winnings—In addition to the Monthly Compensation, the COACH shall five (5%) percent of the ORGANZIATION's total earned prize and/or tournament winnings and the COACH's allocation of such prize and/or tournament shall be paid to the COACH within ten (10) days of the ORGANIZATION's receipt of the applicable prize and/or tournament winnings.

III. **Right to Match**—The ORGANIZATION shall have the right to match any bona fide, arms-length post-Term agreement offer received by the Coach to perform the same or substantially similar professional services described in this agreement for another esports organization (a "Post-Term Services Agreement Offer") during the "Right-to-Match Period." If the COACH or the COACH's agents or representatives receive a Post-Term Services Agreement Offer during the Right-to-Match Period, the COACH shall provide the ORGANIZATION with a summary of the material terms of the Post-Term Services Agreement Offer, and then the ORGANIZATION shall have twenty-one (21) days ("Right-to- Match Period") to match or exceed/improve the terms of the offer contained in the Post-Term Services Agreement Offer. If the ORGANIZATION agrees to meet and/or exceeds/improves on the

Post-Term Services Agreement Offer, the COACH shall enter into an agreement with the ORGANIZATION under the agreed-upon terms and conditions.

Analogous to most professional service contracts, the amounts paid to the professional esports coaches vary and are negotiable. While the exact payment amounts are confidential, some reports claim that a "coach can make anywhere from $30,000 to $50,000 a year" with the possibility for additional revenues if the organization provides them with "a performance bonus [and/or] health insurance." [1044] In most cases, a coach's salary can be paid annually, monthly, or hourly.[1045] The actual rate may vary greatly based on the game that they coach, the team that they are working for, and the time commitment involved.[1046] Additionally, similar to the language above, a coach can typically only coach one team at a time, so they are generally exclusive to the signing organization. Additionally, for top coaches, an organization may include a right of first refusal or matching right, similar to the ones included in some professional gamer deals.

The COACH's Obligations—(a.) The COACH shall not, directly or indirectly, do any act, fail to do any act, or make any statement (either "on the record" and/or "off the record"), which may or will impair, disparage, or otherwise reflect negatively upon the name, reputation, and/or the business interests of the ORGANIZATION and/or the ORGANIZATION's owners, officers, directors, or employees, and/or any of the ORGANIZATION's sponsors, including to avoid using profanity in public comments and in any posted and distributed content and information.

(b.) Except in media interviews pre-approved by the ORGANIZATION, the COACH shall not, at any time during or after the Term, participate in the writing and/or scripting of any book, article, movie, and/or other written or theatrical work that (i) relates to the COACH's services on behalf of the ORGANIZATION or any of the ORGANIZATION's sponsors or (ii) otherwise refers to the ORGANIZATION or any of its sponsors, activities, directors, officers, and/or employees, without the prior written consent of the ORGANIZATION.

(c.) The COACH agrees that the COACH shall be bound by and take no action inconsistent with (i) any and all applicable rules, regulations, and/or instructions of any league, tournament, and/or competition in which the ORGANIZATION participates in; (ii) any rules created by the ORGANIZATION; (iii) the standards of good conduct, fair play, and good sportsmanship; and (iv) by any and all applicable state and/or federal laws.

(d.) The COACH warrants and agrees to refrain from engaging in any conduct constituting match fixing, collusion, and/or gambling with respect to any competition, whether the ORGANIZATION is participating or not.

(e.) The COACH warrants and agrees to cooperate and coordinate with the ORGANIZATION to use any Gear and/or other product(s) provided by the ORGANIZATION's Sponsor(s).

(f.) The COACH shall actively, and including at the specific request of the ORGANIZATION, participate in promotional, marketing, advertising, publicity, and production activities separate and distinct from the COACH's daily routine for the benefit of the ORGANIZATION and the ORGANIZATION's Sponsors at such dates, times, and locations as determined by the ORGANIZATION.

Throughout professional gaming's history, there has been a myriad of betting scandals, including professional gamers betting on competitive play as well as engaging in "match fixing."[1047] More recently, a professional team's analyst, which an individual hired by an organization to help work with the team's coaches, publicly stated that he bet on the outcome of a match where the team that he worked for was competing.[1048] While this particular analyst's contract did not prohibit such actions; due to the existence and rise in such conflicts, many organizations do include such restrictions in their documentation. As exhibited above, many coach and analyst agreements list a variety of forbidden conduct.[1049] Some of these prohibited actions are aimed at preventing match fixing, collusion, and gambling with respect to any esports competition, whether or not the bettor works with or is in anyway affiliated with a participating team.[1050] Other standard clauses could be aimed at determining what statements a coach can make publicly in interviews during their employment as well as regulate any statements or other created works produced after their employment ends.[1051] Essentially, the organization tries to incorporate language that protects its image and prevents any individual with access to the internal workings, such as a coach or analyst presumptively would have, from disclosing or otherwise publicizing sensitive information without the team's approval. Similar to other organized sport coaches, esports coaches are also required to follow any league or tournament rules as well as any instruction provided to them by their hiring organization.

Overall, a professional esports coach or analyst contract is not as elaborate as a typical player one but there are many similarities between them. In particular, both documents provide the team with enormous control over the coach's public comments, especially when referencing the team and the organization's competitive performance.

5.1.3 A Look at On-Air Talent Contracts with an Event, Tournament, or League Organizer

With the continued rise in the frequency and the scope of live esports events, the use of broadcast announcers and shoutcasters has steadily risen.[1052] Similar to other careers within the esports ecosystem, most professional commentators working in the space enter into written agreements with their respective employer.[1053] Since most of these contracts are confidential, this section explores a few select provisions from a major shoutcaster agreement for a large event organizer as well as some of other concepts and considerations for shoutcaster and broadcaster agreements.

Generally, the tournament or league organizer hires shoutcasters and other talents for the event presentation.[1054] In other cases, a television network broadcasting the event may hire the on-air personalities. Similar to an esports coach, the payment rate for esports shoutcasters differs greatly.[1055] The amount that they earn per event can range anywhere from a few hundred to several thousand dollars or more. Sometimes, these fees are paid on a flat fee, event-by-event basis and other times, they are paid at an hourly rate. Thus, it is important that any written broadcaster agreement fully outline the payment terms, including the total fee payable as well as explain how this amount will be calculated and disbursed.[1056]

When determining an appropriate broadcaster fee, there are a variety of factors to consider.[1057] For instance, the payment rate might be based on the length of the event, the game title that they are commentating for, as well as the anticipated competition viewership.[1058] Other relevant factors could include how large the event is, which may be based on the broadcast viewership numbers as well as live event attendance. In addition, the size of the event operator is important, including whether the host is a large game developer or a small local company. This is because a large televised event, such as the *Overwatch League* finals run by a large game publisher (Activision-Blizzard) on ESPN, may provide a larger broadcaster fee than the amount paid to an individual providing the same services at a smaller, non-televised event.[1059] Another consideration when setting an announcer fee is whether the event will be televised. This is because many television networks, especially those with substantial viewership, usually have larger production budgets than most traditional non-televised events possess. Therefore, in these cases, the provided broadcast fee might be larger than those offered to a caster of a non-televised event.

In addition, it is important to examine the distance that the shoutcaster has to travel to provide their services. This is because a caster may try to include their "travel days" when setting their fee quote due to the individual being unable to work elsewhere while traveling.[1060] In particular, the more travel time that is required by the individual, the larger the fee may be. This is especially important if the announcer is required to travel internationally which may add a day or two of travel on either side of the assignment. Thus, another matter that both parties must determine and agree on prior to proceeding is whether the talent will receive additional payment for any travel days or if the provided price quote already factors this amount in.[1061]

Finally, another aspect involved in setting an on-air talent's broadcast fee is the shoutcaster's previous experience and other intangible assets.[1062] For example, a caster's large social media or streaming following might be factored in when setting a fee. This is because it may be assumed that if they have a large following or fandom, then the caster's promotion of their appearance will hopefully mobilize their substantial number of followers to tune in to the event to support the caster. Finally, it is important that an individual is aware that a prize pool's size should not be a determinative factor in deciding on an appropriate rate. This is because the fees paid to on-air talent are usually from a different budget or "pool" of money than where the prize derives. This means that the total prize money has no reflection on the amount that the organizer has budgeted for event production. Overall, there are many external factors that can be considered when setting an appropriate caster fee.

The CASTER's SERVICES The CASTER shall provide the following services ("Services") on behalf of the ORGANIZER as detailed below:

(a.) Shoutcasting and Reporting Services—The CASTER shall perform first-class service customarily appropriate for the shoutcasting, broadcasting, and/or reporting services for the ORGANIZER at "Season 1 of the 2020 Organizer Championship Series" related events, including but not limited to any preseason, regular season, playoffs, and championship finals (individually and collectively, the "Event(s)").

(b.) The CASTER agrees that the CASTER shall attend all and participate in all of the ORGANIZER's Event(s) that the ORGANIZER schedules the CASTER to perform the abovementioned Services during the Term. The CASTER shall provide "sportscaster style" or other industry accepted broadcast commentary services at the ORGANIZER's Event.

(c.) The "shoutcasting and reporting services" herein shall include taking direction from the ORGANIZER during all pre-briefing, preparation, rehearsals, and "test runs" at the ORGANIZER's Event.

(d.) The ORGANIZER shall specify what type of attire is required for on-air appearances at each Event by the CASTER.

(e.) **Term and Scheduling**—The CASTER's Services on behalf of the ORGANIZER will be rendered up to five (5) hours per each Event during each week of the preseason, regular season, playoffs, and championship finals for the duration of "Season 1 of the 2020 Organizer Championship Series" ("Term"). The "Season 1 of the 2020 Organizer Championship Series" shall last for four (4) months from the date of this Agreement.

(f.) **Social Media Promotion**—During the Term of this Agreement, the ORGANIZER shall promote the CASTER on the ORGANIZER's social media accounts and platforms by integrating the CASTER into the ORGANIZER's produced social media content, such as an audiovisual work featuring the CASTER's calls during the Events.

(g.) **Ownership**—The CASTER acknowledges and agrees that any and all tangible and intangible property including but not limited to any on-screen appearances, voice recordings, vocal performances, narrations, catch-phrases, and spoken word recordings created by CASTER in connection with this Agreement ("Work Product") shall be considered "works made for hire" so the Work Product shall be the exclusive property of the ORGANIZER. To the extent that any part of the Work Product does not qualify as a "work made for hire" under applicable law, the CASTER hereby irrevocably assigns, transfers, and conveys in perpetuity to the ORGANIZER and its successors and assigns the entire worldwide right, title, and interest in and to the Work Product.

Another unique facet of esports broadcasting talent relates to the agreement's term. This is because some announcer's contracts may be for a specified time period, such as a calendar year and some may only be for a set number of months or weeks. Conversely, some other individuals may only be hired for a single event, an entire tournament, or for a full season. If the shoutcaster is hired for a single event, the individual would generally receive a set fee to work the entire occasion, no matter the number of hours that they cast for or the rate may solely be an hourly one.[1063]

In addition to including the caster's payment amount and the frequency of such payments, many tournament organizers and event production companies impose a myriad of restrictions and obligations upon the announcer.[1064] Since well-known shoutcasters might have independent sponsorship and brand partnerships as well as engage in their own independent streaming, they may be contractually obligated to disclose any independent sponsorship arrangements to the event organizer as well as to ensure that they include any required advertisement disclosures or hash-tags when producing or promoting any "sponsored" content or posts. These disclosures are explored in more detail later in the text.

Many game developers and tournament organizers differ in their policy regarding on-air talent's ability to monetize their private streaming. Some game developers, such as Riot Games, originally included language in their broadcaster "contracts restricting" the talent from "becoming partnered streamers" and from "accepting donations [through] Twitch."[1065] At the time of this policy, such a restriction "was unheard of within rival publishers in the industry," which, eventually, led to a change in Riot Games' policy to be more in line with other developers.[1066] While this limitation was ultimately rescinded, the existence of such as a restriction is a prime example of how contractual language can affect an individual's other unrelated income streams. It also further highlights the need for a caster to fully understand the language of any agreement they sign as the language may impact their other business avenues.

Many standard broadcasting talent contracts also include provisions preventing actions or comments from a caster that exhibits any "favoritism" in the competition that they are casting for as well as from making any profane or other impermissible statements.[1067] This means the announcer is prohibited from showing any affinity or rooting for one team and not the other. Similar to professional coaches and analysts, many standard shoutcaster contracts prohibit the caster from gambling on an event that they are casting and some may extend this exclusion to prevent gambling on any esports competitions. This is because it is essential that a caster mandates an unbiased telecast and having a gambling or other rooting interest in the contest may jeopardize the competitive integrity of it. Also, since the on-air talent represents the event organizer, they may incorporate requirements on the caster's on-air clothing attire, such as indicated in the sample language above.[1068] Furthermore, as with most general talent agreements, any on-air work including any "unique" catchphrases are owned by the hiring party, the organizer and this includes those individuals in the competitive gaming scene (as exemplified above).[1069] As with many talent agreements, there might be a morals clause that governs the caster's public comments or prohibits against inappropriate behavior.[1070] Morals clauses are discussed in more detail later.

In conclusion, an esports commentator or broadcaster agreement is not as elaborate or in-depth as a typical player one may be but these contracts address some extremely important points which need to be agreed upon to ensure that all parties understand their obligations. Specifically, a proper understanding of the restrictions that a contract imposes on the caster's other streams of income is crucial. A caster should also fully understand the elements that may factor into the determination of a fee for an individual's casting services.[1071]

5.2 Esports Sponsorship and Brand Partnership Contracts

The most common, and in many cases the most lucrative stream of income within the esports space, are those funds generated from sponsorships and brand partnerships. As discussed in earlier sections, professional gamers,

Some Exemplary Esports Sponsors

"Endemic"	"Non-Endemic"
- Gaming Headsets - Computer Monitors - Computer Processors - Gaming Chairs - Controllers - Keyboards & Keycaps - Mice	- Food & Beverage - Alcohol & Beer - Automobile - Watch & Clothing Apparel - Sunglasses - Face & Hair Care Products - Financial & Insurance Institutions
<u>Some Esports "Endemic" Sponsors</u> - HyperX - Scuf Gaming - Intel - Turtle Beach - Logitech - Razer - Steel Series - Respawn - Matrix Keyboards	<u>Some Esports "Non-Endemic" Sponsors</u> - Coca-Cola - Audi - Nike - MasterCard - Chipotle - Red Bull - Doritos - Gillette - GEICO

streamers, and teams, as well as event organizers all rely heavily on third-party brand partnership income.[1072] In recent years, there has been a substantial increase in the number of sponsors as well as in the total value of these partnerships.[1073] This includes endorsements and marketing dollars from both endemic and non-endemic companies in a wide range of industries.[1074] For example, marketing to esports fans appeals to companies like "Arby's, Audi, Coca-Cola, PepsiCo, Gillette and Bud Light" because they all desire to interact with one of the "demographic sweet spot[s,] males between the ages of 21 to 35."[1075] Specifically, this demographic is "increasingly hard to reach via traditional advertising" so these companies have identified new avenues of promotion.[1076] In particular, it is reported that "sponsorship spending will reach $655 million by 2020, while ad spending in the esports industry will climb to $224 million" within the same time period.[1077] In fact, sponsorship and brand activation has become so essential to the esports ecosystem that new rules and city-based franchising have been implemented to provide some stability and predictability for long-term sponsorship deals. Such geographical-based franchising makes it "much more palatable and approachable for brands to come in and invest."[1078] This is because in the previous league structures, teams were subject to potential relegation; however, the newly established franchise leagues removed this element so brands will no longer need to worry about whether "the team is going to exist" when entering into a sponsorship deal.[1079] This section explores some important points that should be included in a brand "pitch" deck as well as reviews some significant provisions and considerations for a sponsorship agreement.

5.2.1 Look at Sponsorship and Investment Pitch Decks for Gaming "Talent," Esports Teams and Event Organizers

In most cases, an individual or organization wishing to approach a brand about a potential marketing or other promotional relationship will present a document referred to as "deck" or "pitch deck."[1080] A deck is a presentation that is created and is provided to a brand in order to pitch or otherwise elaborate on potential sponsorship activation between the parties.[1081] This document is intended to be utilized to present sponsorship options and other industry-focused information to illuminate why a brand should enter into some type of partnership with the pitching party.[1082]

Forbes explains that a business pitch deck should generally "have no more than 19 slides."[1083] According to *Forbes*, the presentation should include a slide that highlights the "problem:" provides a "solution;" discusses the relevant "market;" explains the "product;" mentions any "traction" that the concept is gaining (i.e., "month over month growth of the business"); includes information on the operational "team;" explains the company's "competition;" lists the company's current "financials" and "projections;" and, includes the "amount being raised" and requested within the deck.[1084]

In addition to these suggested slide topics, field-specific information should be provided. As an individual who has reviewed many top esports organizations investment as well as various sponsorship pitch decks created by players, event organizers, and teams, there are some unique facets that should be incorporated to best present the full picture of the pitching party. For instance, when a professional esports team, organizer or gamer is preparing a pitch deck, it is crucial that the preparing party include some past history on the video game title played, including its audience numbers.[1085] A deck could also include examples of prior large competitions within the title with their corresponding prize pools in an effort to explain the potential market place. It is also prudent to include data on the specific party. For example, a team presentation could include background information on the team's history as well as its current management and coaching staff. In the case of a gaming talent deck, it may be advantageous to provide biographical information on the gamer or streamer, including their past competitive history, any unique backstories as well as list any earned national or international ranking or other career milestones. An event organizer may include information and data on past tournament and events they held, including the dates, locations, total prize pools, and total event participant numbers. Additionally, all of these parties should also include links to all of their social media platforms as well as list each platforms' metrics, such as the total follower count and the total content views. In these cases, when these entities are preparing a formal document to present to sponsors, the deck might include information on "website views, click-through rates, the number of tournament spectators or streaming media/TV watchers for the match, and team and player standings" for any league, event, or tournament.[1086]

Similarly, it is prudent for a team, talent-specific, or event organizer deck to provide links to any notable press, awards, or other achievements received by the particular party. This is important so that the brand is aware of these facts when making their determination whether to enter into a partnership. The presentation might also list any of the team, the event producer, or the individual gamer's current and past sponsorships and brand partners. This is beneficial as it highlights the past work undertaken by the party in an effort to establish the level of companies that the presenter associates themselves with as well as to provide insight on the kind of return on investment (ROI) that they have received during prior brand partnerships.

When introducing this information, a party should include examples of any content produced during previous sponsorship campaigns. This could be accomplished by including information on any "Key Performance Indicators" (KPI) related to campaign.[1087] This could be in the form of any metrics on the content viewership as well as information on the impressions earned through the partnership.[1088] Providing this information may be advantageous because most brands have established set key performance indicators that are used to determine the success of a particular marketing campaign and to better understand a partnership's effectiveness.[1089] For example, a campaign's success may hinge on how many original content pieces were generated during the activation, including the number of photographs, video clips, social media posts, Instagram reactions, and Snapchat "stories" published. The success of a campaign might also be indicated by which influencers and other individuals shared the created content as well as through an examination into the total "impressions" and "engagement" figures that the produced content garners. In this context, engagement means how the viewers interacted with the particular piece of content.[1090] For instance, this figure may encompass how many people "click" on the content, including "post" clicks and "link" clicks as well as how many unique as well as total views of the material occurred.[1091] This information might also include how many "shares," "retweets," replies, and comments on the content there were. It might also include an analysis into the "view-through" rate and "watch time" of the piece, such as determining whether a viewer watched 5 seconds and exited out of the content and if a viewer watched the entire clip, half the clip, or any portion of it. Impressions are the total number of views, "clicks," or other interactions by a third party with the activation's content. Impressions are typically calculated by totaling the poster's social media following as well as that of the other individuals who responded or otherwise shared the materials. Thus, all of this information could be provided in a deck to substantiate the success of past brand partnerships. In particular, it is beneficial to note the high level of impressions and unique interactions that the branded content has received (if this occurred).

Additionally, the sponsorship presentation should include details relating to the various sponsorship tiers, "levels," or "packages" that are available to the brand.[1092] This could potentially include listing the sponsorship fees as well as including information on what each sponsorship tier provides the brand.[1093] For example, a sponsoring partner might receive a static logo on the player or team's social media accounts or brand placement in a logo rotator on the team or player's stream.[1094] Another offering could be a more elaborate one that includes logo placement on the team's jerseys as well as product placement of sponsored goods within any created content produced by the team or the gamer, such as any podcasts, videos, or photographs.[1095]

A brand may also want to see the party's upcoming event agenda, including both online and offline events for the next six or twelve months to better understand the potential exposure opportunities that the brand could receive. For instance, in an effort to exemplify the different live events that a jersey sponsor might be featured in, a team might list all of their upcoming tournaments, the tournament's past viewership numbers, the existence of any television or other large broadcast deals for the upcoming events, as well as the size of the prize pool of the event. This might also be done to spotlight the total exposure that the brand could receive as a result of being a partner of the gamer or organization through these events.

The above information is not exhaustive as each situation is different but it is solely intended to provide an overview of some of the types of information that might be included when a competitive gamer, organization, or event organizer prepares a sponsorship pitch deck. Overall, whether a pro gamer, an esports event organizer, or a team is preparing the presentation, it is important to focus on the most impressive and unique facets of the presenter. This is because most brands look for authentic and engaging content with a party who has an active and responsive fan base.

5.2.2 Some Considerations for Sponsorship Agreements with Gaming Talent and Esports Organizations

With the increased frequency of brand partnerships and the potential large sums of money associated with them, all parties involved in these transactions should ensure that all of the endorsement deal points are clearly articulated and negotiated in a written agreement. Building on this point, some key provisions are explored below in an order to highlight some of the issues that might be addressed when an esports gamer or team creates a sponsorship or other brand partnership arrangement.[1096]

One of the essential provisions to negotiate in a sponsorship agreement is the term of the deal. This is the length or duration of the contract.[1097] It is critical to determine this point in advance as it provides the parties with a structure on how the relationship operates. In most arrangements, the term of a sponsorship agreement lasts for a calendar year or is structured as a multi-year deal. In other cases, the agreement's length could be for a set number of weeks or months or just for a pre-determined number of events or "activations" that occur during a specific time period.[1098] In esports, a brand partnership can also exist solely for the length of a specific tournament or series of tournaments or for the duration of an entire professional league or franchise season or many seasons.[1099]

It is also important for the interested parties to address the existence of any renewals or other "options" to extend the partnership.[1100] These individuals should generally agree on who has the right (the option) to renew the contract and on what terms, including whether the extension is on the same financial terms or on different ones than those that the parties originally agreed to.[1101] Some agreements can include set language that provides additional benefits to the party for extending the sponsorship. For example, there could be an additional "bonus" or option payment when the brand renews the term or an increased sponsorship fee to the talent or team during any subsequent extensions.[1102] Alternatively, the sponsored party may receive other benefits as part of a renewal, such as additional free product or a higher commission or product discount rate.

While the exact provisions of an actual major esports talent sponsorship agreement with a brand partner cannot be revealed, below are sample provisions modeled on such an existing deal. The below sample provisions include clauses that examine the term of the agreement as well as incorporating an additional option period to extend the endorsement deal.

> **TERM**—1.1—The Term of this Sponsorship Agreement shall begin on the date hereof and shall continue until the earlier of (i) twelve months (the "Original Term") or (ii) termination of this Agreement pursuant to Sections 1.2 and 1.3 hereof.
>
> 1.2—This Sponsorship Agreement will automatically renew for an additional one (1) year period on the same conditions hereunder unless otherwise terminated by either party upon written notice to the other party at least thirty (30) days prior to the expiration of the Original Term.
>
> 1.3—Either party may terminate this Sponsorship Agreement upon thirty (30) days' written notice to the other (the "Breach Notice"), in the event the other party breaches a material term of this Sponsorship Agreement and fails to cure such breach with thirty (30) days of receipt of the Breach Notice.

The type of sponsorships offered, and the amounts paid by the brand, if any, to a professional team or gamer differ based on a variety of factors. A brand partnership can simply be an unpaid, sponsorship "in kind" where free product is provided to the sponsored party. Some companies may instead offer a team or gamer discounted products, especially if the goods are very expensive. In other cases, a player or organization may be provided with an "affiliate code."[1103] This provides a specific code for a price reduction on the sponsoring company's product when a consumer enters it to purchase the brand's item. The use of the code then provides payment to the code's originator (i.e., the gamer or team) and, in many cases, the payment is the amount that is "discounted." Additionally, a sponsored individual may receive a monthly stipend from the company that could range from a few hundred to several thousand dollars a month or per each marketing campaign. In rare cases, an organization or gamer may enter into an extensive multi-year, million-dollar partnership. Some deals may go even further by offering the sponsored party a residual or royalty payment for the sale of any merchandise or other goods bearing the sponsored player or organization's name, logos, or other protected intellectual property. Overall, the compensation offered to a professional esports team or gamer during a typical promotional campaign can be a mixture of all of the above options. For example, it might include providing the party with free product in addition to a monthly or yearly stipend or sponsorship fee or any other combination that the parties choose.[1104]

Similar to other talent-driven industries, the amount paid to these parties for the brand activation differs based on a number of criteria. While not exhaustive, there are a variety of factors that might be utilized when determining the amount a brand may provide. Some of these include the category exclusivity as well as the length of the activation (i.e., weeks, months, years). Other considerations could include the applicable territory or territories as well as the number and type of deliverables provided by the sponsored party (i.e., how many posts or content pieces are created during the campaign, how often they need to post, etc.).[1105] The player or organization's notoriety, past accomplishments, and social media metrics are also all generally considered.[1106] In most cases, the larger a social media following a party has, the more likely that a higher amount will be paid to them for a sponsorship campaign.[1107] For instance, *USA Today* stated that a typical "baseline rate [paid to an influencer is] about 1 percent of [their] follower counts per sponsored Instagram post, or $100 for every 10,000 followers."[1108] While there is no way to verify the accuracy of this figure, the concept that the larger a social following an influencer, such as an esports team or a player possesses, the more that they can potentially charge for activating and promoting a sponsored product to their followers is prevalent and accepted among many industry professionals.[1109]

In addition, a sponsorship contract should specifically list the amounts to be paid by the sponsor and when those payments are due. It is also prudent to list what type of products the sponsored party would have access to and how many products the brand would provide them with, including the number of free or discounted products included in the sponsorship deal. A brand partnership agreement might also list how often the sponsored party receives free product from the company as well as outline the procedures that the sponsored individual must utilize to request or obtain the sponsored goods. For example, the contract could require that the party provide advanced notice in order for them to receive the promised product from the brand.[1110]

It may also be practical for a sponsorship contract to include language that addresses any expense related to a brand promotional campaign. In many of these cases, the sponsored party may try to insist that any expense is covered by the brand. For instance, if the sponsoring company requires the displaying of any banners or the creation of a specific "branded" giveaway, the agreement may specify who is responsible for providing these items and at whose cost. Generally, the sponsor will most likely be paying or reimbursing the gamer or team for these items, or at least supplying them to the party at no charge. However, this may not always be the case, so it is essential that this information is agreed to by the parties in a signed writing.

Compensation—The COMPANY shall pay the INFLUENCER a one-time fee of ten thousand ($10,000.00) Dollars for the INFLUENCER's obligations under this Sponsorship Agreement. In addition, the COMPANY shall provide up to ten thousand ($10,000.00) dollars' worth of Product to INFLUENCER during the Term. If the INFLUENCER requires additional Product, the COMPANY agrees to offer the INFLUENCER a fifty-percent (50%) discount from any listed retail price on all the COMPANY's items if the INFLUENCER gives the COMPANY written notice of which are items are desired by the INFLUENCER. The COMPANY, at its sole cost, may periodically send the INFLUENCER free product samples of new items in the COMPANY's product lines. Any and all expenses related to the INFLUENCER's performance of any of INFLUENCER's services, obligations, or duties under this Sponsorship Agreement shall be solely paid by the COMPANY.

In general, these types of endorsement and marketing arrangements generally provide the gamer or team with the agreed-upon compensation in exchange for the performance of a specific list of obligations for the sponsoring brand referred to as "deliverables."[1111] Deliverables are the specifics and duties that the sponsored party must adhere to in order to maintain the endorsement. This means that the sponsored party must satisfy these obligations in order to earn their sponsorship fee as well as to receive any complementary products or discounts that they are entitled to as a result of the brand partnership. There are also now esports organizations beginning to "shop" the exclusive naming rights for one of its specific competitive teams.[1112]

It is important to include the party's deliverable obligations in a formal writing executed between the parties so that all the interested parties can easily understand what is required of them. This means that the document should list all of the parameters and requirements of the marketing campaign. For example, the document could list the number and frequency of social media posts that the sponsored party must provide during the activation.[1113] This could include listing a set number of content pieces or posts per week or month or any other proscribed time frame that must be made. The brand partnership document should also include the exact specifications related to any created content, including the size and placement of a brand's logo on any of the created materials. A sponsorship agreement might also regulate the actual content of any published statements made by the party on behalf of the brand. This includes the company potentially providing the team or gamer with a pre-drafted "copy" of the text that must be utilized for any social media posts that they are contracted to make. In other cases, the sponsoring company may require prior approval on any branded content or other sponsored posts made by the other party.[1114]

While there are a variety of different offerings that a sponsored gamer or team can provide to a brand, some of these deliverables could include displaying the sponsoring company's logo on the gamer or organization's official website or on their associated social media platforms (e.g., Twitter, Twitch, Instagram, and Facebook).[1115] Other deliverables might include the specific gamer or team members of an organization participating in live appearances on behalf of the brand at a tournament, trade show, conference, or other similar events.[1116] A sponsored activation with a gamer or organization may also include the creation and social media distribution of unique curated or branded content featuring sponsored product placement.[1117] For instance, a common content piece is an "unboxing" where a product is shown and a review is conducted by the sponsored party and shared to their fans. In other instances, a sponsored party may also be obligated to display and post images of them utilizing the endorsed product on their social media platforms as well as to engage in other sponsored social media posts on behalf of the company. This might include sharing any of the brand partner's product giveaways as well as sharing information on the company's new product releases. Similarly, some brand partnership deliverables may require that the brand's product is placed in any created content or is utilized and visible during any live streams. An esports organization deliverable might include placement of the brand's logo on the organization's official jerseys worn by all of its players as well as on the items sold to their fans. The endorsement deal deliverables might also require that the sponsored team or gamer participate in unique fan "experiences," such as player "meet and greets" as well as hosting sponsored product giveaways and contests on behalf of the sponsoring company.[1118]

Below are sample provisions listing potential deliverables by a party to a brand as well as language granting the sponsoring company category exclusivity.

> **Deliverables**—1.1—The COMPANY desires for the INFLUENCER to publicize and where possible, mention the COMPANY in advertising and on streams in connection with the INFLUENCER's work. From the commencement of the Sponsorship Agreement through the end of the Term, the INFLUENCER grants to the COMPANY a limited license during the Term: (a) to advertise and promote the fact that the COMPANY is an "official headset sponsor of the INFLUENCER;" (b) to use, reproduce, and display the INFLUENCER's likeness, image, and/or gamer-tag in connection with advertising and promotion of the COMPANY's goods for the Term of the Agreement and any extensions/renewals thereof; and (c) to promote the COMPANY's sponsorship, subject to the terms and conditions of use set forth herein.
>
> 1.2—The INFLUENCER will arrange to add the COMPANY's logo to the INFLUENCER's website and include a link to the COMPANY's website (www.WWJHeadset.com). The INFLUENCER will also include the COMPANY's logo on the INFLUENCER's social media platforms, including but not limited to the INFLUENCER's Twitch overlay and/or underlay, Facebook, Instagram, Twitter, YouTube Channel, and/or any other social media or streaming platform that the INFLUENCER utilizes.

1.3—The INFLUENCER shall include the COMPANY's trademarks and logos as designated by the COMPANY and/or other tag line(s) or slogan(s) approved by the COMPANY in all advertising, publicity, and promotion of the INFLUENCER (including, without limitation, any and all internet advertising) in a position and size pre-approved by the COMPANY, and in prominence, position, and size pre-approved by the COMPANY for the duration of the Term of the Sponsorship Agreement.

1.4—The INFLUENCER agrees to show and display the COMPANY's brand name on any banners at any live tournaments, games, matches, appearances, and/or events for the duration of the Term. The COMPANY will provide this banner and any and all other COMPANY "branded" promotional materials, if necessary and required by the COMPANY, at the COMPANY's sole cost.

1.5—The INFLUENCER agrees to hold at least one (1) free product give-away of the COMPANY's Product each month during the Term. Said Product will be provided to the giveaway winner at the COMPANY's sole cost. Any equipment Product provided to the INFLUENCER by the COMPANY shall be delivered F.O.B. Destination and the Product shall be safe, free from defects, and ready to be used by the INFLUENCER.

1.6—During the Term, the INFLUENCER shall make a minimum of one (1) social media post per month containing a photograph of the product received by the INFLUENCER from the COMPANY on all of the INFLUENCER's Social Media platforms including but not limited to the INFLUENCER's Facebook, Instagram, Twitter, Tik Tok, and/or Twitch, within three (3) days of receipt of said product(s) from the COMPANY.

1.7—**Public Appearance**—The INFLUENCER shall permit the COMPANY to set up and operate a booth branded to promote the COMPANY (the "Booth") at one (1) live event featuring the INFLUENCER (the "Appearance") during the Term. The COMPANY shall be permitted to operate the Booth for the purpose of selling, promoting, distributing, and/or giveaways of its Products.

1.8—The COMPANY, at its sole cost, may periodically send the INFLUENCER free product samples of new items that have come into their product line for comment and/or review by the INFLUENCER. Said comment(s) and/or review(s) may be utilized by the COMPANY in any and all printed and/or digital advertisement publicly attributing said comments and/or reviews to the INFLUENCER for the duration of the Term.

1.9—The INFLUENCER hereby agrees that the COMPANY shall own the sole and exclusive sponsorship rights in the category of "Gaming Headsets" (including but not limited to gaming headsets) for the Term and that "Headset" shall be the "Official Gaming Headset" used by the INFLUENCER during the Term. The Agreement shall only be applicable in the defined "territory." The applicable "Territory" hereunder is "only North America."

Another paramount consideration for parties entering into a brand partnership is whether the sponsorship is exclusive or not for a certain category.[1119] For example, if a player or team is sponsored by Volvo, the agreement might provide Volvo with the exclusive rights to the "automobile" category. Such exclusivity enables the sponsoring company to ensure that another competitor's brand (e. g., Audi) is not also displayed, used, or acts as an additional sponsor of the organization or player. Generally, a sponsored party can and will only have one endorsement deal for each type of product.[1120] This means that the team or gamer may only have one non-alcoholic beverage, one alcoholic beverage, one headset sponsor, one gaming chair sponsor, and one nutritional supplement sponsor. Since the actual language utilized determines the extent and scope of the brand's exclusivity, the sponsored party might aim to tailor the language to be as narrow as possible to not prevent them from working with additional brands.[1121] For instance, an energy drink, such as Red Bull, could be seen as different from a non-alcoholic beverage, such as Mountain Dew or Arizona Iced Tea. The latter could be categorized as a juice or a soda and this might be considered a different category than that of an "energy drink." In addition, one brand could be the party's official gaming headset while another company could be their official gaming controller provider as these could be considered separate gaming peripherals.[1122] Thus, the actual structuring of the language included in an agreement is essential as any document should be drafted with this in mind.

In addition to category exclusivity, another crucial consideration in these arrangements is the determination of which territory or geographic areas a deal encompasses. For example, the applicable territory may solely be one country (e.g., Canada or the United States), could be several countries (e.g., Europe, Asia), or might cover the entire "universe" or "world."[1123] This is a very important point that should be negotiated and memorialized in a written document. This is especially true because it may permit the gamer or the organization to "carve-out" and potentially enter into regional, national, as well as international sponsorships with a variety of different brands across the globe.[1124]

It is also important to address how the parties will operate after the expiration or otherwise termination of an existing brand partnership. Some sponsorship agreements may impose non-compete provisions preventing the team or player from working with the brand's competitor for a specific time period after expiration of a sponsorship.[1125] In other cases, there might not be a non-compete clause included in the document at all. In this instance, the professional gamer and organization are free to immediately sign a new contract with any other sponsor in any territory, even a competitor of a prior brand partner. Additionally, in partnerships that only apply to one or a select number of "territories" or geographic areas, a non-compete might be fashioned as to only prevent the sponsored party from working with a previous sponsor's competitor in the excluded areas. This type of provision provides the team and player with the opportunity to immediately enter into partnership arrangements in other territories that are not exempted.

In addition, it is essential that any sponsorship agreement address each party's right to utilize each other's intellectual property ("IP"). This could apply to any of the player, team, and brand logos as well as any provided photographs or other protected audiovisual and visual works. The agreement generally provides each party with the right to use each parties' IP in any created content. Ideally, the sponsored party should have the right to utilize the brand's IP for any purpose that it requires in order to further the goals of the agreement. This could include placing a sponsor's logo on a party's stream overlay or within their social media header or banner.

Another important matter that should be addressed and memorialized is the brand's right to utilize the sponsored party's image and name in association with its product (referred to as their right of publicity). As explored in earlier in this chapter, this right includes permission to utilize the professional team and player's likeness during the sponsorship term as well as lists how matters would proceed after the expiration of an existing endorsement. Generally, a brand owner may prefer for its rights to be extensive with minimal requirements and restrictions on them; conversely, a team or gamer may typically wish to maintain control over the use of their image and name, so an agreement on these points is important. The provision listed below is an example of a clause providing a sponsoring brand with the right to utilize a sponsored party's name and likeness during the term of a sponsorship deal with the company's right terminating upon the expiration of the agreement.

Furthermore, the contract may address whether the sponsoring party or the brand has any approval rights over the player or team's usage in any finished material. It might also be agreed that a party's prior approval is required prior to the publication of any finished content produced through the activation. In these cases, language may be inserted to enable some creative or editorial control over publicized work prior to publication to ensure that all the created works are acceptable and conform to the brand's message.

Rights Granted

(a.) **The INFLUENCER'S Approval Right**—The COMPANY shall have the right to develop, implement and manage in-market and national advertising and publicity and promotional campaigns to promote the sponsorship with the INFLUENCER across various media, subject to the INFLUENCER's prior written approval of any and all printed and/or digital promotional campaign materials containing the INFLUENCER's likeness, including but not limited to any promotional advertisements or created audiovisual or photographic work for the duration of the Term.

(b.) **Name And Likeness**—Both parties hereby agree to grant to the other party a non-exclusive, royalty free, worldwide right and license to use, display, distribute, edit, and otherwise utilize the other party's company name, gamer-tag, logo, likeness, image, photograph, voice, and/or biographical information, in any and all present and future media, on or in connection with any of the Services or other Deliverables under this Sponsorship Agreement, including but not limited to in any broadcast, streaming, webcast or other distribution of any audiovisual, visual, and/or audio work created under this Sponsorship Agreement and in any social media postings, print and online advertising and content, including banners, posters, press releases, and newsletters. Upon expiration or termination of this Sponsorship Agreement, the COMPANY shall immediately cease any and all uses of the INFLUENCER's name, gamer-tag, likeness, and/or biography as well as any statements of association with the INFLUENCER.

In addition to an influencer's deliverables on behalf of a brand and the brand's category exclusivity, the negotiations of provisions relating to the potential early termination of the agreement might also be relevant. In particular, some sponsorship agreements contain a provision identified as a "harmful behavior" or morals clause.[1126] This clause permits a party to immediately terminate an existing arrangement with an individual or a company that "engages in illegal, indecent, immoral, harmful or scandalous behavior or activities."[1127] This contract provision may be utilized in an effort to protect the image and reputation of the involved party.[1128] The existence of such language enables one party to unilaterally terminate the contract when the other party engages in conduct that could have some type of negative impact upon the other party's public reputation.[1129] Furthermore, some agreements may incorporate a "reverse morals clause." This language may be inserted to ensure that these termination provisions apply equally to both parties.[1130] This particular clause provides the sponsored party with the right to terminate a brand partnership agreement if the sponsoring company behaves in a "damaging" way.[1131] This is meant to protect a party's reputation from association with a disgraced company or brand. A sample of this type of clause is depicted below.

> **Harmful Behavior/Morals Clause**—Either Party shall have the right to immediately terminate this Sponsorship Agreement in the event that the other Party, in such Party's reasonable discretion, engages in illegal, indecent, immoral, harmful, or scandalous behavior that brings the other party into public hatred, public disrepute, contempt, scorn, or ridicule, or that will tend to shock, insult, or offend the community or public morals or decency and that may, directly or indirectly, damage such Party's reputation or goodwill or if such party commits an offense involving moral turpitude under federal, state, or local laws or ordinances, or otherwise violates any applicable rules or regulations. In addition, the INFLUENCER shall not engage in any act or conduct and/or make any public derogatory statements which denigrate the COMPANY and/or its brand.

If there is a dispute about the provisions and obligations contained in a sponsorship agreement, it is crucial to incorporate provisions regarding notice and cure of any breach or alleged breach of the document. This is important as it provides both parties to the contract with the opportunity to try to fix or otherwise "cure" any allegedly committed defects. This is a prudent way for the parties to try to ensure that the sponsorship arrangement continues without interruption. It is also judicious to include "choice of law," jurisdiction and venue language so that all parties are aware of what state law applies to the agreement as well as what the appropriate routes for any judicial or other intervention is, if needed.

5.2.3 Some Professional Gamer-Specific Sponsorship Matters

In some situations, an esports organization will permit a signed gamer to seek their own independent sponsorship and brand partners. Similar to the language displayed below, an organization generally requires prior approval before a gamer can enter into an individual sponsorship.[1132] However, even in the instances where the gamer can obtain its own independent sponsorship, the gamer is generally only permitted to work with a brand that is not a competitor of a current organizational sponsor. In addition, an organized league that the professional teams compete in may also impose contractual prohibitions aimed to prevent the gamer from entering into individual sponsored arrangements with specified products or companies. In fact, some of these restrictions may apply to a category that no current sponsor is in but that the parties may intend to enter in the future. As exemplified below, a gamer may be specifically prohibited from working with select products.[1133] For instance, the below provision prevents a professional gamer from entering into a sponsorship agreement for any alcoholic beverages, tobacco and vaping products, casinos and gambling websites, or with any firearm companies.[1134] Furthermore, as mentioned, a professional gamer may also be prohibited from receiving a sponsorship in certain exempt or carved-out categories. These categories may be instead reserved for the professional team that they are signed to or set aside for the specific league that the gamer competes in.[1135]

(a.) **Independent Sponsorships**—The GAMER shall be entitled to seek independent sponsorships with any business or entity that is not a direct or indirect competitor of a current ORGANIZATION Sponsor. The GAMER shall not enter into any independent sponsorship agreements without the prior written consent of the ORGANIZATION, which shall not be unreasonably withheld.

(b.) **Sponsorship Prohibitions**—The GAMER is prohibited from entering into any Independent Sponsorship Agreement with any product or service category included in the "Sponsorship Restricted List" including (i) account selling, sharing, or trading websites, or account hacking; (ii) alcoholic beverages; (iii) drugs (whether legal or illegal) and any products used to consume drugs; (iv) tobacco and/or vaping products; (v) adult-oriented products or services; (vi) gambling and/or casinos (whether legal or illegal); (vii) firearms; and/or (viii) Political candidates or ballot initiatives.

(c.) **Sponsored Categories Reserved for the Organization**—The GAMER is prohibited from entering into any such Independent Sponsorship Agreement with any product or service category including (i) athletic apparel; (ii) energy drinks, soft drinks, and/or water; (iii) computer monitors; (iv) casinos; (v) beer; and/or (vi) wine.

While the exact specifics of most sponsorship arrangements are undisclosed, many of the same requirements and concepts that traditional talent endorsement deals encompass are also incorporated into gaming and esports-driven influencer marketing campaigns. As explored above, the importance of proper documentation listing all of the rights and duties of each party becomes even more important, especially as the brand partnerships continue to expand and establish themselves as one of the largest consistent sources of income for the esports business ecosystem.

5.3 Licensing in Esports

Another important legal aspect of the global esports business is licensing of intellectual property (IP) and the role it plays in the entire professional esports business ecosystem. A "license" is the "permission to act" or the ability to do something.[1136] This "right" is granted by the owner, an individual or company, who has the ability to provide such permission to another party.[1137] There are many different types of licenses and licensing agreements applicable to the esports world, including those related to the licensing of a copyrighted image or other protected IP asset such as a trademark. As mentioned, these are those related to a gaming talent, including their likeness rights as well as the proper use of third-party content and music while streaming and crafting their own separate works. There are also a number of licensing deals between esports organizations and third-party companies for the manufacturing of esports team branded items in a variety of consumer goods. This in addition to the licensing arrangements created by the other major "players" in the esports business sector.

5.3.1 Gaming "Talent" Licensing Matters

5.3.1.1 Likeness Rights As discussed in earlier sections of this work, professional gamers as well as gaming content streamers have certain intellectual property rights in their name, gamer-tag, logo, and other aspects of their individual likeness. These intellectual property and likeness rights may be licensed, assigned, or otherwise transferred by the rights holder (the gamer or streamer) to any other third party, such as a merchandise manufacturer. For example, influential streamer Tyler "Ninja" Blevins licensed his gamer-tag and logo to Red Bull to create an official "gameplay headband" that are available for sale at Walmart retail stores.[1138] He also entered into an endorsement arrangement with Adidas whereby his likeness and gamer-tag were printed on apparel, including a custom sneaker-line.[1139] Other gamers and content creators have also licensed their likeness to collectible creator Youtooz, including 100 Thieves' streamer, Rachell "Valkyrae" Hofstetter.[1140]

Another player-focused licensing deal is the one between content streamer Herschel "DrDisrespect" Beahm and gaming peripheral manufacturer Razer Gaming.[1141] In particular, Razer sells a custom "high-performance" mouse pad featuring the streamer's likeness and name.[1142] In addition, DrDisrespect also secured a licensing "deal with Skybound Entertainment [...] to develop a narrative scripted television series based on his character"[1143] and unique life story as well as a book publishing deal with Gallery Books for the licensing and distribution of his "in-character memoir."[1144] There are also endemic brands such as G Fuel, who has created custom products "inspired" by specific content streamers as well as entire product lines featuring a particular gamer.[1145] For instance, streamer Felix Arvid Ulf "PewDiePie" Kjellberg has licensed his likeness and gamer-tag for use by G Fuel for a custom product line of unique "PewDiePie flavors," including the "*Lingonberry* 12 pack" of cans.[1146]

However, in many cases and as elaborated on in prior chapters, when a professional organization or team signs a gamer, the organization generally receives the exclusive right to license the player's likeness and other intellectual property assets for their sole benefit. In a rare situation, the signed gamer may still possess some of these licensing rights, especially if the arrangement is a non-exclusive one. If so, this carve-out may enable the professional gamer to independently license their likeness rights elsewhere.

5.3.1.2 Music Licensing Another important licensing matter that affects many content makers and streamers is the use of music during their stream as well as for any tracks included in any created content.[1147] The general rule in these situations is that a streamer requires a license from the copyright holder of the song or tracks that they intend to play live during stream or that are included in a created video.[1148] In these cases, a synchronization or "synch" license must be obtained from the proper party.[1149] A synch license is issued by the copyright owner (i.e., a record label or a music publishing company) to allow a third party (the streamer) to "synchronize the musical composition [...] with [an] audio-visual image (the stream or content clip)."[1150] This means that if an individual wants to play a song that is not their own original work that they own all the rights to in a recorded video or live on stream, a proper license must be obtained from the appropriate right owners.[1151]

A streamer's failure to obtain the appropriate rights to a musical recording can lead to the created content being removed for copyright infringement.[1152] In addition, a saved stream may be "muted" or otherwise "blacked out" due to the unauthorized use of a protected work.[1153] For instance, Twitch states that they will "promptly terminate without notice the accounts of those determined [...] to be 'repeat infringers.'"[1154] Additionally, YouTube has established the three "copyright strike" policy.[1155] This policy states that each infringing use earns the account owner a "copyright strike" and once an account receives three copyright strikes within a certain period of time, YouTube will remove "all the videos uploaded to [their] account."[1156] These streaming companies are able to identify and punish infringers because many of these services utilize "automatic content recognition" (ACR) systems that identify any copyrighted content played in a media file.[1157] For example, Twitch works with the company AudibleMagic for its ACR system needs.[1158] This company uses its automatic content recognition system to scan each stream in order to recognize and "mute" or otherwise prevent any infringing content contained in the stream from playing during a re-broadcast.[1159]

Since many prominent streamers and creators generate most of their income from their existing created content, the potential loss of all of their saved work due to such a violation as well as all of the associated viewership metrics and data could be catastrophic to their business and may cause substantial financial losses to the party.[1160] To avoid this potential issue, a variety of options exist to provide gaming streamers and other original content creators with usable music to entertain their live viewers as well as for inclusion in any created works.

One such available option is a "creative commons" license.[1161] The creative commons is a "nonprofit organization that offers royalty-free licenses so that [certain music] can be used without legal retaliation."[1162] However, the potential "downside of using [the] Creative Commons music commons [license] is that most of the [included] songs cannot be used for monetized projects."[1163] This creates a dilemma as most professional streamer and content creators create media in an effort to profit and earn income off their work and they could do not do that if this type of a license is utilized by them.

Since the creative commons license is only available for non-monetized works, the individual might instead look to utilize "royalty-free" tunes.[1164] There are also some musical creations that are completely "copyright free" or "no copyright" ones.[1165] While this is not an official legal term, it accurately describes the type of rights in work. This means that the work is completely free to use because no individual creator is claiming any exclusive rights or any rights at all to the song.[1166] While this is rare, there exist some databases that provide such works for any use by any third party, including commercial purposes.[1167] In addition, there also exist "royalty-free" musical creations that may be available for use in a creator's video or during their stream.[1168] The chief difference between these two is that the royalty-free track might have (and usually does have) an initial license fee or payment of some sort to use the work for any purposes, including for business ones.[1169] This use would be considered royalty free because there would be no additional residual or royalty payments to continue to utilize the originally licensed track.[1170]

In addition to copyright free and royalty free licensed music, a streamer or gaming influencer can also acquire rights to stream "licensed" popular music from an established music library or other licensed catalog.[1171] Many of these music licensing companies provide "blanket" licenses that permit the usage of any media contained in their "library."[1172] In contrast, some other libraries may only issue licenses to a select number of tracks or just one song. In an effort to work with streamers, well-known dance record label Monstercat has created a monthly subscription service.[1173] This service enables a streamer to pay a monthly fee in order to "use Monstercat music on [their] monetized content."[1174] It currently supports music usage on YouTube and Twitch by providing the subscriber with access to "over 2,000 songs across 29 genres of music, from drum & bass through to indie dance tunes and happy hardcore."[1175] The streamer or content creator may then utilize these licensed works "in the background of their content across YouTube and Twitch while keeping all of the revenue for themselves."[1176] Another similar licensing system is Pretzel Rocks.[1177] This company offers similar licensing options, including providing access to a "custom curated music catalog" that the individual can play live on their streams.[1178] Furthermore, Twitch created an "Amazon Music" streaming extension that allows a "streamer" that is also a "Twitch Prime member or [a] Amazon Music Unlimited subscriber" to "play a radio station during their live stream."[1179] However, the major drawback to this Twitch extension is that any stream viewer who is a not a "prime member [or a] Amazon Music Unlimited subscriber" will be unable to listen to the streamed music.[1180] This seems to be a unique way to include popular songs while also minimizing a streamer's costs and potential liability and exposure for utilizing unlicensed music. While these are not the only options, they are examples of mainstream media adapting its current licensing and business model to work within the gaming sphere. It will be interesting to see how this facet continues to develop as more prominent gaming talent utilize third-party original music during their stream and in their created works.

5.3.2 Professional Esports Organizations and Teams Licensing Matters

As discussed in prior chapters, professional esports organizations and teams have intellectual property rights in many aspects of the team's likeness. This could include exclusive rights to their team name, logo, as well as jersey design. Similar to professional gamers, the intellectual property and likeness rights owned by the team are licensable, assignable, and otherwise transferable to any other third party, such as a gaming peripheral manufacturer.

While this has been previously discussed, a fundamental licensing matter integral to the esports business is the third-party use of an organization's protected IP assets. In fact, licensing has become an important stream of revenue with many esports organizations entering agreements with different companies for the use of the team's protected assets. Some of these licensing agreements are simply a direct license of existing intellectual property, such as placing a team logo on a headset or gaming controller. Other arrangements could include "derivative" works based on existing protected content. For example, this might consist of a unique product design featuring a specific team's colors or other re-imagination of their existing organization logo in a new item.[1181]

While some teams may produce merchandise in-house, most teams work with third parties and enter into appropriate licensing arrangements with them. In particular, many esports organizations work with other outside companies so that the team is not "responsible for all of manufacturing and distribution themselves."[1182] Instead, the licensor will typically handle those tasks because most of the time, this is "the licensors' main business" so "they [usually] have all the facilities and infrastructure already in place."[1183] This fact has caused many professional esports teams to enter into licensing deals with third-party clothing and gaming equipment manufacturers and distributors. For example, Misfits Gaming entered into a business venture with the company Outerstuff.[1184] Under this arrangement, Outerstuff designs, manufactures, and markets newly created "Misfits Gaming and

Florida Mayhem licensed apparel."[1185] This arrangement also incorporates "Outerstuff's global operations (including its retail channels in Asia and four other continents) and experience creating and distributing official apparel for the NFL [and] NBA" for the distribution and the sale of the created items.[1186] In addition, the apparel company Champion Athleticwear has created co-branded items with several esports teams available for sale on its website.[1187] This includes licensed goods from esports organizations "Counter Logic Gaming, Dignitas, Spacestation Gaming and the Renegades."[1188] Some other examples of licensing deals include esports organization Cloud9 with Puma for custom apparel and footwear.[1189] There was also a custom "one-off collection" created by Kappa Clothing and Vexed Gaming incorporating the organization's logo into "two t-shirt designs."[1190] Furthermore, Adidas and esports organization Team Vitality created a custom-designed shoe that featured "the team's yellow and black colors, along with geometric shapes that symbolize the teams' bee logo."[1191] The item also includes "the Team Vitality and Adidas logos" on the shoe's tongue.[1192] Finally, many top esports teams, including FaZe Clan, Evil Geniuses, Luminosity, Team Envy, and Splyce, have all licensed their logos for use on Scuf Gaming's custom-created gaming controllers.[1193]

There have also been some other third-party licensing collaborations. For example, esports organization Fnatic collaborated with cartoon *Hello Kitty* to create a line of unique merchandise.[1194] In addition, footwear brand, K-Swiss worked with esports team Immortals Gaming Club to create new "slip-on lightweight sneakers that are designed for those competing in multi-player video games."[1195] Another pop culture brand Hot Wheels released a collaborative toy car with esports organization Spacestation Gaming.[1196] The custom item will be available for purchase "at Walmart, Target, and other major stores stateside."[1197] Additionally, *Overwatch League* franchise NY Excelsior licensed their IP assets to lifestyle brand Mother Design in order to create a unique collaborative merchandise capsule collection.[1198] Mother Design's designer stated that "the goal [of the collaboration] was to build on New York's existing identity as a place for fashion and street wear."[1199] This collaboration is another example of esports organizations looking for new outlets to license their likeness.[1200] Similarly, esports team Astralis "established a partnership with Danish brewery *Royal Unibrew*" to create "its own line of [licensed] soft drinks" featuring the team's name and logo.[1201] As evident by some of these licensing deals, there are many new opportunities for an esports team to expand its existing "footprint" and to collaborate with third parties to leverage that company's followers and to expand the esports team's notoriety.

While many of these agreements differ in structure and content, there are a few consistent provisions included in many standard licensing deals across many talent-driven industries. For clarification, a "licensor" is the party (esports organization) issuing or granting a license to another.[1202] The "licensee" is the person or company (e.g., gaming headset company) that receives the license to the specified work (team name).[1203]

> **Rights Granted**—The Licensor hereby grants to the Licensee the exclusive right and license to use the Licensor's Trademark and associated team name in connection with the design, manufacture, distribution, and sale of the Licensed Product in the Territory under the terms, conditions, and limitations set forth in this Licensing Agreement. Except as otherwise specifically provided in this Licensing Agreement, the Licensee shall not export the Licensed Products from the Territory, and shall not promote to sell or offer for sale any the Licensed Products to any third party which the Licensee knows or has reason to know will sell the Licensed Products outside the Territory.

In order for a licensor to utilize a specific asset, the party must actually receive the right to utilize the asset for the agreed-upon purposes. As exemplified above, the licensing party receives the exclusive right to sell, manufacture, and distribute the product within the agreed-upon geographic territory. In fact, the above language also prevents the licensor from selling or otherwise distributing the product in any territory not agreed upon in the contract by the parties.

> **Quality Control**—The Licensee agrees that the Licensed Products shall be of a high standard and of such style, appearance, and quality as to conform to the standards and specifications reasonably and collectively established by the Licensor and the Licensee; and that the Licensed Products will be manufactured, packaged, sold, distributed, and promoted in accordance with any and all applicable laws and regulations.

An important responsibility that most licensing agreements place upon the licensing party is to provide "quality control" on the produced goods.[1204] This requires the party to ensure that the manufactured goods containing the licensor's protected asset are of the same quality and standards that the product has been provided in previously. Specifically, this means that the licensee must ensure that the proper materials are used, including higher quality ones, if they are required to produce the licensed item.

> **Counterfeit/Infringing Goods**—The Licensee will cooperate with the Licensor to minimize, deter, and prevent the importation into, or sale or manufacture within the Territory of any counterfeit or infringing goods of the same type as the Licensed Products.

Another obligation imposed on many licensees in such agreements is the duty to police and prevent the manufacturing and sale of any infringing or counterfeit goods.[1205] This means that the licensing party must take the necessary steps to pursue and stop any individuals selling or importing infringing or counterfeit (fake) goods. This is also important as U.S. trademark law imposes a duty on a trademark owner to police and protect its mark and lack of which can cause the owner to potentially lose rights in the mark.[1206]

> **Sell-Off Period**—On the expiration or earlier termination of this Licensing Agreement, the Licensee shall be entitled, for a period of no more than sixty (60) days from the date of such termination or expiration, on a non-exclusive basis, to continue to distribute and sell its existing inventory of the Licensed Products. Such sales shall be made in accordance with all of the terms and conditions of this Licensing Agreement.

As displayed above, one more typical provision included in most licensing agreements is a "sell-off" period. This is especially true for any agreement involving any created clothing or other custom memorabilia and items.[1207] This clause permits the licensee to sell any remaining inventory after the expiration of the agreement. It also limits and prevents the party from creating any new merchandise after the deal ends. A licensor may try to limit the time frame that the licensee's sell-off period lasts for. This is because the licensor may want to negotiate a new license with another party, and they may be prevented from doing so until the prior licensee's sell-off period expires. In addition, the licensing party might try to include language that prevents the licensee from selling the remaining merchandise at a substantially reduced rate in an effort to undercut any sales efforts taken by the original party after their exclusive merchandise deal ended.

While there are many provisions in most licensing agreements, it is important that the parties understand their obligations and rights during the term as well as how they are affected when the arrangement expires. As with most business dealings, it is prudent to have a signed writing outlining these matters prior to engaging in any work.

5.3.3 Other Esports Institution Licensing Matters: Esports Teams and Game Publishers

In addition to the traditional licensing agreements related to the broadcast and streaming of the competitions and similar to other areas of the esports ecosystem, esports league organizers and game developers have begun entering into unique licensing arrangements. In particular, some game developers have begun licensing and incorporating third-party content into their titles. Additionally, some franchise league organizers have also created league-wide licensing deals that apply to all of the participating franchises within their league. This includes those parties that are also video-game publishers.

One unique emerging trend has been game developers incorporating and licensing third-party protected intellectual property into their games as well as other "fashionable" brand integrations. For example, Epic Games licensed Keanu Reeves' "John Wick" movie character as a playable in-game skin for its *Fortnite* users.[1208] Similarly, they also licensed all 32 NFL franchise's jerseys as wearable in-game skins for its *Fortnite* players' use.[1209] In addition, as a cross-promotion coinciding with Marvel's *Avengers: Infinity War* movie release, Epic Games also created a playable "Thanos" character which included a usable "Infinity Gauntlet."[1210] This was a similar integration route that Netflix took when promoting the third season of *Stranger Things*.[1211] In particular, Epic Games licensed assets from Netflix and transformed the *Fortnite* gaming experience into the "upside-down" realm.[1212] The activation included providing *Fortnite* gamers with the opportunity to acquire special *Stranger Things* in-game items "from the Item Shop," including "Chief Hopper and Demogorgon outfits and Vines Wraps."[1213] The *Fortnite* creators continued this trend by licensing intellectual property from *Star Wars*.[1214] Specifically, to "celebrate" the premiere of the most recent *Star Wars* movie, the developer incorporated custom in-game skins for movie characters Rey and Finn.[1215] Building from this, the developer of *League of Legends*, Riot Games entered into a licensing arrangement with luxury fashion brand Louis Vuitton.[1216] The deal created a purchasable "prestige" in-game character skin which provided the video-game user with the ability to use a game character with a "weapon covered in the iconic Louis Vuitton pattern."[1217]

This trend does not only apply to video game developers licensing mainstream and pop culture assets. For example, the developer of the *FIFA* soccer series, Electronic Arts licensed the rights to 21 esports organizations' logos and imagery in order to provide its users with the ability to wear custom in-game jerseys featuring their favorite esports team.[1218] The custom jerseys included wearable items from esports organizations such as "Team Vitality, Team Liquid, Team Envy, SK Gaming, Rogue, [...and] Natus Vincere."[1219]

In addition to game developers licensing third-party content in their titles, some of the companies who also act as league organizers have begun operating as licensing agents for its participating franchise teams. For example, the organizer of the *Overwatch League*, Activision-Blizzard licensed all of its participating team's logos to Fanatics so that the company can manufacture, market, and distribute each franchise's apparel.[1220] Similarly, Activision-Blizzard licensed its participating players' likeness to Upper Deck to create "player-signed trading cards that are packaged with swatches of game-worn jersey[s]."[1221] In addition to these league organizers collectively licensing its participating franchises assets to third parties, the *NBA 2K League*, ran by the NBA and game publisher Take Two Interactive have followed suit. In particular, the *NBA 2K League* has entered into league-wide sponsorships with a variety of companies that include each franchise's logo in their created item.[1222] This includes previous and existing licensing deals with Champion Athleticwear for team jerseys and clothing, Scuf Gaming for gaming controllers, Stance Socks for socks, Raynor Gaming for gaming chairs, HyperX for gaming headsets, and restaurant partner Panera.[1223] It is clear that game publishers and competitive gaming league and event organizers are securing many unique licensing opportunities.

5.3.4 Licensing of Broadcasting and Streaming Media Rights by Event Organizers and Game Publishers

Similar to some of the content streaming and broadcasting deals explored earlier, another facet of successful monetization is the potential for a game developer as well as a league or event organizer to license its competitive broadcast.[1224] Today, there are two dominant forms of third-party casters of gaming content. Similar to the initial origins of competitive gaming, television broadcasters still are a major source of content distribution. For example, game creator Electronic Arts licensed the U.S. television broadcast rights to *Turner Esports' ELEAGUE* for all of its *FIFA 20* competitive events.[1225]

Similarly, various games during the third season of the *NBA 2K League* were televised on ESPN 2.[1226] Likewise, the game developer and franchise league organizer for *League of Legends* Championship Series, Riot Games entered into a licensing arrangement with electronic company Panasonic.[1227] This agreement provides on-demand viewing through Panasonic's in-flight airline entertainment systems for all of the developer's "*LCS* and lower-tier *LCS* Academy matches."[1228] This in-flight system is currently available in "more than 300 airline[s]."[1229] These are just two examples of the types of licensing arrangements that developers can enter into, as many more have been previously explored in earlier sections.

Other main distributor of gaming content are live streaming platforms such as Twitch and YouTube Gaming in the United States and Douyu and Huya in China.[1230] There is also a rise in other international and rival competitive gaming streaming platforms that are also securing their own licensing deals.[1231]

As explored earlier, since a game developer legally owns the exclusive rights "to use of game images and video through copyright law," they can determine and limit how their video game is used, including in online videos and in streamed gameplay.[1232] For example, a video game developer may refuse to permit the display of games and might even pursue a stream as an "unauthorized" use of their protected work or in the worst-case scenario, they might "sue [the] unauthorized game streamer."[1233] However, similar to how these companies have dealt with "user-generated content" and mods of their protected software in the past, many game developers are again adjusting their "legal policies" in an attempt to "balance the monetization of streams with facilitating viewership and creativity."[1234] One such shift includes creating revenue share options with existing streaming platforms.[1235] For instance, Japanese game publisher Nintendo had entered into a revenue share deal for any use of their images and audio works on YouTube.[1236] Other developers such as Activision-Blizzard are working with streaming platforms, such as Facebook Gaming to easily incorporate and stream various Activision-Blizzard titles "natively to Facebook."[1237] This means that a "Blizzard client user" can directly "connect their Blizzard account to their Facebook profile" so that "they'll be able to stream live gameplay directly to."[1238] Ultimately, there are a variety of approaches that can be taken, so each publisher may utilize one that best suits their overall community and business growth plan.[1239]

Specifically, these publishing companies have the opportunity to monetize their content across many mediums, including through online streaming and televised broadcast, as well as the option to license content in different individualized geographic territories.[1240] This possibility provides them with ample opportunity to segment off different continents and countries to most effectively earn world wide revenues from their competitive content.[1241]

5.3.5 Licensing of Rights by Event Organizers from Game Publishers

As explored earlier, an event, league, and other competitive gaming tournament producer must acquire a license (sign a contract) with the publisher of the event's game title.[1242] However, the new trend of game developers acting as league and tournament operators obviates that need as the entity already possesses these rights.[1243] It seems that this may be a continuing trend with some major game publishers continuing to develop their own events while at the same time, others seem set on continuing to license the rights to utilize their protected game for a commercial work to others.[1244] Overall, licensing is an integral part of a game developer's success, as this permits them to expand their reach as well as earn substantial new revenues that might not otherwise be available to them or are not part of their current typical business offerings.

6

Some Other Ancillary Esports Legal and Business Topics

This chapter examines some related legal and business topics that have not been previously discussed. This includes exploring the rise of mobile esports as well as the creation and the growth of youth-, high school-, and college-level competitive gaming. It continues by looking at the formation and the development of esports associations and federations, including both national ones as well as international and continent-wide organizations. The chapter also provides information on a gamer's potential "team" of professionals as well as examining some marketing and promotional considerations for social media and livestreaming.

6.1 Mobile Esports

Some Popular Mobile Gaming Titles

- **Arena of Valor (Honor of Kings)**
- **Brawl Stars & Brawlhalla**
- **Clash Royale**
- **PUBG Mobile**
- **Call of Duty Mobile**
- **Free Fire**
- **Guns of Boom**
- **League of Legends: Wild Rift**
- **Teamfight Tactics**
- **Mobile Legends: Bang Bang**

While PC and console-based competitive esports have traditionally dominated the gaming landscape, there has been a recent shift and an explosion in competitive mobile gaming on an individual's smartphone or tablet.[1245] In fact, as of 2018, the "global mobile esports game revenue is $15.32 billion."[1246] The mobile competitive gaming market has continued to grow in the time since, including in many secondary markets such as India, and in many South American countries.[1247] Additionally, there are reportedly "already more gamers on mobile than PC [and] console combined."[1248] Specifically, based on these estimations, there were "around 2.53 billion mobile gamers in the world in 2019, compared to the estimated 1 billion PC gamers and 500 million console gamers."[1249] While there are a variety of reasons for this discrepancy, one of the main explanations for the recent growth of mobile esports is that "almost everyone has a smartphone these days, while PCs and consoles are more expensive and [are] less likely [within] reach at any given moment."[1250]

As explored briefly above, many mobile games have generated substantial sales, including "in-game" items purchased on free-to-play (F2P) titles.[1251] Some of these F2P titles have even spawned their own competitive scenes mirroring those that have existed in the traditional console and PC competitive titles.[1252] The meteoric rise of mobile competitive gaming has led many traditional tournament organizers and game developers to begin organizing competitive esports leagues for some of the larger mobile gaming titles.[1253] For instance, *PlayerUnknown's Battlegrounds* (*PUBG*) *Mobile* has been a highly successful mobile game, including generating over "$1.5 billion" in total revenues so far.[1254] At its initial launch, the game had "over 180 million downloads in Q4 2019," which was "the best quarter for any mobile game since the launch of *Pokémon Go* back in Q3 2016."[1255] This large userbase caused the game's developer to establish their own 2020 "competitive ecosystem," including committing to $5 million dollars in total prize money across "three new leagues."[1256] Furthermore, the potential growth in this sector has caused some esports organizations to sign their own *PUBG Mobile* roster to professionally compete on behalf of the teams, including esports organizations FaZe Clan,[1257] Spacestation Gaming,[1258] and Fnatic.[1259] In addition, Supercell, the developer of two other large mobile games, *Brawl Stars* and *Clash Royale* has established their own competitive leagues, including the *Brawl Stars* Championship[1260] and the *Clash Royale League* (*CRL*).[1261] In fact, the 2020 *Clash Royale League* World finals held in Shanghai, China boosted a "$225,000" total prize pool for its eventual winner.[1262] Some of these newly established leagues, including the *PUGB Mobile World League* have even secured sponsors[1263] and others have secured exclusive streaming rights deals for their competitive gameplay.[1264] Supercell also partnered with tournament organizer DreamHack for its "Dream Hack Mobile Series" in an effort to showcase the competitive mobile esports scene for these two titles.[1265] Building on this, mobile esports growing viewership also provided U.S. broadcaster Turner Sports with the basis for its newest expansion of its existing *ELEAGUE* series.[1266] Specifically, the network licensed the exclusive television rights to Supercell's competitive mobile title *Clash Royale* and their *Clash Royale League*.[1267] The network will display competitive league play on its station as well as debuting the new programming with a "two- hour show [...] on *TBS*."[1268]

Furthermore, the highest grossing mobile game in the world *Arena of Valor* (AoV) (known as *Honor of Kings* in China) has also created its own competitive system.[1269] In fact, based on the game's widespread usage, the developer Tencent embraced competitive play. Specifically, they established their own Chinese competitive circuit, the *King Pro League* (*KPL*).[1270] Additionally, in 2019, the developer also provided "$2.36 M [in] total prize pool money for [the] 2019 *Honor of Kings World Champion Cup*" with the tournament winner earning $1 million of the total prize pool."[1271] The prize pool grew to "$4.6 million" with the winner of the 2020 tournament "tak[ing] home

$1.9 million."[1272] In fact, this large fan base provided esports event organizer Electronic Sports League with the opportunity to establish its own "Arena of Valor" esports competitions.[1273]

Overall, as mobile coverage and availability continues to increase across the world, the use of more smartphones for gaming, including competitive gaming, will surely follow. This is especially true as more individuals receive access to higher data speeds, such as 4G and 5G digital cellular networks. While some mobile esports have come and gone, such as *Vainglory*, the continued success of some other titles such as *Arena of Valor* and *Brawl Stars* provides hope that other titles may follow suit and create competitive tournaments or leagues that are large enough to be televised on prominent U.S. broadcast networks.[1274] In fact, another mobile title Garena International's *Free Fire* currently offers substantial prize pools[1275] as well as previously being "the fourth most-watched video game on the [Twitch] platform."[1276] These facts further highlight the current growth that is happening within the competitive mobile esports scene.[1277]

6.2 The Rise of Global Youth, High School, and College Esports

The text has extensively covered the professional esports scene; however, it is also necessary to explore the development and the expansion of competitive gaming at earlier ages. Particularly, this section examines the growth of youth-, high school-, as well as college-level competitive gaming.[1278] Specifically, youth, high school, and college esports are on the rise in the United States.[1279] In fact, in 2018, the *National Federation of State High School Associations* (NFHS), which is the regulatory body for U.S. high school sports, reported that "72 percent of teens play video games regularly."[1280] There is also evidence of widespread usage of video and computer games by individuals of all age across all segments of the world's population.[1281] In addition, there are also "[n]early 200 colleges in the United States and Canada [that] are actively recruiting and offer scholarships for esports" in a variety of titles (and more being added every year).[1282] These educational institutions are actually competing against other colleges and universities in select games for prizes and scholarship money.[1283] There is also a growing esports scene among many U.S.-based junior colleges, including through the efforts of the esports association "NJCAA Esports."[1284]

The global gaming scene has caused many elementary, middle, and high schools across the country to take notice of the growing competitive gaming scene existing and figuring out ways to incorporate it into their neighborhoods. For instance, the substantial growth in this sector has caused many states to start developing their own school-sponsored esports teams.[1285] One of the central reasons cited by many educators when establishing these gaming programs is that "[e]sports offer a unique pathway to encourage interest in STEM fields such as programming, graphic design, networking, and video game design."[1286] In particular, some studies suggest that "gamer students are primed to pursue STEM in college and careers" as opposed to others who do not participate in esports.[1287] This fact may be beneficial for a child's educational and career development. [1288]

This point has caused many high schools across the country to begin establishing their own esports leagues. "Specifically, as of July 2019, Virginia [and] eight other states [...] officially recognize[d] video gaming as a varsity high school sport."[1289] For example, "four New York City schools in Upper Manhattan" created a new esports league for "New York City middle school students."[1290] The New York State Department of Education has further supported these actions, including by highlighting the Rensselaer City School District.[1291] This New York school district currently "include[s] competitive esports" in its extracurricular club offering to their "425 students [in] grades 7–12."[1292] Additionally, "Fair Haven New Jersey's Knollwood Middle School became one of the first middle schools in the country to have video games" as an official school sport.[1293] Some teachers in New Jersey have gone even further by establishing a "nonprofit organization" to help create "esports" and other "student educational experience[s.]"[1294]

In an effort to continue to grow the competitive youth gaming scene, the National Federation of State High School Associations (NFHS) partnered with tournament platform provider PlayVS in an effort "to introduce esports to high schools and state associations."[1295] The partnership began with "an initial rollout in at least 15 states" with plans to expand into other areas in the future.[1296] This strategic partnership provides each participating school with access to PlayVS' online platform to "build and manage teams, check schedules, and track stats." [1297] In addition to this partnership, other unaffiliated high school esports leagues have arisen. Two well-known ones are the High School Esports League (HSEL)[1298] and the North America Scholastic Esports Federation (NASEF).[1299] These independent associations provide platforms for high schools and other "community-based organizations" to compete against other schools and community groups on.[1300] For instance, all "high schools and community-based organizations located in North America" are eligible to participate in the NASEF.[1301] Furthermore, the primary school competitive landscape continues to evolve with the addition of new competitive gaming titles. For instance, as part of its high school esports program with the NFHS, PlayVS expanded "its tournament and league platforms with the addition of Epic Games' *Fortnite* to its high school game lineup"[1302] as well as with the addition of Riot Games' *League of Legends*.[1303] They also continue further expansion into other games, including establishing the competitive high school *Overwatch* scene.[1304]

In addition to independent organizations establishing and managing the growing youth and high school esports competitive scene, many states have begun launching their own individual programs aimed at this. Some of these states have even enacted their own policies toward which titles will be permissible for competitive gaming. For example, the Kentucky High School Athletic Association ruled that "the video game *Fortnite*" could not be played in any school's "interscholastic e-sports competitions."[1305] Other states have also established their own associations governing the gaming space, including Virginia,[1306] Indiana,[1307] Colorado,[1308] Wisconsin,[1309] Connecticut, [1310] Ohio,[1311] Illinois, [1312] North Dakota,[1313] and Alaska,[1314] to name a few. Furthermore, the California Interscholastic Federation (CIF) has gone one step further by establishing its own separate partnership with PlayVS.[1315] This alliance formed its own extensive "Esports Initiative."[1316] This collaboration is reportedly aimed at providing esports opportunities that comply with the "California Education Code" by "assist[ing] schools statewide by providing [them with] a platform for participation in competitions that include [set] rules, regulations, [and] participation standards."[1317] This new initiative continued to expand, including entering into an official partnership with gaming peripheral company HyperX.[1318] This arrangement enabled HyperX to act as the "official headset, official keyboard, official mouse, and official mousepad of the CIF's new esports program."[1319]

In addition to the growth of high school and middle school esports, many universities and colleges across North America also took note.[1320] In response to this new trend, many educational institutions began offering esports clubs as well as creating their own competitive teams that play against other colleges in organized tournaments and leagues.[1321] These colleges have even begun recruiting former professional gamers to compete on behalf of them.[1322] Some universities that gone through and have also begun including esports in the additional aspects of campus life including through undergraduate or graduate courses, minor degrees and esports certifications, including schools such as Oklahoma City University,[1323] University of Arizona,[1324] Illinois State University,[1325] Northwood University,[1326] Illinois Wesleyan University,[1327] and Arizona State University,[1328] as well as many other educational institutions.[1329] Some universities have taken more elaborate steps, including creating their own dedicated esports and competitive gaming facilities on campus.[1330] For instance, Harrisburg University invested "$750,000" to construct an "on-campus facility."[1331] Some universities have even begun offering academic scholarships to entice esports participants.[1332] In addition, some established college conferences have even created their own competitive esports circuits for its participating universities. For instance, the Eastern College Athletic Conference (ECAC) Esports was established for competitive gameplay between its conference members and is intended to mirror the traditional college sports conferences such as the "BIG 12 Conference." [1333]

In response to the collegiate gaming competitive scene's growth, the National Association of Collegiate Esports (NACE) was formed.[1334] NACE was created to help the "development of esports programs at the collegiate level."[1335] The association currently has over "170 member schools" with over "5000 student-athletes" competing across the United States.[1336] These student-athletes game against other colleges in a variety of titles including *Overwatch, Rocket League, Smite, Fortnite*, and *League of Legends*.[1337] In addition to the NACE, another similar organization that was created is TESPA.[1338] TESPA currently has over "270 chapters across North America" competing in various games including *Overwatch, Hearthstone, Heroes of the Storm*, and *StarCraft II*.[1339]

Another large collegiate competitive league is *the Collegiate Star League (CSL)*.[1340] The *CSL* has "over 70,000 competing students across 1,800 universities in North America" in a variety of titles including "*League of Legends, Dota 2, Counter-Strike: Global Offensive, Fortnite*, [and] *Smash Bros*." [1341] In fact, some of *CSL's* collegiate esports events are presented during DreamHack's events and tournament.[1342] In fact, this league is "the world's largest collegiate gaming league" and; since its inception in 2009, it has awarded "over $600,000 in scholarship money" to competitors.[1343]

While new gaming titles are consistently being added to the competitive college circuit, Riot Games' *League of Legends* has distinguished itself within the college scene.[1344] In particular, the "College *League of Legends*" competitions have over "350 teams competing" in them.[1345] This organized league is a "student-led network of *League of Legends* players on college campuses across the U.S. and Canada" and enables different colleges to compete against each other in various *League of Legends* tournaments.[1346] The league even offers scholarships to winning teams.[1347] With the increasing viewership and interest, some of these collegiate competitions are even televised, such as ESPN's College Esports Championship (CEC).[1348]

In addition to the competitive scene, some colleges across the country have established specific courses in the field, while others have created entire esports degree programs.[1349] In fact, the non-professional gaming scene has become so large that one of the largest gaming streaming platforms, Twitch created its own "Twitch for School" project.[1350] The program provides a participating university student with a "university team page and accompanying [Twitch] channel" as well as with the opportunity for a "fully partnered channel" so that the university earns "revenue" while utilizing it.[1351] Additionally, as part of the program, any participating school would also receive continued support from Twitch.[1352] This might include receiving "swag" as well as potentially "front page [placement ...] to promote" the university's channel.[1353] The "Twitch Student" concept was initially formed by the company in an effort to "empower and give [a] voice to students within the [gaming] industry."[1354] The program was "designed [by Twitch] to create an apparatus for universities, students and teams to facilitate growth in the [esports] realm."[1355] In fact, as a result of this concept, more universities began incorporating esports into their collegiate athletic programs.[1356]

The competitive collegiate scene has not only grown in North America but it has also expanded into many other countries across the globe. This includes the development of university-focused gaming competitions in many nations including Brazil,[1357] France,[1358] Spain,[1359] the United Kingdom,[1360] Ireland,[1361] and Germany.[1362] For example, the University eSport Germany is a "student-initiated startup that organizes eSports competitions for students, primarily from German universities" against other German university students.[1363] Furthermore, Amazon announced the "Amazon University Esports"[1364] partnership that pits universities in the "United Kingdom, Spain and Italy" against each other in a variety of gaming titles, including in *League of Legends*, *Teamfight Tactics*, and *Clash Royale*.[1365] Similar to the United States, some other countries have established organizations to govern collegiate esports within their territory.[1366] This includes the National Student Esports (NSE), who even secured a lucrative partnership with Barclays Bank.[1367] They have also secured a license to operate competitive tournaments, including with Nintendo for its *Super Smash Bros. Ultimate* title.[1368]

Overall, as more and more individuals continue to play video and computer games, the non-professional competitive gaming scene seems primed to continue to grow. Specifically, it is clear that collegiate esports has the potential to become a global force and it might even enable university students from different countries to compete against each other. In fact, as more children grow up with competitive gaming and esports as part of their everyday lives, the more likely it is that these lower-level gaming experiences will continue to expand and rise in importance and scope.

6.3 International and National Esports Associations and Federations

Some Esports Associations & Federations

International	Continental	National
World Esports Association (WESA)	Asian Esports Federation (AESF)	British Esports Association (BEA)
World Esports Consortium (WESCO)	European Esports Federation (EEF)	German Esports Federation (ESBD)
International Esports Federation (ieSF)		Japan Esports (JESU)
Esports Integrity Commission (ESIC)		Israeli Electronic Sport Association (IESA)
		Korean e-Sports Association (KeSPA)
		United States Esports Federation (USeF)

As the professional side of esports and competitive gaming continues to develop and expand internationally, many countries and different geographic areas have begun working together to establish uniform policies applicable to their territories.[1369] This includes these interested parties creating policies that relate to any esports and professional gaming matter within their borders. For example, this might be in the form of establishing participation guidelines for any competitive gaming events operated in their country. These entities include country-specific ones, continent-wide ones, as well as those that govern even larger geographic regions. Some of these groups are even recognized by their own country's public authorities and government.[1370] In addition, there has also been the creation of international bodies meant to govern all international competitive gaming activities. Building off previous attempted organizations such as the *G7* Federation, one such organization that was created is the World Esports Association (WESA).[1371] The WESA was created by event organizer Electronic Sports League (ESL) and several large international esports organizations, including Fnatic, Team Envyus, G2 Esports, FaZe Clan, and SK Gaming.[1372] The WESA established its own standard "rules of conduct and compliance" for all of its participating teams and their respective players.[1373] These rules were promulgated "to protect and to promote the reputation and integrity of eSports."[1374] This association also attempts to regulate and "approve" any "pro league license transfers" between any of its association members in an effort to maintain the integrity of competitive gaming.[1375] Another similar global association, the World Esports Consortium (WESCO) was founded to assist with the "creation of national federations" and "esports laws" as well as to establish set "rules, regulations and [to assist with] legal matters."[1376] Similarly, the International Esports Federation (ieSF) was created to enact "standards for referees, players, [...] titles and competitions."[1377] The ieSF currently consists of over "46 nations" from all across the world, including Argentina, Brazil, Mexico, China, Japan, India, Thailand, Austria, Portugal, Sweden, New Zealand, and the United States.[1378] In 2020, this organization has grown to "72-nations" with the addition of new countries such as "Brunei, Montenegro and Peru."[1379] Finally, the Esports Integrity Commission (ESIC) has also been created.[1380] The ESIC attempts to work on formulating industry regulations, including working on establishing esports talent agent guidelines and has even issued sanctions against "cheating."[1381]

In addition to international organizations, there are also national and continent-wide associations. These associations work to establish policies within their own countries as well as those that apply across their continent. This includes working with the intention of furthering the growth of the professional side of competitive gaming in their respective territories. For example, the Asian Esports Federation (AESF) consists of 45 member countries and is recognized by the Olympic Counsel of Asia.[1382] The AESF "aims to enhance the quality and professional governance of esports [as well as to] support and oversee the development of esports in the Asia region." [1383] Similarly, the European Esports Federation (EEF) was established for analogous purposes.[1384] The federation is composed of "12 national esports federations," including those representing "the UK, Belgium, Germany, Austria, Hungary, France, Russia, Slovenia, Serbia, Sweden, Turkey, and Ukraine."[1385] The European Esports Federation unified all of its participating associations in

"The Berlin Declaration."[1386] In this declaration, all of the signatory members acknowledged their belief "in the values of dedication, commitment, respect, fair play and personal and structural integrity" within esports and that they intend to uphold these values by acting as "the European voice of its national member federations."[1387] The signatory federations representing their individual country's esports interests include the British Esports Association (BEA), the Belgian Esports Federation (BESF), the German Esports Federation (ESBD), the Austrian Esports Federation (ESVÖ), the Hungarian Esports Federation (HUNESZ), France Esports, the Russian Esports Federation (RESF), the Slovenská Asociácia Elektronických Športo (SAEŠ), the Serbian Esports Federation (SESF-RS), Svenska esportsförbundet (Sweden), the Turkish Esports Federation (TESFED), the Ukrainian Esports Federation (UESF), Esports Association Polskam (ESA), Federazione Italiana E-Sports (FIES), eSport Danmark (ESD), the Israeli Electronic Sport Association (IESA), and the Swiss Esports Federation (SeSF).[1388]

In addition, many other countries across the globe have created their own individual societies and other interest groups meant to govern esports within their own countries. For example, Japan Esports (JESU) was established by several interested parties, including game developers Nintendo, Tencent, Capcom, Konami, Sony, and SEGA to "support e-sports player development."[1389] The JESU even created their own "pro license" that must be obtained by an individual in order to earn income as a competitive video gamer.[1390] Other countries have also established their own federations in an effort to "unite all esports stakeholders, including athletes, event organizers, technology producers, innovators and inventors, IP holders, parents, sponsors and fans."[1391] Some of these include the United States Esports Federation (USeF),[1392] the Esports Kenya Federation (ESKF) (a federation registered with Kenya's Ministry of Sports),[1393] the Federación Nacional de Deportes Electrónicos México (FNDEM),[1394] as well as the Thailand Esports Association (TESF) (an association recognized by Sports Authority of Thailand),[1395] to name a few.

Some initiatives that these organizations focus on include working on visa and other immigration reform policies within their countries. These procedures are intended to enable easier foreign access for non-resident competitive gamers wishing to play in a tournament or participate in any other gaming activity in a country. For example, the Germany Esports Federation (ESBD) created a new visa for "esports athletes from outside of the European Union" wishing to compete in esports competitions held in Germany.[1396] These federations also typically work on creating new benefits and other ways of enticing the hosting of major esports events within their country.[1397] Furthermore, some associations may even work toward having their country officially "recognize" esports as a "sport." For example, the Sri Lanka Esports Association (SLESA) achieved this goal within their own country by having esports "officially recognized" as an "official sport" by their government.[1398] Similarly, China's Ministry of Human Resources and Social Security released a statement formally "recognizing" "'esports operators' and 'esports player'" as professions.[1399] Other initiatives include attempts to incorporate esports representatives onto a country's Olympic committee as well as proposing competitive gaming for consideration as an "official" Olympic sport. In fact, this was successfully accomplished in Finland where the "*Finnish Olympic Committee* approved the *Finnish Esports Federation* (SEUL) as a member of the Committee."[1400] This approval might indicate and be seen as a step toward competitive gaming being included in the *Olympic Games* at some point in the future. Overall, as the global esports market continues to grow, there is an increased need for international as well as national regulatory and lobbying bodies. In particular, the establishment of associations that represent the interests of professional gamers, video game and software developers, as well as any other party involved in esports, seems necessary to carefully regulate the growth of competitive gaming. These entities try to accomplish this by working to maintain gaming's competitive integrity as well as attempting to enact accepted rules and regulations for fair play.[1401] These actions are similar to those undertaken by international associations such as the World Anti-Doping Agency (WADA)[1402] and the International Olympic Committee (IOC).[1403] Specifically, these entities try to maintain the competitive integrity within the *Olympic Games* by battling "doping" and any other anti-competitive actions.[1404]

6.4 Esports Professionals

Similar to other talent-based industries, including music, television, and sports, professional video game competitors participating in organized esports may have an individual or a "team" of competent specialists around them to advise and consult with regarding their business, legal, and potentially, their personal matters.[1405] In addition to any players associations available to a professional gamer, it may also be beneficial for a professional gamer to have their own separate, independent professional who is solely loyal to and responsible for assisting that one talent. While this may seem straightforward in today's media-driven and public world where legal and personal issues arise daily, it has become a prevalent practice for many professional gamers, streamers and other gaming talent to review, negotiate, and sign agreements with esports teams and other companies in the space without any independent competent assistance.[1406] This includes players entering into deals without any support from an independent representative, such as a registered talent agent or licensed attorney, advisor or or player association representative.[1407] For example, *Fortnite* streamer Turner "Tfue" Tenney was engaged in litigation with his former organization FaZe Clan over a reportedly "grossly oppressive" and "one-sided" agreement.[1408] Some professional gamers are also failing to properly handle some other aspects of their professional career such as immigration and tax matters.[1409] While it is never required for an individual to obtain any third-party advice, let alone to consult with an attorney or other third-party representative, in many cases, the benefits may outweigh the costs. Specifically, a professional person whose daily job it is it to handle these types of matters may provide a gamer with unique and specialized insight that others may not possess. In fact, it is the norm for an entertainer, athlete, and every other "celebrity" personality to have an individual or even a "team" of professionals assisting them with their legal, business, marketing, public relations, and any other day-to-day needs.[1410] These individuals exist to assist the talent so that they can solely focus on competing in their sport or gaming title.

While a talent may have mastered their craft, there are a variety of other members of a professional esports competitor's "team" that can also support them off the digital gridiron.[1411] These individuals may assist a gamer's career longevity as well as affect their potential current and long-term financial success.[1412] These professionals could include an attorney, a personal manager or other player representative, a business manager, an accountant, an insurance agent, a public relations manager, or any combination of (or all of these).[1413] These additional experts are also similar to the type of individuals that are commonly used by talent in the music, television, and motion picture industries. For instance, in the entertainment business, a personal manager or agent typically handles an entertainer's day-to-day affairs, such as booking hotels, transportation to and from performances and appearances, and the booking of recording sessions. Their representative might also assist in handling any press and sponsorship inquiries as well as any other personal affairs that the talent does not have time to handle. This is similar to how a player representative or manager can operate on behalf of a gamer. For instance, this individual could assist the gamer with contract review and negotiation of a deal, with the creation of sponsorship "deliverables" as well as with any tournament or other event and appearance travel logistics. This is in addition to the representative potentially acting as a buffer between the gamer and other parties, such as the press or media, league organizers, and sponsoring brands. While their application and use in esports is not as widespread, it is now becoming the norm for some top gaming talent to utilize independent, competent, third-party representatives in the advancement of their professional gaming careers.[1414] Some of these independent player representative duties are explored below in more detail.

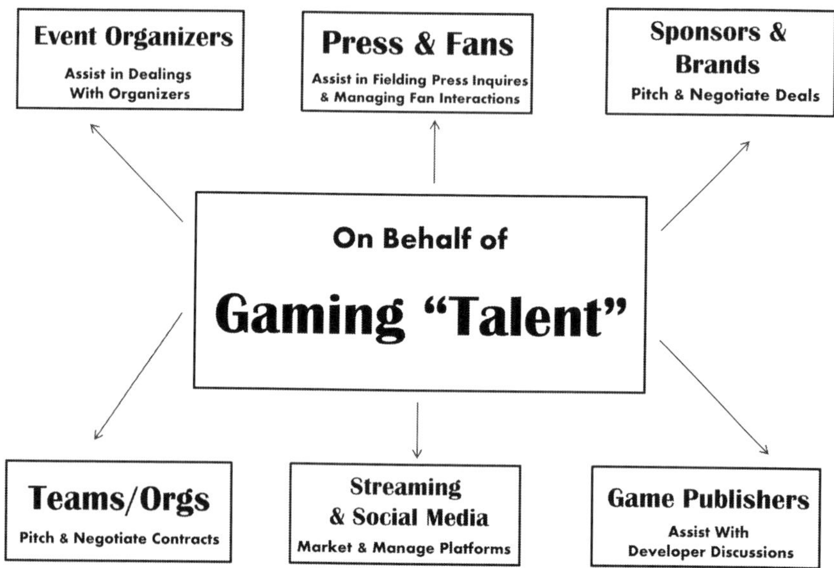

Similar to a player representative in other major North American professional sports, one of the primary tasks of an esports player representative is the negotiation of the gamer's player contract with the organization. In most instances, a qualified professional may be beneficial for the gamer to consult to fully understand each clause contained in the agreement. This includes the player receiving specialized insight from the retained professional into how to best negotiate a specific contract to benefit the gamer as much as possible.[1415]

In the last few years, there have also been several potentially preventable situations that might have theoretically been avoided if independent counsel was consulted. One of these consistent mistakes is the absence of contract assistance on behalf of a player causing the organization to retain provisions that dramatically favor them. As discussed earlier, one of the important clauses that can significantly impact a gamer's career is the "buy-out" clause. This provision generally provides the player's original team with the ability to require a specific payment amount prior to releasing the player from their existing contract. Therefore, a contract that contains a substantial buy-out may inhibit the gamer's ability to play for another organization without a huge financial commitment by the new team (which the team might not want to make). For example, esports organization FaZe Clan paid one of the largest player buyouts ever, a reported $500,000 buyout paid for pro gamer Nikola "Niko" Kovač.[1416] Later, esports organization Cloud9 spent a reported "$1.5 million buyout" for Dignitas' *League of Legends* player, Philippe "Vulcan" Laflamme.[1417] Similarly, esports organization G2 Esports reportedly set a "staggering buyout price of around $800,000" for each of its gamers, Nathan "NBK" Schmitt and Dan "apEX" Madesclaire.[1418] In these cases, if these gamers desired to be moved elsewhere, the purchasing team would need to pay this amount. However, if the purchase fee was too costly, then this fact may prevent the gamer from being bought out, which prevents them from playing for another team.

In addition to contract guidance, a player representative also might assist a player in locating a new team if they are a "free agent" or if they are a new gamer (just starting out on their professional gaming career). In fact, many top esports player representatives have access to and work with many esports team organization owners and managers.[1419] These are the individuals who handle or assist in the organization's personnel decisions as well as advise the team on which gaming titles to field squads in. This network is similar to the one that a Hollywood talent representative might have for an actor that they are representing.

Another unique characteristic of a player representative is the ability and desire to build a marketable "brand" based around their talent. This is because it coincides with a representative's goal of building and developing their signed talent's individual, stand-alone marketability, and value. As we explored earlier, sponsorship and brand partnerships are a highly lucrative area that is central to many top gaming talent's earnings, so it must be approached professionally. In addition, many established esports talent representatives also have access to both endemic and non-endemic brands. This access provides these individuals with the ability to potentially bring both organizational-wide as well as individual-based sponsorship opportunities that many players and even some organizations may not have access to. Therefore, in many cases, a connected player representative is also well versed in "pitching" and negotiating marketing and endorsement opportunities on behalf of their gaming talent.

In addition to a veteran player representative's prowess and knowledge in contract negotiations as well as in sponsorship identification, most are also adept at and familiar with conversing with the game developers as well as the tournament and league organizers. They are also usually knowledgeable of any applicable rules and regulations, including the tax and visa requirements of the industry. As discussed earlier, the proper work authorization could be the difference between playing in a tournament or not. In some cases, the representative may also act as a "buffer" to the outside world of press, journalists, and fans. Whether it is a player agent or other independent press relations specialists, these independent consultants can provide additional media training as well as crisis management assistance to ensure that a gamer is able to handle all that is thrown at them, especially during a time of turmoil or stress. Specifically, the use of a competent public relations professional or another independent representative could be a tremendous asset to a gamer and could hopefully help them avoid some of the recent scandals that emerged as a result of an esports professional's conduct. For example, former *Overwatch League* professionals Felix "xQc" Lengyel[1420] and Timo "Taimou" Kettunen[1421] both encountered problems for derogatory comments that each of them made in the heat of the moment during a competition. These comments caused Felix "xQc" Lengyel to be suspended and fined and, subsequently, terminated for his continuous "disparaging language."[1422] It is apparent that a seasoned professional in these gamers' corner might have provided valuable insight and training on how to best handle these stressful situations. For instance, they could have provided techniques and advice to the gamer on how to optimally respond to their opponents while under high-pressure conditions. The professional is also able to "pitch" the gamer to various publications and podcasts for interviews and appearances to promote the player in order to build their personal "brand" and in an effort to increase their social media metrics (which may help their income opportunities).

Finally, many independent professionals are connected with a variety of other skilled professionals, including tax specialists and accountants. These professionals can assist in filing and preparing a player's personal income tax and with any other related business and legal matters such as protecting the player "brand" and intellectual property protections if that professional is not able to handle it on their own.

In addition to an attorney or other independent talent representative, a business manager (who may also be a tax specialist) or an accountant are also both extremely beneficial and are standard in many professional's careers. A business manager may assist a gamer in collecting all their owed salary, tournament winnings, as well as any owed appearance and sponsorship fees. These professionals could also be utilized to potentially track and pay a professional gamer's personal bills as well as handle any tax and accounting matters related to any prize money or other income earned. This individual could be important to ensuring that a professional gamer is fully compliant with their tax obligations for their gaming income. As explored earlier, this includes the paying of taxes on the gamer's tournament winnings, player salaries, streaming money, as well as any sponsorship fees and any related fringe benefits, such as free mileage earned as part of an endorsement deal with an airline. As these matters become even more complicated, a competent third party may provide additional value, especially when several states or countries are entitled to taxes from a gamer.

While there are obvious drawbacks to a third-party representative consulting and representing a gamer, such as added costs, the potential downfalls that may occur as a result of a miscue could have wide-reaching negative implications. Additionally, while a gamer may see the additional expense that a professional representative may impose as prohibitive, the long-term value, experience, and connections that they possess could be infinitely more valuable to the gamer's long-term career advancement and could justify this expense. As a warning, there will always be unscrupulous and less than competent advisers; however, for the most part, the competent and top-quality ones usually rise to the top.[1423]

In addition to receiving recommendations and researching a potential professional prior to engaging them, there are other ways a gamer may try to protect themselves. For example, if a player is signed to a talent agency or management company, especially one with several agents, managers, or other business personnel, it might be beneficial for them to include a "key man" clause. This clause is exemplified below and is intended to protect the professional's relationship with a particular individual. It states that that the personal manager (the key man) must represent the gamer or else the player may terminate the representation contract. This provision may be applicable in situations where the key man is deceased, is terminated, or is otherwise no longer affiliated with the management company that the gamer is signed to. For this clause to be operative, the particular individual (the key man) needs to be listed by name in the agreement. However, it is important to note that the inclusion of this language does not obligate the gamer to leave the management company; instead, it just provides the player with the opportunity and right to do so if they choose to.

> **Key Man**: During the Term, "Justin M. Jacobson, Esq." shall be primarily responsible for the Manager's activities under this Management Agreement. Notwithstanding the foregoing, it is understood and agreed that "Justin M. Jacobson, Esq." may delegate day-to-day responsibilities to other employees of the Manager provided "Justin M. Jacobson, Esq." remains primarily responsible for the activities and services provided by the Manager. Notwithstanding anything to the contrary contained herein, in the event that "Justin M. Jacobson, Esq." ceases to be employed by the Manager or shall cease to be primarily responsible for the Manager's activities hereunder ("Key-Man Event"),

then the GAMER shall have the right to immediately terminate this Management Agreement effective upon the date of the GAMER's notice to the Manager of such Key-Man Event.

In conclusion, as the esports business continues to expand and as more stakeholders continue to earn larger sums, the need for competent, unbiased representatives to protect, advise, and develop professional gaming talent becomes more apparent.[1424] In fact, to date, more and more esports talent agents and other professionals specializing in the field are continuously emerging and providing this type of assistance.[1425]

6.5 Marketing and Promotions Legal Considerations for Social Media and Streaming

Some "Influencer" Disclosure Tips

- **Disclose Your Honest Opinion**
- **Use #Ad or #Sponsored On All Applicable Posts**
- **Make It Obvious A Relationship Exists With The Product or Brand** (Free Product Counts!)
- **Put "Sponsored" In The Message Itself** (The "About Me" or "Video Description" Isn't Enough)
- **Include "Ad" Superimposed On an "Instagram Story" and in a Video Post**
- **For Video Content Include Both Audio & Video Sponsor Notice**
- **Repeat Sponsored Ad Read Periodically During A Live Stream**

The worldwide rise in the use of live streaming, social media, and other online platforms has led to the creation of new influential individuals, commonly referred to as "influencers." An influencer is "a person who is able to generate interest in something (such as a consumer product) by posting about it on social media."[1426] These influencers can be a celebrity or any other famous or notable person, including professional athletes, musicians, models, food and fashion bloggers, and, now, professional gamers, streamers, and content creators.[1427] In recent years, there has been a significant rise in the number of people across the world claiming to be influencers. Some of these people have actually begun earning substantial sums for posting about a sponsored product on their social media or utilizing it on a social streaming platform.[1428] As we have explored in earlier sections, the gaming world is no different. This is because professional gamers, streamers, content creators, and esports teams all utilize brand partnerships and ambassadorships in their business model, especially digitally and online-driven campaigns.[1429] This includes extensive use of social media platforms such as YouTube, Twitch, Instagram, and the quickly emerging Tik Tok.[1430] Coincidentally, in most cases, these income streams happen to account for a substantial portion of many of these individual and team's yearly income.

With the rapid growth of this segment, many people are trying to capitalize on their own followings, including individuals with small followings, sometimes referred to as "microinfluencers" or "nanoinfluencers."[1431] This rise has caused many regulatory bodies to take notice and begin monitoring and policing how an influencer interacts with those that they intend to "influence." In the United States, the Federal Trade Commission (FTC) is the regulatory agency responsible for establishing policies and enacting legislation to govern these types of influencers' public actions.[1432] In particular, under Section 5 of the *FTC Act*, the FTC specifically governs these social media statements made by influencers as the section covers the "Use of Endorsements and Testimonials in Advertising."[1433] The Act sets out the "general principles" used for "evaluating endorsements and testimonials" as well as those examined when determining whether or not a specific public "endorsement or testimonial" made by a party is "deceptive."[1434]

The FTC has enacted guidelines specifically applicable and targeted at social media and streaming influencers.[1435] These procedures list "the various ways that an influencer's relationship with a brand would make [a] disclosure necessary."[1436] For instance, one important rule is that any post or other public statement made by the influencer must be true and actually "reflect the honest opinions, findings, beliefs, or experience of the endorser."[1437] This means that the party cannot make any "false or unsubstantiated statements" about the product or service they post or otherwise endorse.[1438]

As explained in the "Disclosure 101 for Social Media Influencers" document, if an individual "endorse[s] a product through social media," the poster must "make it obvious" to the public that a "relationship with the brand" exists.[1439] This means that the influencer is responsible for and must publicly disclose the existence of a sponsorship relationship in cases where the influencer has a "material connection" to the brand.[1440] A "material connection" is found when a "personal, family or employment or financial relationship" exists between the influencer and the company.[1441] This means that a disclosure is required, even if the brand is only providing the influencer with "free or discounted products or services."[1442] Furthermore, if a material connection exists between the parties, then a disclosure is also required even if the influencer is just "tagging a brand" that they are currently wearing without mentioning them within the content of a social media post.[1443] This is because the influencer's action of "tagging" the brand could be seen as an endorsement of the product that may "require a disclosure" when such a material connection exists between the poster and the brand.[1444] While there is no bright-line rule for how and what a social media or streaming "disclosure" must contain, the FTC has articulated some guiding principles. For instance, the disclosure must be placed in a position that it is not "hard to miss."[1445] This could include placing the required disclosure within the "endorsement message itself," such as within the body of the post or listed in the stream's title and it will not be satisfied by solely listing this information on an "ABOUT ME or profile page."[1446] Additionally, if the endorsement is included in a "picture on a platform like Snapchat" or is inserted in an "Instagram story," then, the influencer must "superimpose the disclosure over the picture" to ensure that "viewers have enough time to notice and read it."[1447] Similarly, if an endorsement is made in a video, then the required disclosure must be placed within the actual video and should "not just [be listed] in the description uploaded with the video."[1448] It might also be prudent for an influencer to make any required disclosure "notice" in "both audio and video" form in case some viewers "watch [the content] without sound."[1449] Furthermore, if a product testimonial is made on or during a live stream, such as during a Twitch broadcast, any required disclosure statement must be repeated "periodically so [that any] viewers who only see part of the stream" and tune in later, will hear and receive notice of it.[1450] In addition, some products may also require another specific disclaimer in addition to the required disclosures. For instance, if a person is promoting a product that contains nicotine, such as tobacco, vapes, or e-cigarettes, then an additional disclosure that states that the product contains nicotine is required.[1451] Thus, an influencer who works with a sponsoring vape company must disclose the existence of the sponsorship in a social media post as well as include a disclaimer regarding the product's actual contents (that it contains nicotine).[1452]

When making the required disclosure statement, the information must include "simple and clear language."[1453] It also must be made "in the same language as the endorsement itself."[1454] Furthermore, the use and inclusion of terms such as "'advertisement,' 'ad,' and 'sponsored,'" "ambassador" or "partner," as well as hash-tags such as "#ad or #sponsored" may suffice.[1455] Since the FTC governs testimonials and endorsements, it is essential that the influencer only endorses products that they have actual "experience" with. This means the individual should not fabricate claims about a product that "require proof the advertiser doesn't have" or must not say something is great when it is not.[1456] The FTC has made some "Frequently Asked Questions" available to explain the applicability of these laws to a social media influencer's posts.[1457]

Another legal matter related to the world of social media and "influencers" is the trend of "fake" follower and "like" purchasing.[1458] In fact, two leading social media platforms have acknowledged the existence of millions of "fake" profiles on their respective sites. For example, Facebook has stated that "up to 60 million automated accounts roam" its platform and Twitter has stated that "nearly 15 percent [of its "active" users] are [actually] automated accounts designed to simulate real people."[1459] The practice of purchasing followers emerged due to the accepted assumption that "a bigger following might mean something" and that an influencer's large social media numbers might inform "you (the consumer)" about the "legitimacy or how good" a product or service is.[1460] This notion caused many celebrity influencers to utilize third-party services intended to grow their social media "followers" in hope of increasing the paid sponsorship opportunities that they could receive. In response to this wide- spread industry practice of purchasing fake "followers" and "likes," the FTC began regulating this practice in order to protect the consuming public from false statements by influential figures.[1461] Specifically, the federal agency brought charges against an alleged company who engaged in such actions.[1462] In the aforementioned case, this entity was found guilty of selling "fake indicators of social media influence."[1463] This company's actions were seen as a violation because these fabricated indicators "are important metrics that businesses and individuals use in making hiring, investing, purchasing, licensing, and viewing decisions."[1464] In particular, this company's actions permitted its "buyers to deceive potential clients, investors, partners, and employees" by providing "their customers with the means and instrumentalities to commit deceptive acts or practices, which is itself a deceptive act or practice in violation of the FTC Act."[1465]

As evident from the FTC's actions, the required disclosures are crucial to an influencer's sustained profitability. This applies to situations where the endorser merely posts a picture of themselves in some product that they received for free to the paid use of product that is promoted during an individual's live stream. Ultimately, if a streamer or content creator fails to include the proper notices, they could subject themselves to liability under the *FTC Act*. Furthermore, if an individual engages in deceptive or other misleading tactics, they can be exposed to potential criminal and civil liability as well as potential monetary repercussions for making false statements or failing to actually utilize a product that they claim to enjoy.

6.6 Conclusion

6.6.1 The Future of the Business of Esports

As we enter the end of 2020, and the COVID-19 health crisis is still taking its toll on the recreational and entertainment worlds of many across the world, esports and gaming have become a normal daily outlet for many individuals, including a myriad of professional athletes, musicians, and other entertainment industry celebrities.[1466] In my estimation, this seems to be the new trend as it seems that there will be more merging of the traditional entertainment, music, sports and politics into the esports and gaming world.[1467] This includes more musicians, politicians, and athletes utilizing live streaming platforms for gaming content such as Twitch as well as more celebrity-filled competitive and charity gaming tournaments.[1468] Furthermore, some esports organizations are partnering with traditional entertainment companies such as record labels to create unique content and other entertainment activations.[1469] Finally, another unique facet that is sure to evolve is the use of "in-game" music, especially in *NBA 2K* series.[1470] For instance, the *NBA 2K13* title featured an in-game music soundtrack music "executive produced" by music icon Jay-Z where he actually selected the music that the gamer heard while playing the game.[1471] Following this, additional entertainers came such as executive production by Pharrell (*NBA 2K15*),[1472] and song "curation" by popular DJs DJ Mustard, DJ Khaled, and DJ Premier (*NBA 2K16*).[1473] Finally, most recently, *NBA 2K20* title took this music integration further by adding a way to add new songs to the game over time.[1474] To do this, the game publisher Take Two Interactive actually partnered with entertainment company United Masters to select ten new songs from unsigned talent to be added to the game for in-game enjoyment.[1475] This year's new *NBA 2K21* track list has already been released and it even features tracks from the game's cover NBA athlete and aspiring rapper, Damian Lillard of the *Portland Trailblazers*.[1476] It is clear that entertainment, music, and other areas of pop culture are poised to continue to melt and build off each other.

In addition, there seems to also be a trend for more "entertainment"-focused esports organizations such as FaZe Clan[1477] and as well as the creation of new teams dedicated to combat "toxicity," bring "acceptance" and "inclusiveness," such as the newly incarnated X Set esports organization.[1478] Additionally, the trend for additional television channels solely dedicated to esports and competitive gaming is sure to continue, especially online with VENN and its substantial investment and the return of *G4* under Comcast.[1479]

The world of competitive video gaming and professional esports continues to evolve on a daily basis. It should also continue to expand overseas to other markets such as India, Australia, and Latin America.[1480] These future changes also include the constant addition of new competitive titles coming to the forefront as well as existing competitive games being replaced by these newer ones. There is also a constant flow of new business deals for the various players of the esports business "ecosystem." In conclusion, as the esports global market continues to grow, additional legal matters will be determined and come to the forefront.

References

1. Paul 'Redeye' Chaloner, *This is Esports (and How to Spell it)*, 25 (Bloomsbury Sport 2020); See also Tobias M. Scholz, *eSports is Business: Management in the World of Competitive Gaming*, 20 (Palgrave Macmillan 2019); Lawrence Phillips, *The History of Esports*, Hotspawn (Apr. 1, 2020), https://www.hotspawn.com/guides/the-history-of-esports; British Esports Association, *A Brief History of Esports and Video Games*, https://britishesports.org/news/a-brief-history-of-esports-and-video-games (last visited Jul. 2, 2020).
2. Chris Baker, *Stewart Brand Recalls First 'Spacewar' Video Game Tournament*, Rolling Stone (May 25, 2016), https://www.rollingstone.com/culture/culture-news/stewart-brand-recalls-first-spacewar-video-game-tournament-187669; See also Lawrence Phillips, *The History of Esports*, Hotspawn (Apr. 1, 2020), https://www.hotspawn.com/guides/the-history-of-esports.
3. Chris Baker, *Stewart Brand Recalls First 'Spacewar' Video Game Tournament*, Rolling Stone (May 25, 2016), https://www.rollingstone.com/culture/culture-news/stewart-brand-recalls-first-spacewar-video-game-tournament-187669/; See also Lawrence Phillips, *The History of Esports*, Hotspawn (Apr. 1, 2020), https://www.hotspawn.com/guides/the-history-of-esports.
4. Paul 'Redeye' Chaloner, *This is Esports (and How to Spell it)*, 25 (Bloomsbury Sport 2020); See also Sigma Klim, *The First-Ever Esports Tournament in the World Featured Space Invaders*, Guru Gamer (Sept. 3, 2019), https://gurugamer.com/viral/the-first-ever-esports-tournament-in-the-world-featured-space-invaders-5983.
5. Paul 'Redeye' Chaloner, *This is Esports (and How to Spell it)*, 25 (Bloomsbury Sport 2020); See also Tobias M. Scholz, *eSports is Business: Management in the World of Competitive Gaming*, 20 (Palgrave Macmillan 2019); Lawrence Phillips, *The History of Esports*, Hotspawn (Apr. 1, 2020), https://www.hotspawn.com/guides/the-history-of-esports; Atari Women, *Rebecca Heineman* http://www.atariwomen.org/stories/rebecca-heineman, (last visited Oct. 22, 2020).
6. Paul 'Redeye' Chaloner, *This is Esports (and How to Spell it)*, 27 (Bloomsbury Sport 2020); See also The Golden Age Arcade Historian, *The Atari $50,000 Centipede Fiasco*, http://allincolorforaquarter.blogspot.com/2012/11/the-atari-50000-centipede-fiasco.html (last visited Jul. 16, 2020; Rotheblog, *Atari Could Have Revolutionized Social Gaming in 1981*, http://www.rotheblog.com/2012/11/arcade-history/atari-couldve-cashed-in-1981-world-championships (last visited Jul. 16, 2020).
7. Paul 'Redeye' Chaloner, *This is Esports (and How to Spell it)*, 27 (Bloomsbury Sport 2020).
8. T.L. Taylor, *Raising the Stakes: E-Sports and the Professionalization of Computer Gaming*, 5 (The MIT Press 2012); Paul 'Redeye' Chaloner, *This is Esports (and How to Spell it)*, 29 (Bloomsbury (Sport 2020)); Lawrence Phillips, *The History of Esports*, Hotspawn (Apr. 1, 2020), https://www.hotspawn.com/guides/the

-history-of-esports; See also Jason Bennett, *Greg Sakundiak Makes 40 Years a Perfect Pac-Man Moment*, Twin Galaxies (Jun. 6, 2020), https://www.twingalaxies.com/feed_details.php/6122/greg-sakundiak-makes-40-years-a-perfect-pac-man-moment.

9. T.L. Taylor, *Raising the Stakes: E-Sports and the Professionalization of Computer Gaming*, 5 (The MIT Press 2012); See also Lawrence Phillips, *The History of Esports*, Hotspawn (Apr. 1, 2020), https://www.hotspawn.com/guides/the-history-of-esports; Twin Galaxies, *What is Twin Galaxies?*, https://www.twingalaxies.com/wiki_index.php?title=Policy:What-is-Twin-Galaxies (last visited Jul. 16, 2020).
10. Lawrence Phillips, *The History of Esports*, Hotspawn (Apr. 1, 2020); See also Stephen Totilo, *You Cannot Top the New Pac-Man World Record*, Kotaku (Jan. 11, 2012), https://kotaku.com/you-cannot-top-the-new-pac-man-world-record-5875131.
11. Lawrence Phillips, *The History of Esports*, Hotspawn (Apr. 1, 2020); See also T.L. Taylor, *Raising the Stakes: E-Sports and the Professionalization of Computer Gaming*, 5 (The MIT Press 2012); Tobias M. Scholz, *eSports is Business: Management in the World of Competitive Gaming*, 20 (Palgrave Macmillan 2019); Luke Plunkett, *Arcades Don't Make for Good TV (But Starcades Do)*, Kotaku (Jun. 14, 2011), https://kotaku.com/arcades-dont-make-for-good-tv-but-starcades-do-5811611.
12. Lawrence Phillips, *The History of Esports*, Hotspawn (Apr. 1, 2020); See also T.L. Taylor, *Raising the Stakes: E-Sports and the Professionalization of Computer Gaming*, 5 (The MIT Press 2012); Tobias M. Scholz, *eSports is Business: Management in the World of Competitive Gaming*, 20 (Palgrave Macmillan 2019); Luke Plunkett, *Arcades Don't Make for Good TV (But Starcades Do)*, Kotaku (Jun. 14, 2011), https://kotaku.com/arcades-dont-make-for-good-tv-but-starcades-do-5811611.
13. Luke Plunkett, *Arcades Don't Make for Good TV (But Starcades Do)*, Kotaku (Jun. 14, 2011), https://kotaku.com/arcades-dont-make-for-good-tv-but-starcades-do-5811611.
14. Paul 'Redeye' Chaloner, *This is Esports (and How to Spell it)*, 30 (Bloomsbury Sport 2020); See also The Golden Age Arcade Historian, *The Electronic Circus*, https://allincolorforaquarter.blogspot.com/2013/03/the-electronic-circus.html (last visited Jul. 16, 2020).
15. Paul 'Redeye' Chaloner, *This is Esports (and How to Spell it)*, 31 (Bloomsbury Sport 2020).
16. Paul 'Redeye' Chaloner, *This is Esports (and How to Spell it)*, 31 (Bloomsbury Sport 2020); See also U.S. National Video Game Team, *History*, https://www.usnationalvideogameteam.com/history (last visited Jul. 16, 2020).
17. *Id.*
18. *Id.*
19. Shawn Knight, *'King of Kong' Billy Mitchell is Back in the Record Books at Guinness*, Tech Spot (Jun. 19, 2020), https://www.techspot.com/news/85705-guinness-reinstates-billy-mitchell-donkey-kong-pac-man.html.
20. Paul 'Redeye' Chaloner, *This is Esports (and How to Spell it)*, 31 (Bloomsbury Sport 2020).
21. Paul 'Redeye' Chaloner, *This is Esports (and How to Spell it)*, 32 (Bloomsbury Sport 2020); See also U.S. National Video Game Team, *History*, https://www.usnationalvideogameteam.com/history (last visited Jul. 16, 2020).

22. Paul 'Redeye' Chaloner, *This is Esports (and How to Spell it)*, 33 (Bloomsbury Sport 2020); See also U.S. National Video Game Team, *History*, https://www.usnationalvideogameteam.com/history (last visited Jul. 16, 2020).
23. *Id.*
24. Paul 'Redeye' Chaloner, *This is Esports (and How to Spell it)*, 34 (Bloomsbury Sport 2020); See also U.S. National Video Game Team, *History*, https://www.usnationalvideogameteam.com/history (last visited Jul. 16, 2020); Jason Fell, *Founder Eyes December Relaunch for EGM*, Folio (Sept. 4, 2009), https://www.foliomag.com/founder-eyes-december-relaunch-egm.
25. Paul 'Redeye' Chaloner, *This is Esports (and How to Spell it)*, 34 (Bloomsbury Sport 2020); See also U.S. National Video Game Team, *History*, https://www.usnationalvideogameteam.com/history (last visited Jul. 16, 2020).
26. *Id.*
27. Paul 'Redeye' Chaloner, *This is Esports (and How to Spell it)*, 34 (Bloomsbury Sport 2020); See also I.M.D.B., *The Wizard*, https://www.imdb.com/title/tt0098663/ (last visited Jul. 10, 2020).
28. Paul 'Redeye' Chaloner, *This is Esports (and How to Spell it)*, 35 (Bloomsbury Sport 2020).
29. Paul 'Redeye' Chaloner, *This is Esports (and How to Spell it)*, 35 (Bloomsbury Sport 2020); IGN, *Nintendo World Championships 1990*, https://www.ign.com/games/nintendo-world-championships-1990-nes (last visited Jul. 16, 2020); Super Mario Wiki, *Nintendo World Championships 1990*, https://www.mariowiki.com/Nintendo_World_Championships_1990 (last visited Jul. 16, 2020).
30. Paul 'Redeye' Chaloner, *This is Esports (and How to Spell it)*, 35 (Bloomsbury Sport 2020); See also Lawrence Phillips, *The History of Esports*, Hotspawn (Apr. 1, 2020), https://www.hotspawn.com/guides/the-history-of-esports.
31. Paul 'Redeye' Chaloner, *This is Esports (and How to Spell it)*, 35 (Bloomsbury Sport 2020).
32. Lawrence Phillips, *The History of Esports*, Hotspawn (Apr. 1, 2020), https://www.hotspawn.com/guides/the-history-of-esports; See also See also Darren Murph, *World's "Only" PowerFest '94 SNES Cartridge Up for Auction*, Engadget (Apr. 27, 2007), https://www.engadget.com/2007-04-27-worlds-only-powerfest-94-snes-cartridge-up-for-auction.html; Super Mario Wiki, *Nintendo PowerFest '94*, https://www.mariowiki.com/Nintendo_PowerFest_%2794 (last visited Jul. 10, 2020).
33. Lawrence Phillips, *The History of Esports*, Hotspawn (Apr. 1, 2020), https://www.hotspawn.com/guides/the-history-of-esports; See also See also Darren Murph, *World's "Only" PowerFest '94 SNES Cartridge Up for Auction*, Engadget (Apr. 27, 2007), https://www.engadget.com/2007-04-27-worlds-only-powerfest-94-snes-cartridge-up-for-auction.html; Super Mario Wiki, *Nintendo PowerFest '94*, https://www.mariowiki.com/Nintendo_PowerFest_%2794 (last visited Jul. 10, 2020).
34. Paul 'Redeye' Chaloner, *This is Esports (and How to Spell it)*, 120 (Bloomsbury Sport 2020); CAPCOM, History, http://www.capcom.co.jp/ir/english/company/history.html?tab=1 (last visited Jul. 10, 2020).
35. Brad Jones, *Who Threw that Punch? Capcom Puts 25-Year-Old 'Street Fighter II' Mystery to Rest*, Digital Trends (May 27, 2016), https://www.digitaltrends.com/gaming/street-fighter-2-characters-mystery.

36. ESPN Esports Staff, *The Best Fighting Game Moments We've Ever Seen*, ESPN (May 12, 2020), https://www.espn.com/esports/story/_/id/29162565/the-best-fighting-game-moments-ever-seen.
37. Paul 'Redeye' Chaloner, *This is Esports* (*and How to Spell it*), 119 (Bloomsbury Sport 2020).
38. Tobias M. Scholz, *eSports is Business: Management in the World of Competitive Gaming*, 21 (Palgrave Macmillan 2019); See also Lawrence Phillips, *The History of Esports*, Hotspawn (Apr. 1, 2020), https://www.hotspawn.com/guides/the-history-of-esports; Brandon Brathwaite, *OPINION*: *The Past, Present, and Future of Evo Makes It Prime for Investment*, The Esports Observer (Jul. 23, 2018), https://esportsobserver.com/opinion-evo-prime-for-investors).
39. Paul 'Redeye' Chaloner, *This is Esports* (*and How to Spell it*), 117 (Bloomsbury Sport 2020); T.L. Taylor, *Raising the Stakes*: *E-Sports and the Professionalization of Computer Gaming*, 204 (The MIT Press 2012); See also Brian Crecente, *Fighting to Play: The History of the Longest Lived Fighting Game Tournament in the World*, Kotaku (Oct. 6, 2008), https://kotaku.com/fighting-to-play-the-history-of-the-longest-lived-figh-5054856.
40. T.L. Taylor, *Raising the Stakes: E-Sports and the Professionalization of Computer Gaming*, 6 (The MIT Press 2012); See also British Esports Association, *Quake*, https://britishesports.org/games/quake (last visited Jul. 16, 2020).
41. John Davison, *How 'Quake' Changed Video Games Forever*, Rolling Stone (Jun. 22, 2016, https://www.rollingstone.com/culture/culture-news/how-quake-changed-video-games-forever-187984; See also Timothy Lee, *Can Quake Make a Comeback?*, ESPN (Aug. 14, 2017), https://www.espn.com/esports/story/_/id/20345096/quake-champions-quake-make-comeback.
42. Paul 'Redeye' Chaloner, *This is Esports (and How to Spell it)*, 43 (Bloomsbury (Sport 2020)); Lawrence Phillips, *The History of Esports*, Hotspawn (Apr. 1, 2020), https://www.hotspawn.com/guides/the-history-of-esports; See also iD Software, *What We Do*, https://www.idsoftware.com/en-us#section-games (last visited Jul. 9, 2020).
43. Paul 'Redeye' Chaloner, *This is Esports* (*and How to Spell it*), 43 (Bloomsbury Sport 2020); Tobias M. Scholz, *eSports is Business*: *Management in the World of Competitive Gaming*, 82 (Palgrave Macmillan 2019); See also John Davison, *How 'Quake' Changed Video Games Forever*, Rolling Stone (Jun. 22, 2016, https://www.rollingstone.com/culture/culture-news/how-quake-changed-video-games-forever-187984; Chris Baker, *Meet Dennis 'Thresh' Fong, the Original Pro Gamer*, Rolling Stone (Aug. 30, 2016), https://www.rollingstone.com/culture/culture-news/meet-dennis-thresh-fong-the-original-pro-gamer-103208; See also William Collis, *The Book of Esports*, 45 (Rosetta Books 2020).
44. Paul 'Redeye' Chaloner, *This is Esports* (*and How to Spell it*), 42 (Bloomsbury Sport 2020); Tobias M. Scholz, *eSports is Business*: *Management in the World of Competitive Gaming*, 21 (Palgrave Macmillan 2019); See also Chris Baker, *Meet Dennis 'Thresh' Fong, the Original Pro Gamer*, Rolling Stone (Aug. 30, 2016), https://www.rollingstone.com/culture/culture-news/meet-dennis-thresh-fong-the-original-pro-gamer-103208.
45. Paul 'Redeye' Chaloner, *This is Esports* (*and How to Spell it*), 42 (Bloomsbury Sport 2020); Tobias M. Scholz, *eSports is Business*: *Management in the World of Competitive Gaming*, 21 (Palgrave Macmillan 2019).

46. Lawrence Phillips, *The History of Esports*, Hotspawn (Apr. 1, 2020), https://www.hotspawn.com/guides/the-history-of-esports; See also TL.net, *eSports: A Short History of Nearly Everything by Lari Syrota*, https://tl.net/forum/starcraft-2/249860-esports-a-short-history-of-nearly-everything (last visited Jul. 24, 2020).
47. Paul 'Redeye' Chaloner, *This is Esports (and How to Spell it)*, 42 (Bloomsbury Sport 2020); Tobias M. Scholz, *eSports is Business: Management in the World of Competitive Gaming*, 21 (Palgrave Macmillan 2019); T.L. Taylor, *Raising the Stakes: E-Sports and the Professionalization of Computer Gaming*, 7 (The MIT Press 2012); See also Chris Baker, *Meet Dennis 'Thresh' Fong, the Original Pro Gamer*, Rolling Stone (Aug. 30, 2016), https://www.rollingstone.com/culture/culture-news/meet-dennis-thresh-fong-the-original-pro-gamer-103208.
48. Lawrence Phillips, *The History of Esports*, Hotspawn (Apr. 1, 2020), https://www.hotspawn.com/guides/the-history-of-esports; See also Chris Baker, *Meet Dennis 'Thresh' Fong, the Original Pro Gamer*, Rolling Stone (Aug. 30, 2016), https://www.rollingstone.com/culture/culture-news/meet-dennis-thresh-fong-the-original-pro-gamer-103208.
49. Paul 'Redeye' Chaloner, *This is Esports (and How to Spell it)*, 44 (Bloomsbury Sport 2020); Tobias M. Scholz, *eSports is Business: Management in the World of Competitive Gaming*, 21 (Palgrave Macmillan 2019); Cyber Professional league, *CPL World Tour*, http://www.cplworldtour.com (last visited Jul. 16, 2020); See also Vic Hood, *Esports: Everything You Need to Know*, TechRadar (Oct. 16, 2018), https://www.techradar.com/news/esports-everything-you-need-to-know.
50. Paul 'Redeye' Chaloner, *This is Esports (and How to Spell it)*, 44 (Bloomsbury Sport 2020); Tobias M. Scholz, *eSports is Business: Management in the World of Competitive Gaming*, 21 (Palgrave Macmillan 2019); T.L. Taylor, *Raising the Stakes: E-Sports and the Professionalization of Computer Gaming*, 7 (The MIT Press 2012); See also John Gaudiosi, CPL *Founder Angel Munoz Explains Why He Left ESports and Launched Mass Luminosity*, Forbes (Apr. 9, 2013), https://www.forbes.com/sites/johngaudiosi/2013/04/09/cpl-founder-angel-munoz-explains-why-he-left-esports-and-launched-mass-luminosity/#6e8c42ca648e; Jeffrey R. Young, *Putting Your Face Inside a Video Game*, N.Y. Times (Aug. 9, 2001), https://www.nytimes.com/2001/08/09/technology/circuits/putting-your-face-inside-a-video-game.html.
51. Paul 'Redeye' Chaloner, *This is Esports (and How to Spell it)*, 46 (Bloomsbury Sport 2020); British Esports Association, *A Brief History of Esports and Video Games*, https://britishesports.org/news/a-brief-history-of-esports-and-video-games (last visited Jul. 2, 2020); See also CPL World Tour, *Main Page*, http://www.cplworldtour.com (last visited Jul. 10, 2020).
52. Tobias M. Scholz, *eSports is Business: Management in the World of Competitive Gaming*, 21 (Palgrave Macmillan 2019); See also Greg Miller, *Out of the Arcade*, L.A. Times (Nov. 3, 1997), https://www.latimes.com/archives/la-xpm-1997-nov-03-fi-49823-story.html; Darren Allen, *How Esports Are Taking Over the World*, Tech Radar (Mar. 25, 2019), https://www.techradar.com/news/how-esports-are-taking-over-the-world).
53. Tobias M. Scholz, *eSports is Business: Management in the World of Competitive Gaming*, 21 (Palgrave Macmillan 2019); See also Greg Miller, *Out of the Arcade*, L.A. Times (Nov. 3, 1997), https://www.latimes.com/archives/la-xpm-1997-nov-03-fi-49823-story.html.

54. Tobias M. Scholz, *eSports is Business: Management in the World of Competitive Gaming*, 21 (Palgrave Macmillan 2019).
55. Tobias M. Scholz, *eSports is Business: Management in the World of Competitive Gaming*, 21 (Palgrave Macmillan 2019); See also ESL Gaming GmBH, *Our Story*, https://about.eslgaming.com/history (last visited Jul. 16, 2020; ISPO Sports Business Network, *The History of the Origin of eSports*, https://www.ispo.com/en/markets/history-origin-esports (last visited Jul. 9, 2020).
56. Tobias M. Scholz, *eSports is Business: Management in the World of Competitive Gaming*, 21 (Palgrave Macmillan 2019); See also ISPO Sports Business Network, *The History of the Origin of eSports*, https://www.ispo.com/en/markets/history-origin-esports (last visited Jul. 9, 2020); Modern Times Group, *MTG Completes the Acquisition of Turtle Entertainment* (Sept. 1, 2015), https://www.mtg.com/press-releases/mtg-completes-the-acquisition-of-turtle-entertainment (last visited Jul. 10, 2020).
57. T.L. Taylor, *Raising the Stakes: E-Sports and the Professionalization of Computer Gaming*, 13 (The MIT Press 2012); See also David O' Keefe, *How Blizzard's StarCraft Became South Korea's National Pastime*, The Esports Observer (Oct. 29, 2018), https://esportsobserver.com/starcraft-ii-esports-essentials.
58. Paul 'Redeye' Chaloner, *This is Esports (and How to Spell it)*, 49 (Bloomsbury (Sport 2020)); Lawrence Phillips, *The History of Esports*, Hotspawn (Apr. 1, 2020), https://www.hotspawn.com/guides/the-history-of-esports; See also David O' Keefe, *How Blizzard's StarCraft Became South Korea's National Pastime*, The Esports Observer (Oct. 29, 2018), https://esportsobserver.com/starcraft-ii-esports-essentials.
59. Paul 'Redeye' Chaloner, *This is Esports (and How to Spell it)*, 50 (Bloomsbury Sport 2020); Tobias M. Scholz, *eSports is Business: Management in the World of Competitive Gaming*, 22 (Palgrave Macmillan 2019); T.L. Taylor, *Raising the Stakes: E-Sports and the Professionalization of Computer Gaming*, 18 (The MIT Press 2012); See also Dot Esports Staff, *The Evolution of eSports*, Dot Esports (Jul. 22, 2015), https://dotesports.com/news/the-evolution-of-esports-7693.
60. Paul 'Redeye' Chaloner, *This is Esports (and How to Spell it)*, 50 (Bloomsbury Sport 2020); T.L. Taylor, *Raising the Stakes: E-Sports and the Professionalization of Computer Gaming*, 25 (The MIT Press 2012); See also Valentina Popova, *Esports and Gaming Culture in South Korea: A "National Pastime" or Addictive Disease?*, NOVAsia (Nov. 13, 2018), http://novasiagsis.com/esports-gaming-culture-south-korea-national-pastime-addictive-disease.
61. Paul 'Redeye' Chaloner, *This is Esports (and How to Spell it)*, 50 (Bloomsbury Sport 2020); See also LinkedIn, *Korea e-Sports Association: Overview*, https://www.linkedin.com/company/korea-e-sports-association/about (last visited Jul. 16, 2020).
62. Paul 'Redeye' Chaloner, *This is Esports (and How to Spell it)*, 52 (Bloomsbury Sport 2020); T.L. Taylor, *Raising the Stakes: E-Sports and the Professionalization of Computer Gaming*, 167 (The MIT Press 2012); See also Kwanghee Woo, *StarCraft: Remastered Hasn't Changed How Korea Feels about StarCraft*, P.C. Gamer (Aug. 23, 2017), https://www.pcgamer.com/starcraft-remastered-hasnt-changed-how-korea-feels-about-starcraft; See also William Collis, *The Book of Esports*, 51 (Rosetta Books 2020).

63. Paul 'Redeye' Chaloner, *This is Esports* (*and How to Spell it*), 52 (Bloomsbury Sport 2020); T.L. Taylor, *Raising the Stakes*: *E-Sports and the Professionalization of Computer Gaming*, 91 (The MIT Press 2012); Tobias M. Scholz, *eSports is Business: Management in the World of Competitive Gaming*, 27 (Palgrave Macmillan 2019); See also William Collis, *The Book of Esports*, 53 (Rosetta Books 2020).
64. Paul 'Redeye' Chaloner, *This is Esports* (*and How to Spell it*), 52 (Bloomsbury Sport 2020); Tobias M. Scholz, *eSports is Business*: *Management in the World of Competitive Gaming*, 27 (Palgrave Macmillan 2019); See also Liquipedia, *Boxer*, https://liquipedia.net/starcraft2/BoxeR (last visited Jul. 20, 2020).
65. Paul 'Redeye' Chaloner, *This is Esports* (*and How to Spell it*), 43 (Bloomsbury Sport 2020); British Esports Association, *A Brief History of Esports and Video Games*, https://britishesports.org/news/a-brief-history-of-esports-and-video-g ames (last visited Jul. 2, 2020); See also Counter-Strike: Global Offensive, *History*, https://blog.counter-strike.net/index.php/history/ (last visited Jul. 9, 2020).
66. Paul 'Redeye' Chaloner, *This is Esports* (*and How to Spell it*), 43 (Bloomsbury Sport 2020).
67. Id.; See also Counter-Strike: Global Offensive, *History*, https://blog.counter -strike.net/index.php/history (last visited Jul. 9, 2020); Alex Mcalpine, *What Makes Counter-Strike an Ageless Classic in Esports?*, ESTNN (May 20, 2020), https://estnn.com/what-makes-counter-strike-an-ageless-classic-in-esports.
68. Tobias M. Scholz, *eSports is Business: Management in the World of Competitive Gaming*, 24 (Palgrave Macmillan 2019); Paul 'Redeye' Chaloner, *This is Esports (and How to Spell it)*, 43 (Bloomsbury Sport 2020); See also Counter-Strike: Global Offensive, *History*, https://blog.counter-strike.net/index.php/history (last visited Jul. 9, 2020).
69. Paul 'Redeye' Chaloner, *This is Esports* (*and How to Spell it*), 43 (Bloomsbury Sport 2020); Tobias M. Scholz, *eSports is Business*: *Management in the World of Competitive Gaming*, 24 (Palgrave Macmillan 2019); See also Thomas Llewellyn, *The Rise of an Esports Phenomenon*, Science & Media Museum (Sept. 17, 2018), https://blog.scienceandmediamuseum.org.uk/counter-str ike-esports; Alex Mcalpine, *What Makes Counter-Strike an Ageless Classic in Esports?*, ESTNN (May 20, 2020), https://estnn.com/what-makes-counter-str ike-an-ageless-classic-in-esports.
70. T.L. Taylor, *Raising the Stakes: E-Sports and the Professionalization of Computer Gaming*, 12 (The MIT Press 2012); See also Ryan Taljonick, *Why Counter-Strike is One of the Greatest Games Ever Made*, Game Radar (Nov. 7, 2012), https ://www.gamesradar.com/why-counter-strike-one-greatest-games-ever-made.
71. Paul 'Redeye' Chaloner, *This is Esports* (*and How to Spell it*), 109 (Bloomsbury Sport 2020); See also Counter-Strike: Global Offensive, *History*, https://blog .counter-strike.net/index.php/history/ (last visited Jul. 9, 2020).
72. Paul 'Redeye' Chaloner, *This is Esports* (*and How to Spell it*), 45 (Bloomsbury Sport 2020); See also ESL Gaming, *Johnathan "Fatal1ty" Wendel to Be Inducted into Esports Hall of Fame at Intel Extreme Masters Chicago 2018*, https://www .eslgaming.com/article/johnathan-fatal1ty-wendel-be-inducted-esports-hall-fame-intel-extreme-masters-chicago-2018-4119 (last visited Jul. 16, 2020).

73. Paul 'Redeye' Chaloner, *This is Esports* (*and How to Spell it*), 45 (Bloomsbury Sport 2020); TL.net, *eSports: A Short History of Nearly Everything by Lari Syrota*, https://tl.net/forum/starcraft-2/249860-esports-a-short-history-of-nearly-everything (last visited Jul. 24, 2020); See also Jennifer Ho, *CPL Announces US Events*, Game Spot (May 17, 2006), https://www.gamespot.com/articles/cpl-announces-us-events/1100-2576493.
74. Paul 'Redeye' Chaloner, *This is Esports* (*and How to Spell it*), 45 (Bloomsbury Sport 2020); See also Johnathan (Fatal1ty) Wendel, *The Original*, The Players' Tribune (Dec. 23, 2016), https://www.theplayerstribune.com/en-us/articles/fatal1ty-esports-the-original.
75. Alex Prewitt, *Fatal1ty, E-sports' Original Star, Goes Corporate as Sport Enters New Era*, Sports Illustrated (Jun. 30, 2016), https://www.si.com/more-sports/2016/06/30/fatal1ty-esports-professional-gaming-prize-money-motherboards.
76. Paul 'Redeye' Chaloner, *This is Esports* (*and How to Spell it*), 45 (Bloomsbury Sport 2020); See also Fatal1ty, *The Brand*, https://fatal1ty.com/the-brand (last visited Jul. 16, 2020).
77. Paul 'Redeye' Chaloner, *This is Esports* (*and How to Spell it*), 45 (Bloomsbury Sport 2020); T.L. Taylor, *Raising the Stakes*: *E-Sports and the Professionalization of Computer Gaming*, 85 (The MIT Press 2012); See also I.M.D.B, *"True Life I'm a Gamer (TV Episode 2003)*, https://www.imdb.com/title/tt1998106 (last visited Jul. 6, 2020); N.Y. Times, *Video Games Go Pro: Fatal1ty* (Dec. 4, 2005), https://www.nytimes.com/video/technology/1194817098688/fatal1ty.html.
78. Tobias M. Scholz, *eSports is Business: Management in the World of Competitive Gaming*, 22 (Palgrave Macmillan 2019); T.L. Taylor, *Raising the Stakes: E-Sports and the Professionalization of Computer Gaming*, 10 (The MIT Press 2012); See also World Cyber Games, *About*, https://www.wcg.com/2019/about/about-wcg?lang=en (last visited Jul. 16, 2020).
79. Tobias M. Scholz, *eSports is Business: Management in the World of Competitive Gaming*, 22 (Palgrave Macmillan 2019); T.L. Taylor, *Raising the Stakes: E-Sports and the Professionalization of Computer Gaming*, 22 (The MIT Press 2012).
80. *Id.* at 205.
81. Paul 'Redeye' Chaloner, *This is Esports (and How to Spell it)*, 46 (Bloomsbury (Sport 2020)); TL.net, *eSports: A Short History of Nearly Everything by Lari Syrota*, https://tl.net/forum/starcraft-2/249860-esports-a-short-history-of-nearly-everything (last visited Jul. 24, 2020); Trey Walker, *The World Cyber Games Tournament Begins*, Game Spot (Dec. 6, 2001), https://www.gamespot.com/articles/the-world-cyber-games-tournament-begins/1100-2830722; See also WCG Official Website, *WCG History*, https://web.archive.org/web/20120117111201/http://www.wcg.com/6th/history/wcgchallenge/wcgchallenge.asp (last visited Jul. 6, 2020).
82. TL.net, *eSports: A Short History of Nearly Everything by Lari Syrota*, https://tl.net/forum/starcraft-2/249860-esports-a-short-history-of-nearly-everything (last visited Jul. 24, 2020); Trey Walker, *The World Cyber Games Tournament Begins*, Game Spot (Dec. 6, 2001), https://www.gamespot.com/articles/the-world-cyber-games-tournament-begins/1100-2830722; See also Liquipedia, *2001 CPL Winter Championship*, https://liquipedia.net/counterstrike/2001_CPL_Winter_Championship (last visited Jul. 6, 2020).

83. Paul 'Redeye' Chaloner, *This is Esports* (*and How to Spell it*), 46 (Bloomsbury Sport 2020); T.L. Taylor, *Raising the Stakes*: *E-Sports and the Professionalization of Computer Gaming*, 8 (The MIT Press 2012).
84. Paul 'Redeye' Chaloner, *This is Esports* (*and How to Spell it*), 46 (Bloomsbury Sport 2020); T.L. Taylor, *Raising the Stakes*: *E-Sports and the Professionalization of Computer Gaming*, 8 (The MIT Press 2012); See also Danl Haas, *Playing with Others: The Cyberathlete Amateur League*, Destructoid (Jan. 29, 2009), https://www.destructoid.com/playing-with-others-the-cyberathlete-amateur-league-117785.phtml.
85. Tobias M. Scholz, *eSports is Business: Management in the World of Competitive Gaming*, 21 (Palgrave Macmillan 2019); T.L. Taylor, *Raising the Stakes: E-Sports and the Professionalization of Computer Gaming*, 145 (The MIT Press 2012); Paul 'Redeye' Chaloner, *This is Esports (and How to Spell it)*, 47 (Bloomsbury Sport 2020); See also Major League Gaming, *Home Page*, https://www.mlg.com/ (last visited Jul. 16, 2020); Esports.net, *Major League Gaming*, https://www.esports.net/wiki/tournaments/major-league-gaming (last visited Jul. 17, 2020).
86. Imad Khan, *Melee Has Dominated the Smash Esports Scene for Nearly Two Decades. Its Reign May Be Over*, Launcher (Jan. 28, 2020), https://www.washingtonpost.com/video-games/esports/2020/01/28/melee-has-dominated-smash-esports-scene-nearly-two-decades-its-reign-may-be-over; See also Eli Hunt, *Wide World of Esports: Super Smash Brothers, the esport*, UT Daily Beacon (Sept. 24, 2019), http://www.utdailybeacon.com/opinion/columns/wide-world-of-esports-super-smash-brothers-the-esport/article_76a27f30-ded1-11e9-bdbe-935f9f30b8ef.html.
87. Paul 'Redeye' Chaloner, *This is Esports* (*and How to Spell it*), 125 (Bloomsbury Sport 2020); See also IGN Staff, *Smashing Success*, IGN (Oct. 28, 1999), https://www.ign.com/articles/1999/10/29/smashing-success-2.
88. Nintendo, *Smash Bros. DOJO!!*, https://www.smashbros.com/wii/en_us/index.html (last visited Jul. 10, 2020); Nintendo, *Super Smash Brothers Ultimate*, https://www.smashbros.com/en_US/index.html (last visited Jul. 10, 2020); See also Imad Khan, *Melee Has Dominated the Smash Esports Scene for Nearly Two Decades. Its Reign May Be Over*, Launcher (Jan. 28, 2020), https://www.washingtonpost.com/video-games/esports/2020/01/28/melee-has-dominated-smash-esports-scene-nearly-two-decades-its-reign-may-be-over; Jonah Lee-Ash, *Super Smash Bros. Melee - History of Smash*, Akshon Esports (Feb. 19, 2019), https://www.akshonesports.com/2019/02/super-smash-bros-melee-history-of-smash.
89. Paul 'Redeye' Chaloner, *This is Esports* (*and How to Spell it*), 126 (Bloomsbury Sport 2020); See also Esportspedia, *MLG New York Championships 2004*, https://www.esportspedia.com/halo/MLG_New:York_Championships_2004 (last visited Jul. 10, 2020); Liquipedia Smash Wiki, *MLG New York 2004*, https://liquipedia.net/smash/MLG/2004/New:York (last visited Jul. 10, 2020).
90. East Point Pictures, *The Smash Brothers*, http://www.eastpointpictures.com/documentary (last visited Jul. 10, 2020); Steven Rodriguez, *Super Smash Bros. Melee at Evolution 2007*, Nintendo World Report (Feb. 14, 2007), http://www.nintendoworldreport.com/news/12909/super-smash-bros-melee-at-evolution-2007; See also Liquipedia Smash-Wiki, *Evo World 2007*, https://liquipedia.net/smash/EVO/2007/World (last visited Jul. 10, 2020).

91. Sean Smith, *Super Smash Bros. Melee Smash Records at Evo*, GodIsAGeek.com (Jul. 15, 2013), https://www.godisageek.com/2013/07/super-smash-bros-melee-smashes-records-evo; See also Owen Good, *All the Memories of an Unforgettable EVO 2013 Are in this Superb Video*, Kotaku (Jul. 21, 2013), https://kotaku.com/all-the-memories-of-an-unforgettable-evo-2013-are-in-th-857531465; SmashWiki, *Tournament: EVO 2013*, https://www.ssbwiki.com/Tournament:EVO_2013 (last visited Jul. 10, 2020).
92. Paul 'Redeye' Chaloner, *This is Esports (and How to Spell it)*, 128 (Bloomsbury Sport 2020); Shabana Arif, *EVO 2019 Fighting Tournament Lineup Drops Smash Bros. Melee in Favor of Ultimate*, IGN (Feb. 27, 2019), https://www.ign.com/articles/2019/02/27/evo-2019-fighting-tournament-lineup-drops-smash-bros-melee-in-favor-of-ultimate.
93. East Point Pictures, *The Smash Brothers*, http://www.eastpointpictures.com/documentary (last visited Jul. 10, 2020; See also Garrett Jutte, *Nintendo GameCube Classic Super Smash Bros. Melee Gets Fan Made Documentary*, Liberty Voice (Nov. 30, 2013), https://guardianlv.com/2013/11/nintendo-gamecube-classic-super-smash-bros-melee-gets-fan-made-documentaryvideo.
94. Patricia Hernandez, *A Fascinating Look at the World's Best Super Smash Bros. Players*, Kotaku (Oct. 16, 2013), https://kotaku.com/http-youtu-be-6tgwh-qxpv8-a-smashing-documentary-che-1446707322; East Point Pictures, *The Smash Brothers*, http://www.eastpointpictures.com/documentary (last visited Jul. 10, 2020).
95. Tobias M. Scholz, *eSports is Business: Management in the World of Competitive Gaming*, 23 (Palgrave Macmillan 2019); TL.net, *eSports: A Short History of Nearly Everything by Lari Syrota*, https://tl.net/forum/starcraft-2/249860-esports-a-short-history-of-nearly-everything (last visited Jul. 24, 2020).
96. Tobias M. Scholz, *eSports is Business: Management in the World of Competitive Gaming*, 23 (Palgrave Macmillan 2019); TL.net, *eSports: A Short History of Nearly Everything by Lari Syrota*, https://tl.net/forum/starcraft-2/249860-esports-a-short-history-of-nearly-everything (last visited Jul. 24, 2020); See also EsportsEarnings.com, *Element—Ola Moum*, https://www.esportsearnings.com/players/4321-element-ola-moum/team-history (last visited Jul. 6, 2020).
97. Paul 'Redeye' Chaloner, *This is Esports (and How to Spell it)*, 47 (Bloomsbury Sport 2020).
98. T.L. Taylor, *Raising the Stakes: E-Sports and the Professionalization of Computer Gaming*, 146 (The MIT Press 2012); TL.net, *eSports: A Short History of Nearly Everything by Lari Syrota*, https://tl.net/forum/starcraft-2/249860-esports-a-short-history-of-nearly-everything (last visited Jul. 24, 2020); See also E.S.W.C., *About ESWC*, https://www.eswc.com/page/about-eswc (last visited Jul. 16, 2020).
99. TL.net, *eSports: A Short History of Nearly Everything by Lari Syrota*, https://tl.net/forum/starcraft-2/249860-esports-a-short-history-of-nearly-everything (last visited Jul. 24, 2020); See also E.S.W.C., *About ESWC*, https://www.eswc.com/page/about-eswc (last visited Jul. 16, 2020).
100. Paul 'Redeye' Chaloner, *This is Esports (and How to Spell it)*, 53 (Bloomsbury Sport 2020); Tobias M. Scholz, *eSports is Business: Management in the World of Competitive Gaming*, 22 (Palgrave Macmillan 2019); See also Tom McNamara,

2004 World Cyber Games Grand Final Preview, IGN (Jun. 16, 2012), https://www.ign.com/articles/2004/10/06/2004-world-cyber-games-grand-final-preview.

101. Paul 'Redeye' Chaloner, *This is Esports (and How to Spell it)*, 53 (Bloomsbury Sport 2020); Tobias M. Scholz, *eSports is Business: Management in the World of Competitive Gaming*, 27 (Palgrave Macmillan 2019); See also WCG, 2004 San Francisco, https://www.wcg.com/2019/history/view/wcg-2004-san-francisco?lang=en (last visited Jul. 16, 2020).
102. T.L. Taylor, *Raising the Stakes: E-Sports and the Professionalization of Computer Gaming*, 23 (The MIT Press 2012); TL.net, *eSports: A Short History of Nearly Everything by Lari Syrota*, https://tl.net/forum/starcraft-2/249860-esports-a-short-history-of-nearly-everything (last visited Jul. 24, 2020); See also World Cyber Games, *2008 KÖLN*, https://www.wcg.com/2019/history/view/wcg-2008-koln?lang=en (last visited on Jul. 9, 2020); See also IGN Staff, *World Cyber Games Announces Official 2008 Global Tournament Games* (Mar. 17, 2008), https://www.ign.com/articles/2008/03/17/world-cyber-games-announces-official-2008-global-tournament-games; Liquipedia, *World Cyber Games 2008*, https://liquipedia.net/warcraft/World_Cyber_Games/2008 (last visited on Jul. 9, 2020).
103. Paul 'Redeye' Chaloner, *This is Esports (and How to Spell it)*, 55 (Bloomsbury Sport 2020).
104. *Id.* at 123; Chris Baker, *Flashback: Why 2004 'Street Fighter' Match is Esports' Most Thrilling Moment*, Rolling Stone (Jul. 21, 2016), https://www.rollingstone.com/culture/culture-news/flashback-why-2004-street-fighter-match-is-esports-most-thrilling-moment-103566; See also Arash Markazi, *Daigo and JWong: The Legacy of Street Fighter's Moment 37*, ESPN (Aug. 25, 2016), https://www.espn.com/esports/story/_/id/17391663/daigo-jwong-legacy-street-fighter-moment-37; Stephen Kleckner, *Spotlight on the Evolution 2K4 Fighting Game Tournament*, Game Spot (Aug. 18, 2004), https://www.gamespot.com/articles/spotlight-on-the-evolution-2k4-fighting-game-tournament/1100-6103845.
105. Chris Baker, *Flashback: Why 2004 'Street Fighter' Match Is Esports' Most Thrilling Moment*, Rolling Stone (Jul. 21, 2016), https://www.rollingstone.com/culture/culture-news/flashback-why-2004-street-fighter-match-is-esports-most-thrilling-moment-103566.
106. *Id.*
107. Paul 'Redeye' Chaloner, *This is Esports (and How to Spell it)*, 123 (Bloomsbury Sport 2020); Chris Baker, *Flashback: Why 2004 'Street Fighter' Match is Esports' Most Thrilling Moment*, Rolling Stone (Jul. 21, 2016), https://www.rollingstone.com/culture/culture-news/flashback-why-2004-street-fighter-match-is-esports-most-thrilling-moment-103566.
108. *Id.*
109. *Id.*
110. BusinessWire, *The Cyberathlete Professional League $1·000·000 World Tour Finals to Culminate Nov. 22, 2005, in New York City as MTV Televises All the Action*, https://www.businesswire.com/news/home/20051012005278/en/Cyberathlete-Professional-League-1000000-World-Tour-Finals (last visited Jul. 16, 2020).

111. Paul 'Redeye' Chaloner, *This is Esports (and How to Spell it)*, 59 (Bloomsbury Sport 2020); Tobias M. Scholz, *eSports is Business: Management in the World of Competitive Gaming*, 25 (Palgrave Macmillan 2019).
112. Paul 'Redeye' Chaloner, *This is Esports (and How to Spell it)*, 59 (Bloomsbury Sport 2020); Tobias M. Scholz, *eSports is Business: Management in the World of Competitive Gaming*, 25 (Palgrave Macmillan 2019); See also Johnathan (Fatal1ty) Wendel, *The Original*, The Players' Tribune (Dec. 23, 2016), https://www.theplayerstribune.com/en-us/articles/fatal1ty-esports-the-original; GamesIndustry.biz, *Fatal1ty Takes Home $150,000 1st Prize in CPL World Tour Finals Championship*, https://www.gamesindustry.biz/articles/fatal1ty-takes-home-150000-1st-prize-in-cpl-world-tour-finals-championship (last visited Jul. 16, 2020).
113. Paul 'Redeye' Chaloner, *This is Esports (and How to Spell it)*, 62 (Bloomsbury Sport 2020); Tobias M. Scholz, *eSports is Business: Management in the World of Competitive Gaming*, 25 (Palgrave Macmillan 2019); See also Gamesindustry.biz, *Auravision Announces Fatal1ty Brand Partners as a Major Sponsor for World Series of Video Games*, https://www.gamesindustry.biz/articles/auravision-announces-fatal1ty-brand-partners-as-a-major-sponsor-for-world-series-of-video-games (last visited Jul. 16, 2020).
114. Paul 'Redeye' Chaloner, *This is Esports (and How to Spell it)*, 62 (Bloomsbury Sport 2020); See also Liquipedia, *2006 Intel Summer Championship*, https://liquipedia.net/counterstrike/2006_Intel_Summer_Championship (last visited Jul. 8, 2020).
115. Paul 'Redeye' Chaloner, *This is Esports (and How to Spell it)*, 63 (Bloomsbury Sport 2020).
116. Tobias M. Scholz, *eSports is Business: Management in the World of Competitive Gaming*, 25 (Palgrave Macmillan 2019); See also Robert Briel, *Giga TV ceases broadcasts*, BroadbandTVNews (Mar. 31, 2009), https://www.broadbandtvnews.com/2009/03/31/giga-tv-ceases-broadcasts.
117. Paul 'Redeye' Chaloner, *This is Esports (and How to Spell it)*, 63 (Bloomsbury Sport 2020); See also Tim Surette, *MLB Nabs TV, Mobile Deal*, Game Spot (Apr. 17, 2006), https://www.gamespot.com/articles/mlg-nabs-tv-mobile-deal/1100-6147757.
118. Paul 'Redeye' Chaloner, *This is Esports (and How to Spell it)*, 63 (Bloomsbury Sport 2020); T.L. Taylor, *Raising the Stakes: E-Sports and the Professionalization of Computer Gaming*, 147 (The MIT Press 2012); Tobias M. Scholz, *eSports is Business: Management in the World of Competitive Gaming*, 26 (Palgrave Macmillan 2019); See also DIRECTV, *CGS*, https://www.directv.com/DTVAPP/global/contentPage.jsp?assetId=2950003 (last visited Jul. 16, 2020).
119. Paul 'Redeye' Chaloner, *This is Esports (and How to Spell it)*, 63 (Bloomsbury Sport 2020); T.L. Taylor, *Raising the Stakes: E-Sports and the Professionalization of Computer Gaming*, 138 (The MIT Press 2012); See also Lawrence Phillips, *CGS: A Concept "Ahead of Its Time,"* Hotspawn (Apr. 15, 2020), https://www.hotspawn.com/guides/championship-gaming-series-ahead-of-its-time.
120. Paul 'Redeye' Chaloner, *This is Esports (and How to Spell it)*, 63 (Bloomsbury Sport 2020); T.L. Taylor, *Raising the Stakes: E-Sports and the Professionalization of Computer Gaming*, 138 (The MIT Press 2012); See also Ryan Kim, *League Beginning for Video Gamers*, S.F. Gate (Jun. 11, 2007), https://www.sfgate.com/business/article/League-beginning-for-video-gamers-2587547.php.

121. Paul 'Redeye' Chaloner, *This is Esports (and How to Spell it)*, 65 (Bloomsbury Sport 2020); T.L. Taylor, *Raising the Stakes: E-Sports and the Professionalization of Computer Gaming*, 218 (The MIT Press 2012).
122. Paul 'Redeye' Chaloner, *This is Esports (and How to Spell it)*, 66 (Bloomsbury Sport 2020); T.L. Taylor, *Raising the Stakes: E-Sports and the Professionalization of Computer Gaming*, 247 (The MIT Press 2012); See also Tameka Kee, *Championship Gaming Series Closes Down*, CBS News (Nov. 19, 2008), https://www.cbsnews.com/news/championship-gaming-series-closes-down.
123. Paul 'Redeye' Chaloner, *This is Esports (and How to Spell it)*, 66 (Bloomsbury Sport 2020); T.L. Taylor, *Raising the Stakes: E-Sports and the Professionalization of Computer Gaming*, 233 (The MIT Press 2012); Tobias M. Scholz, eSports is Business: Management in the World of Competitive Gaming, 26 (Palgrave Macmillan 2019).
124. Paul 'Redeye' Chaloner, *This is Esports (and How to Spell it)*, 66 (Bloomsbury Sport 2020); T.L. Taylor, *Raising the Stakes: E-Sports and the Professionalization of Computer Gaming*, 233 (The MIT Press 2012); Tobias M. Scholz, *eSports is Business: Management in the World of Competitive Gaming*, 26 (Palgrave Macmillan 2019); See also Michael McWhertor, *Championship Gaming Series Coming to G4*, Kotaku (Jun. 16, 2008), https://kotaku.com/championship-gaming-series-coming-to-g4-5016946.
125. Seth Schiesel, *Video Game Matches to Be Televised on CBS*, N.Y. Times (Jul. 28, 2007), https://www.nytimes.com/2007/07/28/arts/television/28vide.html.
126. Jon Robinson, *Madden Nation: ESPN and EA Team for Reality Show*, IGN (Dec. 7, 2005), https://www.ign.com/articles/2005/12/07/madden-nation.
127. *Id.*
128. T.L. Taylor, *Raising the Stakes: E-Sports and the Professionalization of Computer Gaming*, 211 (The MIT Press 2012); See also Seth Schiesel, *Video Game Matches to Be Televised on CBS*, N.Y. Times (Jul. 28, 2007), https://www.nytimes.com/2007/07/28/arts/television/28vide.html; Michael McWhertor, *Championship Gaming Series Coming to G4*, Kotaku (Jun. 16, 2008), https://kotaku.com/championship-gaming-series-coming-to-g4-5016946.
129. T.L. Taylor, *Raising the Stakes: E-Sports and the Professionalization of Computer Gaming*, 153 (The MIT Press 2012); Tobias M. Scholz, *eSports is Business: Management in the World of Competitive Gaming*, 28 (Palgrave Macmillan 2019); See also S.K. Gaming, *Launch of G7 Federation*, https://www.sk-gaming.com/content/4537-launch-of-g7-federation (last visited Jul. 9, 2020).
130. T.L. Taylor, *Raising the Stakes: E-Sports and the Professionalization of Computer Gaming*, 175 (The MIT Press 2012); Tobias M. Scholz, *eSports is Business: Management in the World of Competitive Gaming*, 28 (Palgrave Macmillan 2019); See also S.K. Gaming, *Launch of G7 Federation*, https://www.sk-gaming.com/content/4537-launch-of-g7-federation (last visited Jul. 9, 2020).
131. T.L. Taylor, *Raising the Stakes: E-Sports and the Professionalization of Computer Gaming*, 175 (The MIT Press 2012); Tobias M. Scholz, *eSports is Business: Management in the World of Competitive Gaming*, 28 (Palgrave Macmillan 2019).
132. Tobias M. Scholz, *eSports is Business: Management in the World of Competitive Gaming*, 28 (Palgrave Macmillan 2019); See also TL.net, *eSports: A Short History of Nearly Everything by Lari Syrota*, https://tl.net/forum/starcraft-2/249860-esports-a-short-history-of-nearly-everything (last visited Jul. 24, 2020);

George Miller, *Five New Members Join IESF*, European Gaming (Jun. 30, 2020), https://europeangaming.eu/portal/latest-news/2020/06/30/73275/five-new-members-join-iesf.

133. Paul 'Redeye' Chaloner, *This is Esports (and How to Spell it)*, 76 (Bloomsbury Sport 2020).
134. StarCraft II, *Official Game Site*, https://starcraft2.com/en-us (last visited Jul. 25, 2020).
135. Paul 'Redeye' Chaloner, *This is Esports (and How to Spell it)*, 76 (Bloomsbury Sport 2020); Tobias M. Scholz, *eSports is Business: Management in the World of Competitive Gaming*, 31 (Palgrave Macmillan 2019); See also Kevin Hovdestad, *The Rise and Fall of StarCraft II as an eSport*, IGN (May 7, 2020), https://www.ign.com/articles/2016/03/22/the-rise-and-fall-of-starcraft-ii-as-an-esport.
136. Paul 'Redeye' Chaloner, *This is Esports (and How to Spell it)*, 76 (Bloomsbury Sport 2020).
137. Paul 'Redeye' Chaloner, *This is Esports (and How to Spell it)*, 77 (Bloomsbury Sport 2020).
138. Id.; See also Tom Goldman, *Blizzard Prepares to Sue Over Illegal StarCraft TV Broadcasts*, The Escapist (Dec. 4, 2010), https://v1.escapistmagazine.com/news/view/105854-Blizzard-Prepares-to-Sue-Over-Illegal-StarCraft-TV-Broadcasts; Max Miroff, Note, *Tiebreaker: An Antitrust Analysis of Esports*, 52 Colum. J.L. & Soc. Probs. 2, 181 (2018).
139. David O' Keefe, *How Blizzard's StarCraft Became South Korea's National Pastime*, The Esports Observer (Oct. 29, 2018), https://esportsobserver.com/starcraft-ii-esports-essentials.
140. Paul 'Redeye' Chaloner, *This is Esports (and How to Spell it)*, 78 (Bloomsbury Sport 2020).
141. David O' Keefe, *How Blizzard's StarCraft Became South Korea's National Pastime*, The Esports Observer (Oct. 29, 2018), https://esportsobserver.com/starcraft-ii-esports-essentials.
142. TL.net, *eSports: A Short History of Nearly Everything by Lari Syrota*, https://tl.net/forum/starcraft-2/249860-esports-a-short-history-of-nearly-everything (last visited Jul. 24, 2020); See also *Liquipedia, Global StarCraft II League*, https://liquipedia.net/starcraft2/Global_StarCraft_II_League (last visited Jul. 13, 2020).
143. Paul 'Redeye' Chaloner, *This is Esports (and How to Spell it)*, 80 (Bloomsbury Sport 2020); Christina Kelly, *Scarlett Named Highest-Earning Female Esports Player*, ESPN (Nov. 13, 2016, https://www.espn.com/espnw/sports/story/_/id/18039852/guinness-world-records-starcraft-ii-scarlett-highest-paid-female-esports-player.
144. Paul 'Redeye' Chaloner, *This is Esports (and How to Spell it)*, 80 (Bloomsbury Sport 2020); See also Imad Khan, *Scarlett Becomes First Woman to Win Major StarCraft II Tournament*, ESPN (Feb. 7, 2018), https://www.espn.com/esports/story/_/id/22358896/scarlett-becomes-first-woman-win-major-starcraft-ii-tournament; Dot Esports Staff, *Meet Scarlett, the 20-Year-Old Woman Who's Blazing Trails in 'StarCraft,'* Dot Esports (Dec. 21, 2013), https://dotesports.com/general/news/sasha-scarlett-hostyn-starcraft-esports.
145. Paul 'Redeye' Chaloner, *This is Esports (and How to Spell it)*, 70 (Bloomsbury Sport 2020); James Cook, *Twitch Founder: We Turned A 'Terrible Idea' into a Billion-Dollar Company*, Business Insider (Oct. 20, 2014), https://www.businessinsider.com/the-story-of-video-game-streaming-site-twitch-2014-10.

146. Tobias M. Scholz, *eSports is Business: Management in the World of Competitive Gaming*, 32 (Palgrave Macmillan 2019); See also Rachel Weber, *Justin.tv Becomes Twitch Interactive*, Gamesindustry.biz (Feb. 10, 2014), https://www.gamesindustry.biz/articles/2014-02-10-justin-tv-becomes-twitch-interactive; Businesswire, *Justin.tv Launches TwitchTV, the World's Largest Competitive Video Gaming Network* (Jun. 6, 2011), https://www.businesswire.com/news/home/20110606005437/en/Justin.tv-Launches-TwitchTV-World%E2%80%99s-Largest-Competitive-Video (last visited Jul. 16, 2020); See also William Collis, *The Book of Esports*, 39 (Rosetta Books 2020).

147. Paul 'Redeye' Chaloner, *This is Esports (and How to Spell it)*, 72 (Bloomsbury Sport 2020); Tobias M. Scholz, *eSports is Business: Management in the World of Competitive Gaming*, 32 (Palgrave Macmillan 2019); See also Darren Geeter, *Twitch Created a Business around Watching Video Games—Here's How Amazon Has Changed the Service Since Buying it in 2014*, CNBC (Feb. 26, 2019), https://www.cnbc.com/2019/02/26/history-of-twitch-gaming-livestreaming-and-youtube.html.

148. Paul 'Redeye' Chaloner, *This is Esports (and How to Spell it)*, 73 (Bloomsbury Sport 2020); Tobias M. Scholz, *eSports is Business: Management in the World of Competitive Gaming*, 32 (Palgrave Macmillan 2019).

149. Paul 'Redeye' Chaloner, *This is Esports (and How to Spell it)*, 79 (Bloomsbury Sport 2020).

150. Tobias M. Scholz, *eSports is Business: Management in the World of Competitive Gaming*, 33 (Palgrave Macmillan 2019).

151. *Id.*

152. Paul 'Redeye' Chaloner, *This is Esports (and How to Spell it)*, 70 (Bloomsbury Sport 2020); Tobias M. Scholz, *eSports is Business: Management in the World of Competitive Gaming*, 34 (Palgrave Macmillan 2019); See also Alyson Shontell, *Twitch CEO: Here's Why We Sold to Amazon for $970 Million*, Business Insider (Aug. 25, 2014), https://www.businessinsider.com/twitch-ceo-heres-why-we-sold-to-amazon-for-970-million-2014-8.

153. Paul 'Redeye' Chaloner, *This is Esports (and How to Spell it)*, 78 (Bloomsbury Sport 2020).

154. Id.; See also Red Bull, *Meet the First eSports Entrepreneur*, https://www.redbull.com/gb-en/esports-entrepreneur-sean-plott-gaming-star-craft (last visited Jul. 16, 2020).

155. Paul 'Redeye' Chaloner, *This is Esports (and How to Spell it)*, 78 (Bloomsbury Sport 2020).

156. Id.; See also Shawn Farner, *The Untold Truth of Sean 'Day9' Plott*, SVG (Aug. 10, 2018), https://www.svg.com/131041/the-untold-truth-of-sean-day9-plott.

157. Paul 'Redeye' Chaloner, *This is Esports (and How to Spell it)*, 78 (Bloomsbury Sport 2020); See also Shawn Farner, *The Untold Truth of Sean 'Day9' Plott*, SVG (Aug. 10, 2018), https://www.svg.com/131041/the-untold-truth-of-sean-day9-plott.

158. Paul 'Redeye' Chaloner, *This is Esports (and How to Spell it)*, 82 (Bloomsbury (Sport 2020)); Lawrence Phillips, *The History of Esports*, Hotspawn (Apr. 1, 2020), https://www.hotspawn.com/guides/the-history-of-esports; See also Mike Minotti, *The History of MOBAs: From Mod to Sensation*, Venture Beat (Sept. 1, 2014), https://venturebeat.com/2014/09/01/the-history-of-mobas-from-mod-to-sensation; See also William Collis, *The Book of Esports*, 60-61 (Rosetta Books 2020).

159. Paul 'Redeye' Chaloner, *This is Esports* (*and How to Spell it*), 92 (Bloomsbury Sport 2020); See also Riot Games, Welcome to League of Legends, https://play.na.leagueoflegends.com/en_US (last visited Jul. 25, 2020); IGN Staff, *Riot Games Brings League of Legends to PAX 2009*, IGN (Jul. 13, 2016), https://www.ign.com/articles/2009/09/01/riot-games-brings-league-of-legends-to-pax-2009; See also William Collis, *The Book of Esports*, 66 (Rosetta Books 2020).
160. Paul 'Redeye' Chaloner, *This is Esports* (*and How to Spell it*), 92 (Bloomsbury Sport 2020); See also Imad Khan, *More than One Percent of the Global Population is Playing 'League of Legends,'* Digital Trends (Sept. 16, 2016), https://www.digitaltrends.com/gaming/league-of-legends-100-million-players.
161. Paul 'Redeye' Chaloner, *This is Esports* (*and How to Spell it*), 90 (Bloomsbury Sport 2020); See also Chris Thursten, *Dota 2 Release Date Set for this Summer*, P.C. Gamer (Jun. 17, 2013), https://www.pcgamer.com/uk/dota-2-release-date-set-for-this-summer.
162. Riot Games, *Home of the LCS (League of Leagends Championship Series)*, https://nexus.leagueoflegends.com/en-us/esports (last visited Jul. 16, 2020).
163. Tobias M. Scholz, *eSports is Business: Management in the World of Competitive Gaming*, 32 (Palgrave Macmillan 2019); Eric Van Allen, *How Exactly Does Dota 2 Come Up with Over $20 Million in Prizes for Its Biggest Event?*, Kotaku (Jul. 13, 2017), https://compete.kotaku.com/how-exactly-does-dota-2-come-up-with-over-20-million-i-1796879005.
164. Tobias M. Scholz, *eSports is Business: Management in the World of Competitive Gaming*, 32 (Palgrave Macmillan 2019); TL.net, *eSports: A Short History of Nearly Everything by Lari Syrota*, https://tl.net/forum/starcraft-2/249860-esports-a-short-history-of-nearly-everything (last visited Jul. 24, 2020); See also S.K. Gaming, *ESWC 2008 Grand Final—DotA*, https://www.sk-gaming.com/event/1099-eswc-2008-grand-final/tournament/119-dota (last visited Jul. 16, 2020).
165. Valve, *Dota 2—The International*, https://www.dota2.com/international/overview (last visited Jul. 16, 2020).
166. Noah Smith, *How the League of Legends World Championship Became the Super Bowl of Esports*, Launcher (Nov. 7, 2019), https://www.washingtonpost.com/video-games/esports/2019/11/07/how-league-legends-world-championship-became-super-bowl-esports.
167. Lawrence Phillips, *The History of Esports*, Hotspawn (Apr. 1, 2020), https://www.hotspawn.com/guides/the-history-of-esports; Paul 'Redeye' Chaloner, *This is Esports (and How to Spell it)*, 92 (Bloomsbury Sport 2020); Noah Smith, *How the League of Legends World Championship became the Super Bowl of esports*, Launcher (Nov. 7, 2019), https://www.washingtonpost.com/video-games/esports/2019/11/07/how-league-legends-world-championship-became-super-bowl-esports.
168. Paul 'Redeye' Chaloner, *This is Esports* (*and How to Spell it*), 110 (Bloomsbury Sport 2020); Tobias M. Scholz, *eSports is Business*: *Management in the World of Competitive Gaming*, 34 (Palgrave Macmillan 2019); See also Jess Wells, *Dota 2's the International: Winners, Teams, Prize Pools, and More*, The Load Out (May 1, 2020), https://www.theloadout.com/tournaments/the-international/dota-2-ti.

169. Paul 'Redeye' Chaloner, *This is Esports (and How to Spell it)*, 92 (Bloomsbury Sport 2020); Tobias M. Scholz, *eSports is Business: Management in the World of Competitive Gaming*, 29 (Palgrave Macmillan 2019); See also Andy Chalk, *Intel Extreme Masters Will not Feature League of Legends Events this Season*, P.C. Gamer (May 23, 2017), https://www.pcgamer.com/uk/intel-extreme-masters-will-not-feature-league-of-legends-events-this-season.
170. Paul 'Redeye' Chaloner, *This is Esports (and How to Spell it)*, 92 (Bloomsbury Sport 2020); Tobias M. Scholz, *eSports is Business: Management in the World of Competitive Gaming*, 31 (Palgrave Macmillan 2019); See also Riot Games, *Home of the LCS (League of Legends Championship Series)*, https://nexus.leagueoflegends.com/en-us/esports (last visited Jul. 16, 2020); See also William Collis, *The Book of Esports*, 71 (Rosetta Books 2020).
171. Paul 'Redeye' Chaloner, *This is Esports (and How to Spell it)*, 92 (Bloomsbury Sport 2020); Tobias M. Scholz, *eSports is Business: Management in the World of Competitive Gaming*, 31 (Palgrave Macmillan 2019); See also Riot Games, *Home of the LCS (League of Legends Championship Series)*, https://nexus.leagueoflegends.com/en-us/esports (last visited Jul. 16, 2020).
172. Tobias M. Scholz, *eSports is Business: Management in the World of Competitive Gaming*, 31 (Palgrave Macmillan 2019).
173. Paul Tassi, *League of Legends Finals Sells Out LA's Staples Center in an Hour*, Forbes (Aug. 24, 2013), https://www.forbes.com/sites/insertcoin/2013/08/24/league-of-legends-finals-sells-out-las-staples-center-in-an-hour/#126ded0f32b8.
174. Paul Tassi 40,*000 Korean Fans Watch SSW Win 2014 'League of Legends' World Championship*, Forbes (Oct. 19, 2014), https://www.forbes.com/sites/insertcoin/2014/10/19/40000-live-korean-fans-watch-ssw-win-2014-league-of-legends-world-championship/#6c705bb0735f.
175. *Id.*
176. Austin Goslin, *The 2018 League of Legends World Finals Had Nearly 100 Million Viewers*, Rift Herald (Dec. 11, 2018), https://www.riftherald.com/2018/12/11/18136237/riot-2018-league-of-legends-world-finals-viewers-prize-pool.
177. Tobias M. Scholz, *eSports is Business: Management in the World of Competitive Gaming*, 33 (Palgrave Macmillan 2019); See also HLTV.org, *CS:Go Released*, https://www.hltv.org/news/8972/csgo-released (last visited Jul. 16, 2020).
178. Tobias M. Scholz, *eSports is Business: Management in the World of Competitive Gaming*, 32 (Palgrave Macmillan 2019).
179. Tobias M. Scholz, *eSports is Business: Management in the World of Competitive Gaming*, 33 (Palgrave Macmillan 2019); Paul 'Redeye' Chaloner, *This is Esports (and How to Spell it)*, 99 (Bloomsbury Sport 2020).
180. Shaun Prescott, *Twitch Users Watched 459,366 Years Worth of Content in 2015*, P.C. Gamer (Feb. 11, 2016), https://www.pcgamer.com/twitch-users-watched-459366-years-worth-of-content-in-2015.
181. Evan Lahti, *Valve Puts in $1 Million for All Future Major CS:GO Tournaments*, P.C. Gamer (Feb. 23, 2016), https://www.pcgamer.com/valve-all-major-csgo-tournaments-will-be-1-million; See also CounterStrike: Global Offensive, *Major Growth—02.23.2016*, https://blog.counter-strike.net/index.php/2016

/02/13658 (last visited Jul. 17, 2020; Counter-Strike: Global Offensive, *MLG Columbus 2016*, https://blog.counter-strike.net/index.php/2015/11/13096 (last visited Jul. 17, 2020).

182. Halo, *Halo Championship Series Announced*, https://www.halowaypoint.com/en-us/news/halo-championship-series-announced (last visited Jul. 17, 2020); See Jasmine Henry, *Microsoft Launching 'Halo Championship Series' eSports League*, Game Rant (Nov. 6, 2014), https://gamerant.com/halo-championship-series-esports-league.
183. Paul 'Redeye' Chaloner, *This is Esports (and How to Spell it)*, 97 (Bloomsbury Sport 2020); Overwatch, *Home Page*, https://playoverwatch.com (last visited Jul. 17, 2020); See also William Collis, *The Book of Esports*, 74 (Rosetta Books 2020).
184. Paul 'Redeye' Chaloner, *This is Esports (and How to Spell it)*, 99 (Bloomsbury Sport 2020); See also Dan Szymborski, *Blizzard to Create Professional Overwatch League*, ESPN (Nov. 4, 2016), https://www.espn.com/esports/story/_/id/17968297/blizzard-announces-professional-overwatch-league; See also William Collis, *The Book of Esports*, 76 (Rosetta Books 2020).
185. FIFA, *FIFA eWorld Cup*, https://www.fifa.com/fifaeworldcup (last visited Jul. 17, 2020).
186. E.A. Sports, *Madden Bowl*, https://www.ea.com/games/madden-nfl/madden-nfl-20/compete/events/madden-nfl-20-bowl (last visited Jul. 17, 2020).
187. See also William Collis, *The Book of Esports*, 161 (Rosetta Books 2020); Brian Mazique, *'NBA 2K19's $250,000 MyTeam Unlimited Tournament is Packed with NBA 2K Leaguers*, Forbes (Jan. 31, 2019), https://www.forbes.com/sites/brianmazique/2019/01/31/nba-2k19s-250000-myteam-unlimited-tournament-is-packed-with-nba-2k-leaguers/#1718ce1a1bf6; Eli Becht, *NBA 2K20 MyTEAM Unlimited $250,000 Tournament Revealed*, Heavy (Oct. 8, 2019), https://heavy.com/games/2019/10/nba-2k20-myteam-tournament; See also NBA 2K20, *MyTeam Unlmited $250,000 Tournament*, https://nba.2k.com/2k20/en-US/news/myteam-unlimited-250-000-tournament (last visited Jul. 17, 2020); See also Eddie Makuch, *Here's How Much Money Take-Two Makes from Microtransactions and Which Games Are the Biggest*, Game Spot (May 20, 2020), https://www.gamespot.com/articles/heres-how-much-money-taketwo-makes-from-microtrans/1100-6477537.
188. M.P.B.A., My Player Basketball Association, https://www.mpba2kevents.com (last visited Jul. 17, 2020).
189. Jonathan Raber, *The True OG: A Conversation with Nets GC GM Ivan Curtiss*, NBA 2K League (Apr. 12, 2019), https://2kleague.nba.com/news/the-true-og-a-conversation-with-nets-gc-gm-ivan-curtiss; Doyle Rader, *LT Fairley Named New Head Coach of Mavs Gaming*, Forbes (Nov. 9, 2018), https://www.forbes.com/sites/doylerader/2018/11/09/lt-fairley-named-new-head-coach-of-mavs-gaming/#465636e95980.
190. WR League, *About Us*, https://wr-league.com (last visited Jul. 27, 2020); See also WR Pro-Am League (@WRroamleague), Twitter (Apr. 2015), https://twitter.com/WRProAmLeague.
191. EV - WR (@EvThatGuy), Twitter (Jun. 2010), https://twitter.com/EvThatGuy; See also Lux-WR (@deluxpike10), Twitter (May 2016), https://twitter.com/deluxpike10.
192. M.P.B.A., *About Us*, https://www.mpba2kevents.com/aboutus (last visited Jul. 17, 2020).

193. Ivan Curtiss (@OGKINGCURT), Twitter (Apr. 5, 2018, 5:55pm), https://twitter.com/OGKINGCURT/status/982013818393022464; See also EV - WR (@EvThatGuy), Twitter (Jul. 15, 2020, 12:38pm), https://twitter.com/EvThatGuy/status/1283440801608073216.
194. Brian Mazique, *'NBA2K19' Neighborhood, PARK, Pro-Am, Jordan Rec Center, 3-On-3 Crews, and New Mini-Games Revealed*, Forbes (Aug. 30, 2018), https://www.forbes.com/sites/brianmazique/2018/08/30/nba2k19-neighborhood-park-pro-am-jordan-rec-center-3-on-3-crews-and-new-mini-games-revealed/#12f9ce0e3c85; See also Justin M. Jacobson, *Getting Ready for Season Three of the NBA 2K League*, Dimer 2K (Jun. 24, 2019), https://dimer2k.com/2019/06/24/getting-ready-for-season-three-of-the-nba-2k-league.
195. Josiah Cohen, WGS Invitational Tournament: Xbox One Player Bios, Dimer 2K (Nov. 6, 2019), https://dimer2k.com/2019/11/06/wgs-invitational-tournament-xbox-one-player-bios; Josiah Cohen, *WGS Invitational Tournament: PS4 Player Bios*, Dimer 2K (Oct. 30, 2019), https://dimer2k.com/2019/10/30/wgs-invitational-tournament-ps4-player-bios; See also WR League, *WGS Invitational: Powered by WR League*, https://tournaments.wr-league.com/WGS (last visited Jul. 27, 2020).
196. WR League, *CLTX Gaming Two-Way Tourney*, https://tournaments.wr-league.com/CLTX (last visited Jul. 27, 2020); See also Toornament, *CLTX Gaming Two-Way Tourney*, https://www.toornament.com/en_US/tournaments/2921023089233772544/stages/2921025532260687872 (last visited Jul. 27, 2020).
197. Brian Mazique, *NBA 2K16 Road to the Finals: Prize Money and Format for New eSports Event*, The Bleacher Report (Feb. 1, 2016), https://bleacherreport.com/articles/2612674-nba-2k16-road-to-the-finals-prize-money-and-format-for-new-esports-event
198. Andrew Lynch, *NBA 2K16's First eSports Event Started with Kobe and Ended with $250,000*, Fox News (Jun. 3, 2016), https://www.foxsports.com/nba/story/nba-2k16-kobe-bryant-esports-road-to-the-finals-250-000-grand-prize-rick-fox-060316; See also Brian Mazique, *'NBA 2K16': Road to the Finals Remaining Schedule for eSports Event*, Forbes (Apr. 4, 2016), https://www.forbes.com/sites/brianmazique/2016/04/04/nba-2k16-road-to-the-finals-remaining-schedule-for-esports-event/#36d0e3ed11c7.
199. Steve Noah, *NBA 2K17 All-Star Tournament Announced, NBA 2K Pro-Am Winner Receives $250,000 & More*, Operation Sports (Dec. 14, 2016), https://www.operationsports.com/nba-2k17-all-star-tournament-announced-nba-2k-pro-am-winner-receives-250000-more; See also The Industry Cosign, *NBA 2K17 All-Star Tournament*, https://www.theindustrycosign.com/nba-2k17-star-tournament (last visited Jul. 20, 2020).
200. Neil Davidson, *NBA 2K League Season Full of Hope and Confidence*, The Canadian Press (May 4, 2020), https://www.thestar.com/sports/basketball/2020/05/04/raptors-uprising-gc-enters-nba-2k-league-season-full-of-hope-and-confidence.html; Steve Noah, *NBA 2K17 All-Star Tournament Announced, NBA 2K Pro-Am Winner Receives $250,000 & More*, Operation Sports (Dec. 14, 2016), https://www.operationsports.com/nba-2k17-all-star-tournament-announced-nba-2k-pro-am-winner-receives-250000-more.
201. Imad Khan, *Adam Silver Vows to Develop Esports Entity as 'Fourth League in Our Family*,' ESPN (Apr. 4, 2018), https://www.espn.com/esports/story/_/id/

23029042/nba-commissioner-adam-silver-welcomes-fourth-league-nba-2k-esports-league.

202. NBA 2K League, *League Info*, https://2kleague.nba.com/league-info (last visited Jul. 17, 2020).
203. Alex Kennedy, *FAQ: Everything You Need to Know about the New NBA 2K League*, HoopsHype (Apr. 4, 2018), https://hoopshype.com/2018/04/04/faq-everything-you-need-to-know-about-the-new-nba-2k-league; See also NBA 2K League, *NBA 2K League Holds Inaugural Draft—Dimez Selected No. 1 Overall*, https://2kleague.nba.com/news/nba-2k-league-holds-inaugural-draft-dimez-selected-no-1-overall (last visited Apr. 4, 2018); See also Lisa Marie Segarra, *Meet the Pro Video Gamer Known as the 'LeBron of NBA 2K,'* Yahoo! (Apr. 9, 2019), https://finance.yahoo.com/news/meet-pro-video-gamer-known-150004287.html.
204. Xing Li, *Jazz Gaming Select Ria First Overall in the NBA 2K League Season Two Draft*, Dot Esports (Mar. 5, 2019), https://dotesports.com/general/news/nba-2k-league-season-two-draft-results; Stefanie Fogel, *NBA 2K League Adds Four Expansion Teams for 2019 Season*, Variety (Aug. 15, 2018), https://variety.com/2018/gaming/news/nba-2k-league-expansion-teams-1202906201.
205. Jeff Eisenband, *Mootyy: From Getting Bullied to Being Kristaps Porzingis of NBA 2K League*, The Post Game (Apr. 3, 2018), http://www.thepostgame.com/mootyy-bullying-nba-2k-league-draft-prospect.
206. Steve Noah, *T-Wolves Gaming Wins 2019 NBA 2K League Championship*, Operation Sports (Aug. 4, 2019), https://www.operationsports.com/t-wolves-gaming-wins-2019-nba-2k-league-championship.
207. ESPN.com, *oLARRY Wins Inaugural ESPY for Best Esports Moment*, ESPN (Jul. 10, 2019), https://www.espn.com/esports/story/_/id/27162597/olarry-wins-inaugural-espy-best-esports-moment.
208. Brian Mazique, *NBA 2K League Expands with Reported $25 Million Deal with Gen.G.* Forbes (Sept. 26, 2019), https://www.forbes.com/sites/brianmazique/2019/09/26/nba-2k-league-expands-with-reported-25-million-deal-with-geng/#5d1745854985; Reuters, *NBA 2K League Announces Shanghai Team for 2020 Season*, ESPN (Sept. 26, 2019), https://www.espn.com/esports/story/_/id/27709528/nba-2k-league-announces-shanghai-team-2020-season.
209. Richard Lawler, *NBA 2K League Comes to Traditional TV on ESPN2*, Engadget (May 5, 2020), https://www.engadget.com/nba-2-k-league-comes-to-broadcast-tv-on-espn-2-021125286.html; See also Olivia Wilson, *ESPN2 to Air First U.S. Linear Telecast of NBA 2K League Live Tonight*, ESPN (May 5, 2020), https://espnpressroom.com/us/press-releases/2020/05/espn2-to-air-first-u-s-linear-broadcast-of-nba-2k-league-live-tonight.
210. NBA 2K League, *NBA 2K League to Host First Qualifying Event in Europe*, https://2kleague.nba.com/news/european-invitational (last visited Jul. 25, 2020).
211. Bayern Ballers Gaming, *Home Page*, https://www.bayernballers.com (last visited Jul. 17, 2020); See also Bayern Ballers Gaming (@Bayernballers), Twitter (Jul. 2019), https://twitter.com/bayernballers.
212. FIBA Basketball, *17 National Teams to Participate in Inaugural FIBA Esports Open 2020*, http://www.fiba.basketball/news/17-national-teams-to-participate-in-inaugural-fiba-esports-open-2020 (last visited Jul. 22, 2020); See also ESPN5, *FIBA Esports Open 2020: Team Pilipinas Clinches Southeast Asia Title*

with Sweep of Indonesia, ESPN (Jun. 22, 2020), https://www.espn.com/basketball/story/_/id/29346373/team-pilipinas-sweeps-indonesia-fiba-esports-open-2020.S.

213. Eddie Moran, *NBA 2K League Aiming for International Expansion*, Front Office Sports (Dec. 12, 2019), https://frntofficesport.com/nba-2k-league-expansion; See also Reuters, *NBA 2K League Announces Shanghai Team for 2020 Season*, ESPN (Sept. 26, 2019), https://www.espn.com/esports/story/_/id/27709528/nba-2k-league-announces-shanghai-team-2020-season; Patrick Murray, *With The Growth Of Esports, NBA 2K League Is Taking Off*, Forbes (Oct. 11, 2020), https://www.forbes.com/sites/patrickmurray/2020/10/11/with-the-growth-of-esports-nba-2k-league-is-taking-off/#1f3108ff23b6.
214. Lawrence Phillips, *The History of Esports*, Hotspawn (Apr. 1, 2020), https://www.hotspawn.com/guides/the-history-of-esports.
215. Scott Heinrich, *Esports Ride Crest of a Wave as Figures Rocket during Covid-19 Crisis*, The Guardian (Apr. 10, 2020), https://www.theguardian.com/sport/2020/apr/11/esports-ride-crest-of-a-wave-as-figures-rocket-during-covid-19-crisis; See also Shawn Smith, *A Pandemic Proved that Esports is More Vital than Ever for Entertainment | Opinion*, GamesIndustry.biz (Apr. 7, 2020), https://www.gamesindustry.biz/articles/2020-04-01-a-pandemic-proved-that-esports-is-more-vital-than-ever-for-entertainment-opinion.
216. ESPN, *Nets' Kevin Durant Leads Field of 16 in NBA 2K20 Tournament on ESPN*, ESPN (Mar. 31, 2020), https://www.espn.com/nba/story/_/id/28978225/nets-kevin-durant-leads-field-16-nba-2k20-tournament-espn); See also Max Thielmeyer, *'Rocket League' World Championship to Air during ESPN Esports Day*, Forbes (Apr. 4, 2020), https://www.forbes.com/sites/maxthielmeyer/2020/04/04/rocket-league-world-championship-to-air-during-espn-esports-day/#28778f6e32b7.
217. Phil "DrPhill" Alexander, *Esports for Dummies*, 8 (Wiley 2020). See also Robert Zak, *How to Start Watching Esports*, Tech Radar (Mar. 18, 2019), https://www.techradar.com/how-to/how-to-start-watching-esports.
218. Phil "DrPhill Alexander, *Esports for Dummies*, 8 (Wiley 2020); See also Ben Casselman, *Resistance is Futile: eSports is Massive ... and Growing*, ESPN (May 22, 2015), https://www.espn.com/espn/story/_/id/13059210/esports-massive-industry-growing.
219. Dean Takahashi, *Newzoo: Global esports Will Top $1 Billion in 2020, with China as the Top Market*, Venture Beat (Feb. 25, 2020), https://venturebeat.com/2020/02/25/newzoo-global-esports-will-top-1-billion-in-2020-with-china-as-the-top-market; See also Newszoo, *Newzoo's Esports Consumer Predictions for 2021: A Quarter of the World's Population Will Be Aware of Esports*, https://newzoo.com/insights/articles/newzoos-esports-consumer-predictions-for-2021-a-quarter-of-the-worlds-population-will-be-aware-of-esports (last visited Jul. 23, 2020).
220. 2019 *Essential Facts about the Computer and Video Game Industry*, https://www.theesa.com/esa-research/2019-essential-facts-about-the-computer-and-video-game-industry (last visited Feb. 5, 2020).
221. Phil "DrPhill" Alexander, *Esports for Dummies*, 75 (Wiley 2020).
222. Adam Fitch, *The International 8 Has the Biggest Prize Pool in Esports*, Esports Insider (Aug. 21, 2018), https://esportsinsider.com/2018/08/the-international-8-prize-pool.

223. Marta Juras, *Most Watched*, Dot Esports (Dec. 27, 2019), https://dotesports.com/streaming/news/most-watched-esports-events-2019.
224. Adam Fitch, *Fortnite World Cup Details Revealed with $30 Million Prize Pool*, Esports Insider (Feb. 22, 2019), https://esportsinsider.com/2019/02/fortnite-world-cup-prize-pool.
225. Sarah Perez, *Twitch Breaks Records Again in Q2, Topping 5B Total Hours Watched*, TechCrunch (Jul. 1, 2020), https://techcrunch.com/2020/07/01/twitch-breaks-records-again-in-q2-topping-5b-total-hours-watched.
226. Paul Tassi, *40,000 Korean Fans Watch SSW Win 2014 'League of Legends' World Championship*, Forbes (Oct. 19, 2014), https://www.forbes.com/sites/insertcoin/2014/10/19/40000-live-korean-fans-watch-ssw-win-2014-league-of-legends-world-championship/#6c705bb0735f).
227. Kennedy Rose, *Despite Loss, the Fusion Solidify a Place for Philadelphia in Esports World (Video),* Philadelphia Business Journal (Jul. 7, 2018), https://www.bizjournals.com/philadelphia/news/2018/07/31/overwatch-spitfire-fusion-grand-finals-barclays.html.
228. ESPN.com, *Overwatch League Comes to ESPN, Disney and ABC* (Jul. 11, 2018), https://www.espn.com/esports/story/_/id/24062274/overwatch-league-comes-espn-disney-abc.
229. Noah Davis, *Jay Ajayi Joins Philadelphia Union's eMLS Team to Become the Prototype of a New Kind of Dual-Sport Athlete*, ESPN (Jan. 8, 2020), https://www.espn.com/soccer/philadelphia-union/story/4028920/jay-ajayi-joins-philadelphia-unions-emls-team-to-become-the-prototype-of-a-new-kind-of-dual-sport-athlete.
230. Logan McLaughlin, *A Taxonomy of Esports Games*, FANAI (Sept. 3, 2019), https://www.fanai.io/a-taxonomy-of-esports-games.
231. Id.; See also Phil "DrPhill" Alexander, *Esports for Dummies*, 8 (Wiley 2020); See also See also William Collis, *The Book of Esports*, 142 (Rosetta Books 2020).
232. Phil "DrPhill Alexander, *Esports for Dummies*, 77, 80 (Wiley 2020); See also Dot Esports Staff, *The Evolution of eSports*, Dot Esports (Jun. 22, 2015), https://dotesports.com/news/the-evolution-of-esports-7693).
233. Phil "DrPhill" Alexander, *Esports for Dummies*, 80 (Wiley 2020).
234. Phil "DrPhill" Alexander, *Esports for Dummies*, 74 (Wiley 2020)
235. Phil "DrPhill" Alexander, *Esports for Dummies*, 77 (Wiley 2020); Logan McLaughlin, *A Taxonomy of Esports* Games, FANAI (Sept. 3, 2019), https://www.fanai.io/a-taxonomy-of-esports-games.
236. Phil "DrPhill" Alexander, *Esports for Dummies*, 77 (Wiley 2020).
237. Phil "DrPhill" Alexander, *Esports for Dummies*, 118, 120 (Wiley 2020); See also William Collis, *The Book of Esports*, 108 (Rosetta Books 2020).
238. Phil "DrPhill" Alexander, *Esports for Dummies*, 118 (Wiley 2020); See also Steve Rousseau, *Everything You Want to Know about 'Fortnite,' The Video Game Drake Played*, Digg (Jun. 26, 2019), https://digg.com/2018/what-is-fortnite.
239. Phil "DrPhill" Alexander, *Esports for Dummies*, 49 (Wiley 2020).
240. Phil "DrPhill" Alexander, *Esports for Dummies*, 49 (Wiley 2020); See also Dot Esports Staff, *The Evolution of eSports*, Dot Esports (Jun. 22, 2015), https://dotesports.com/news/the-evolution-of-esports-7693).
241. Phil "DrPhill" Alexander, *Esports for Dummies*, 50 (Wiley 2020).

242. Phil "DrPhill Alexander, *Esports for Dummies*, 53 (Wiley 2020); See also Dot Esports Staff, *The Evolution of eSports*, Dot Esports (Jun. 22, 2015), https://dotesports.com/news/the-evolution-of-esports-7693).
243. Phil "DrPhill" Alexander, *Esports for Dummies*, 53 (Wiley 2020).
244. Phil "DrPhill" Alexander, *Esports for Dummies*, 55 (Wiley 2020).
245. Phil "DrPhill" Alexander, *Esports for Dummies*, 129, 130 (Wiley 2020); See also William Collis, *The Book of Esports*, 96 (Rosetta Books 2020).
246. EA Sports, *Madden Bowl*, https://www.ea.com/games/madden-nfl/madden-nfl-20/compete/events/madden-nfl-20-bowl (last visited Jul. 24, 2020).
247. NBA 2K League, *Home Page*, https://2kleague.nba.com (last visited Jul. 24, 2020).
248. NHL, *World Gaming Championship to Resume with Regionals*, https://www.nhl.com/news/world-gaming-championship-regionals/c-317606560 (last visited Jul. 24,2020).
249. Phil "DrPhill" Alexander, *Esports for Dummies*, 101, 104, 109 (Wiley 2020).
250. Formula 1 Esports Series, *Home Page*, https://f1esports.com/ (last visited Feb. 5, 2020); See also Dot Esports Staff, *The Evolution of eSports*, Dot Esports (Jun. 22, 2015), https://dotesports.com/news/the-evolution-of-esports-7693).
251. Logan McLaughlin, *A Taxonomy of Esports Games*, FANAI (Sept. 3, 2019), https://www.fanai.io/a-taxonomy-of-esports-games; See also Phil "DrPhill" Alexander, *Esports for Dummies*, 114 (Wiley 2020); Mitch Reames, *Behind XSET's Rocket League Entrance Following Sweeping Changes to RLCS*, Esports Insider (Jul. 27, 2020), https://esportsinsider.com/2020/07/rocket-league-xset-rlcs.
252. Phil "DrPhill Alexander, *Esports for Dummies*, 87, 94 (Wiley 2020); See also Dot Esports Staff, *The Evolution of eSports*, Dot Esports (Jun. 22, 2015), https://dotesports.com/news/the-evolution-of-esports-7693).
253. Phil "DrPhill Alexander, *Esports for Dummies*, 93 (Wiley 2020); See also Dot Esports Staff, *The Evolution of eSports*, Dot Esports (Jun. 22, 2015), https://dotesports.com/news/the-evolution-of-esports-7693.
254. Techopedia, *Role-Playing Game (RPG)*, https://www.techopedia.com/definition/27052/role-playing-game-rpg (last visited Jul. 23, 2020); See also IGN, *Top 100 RPGS Of All Time*, https://www.ign.com/lists/top-100-rpgs (last visited Jul. 23, 2020).
255. Phil "DrPhill Alexander, *Esports for Dummies*, 11 (Wiley 2020); See also Farming Simulator League, *Start*, https://fsl.giants-software.com (last visited Jul. 23, 2020).
256. Tobias Seck, *Q2 2020's Most Impactful PC Games: Riot Games Seizes Esports World Domination, Continuing COVID-19 Impact*, The Esports Observer (Jul. 22, 2020), https://esportsobserver.com/q2-2020-impact-index; See also See also William Collis, *The Book of Esports*, 118 (Rosetta Books 2020).
257. Fox Sports Asia, *The Rise of Mobile Esports in 2018* (Apr. 9, 2018), https://www.foxsportsasia.com/esports/839328/rise-mobile-esports-2018.
258. Adam Fitch, *Farming Simulator Launching €250,000 Esports League*, Esports Insider (Jan. 23, 2019), https://esportsinsider.com/2019/01/farming-simulator-league-announced; See also Jeremy Ainsworth, *Farming Simulator League Roots Itself at IEM Katowice*, Esports Insider (Dec. 23, 2019), https://esportsinsider.com/2019/12/farming-simulator-league-iem-katowice.

259. Riot Games, *VALORANT*, https://playvalorant.com/en-us (last visited Jul. 23, 2020); See also Graham Ashton, *Sizing Up the VALORANT Esports Scene, So Far*, The Esports Observer (Jul. 8, 2020), https://esportsobserver.com/valorant-proves-popular-with-esports-teams; Patrick Kobek, *VALORANT vs CS:GO: An Early Comparison*, The Gamer (Apr. 16, 2020), https://www.thegamer.com/valorant-vs-counter-strike-counterstrike-csgo.
260. Mike Stubbs, *TSM Unveil Stacked 'Valorant' Roster Featuring Subroza and Wardell*, Forbes (May 23, 2020), https://www.forbes.com/sites/mikestubbs/2020/05/23/tsm-unveil-stacked-valorant-roster-featuring-subroza-and-wardell/#5af698e35766; See also Tyler Erzberger, *G2 Esports Sign Mixwell for VALORANT Squad*, ESPN (Jun. 16, 2020), https://www.espn.com/esports/story/_/id/29317826/g2-esports-sign-mixwell-valorant-squad; Tyler Erzberger, *An Inside Look at the VALORANT Bootcamp*, ESPN (Apr. 3, 2020), https://www.espn.com/esports/story/_/id/28991386/an-look-valorant-bootcamp.
261. Kevin Hitt, *Riot Games Launches VALORANT Ignition Series to Jumpstart Ecosystem*, The Esports Observer (Jun. 16, 2020), https://esportsobserver.com/valorant-ignition-series; See also Mike Stubbs, *G2 Esports Win the $50,000 WePlay 'Valorant' Invitational Tournament*, Forbes (Jul. 19, 2020), https://www.forbes.com/sites/mikestubbs/2020/07/19/g2-esports-win-the-50000-weplay-valorant-invitational-tournament/#62e9e94f2748; Kevin Hitt, *Riot Games Announces New Valorant Twitch Rivals Tournament for Title's Official Release*, The Esports Observer (May 28, 2020), https://esportsobserver.com/riot-games-valorant-tournament; See also Kevin Hitt, *FaZe Clan's VALORANT Ignition Series Tournament Sees Largest Prize Offering to Date*, The Esports Observer (Jul. 28, 2020), https://esportsobserver.com/faze-clans-ignition-series/.
262. Preston Byers, *Sentinels Signs Sinatraa, ShahZaM, Zombs, and SicK to VALORANT Roster*, Dot Esports (Apr. 28, 2020), https://dotesports.com/valorant/news/sentinels-signs-sinatraa-shahzam-zombs-and-sick-to-valorant-roster; See also Jacob Wolf and Tyler Erzberger, *Sources: Overwatch League MVP Sinatraa to Retire, Join Sentinels VALORANT Team*, ESPN (Apr. 28, 2020), https://www.espn.com/esports/story/_/id/29109603/sources-overwatch-league-mvp-sinatraa-retire-join-sentinels-valorant-team; Andrew Webster, *Overwatch's Biggest Star is Moving to Valorant*, The Verge (Apr. 28, 2020), https://www.theverge.com/2020/4/28/21240497/overwatch-league-sinatraa-leaving-sf-shock-valorant.
263. Mike Stubbs, *'Valorant' Teams Already Have $25K a Month Salaries According to Report*, Forbes (Jul. 8, 2020), https://www.forbes.com/sites/mikestubbs/2020/07/08/valorant-teams-already-have-25k-a-month-salaries-according-to-report/#6434d82374c2; See also Graham Ashton, *Sizing Up the VALORANT Esports Scene, So Far*, The Esports Observer (Jul. 8, 2020), https://esportsobserver.com/valorant-proves-popular-with-esports-teams.
264. Pete Volk, *Why 'Valorant' is Poised to Be the Next Big Esport*, SB Nation (Apr. 28, 2020), https://www.sbnation.com/2020/4/28/21209730/valorant-esports-future-hype-riot-games; See also Riot Games, *Valorant Esports and Community Competition*, https://playvalorant.com/en-us/news/dev/valorant-esports-and-community-competition (last visited Jul. 24, 2020).
265. Max Miceli, *Esports Essentials: How Twitch Streamers Make Money Off of Sponsorships*, The Esports Observer (Mar. 30, 2019), https://esportsobserver.com/twitch-streamers-sponsorships; See also Darren Geeter, *Here's How*

Gamers Make Money, CNBC (Nov. 16, 2018), https://www.cnbc.com/2018/11/16/esports-twitch-youtube-gamers-fortnite-gaming.html.

266. Paul 'Redeye' Chaloner, *This is Esports (and How to Spell it)*, 178 (Bloomsbury Sport 2020).
267. Paul 'Redeye' Chaloner, *This is Esports (and How to Spell it)*, 179 (Bloomsbury Sport 2020); Tobias M. Scholz, *eSports is Business: Management in the World of Competitive Gaming*, 67 (Palgrave Macmillan 2019).
268. Brian O' Connell, *How Much Do eSports Players Make?*, The Street (Feb. 12, 2020), https://www.thestreet.com/personal-finance/how-much-do-esports-players-make-15126931.
269. Paul 'Redeye' Chaloner, *This is Esports (and How to Spell it)*, 180 (Bloomsbury Sport 2020); Tobias M. Scholz, *eSports is Business: Management in the World of Competitive Gaming*, 67 (Palgrave Macmillan 2019).
270. Nicholas Barth, *The Average Salary of an LCS Player is Very Impressive*, Twin Galaxies (Apr. 25, 2019), https://www.twingalaxies.com/feed_details.php/5090/the-average-salary-of-an-lcs-player-is-very-impressive; See also Monte Cristo (@MonteCristo), Twitter (May 27, 2020, 3:15pm), https://twitter.com/MonteCristo/status/1265723381401317377.
271. Tobias M. Scholz, *eSports is Business: Management in the World of Competitive Gaming*, 68 (Palgrave Macmillan 2019).
272. Liz Richardson, *Overwatch League Reveals Player Contract Status for Entire League*, Dot Esports (Oct. 4, 2019), https://dotesports.com/overwatch/news/overwatch-league-reveals-player-contract-status-for-entire-league.
273. Jacob Wolf, *NRG Signs 17-Year-Old Overwatch Pro Sinatraa for $150K*, ESPN (Sep. 3, 2017), https://www.espn.com/esports/story/_/id/20564135/nrg-signs-17-year-old-overwatch-pro-sinatraa-150k.
274. *Id.*
275. Tyler Erzberger, *Faker's Groundbreaking New Contract—From T1 Superstar to Part-Owner*, ESPN (Feb. 17, 2020), https://www.espn.com/esports/story/_/id/28724101/faker-groundbreaking-new-contract-t1-superstar-part-owner.
276. Thomas Lace, *Bjergsen Becomes Part-Owner of TSM*, Esports Insider (Oct. 15, 2019), https://esportsinsider.com/2019/10/bjergsen-tsm-part-owner/.
277. Paul 'Redeye' Chaloner, *This is Esports (and How to Spell it)*, 182 (Bloomsbury Sport 2020).
278. *Top 100 Highest Overall Earnings*, https://www.esportsearnings.com/players (last visited Feb. 5, 2020).
279. Paul 'Redeye' Chaloner, *This is Esports (and How to Spell it)*, 179 (Bloomsbury Sport 2020).
280. Max Miceli, *TimTheTatman Partners with Charmin for Non-endemic Sponsored Stream*, Dot Esports (Jul. 14, 2020), https://dotesports.com/streaming/news/timthetatman-partners-with-charmin-for-non-endemic-sponsored-stream.
281. Graham Ashton, *Misfits Gaming Group and Matrix Keyboards to Build Custom Player Products*, The Esports Observer (Mar. 10, 2020), https://esportsobserver.com/misfits-gaming-matrix-keyboards.
282. Paul 'Redeye' Chaloner, *This is Esports (and How to Spell it)*, 181 (Bloomsbury Sport 2020).
283. Twitch, *Subscriber Emoticon Guide for Partners and Affiliates*, https://help.twitch.tv/s/article/subscriber-emoticon-guide (last visited Feb. 5, 2020).
284. Twitch, *Purchase Bits*, https://www.twitch.tv/bits (last visited Feb. 5, 2020).

285. *Id.*
286. *Id.*
287. Jesse Aaron, *How Much Can You Make Streaming as a Professional Video Gamer?*, Huffington Post (Mar. 27, 2015), https://www.huffpost.com/entry/how-much-can-you-make-str_b_6926362.
288. Twitch, *Twitch Partner Program*, https://www.twitch.tv/p/partners/ (last visited Feb. 5, 2020).
289. *Id.*
290. Justin M. Jacobson, *Legal & Business Tips for Musicians on Twitch*, Tunecore (Apr. 2, 2020), https://www.tunecore.com/blog/2020/04/legal-business-tips-for-musicians-on-twitch.html.
291. Steven Van Sloun, *Esports Franchise Economics*, Loup Ventures (Mar. 9, 2018), https://loupventures.com/esports-franchise-economics.
292. Twitch, *Subscriber Emoticon Guide for Partners and Affiliates*, https://help.twitch.tv/s/article/subscriber-emoticon-guide (last visited Feb. 5, 2020).
293. Twitch, *Twitch Partner Program*, https://www.twitch.tv/p/partners/ (last visited Feb. 5, 2020); See also Justin M. Jacobson, *Legal & Business Tips for Musicians on Twitch*, Tunecore (Apr. 2, 2020), https://www.tunecore.com/blog/2020/04/legal-business-tips-for-musicians-on-twitch.html.
294. Jesse Aaron, *How Much Can You Make Streaming as a Professional Video Gamer?*, Huffington Post (Mar. 27, 2015), https://www.huffpost.com/entry/how-much-can-you-make-str_b_6926362.
295. *Id.*
296. Matt Greco, *Watch Me Play Video Games! Amazon's Twitch Platform Draws Users and Dollars*, CNBC (May 14, 2016), https://www.cnbc.com/2016/05/13/amazons-twitch-streamers-can-make-big-bucks.html.
297. Tobias M. Scholz, *eSports is Business: Management in the World of Competitive Gaming*, 68 (Palgrave Macmillan 2019).
298. Justin M. Jacobson, *Legal & Business Tips for Musicians on Twitch*, Tunecore (Apr. 2, 2020), https://www.tunecore.com/blog/2020/04/legal-business-tips-for-musicians-on-twitch.html.
299. Erin M. Jacobson, *How Amazon's Twitch.tv Cheats Music Creators*, Forbes (Jul. 31, 2018), https://www.forbes.com/sites/legalentertainment/2018/07/31/how-amazons-twitch-tv-cheats-music-creators/#58450f4916aa.
300. Streamlabs, *Streamlabs Donations*, https://streamlabs.com/donations (last visited Feb. 5, 2020).
301. Morgan Stanley, *The World of Games: eSports from Wild West to Mainstream*, at 22 (Oct. 12, 2018), https://www.goldmansachs.com/insights/pages/infographics/e-sports/report.pdf; See also Morgan Stanley, *Esports Joins the Big Leagues*, *https://www.goldmansachs.com/insights/pages/infographics/e-sports/*; https://theoutline.com/sponsor/goldman-2019/858b1144.
302. *Id.*
303. Phil "DrPhill" Alexander, *Esports for Dummies*, 154 (Wiley 2020).
304. Coco Huang, FaZe Clan Takes Ownership Stake in CTRL, L.A, *Business Journal* (Jun. 26, 2020), https://labusinessjournal.com/news/2020/jun/26/fazeclan-takes-ownership-stake-ctrl; See also Adam Finch, *Skyler Johnson on CTRL's Inception, Place in Esports*, The Esports Insider (Oct. 29, 2019), https://esportsinsider.com/2019/10/skyler-johnson-ctrl-interview; Jacob Wolf, *Team EnVyUs to Receive $35 Million Investment from Hersh Family Investments,*

Sources Say, ESPN (Aug. 8, 2017), https://www.espn.com/esports/story/_/id/20283637/team-envyus-receive-35-million-investment-hersh-family-investments-sources-say.
305. Fatal1ty, *Fatal1ty Gaming Products*, https://fatal1ty.com/the-products (last visited Jul. 26, 2020).
306. Kevin Hitt, *Top 10 Esports Players of 2020 by Total Prize Winnings*, The Esports Observer (Dec. 26, 2019), https://esportsobserver.com/top-10-esports-players-2019.
307. *Id.*
308. Phil "DrPhill" Alexander, *Esports for Dummies*, 222 (Wiley 2020).
309. Id.; See also Joshua Nino De Guzman, *What Makes a Good eSports Coach?*, Red Bull (Jul. 23, 2014), https://www.redbull.com/gb-en/what-makes-a-good-esports-coach.
310. Phil "DrPhill Alexander, *Esports for Dummies*, 222 (Wiley 2020); See also Stephen Chiu, *Coaches across Esports*, ESPN (Aug. 22, 2016), https://www.espn.com/esports/story/_/id/17365945/coaches-esports.
311. Leonardo Biazzi, *HUNDEN Retires as a Pro CS:GO Player to Become Heroic's Head Coach*, Dot Esports (Apr. 29, 2020), https://dotesports.com/counter-strike/news/hunden-retires-as-a-pro-csgo-player-to-become-heroics-head-coach; See also Dennis Gonzales, *Former CS Pro Rambo to Coach MVP Project*, The Score (Oct. 14, 2016), https://www.thescoreesports.com/csgo/news/11009-former-cs-pro-rambo-to-coach-mvp-project.
312. British Esports Association, *Esports Job Spotlight: Coach / Analyst*, https://britishesports.org/careers/coach-analyst (last visited Jul. 25, 2020).
313. Laura Lorenzetti, *You Can Make $50,000 a Year as a Video Game Coach*, Fortune (Jul. 29, 2015), https://fortune.com/2015/07/29/video-game-coach-salary.
314. Emily Gera, *Top 'Fortnite' Streamer DrLupo Will Train New Rogue 2019 Team*, Variety (Feb. 27, 2019), https://variety.com/2019/gaming/news/fortnite-drlupo-junior-rogue-1203150682; See also Imad Khan, *Rogue, DrLupo Aim to Mentor Kids in Fortnite, Esports*, ESPN (Sept. 21, 2018), https://www.espn.com/esports/story/_/id/24756765/rogue-drlupo-aim-mentor-kids-fortnite-esports.
315. Tobias M. Scholz, *eSports is Business: Management in the World of Competitive Gaming*, 68 (Palgrave Macmillan 2019).
316. Natalie Robehmed and Madeline Berg, *Highest Paid YouTube Stars 2018: Markiplier, Jake Paul, PreDiePie and More*, Forbes (Dec. 3, 2018), https://www.forbes.com/sites/natalierobehmed/2018/12/03/highest-paid-youtube-stars-2018-markiplier-jake-paul-pewdiepie-and-more/#47f38b60909a.
317. Matt Perez, *Top-Earning Video Gamers: The Ten Highest-Paid Players Pocketed More than $120 Million in 2019*, Forbes (Jan. 29, 2020), https://www.forbes.com/sites/mattperez/2020/01/29/top-earning-video-gamers-the-ten-highest-paid-players-pocketed-more-than-120-million-in-2019/#1dc713b4880b; See also Joe Price, *Here Are the Top-Earning Gamers in the World According to 'Forbes,'* Complex (Jan. 29, 2020), https://www.complex.com/pop-culture/2020/01/top-earning-gamers-in-world-forbes-list; Andy Chalk, *Ninja's Sponsored Apex Legends Launch Stream Cost EA $1 Million, Reuters Report Says*, P.C. Gamer (Mar. 13, 2019), https://www.pcgamer.com/ninjas-sponsored-apex-legends-launch-stream-cost-ea-dollar1-million-reuters-report-says.

318. Julie Alexander, *Ninja Left Twitch Because His Brand Was Too Big for Gaming*, The Verge (Oct. 4, 2019), https://www.theverge.com/2019/10/4/20898907/ninja-twitch-contract-mixer-streaming-microsoft-amazon.
319. Janko Roettgers, *Ninja is Ditching Amazon's Twitch for Microsoft's Mixer*, Variety (Aug. 1, 2019), https://variety.com/2019/digital/news/ninja-mixer-twitch-1203288169; See also Fraser Brown, *Ninja Allegedly Made $20-30 Million by Moving to Mixer*, P.C. Gamer (Jan. 28, 2020), https://www.pcgamer.com/ninja-allegedly-made-dollar20-30-million-by-moving-to-mixer.
320. Matt Perez, *Top-Earning Video Gamers: The Ten Highest-Paid Players Pocketed More than $120 Million in 2019*, Forbes (Jan. 29, 2020), https://www.forbes.com/sites/mattperez/2020/01/29/top-earning-video-gamers-the-ten-highest-paid-players-pocketed-more-than-120-million-in-2019/#1dc713b4880b.
321. *Id.*
322. Alex Stedman, *Twitch Superstar Michael 'Shroud' Grzesiek joins Mixer as Exclusive Streamer*, Variety (Oct. 24, 2019), https://variety.com/2019/digital/news/shroud-mixer-twitch-microsoft-amazon-1203382359; See also Corinne Reichert, *Microsoft Shuts Down Mixer, Partners with Facebook for Gaming Streams*, CNET (Jun. 22, 2020), https://www.cnet.com/news/microsoft-shuts-down-mixer-partners-with-facebook-for-gaming-streams.
323. Trent Murray, *Streamer Disguised Toast Signs Exclusive Deal with Facebook Gaming*, The Esports Observer (Nov. 22, 2019), https://esportsobserver.com/disguised-toast-facebook-gaming.
324. Todd Spangler, *Corinna Kopf Leaving Twitch to Stream Exclusively on Facebook Gaming*, Variety (Dec. 27, 2019), https://variety.com/2019/digital/news/corinna-kopf-facebook-gaming-leaving-twitch-1203451910.
325. Mitch Reames, *How One Company Orchestrated a Talent War between Twitch, Mixer, and YouTube*, The Verge (Jan. 6, 2020), https://www.theverge.com/creators/2020/1/6/21051500/loaded-streamer-talent-agency-twitch-mixer-youtube-ninja-shroud-courage; See also Kevin Webb, *Ninja Ditching Twitch for Microsoft's Mixer Was a Brilliant Decision*, Business Insider (Aug. 4, 2019), https://www.businessinsider.com/ninja-leaving-twitch-brilliant-move-2019-8.
326. CORSAIR, *CORSAIR Streamer Program*, https://www.corsair.com/us/en/streamers (last visited Jul. 29, 2020); See also Rory Young, *Twitch Streamer Describes McDonald's Sponsored Stream Gone Wrong*, Game Rant (Oct. 6, 2019), https://gamerant.com/twitch-jericho-mcdonalds-sponsorship.
327. Robert Williams, *Zaxby's Signs Twitch Streamer SypherPK to Exclusive Sponsorship Deal*, Mobile Marketer (Jul. 8, 2020), https://www.mobilemarketer.com/news/zaxbys-signs-twitch-streamer-sypherpk-to-exclusive-sponsorship-deal/581192.
328. Geoff Weiss, *Gaming Luminaries Ninja, DrLupo, and CouRage Sign with Talent Management Firm 'Loaded'*, Tubefilter (Mar. 7, 2019), https://www.tubefilter.com/2019/03/07/ninja-drlupo-courage-talent-management-loaded.
329. *Esports Playbook for Brands 2019* (The Nielsen Company, New York, NY), Mar. 2019, at 20.
330. Max Miceli, *EA Sets Up Sponsored Streams with Top Twitch Content Creators for Apex Legends Season 4 Release*, Dot Esports (Feb. 4, 2020), https://dotesports.com/apex-legends/news/ea-sets-up-sponsored-streams-with-top-twitch-content-creators-for-apex-legends-season-4-release.

331. Kevin Webb, *Ninja, the World's Most Popular Gamer, Makes $500,000 Every Month Paying 'Fortnite' – Here's How He Does it*, Business Insider (Jan. 31, 2020), https://www.businessinsider.com/ninja-tyler-blevins-twitch-subscribers-fortnite-drake-youtube-2018-3.
332. Ben Fischer, *Ninja to Be Featured on Red Bull Cans*, The Esports Observer (Mar. 27, 2019), https://esportsobserver.com/ninja-red-bull-drink-deal.
333. Uber Eats, *Here's What Ninja Eats When He's Streaming 300 Hours a Month*, https://www.ubereats.com/blog/en-US/ninja-partnership (last visited Feb. 5, 2020).
334. Postmates, *Shroud X Postmates—How to Order Like a Pro Gamer*, https://blog.postmates.com/shroud-x-postmates-how-to-order-like-a-pro-gamer-1af6aa23365a (last visited Feb. 5, 2020).
335. Max Moeller, *State Farm Has Revealed Their First Ever Sponsorship with an Individual Esports Player, Benjamin DrLupo* Lupo, The Sub Nation (Feb. 5, 2019), https://thesubnation.com/state-farm-announces-sponsorship-esports-player-drlupo.
336. Olga Kharif, *Inside the $1.5 Billion Market for Streamer-Branded Merchandise*, Bloomberg News (Apr. 22, 2020), https://www.bloomberg.com/news/articles/2020-04-22/inside-the-1-5-billion-market-for-streamer-branded-merchandise.
337. Official DanTDM, *Official DanTDM Shop*, https://uk.dantdmshop.com (last visited Feb. 5, 2020).
338. Natalie Robehmed and Madeline Berg, *Highest Paid YouTube Stars 2018: Markiplier, Jake Paul, PreDiePie and More*, Forbes (Dec. 3, 2018), https://www.forbes.com/sites/natalierobehmed/2018/12/03/highest-paid-youtube-stars-2018-markiplier-jake-paul-pewdiepie-and-more/#47f38b60909a.
339. Matt Perez, *Top-Earning Video Gamers: The Ten Highest-Paid Players Pocketed More than $120 Million in 2019*, Forbes (Jan. 29, 2020), https://www.forbes.com/sites/mattperez/2020/01/29/top-earning-video-gamers-the-ten-highest-paid-players-pocketed-more-than-120-million-in-2019/#1dc713b4880b.
340. J!NX, *Official Shroud Apparel, Accessories & More*, https://www.jinx.com/collections/shroud (last visited Feb. 5, 2020).
341. Stephanie Fogel, *Over 200 Custom Twitch Streaming Skins Coming to 'PUBG'*, Variety (Sep. 14, 2018), https://variety.com/2018/gaming/news/twitch-pubg-custom-skins-1202942291.
342. *Id.*
343. Epic Games, *Fortnite Icon Series*, https://www.epicgames.com/fortnite/en-US/news/icon-series (last visited Feb. 5, 2020).
344. Id.; See also Ninja (@Ninja), Twitter (Jan. 15, 2020, 10:09am), https://twitter.com/ninja/status/1217463951044366337.
345. Dean Takahashi, *Our Deep Dive into How Esports Broadcasting Differs from Traditional Sports*, Venture Beat (Apr. 13, 2019), https://venturebeat.com/2019/04/13/our-deep-dive-into-how-esports-broadcasting-differs-from-traditional-sports.
346. Phil "DrPhill Alexander, *Esports for Dummies*, 222 (Wiley 2020); See also Alana Thompson, *How Esports Casters Change the Game*, Esportz Network (Jul. 17, 2020), https://www.esportznetwork.com/how-esports-casters-shoutcasters-change-the-game.

347. BBC Newsround, *eSports: What is Shoutcasting?*, https://www.bbc.co.uk/newsround/39514973 (last visited Feb. 5, 2020); See also Anushia Kandasivam, *Who Are Shoutcasters and What Are They?*, Digital News Asia (Jul. 7, 2017), https://www.digitalnewsasia.com/digital-economy/who-are-shoutcasters-and-what-are-they.
348. Tobias M. Scholz, *eSports is Business: Management in the World of Competitive Gaming*, 70 (Palgrave Macmillan 2019); See also ESPN Esports Staff, *League of Legends Caster Jatt to Coach Team Liquid*, ESPN (May 4, 2020), https://www.espn.com/esports/story/_/id/29133065/league-legends-caster-jatt-coach-team-liquid.
349. University of Oklahoma, *Shoutcasting Program—Sooner Esports*, https://www.sooneresports.org/shoutcasting-program (last visited Feb. 5, 2020).
350. Phil "DrPhill" Alexander, *Esports for Dummies*, 222 (Wiley 2020).
351. Dean Takahashi, *Our Deep Dive into How Esports Broadcasting Differs from Traditional Sports*, Venture Beat (Apr. 13, 2019), https://venturebeat.com/2019/04/13/our-deep-dive-into-how-esports-broadcasting-differs-from-traditional-sports.
352. Adam Starkey, *How to Become a Professional Esports Shoutcaster: 7 Tips from the Experts*, Metro U.K. (Oct. 6, 2017), https://metro.co.uk/2017/10/06/how-to-become-a-professional-esports-shoutcaster-7-tips-from-the-experts-6974731.
353. Tobias M. Scholz, *eSports is Business: Management in the World of Competitive Gaming*, 63 (Palgrave Macmillan 2019).
354. Phil "DrPhill Alexander, *Esports for Dummies*, 222 (Wiley 2020); See also Adam Fitch, *GumGum Sports Reveals Esports Social Rankings for Q2 2019*, Esports Insider (Aug. 29, 2019), https://esportsinsider.com/2019/08/gumgum-rankings-q2-2019; Bräutigam, *FaZe Dominates All Competitors in Esports Social Media Rankings*, Dot Esports (Feb. 15, 2017), https://dotesports.com/business/news/most-influential-esports-brands-social-media-followers-4766.
355. Jay Hunter, *Inside Esports: An Interview with Videographer Sean Do*, The Gamer (May 1, 2020), https://www.thegamer.com/inside-esports-interview-videographer-sean-do.
356. Kengo Miyakoshi, *The Economics of Esports*, U.S.C. Economics Review (Jan. 4, 2019), https://usceconreview.com/2019/01/04/the-economics-of-esports.
357. Kaylee Fagan, *Full Benefits, 6-Figure Salaries, 401Ks and Nutritionists—2 Professionals Reveal What It's Really Like to be Paid to Play Video Games for a Living*, Business Insider (Jul. 27, 2020), https://www.businessinsider.com/what-its-like-to-play-in-the-overwatch-league-2018-4.
358. Tobias M. Scholz, *eSports is Business: Management in the World of Competitive Gaming*, 65 (Palgrave Macmillan 2019).
359. *Id.*
360. NVIDIA, *NVIDIA to Open GeForce Esports Boot Camps in Munich and Shanghai*, https://blogs.nvidia.com/blog/2018/08/09/geforce-esports-boot-camps-munich-and-shanghai (last visited Feb. 5, 2020); See also P.C. Gamer, *An Esports Bootcamp that's Worth Sweating Over*, https://www.pcgamer.com/an-esports-bootcamp-thats-worth-sweating-over (last visited Feb. 5, 2020).
361. Steven Van Sloun, *Esports Franchise Economics*, Loup Ventures (Mar. 9, 2018), https://loupventures.com/esports-franchise-economics.
362. Matt Perez, *Michael Jordan Esports, Invests in Team Liquid's Parent Company*, Forbes (Oct. 25, 2018), https://www.forbes.com/sites/mattperez/2018/10/25/michael-jordan-enters-esports-invests-in-team-liquids-parent-company

#1233ee8f69bf; *See* Matt Perez, *Esports Company TSM Raises $37 Million, Investors Include Stephen Curry, Steve Young*, Forbes (Jul. 24, 2018), https://www.forbes.com/sites/mattperez/2018/07/24/tsm-raises-37-million-investors-include-stephen-curry-jerry-yang/#2a8ac2187f8a; See also Tom Huddleston Jr., *From Michael Jordan to Drake: The Athletes and Celebs Who Invested Millions in Esports in 2018*, CNBC News (Dec. 27, 2018), https://www.cnbc.com/2018/12/19/from-michael-jordan-to-drake-athletes-celebrities-invested-millions-esports.html.

363. Laura Byrne, *Will Smith Invests as Gen. G Announce $46m Funding Round*, Esports Insider (Apr. 17, 2019), https://esportsinsider.com/2019/04/will-smith-invests-as-gen-g-announce-46m-funding-round.
364. Adel Chouadria, *Yankees Announce Investment in Echo Fox Parent Company*, ESPN (Oct. 19, 2017), https://www.espn.com/esports/story/_/id/21078265/new-york-yankees-announce-investment-vision-esports-echo-fox.
365. Jacob Wolf, *Echo Fox Ownership Group Vision Esports Raises $38 Million*, ESPN (Feb. 22, 2018), https://www.espn.com/esports/story/_/id/22543627/echo-fox-ownership-group-vision-esports-raises-38-million-kevin-durant-odell-beckham-jr-more.
366. Jacob Wolf, *Lynch, Strahan, J.Lo Part of $15 Million Investment in NRG Esports*, ESPN (Sep. 28, 2017), https://www.espn.com/esports/story/_/id/20851460/marshawn-lynch-rod-part-15-million-investment-round-nrg-esports.
367. Adam Fitch, *FaZe Clan details $40 million Series A funding round*, Esports Insider (Apr. 17, 2020), https://esportsinsider.com/2020/04/faze-clan-series-a; Tobias Deck, *American Rapper Offset Makes Investment in FaZe Clan*, The Esports Observer (Aug. 16, 2019), https://esportsobserver.com/offset-investment-faze-clan; Christina Settimi, *Philadelphia 76ers Star Ben Simmons Is Latest Athlete To Invest*, Forbes (Aug. 25, 2020), https://www.forbes.com/sites/christinasettimi/2020/08/25/philadelphia-76ers-star-ben-simmons-is-latest-athlete-to-invest-in-faze-clan; Jacob Wolf, *Music producer and DJ Steve Aoki invests in team Rogue*, ESPN (Oct. 1, 2016), https://www.espn.com/esports/story/_/id/17689712/music-producer-dj-steve-aoki-invests-team-rogue; Stefanie Fongel, *Imagine Dragons Invests in Esports Company ReKTGlobal and Team Rogue*, Variety (May 1, 2018), https://variety.com/2018/gaming/news/imagine-dragons-rektglobal-team-rogue-1202793671; Adam Fitch, *ReKTGlobal receives investment from Landon Collins*, Esports Insider (Nov. 14, 2019), https://esportsinsider.com/2019/11/rektglobal-landon-collins
368. Kevin Hitt, *Top 10 Esports Players of 2020 by Total Prize Winnings*, The Esports Observer (Dec. 26, 2019), https://esportsobserver.com/top-10-esports-players-2019.
369. *Id.*
370. *Id.*; See also Jordan Baranwoski, *The Truth about the Richest Esports Team Ever*, Looper (May 5, 2020), https://www.looper.com/206999/the-truth-about-the-richest-esports-team-ever.
371. T.L. Taylor, *Raising the Stakes: E-Sports and the Professionalization of Computer Gaming*, 195 (The MIT Press 2012).
372. Tobias M. Scholz, *eSports is Business: Management in the World of Competitive Gaming*, 65 (Palgrave Macmillan 2019).
373. Fnatic, *Fnatic Shop*, https://us-shop.fnatic.com (last visited Feb. 5, 2020).

374. Rogue Nation, *Official Fan Membership of Team Rogue*, https://www.roguenation.gg (last visited Jul. 26, 2020).
375. Andrew Hayward, *Rogue Launches Rogue Nation Fan Club Premium Subscriptions*, The Esports Observer (Jul. 26, 2019), https://esportsobserver.com/rogue-nation-fan-club.
376. *Id.*
377. Adam Fitch, *Simplicity Set to Open Five Esports Gaming Centers*, Esports Insider (Mar. 29, 2019), https://esportsinsider.com/2019/03/simplicity-esports-gaming-centers; Crystal Mills, *Simplicity Esports Acquires Texas-Based Esports Centre*, Esports Insider (Jul. 6, 2020), https://www.esportsinsider.com/2020/07/simplicity-esports-gaming-center; See also Simplicity Esports, *About*, https://ggsimplicity.com/about (last visited Jul. 26, 2020); PLAYlive Nation, *Locations*, https://playlivenation.com/locations?simplicity (last visited Jul. 26, 2020).
378. Rodrigo Guerra, *Grizzlies Minority Owner's Company Simplicity Esports to Run Brazil's Flamengo eSports*, ESPN Brazil (Jan. 14, 2020), https://tv5.espn.com/esports/story/_/id/28484807/grizzlies-minority-owner-company-simplicity-esports-run-brazil-flamengo-esports.
379. Cody Luongo, *Vindex*'s *Belong to Establish Gaming Venues in NYC through Andbox Deal*, Esports Insider (Jul. 29, 2020), https://www.esportsinsider.com/2020/07/vindex-belong-andbox; See also Cody Luongo, *Envy Gaming and Belong Partner to Bring Gaming Centres to North Texas*, Esports Insider (Jul. 29, 2020), https://esportsinsider.com/2020/07/envy-gaming-belong.
380. Rocket League, *The Esports Shop: A Closer Look*, https://www.rocketleague.com/news/esports-shop-a-closer-look (last visited Feb. 5, 2020).
381. *Id.*
382. Andrew Hayward, *Ubisoft Reveals 14 Teams for Rainbow Six Siege Revenue-Share Pilot Program Phase*, The Esports Observer (Aug. 19, 2019), https://esportsobserver.com/r6pl-phase-two-teams.
383. *Id.*
384. Andrew Hayward, *Gears 5 Adds Esports Items for NRG, Ghost, Reciprocity, and Rise Nation*, The Esports Observer (Nov. 12, 2019), https://esportsobserver.com/gears5-esports-dlc.
385. Adam Fitch, *Sources: The Numbers behind PUBG's Esports Revenue Sharing in 2019*, The Esports Insider (Jan. 14, 2020), https://esportsinsider.com/2020/01/pubg-esports-revenue-share-numbers.
386. *Id.*
387. *Id.*
388. *Id.*
389. *Id.*
390. Dean Takahashi, *Team Liquid's Steve Arhancet Tells Us How to Run an Esports Team*, Venture Beat (Apr. 28, 2017), https://venturebeat.com/2017/04/28/team-liquids-steve-arhancet-tells-us-how-to-run-an-esports-team.
391. Tobias M. Scholz, *eSports is Business: Management in the World of Competitive Gaming*, 82 (Palgrave Macmillan 2019).
392. *Id.*

393. E.J. Schultz, *How an Esports League is Changing to Lure Brand Sponsors*, Advertising Age (Jun. 1, 2017), https://adage.com/article/cmo-strategy/esports-league-changing-lure-brand-sponsors/309241.
394. Kevin Tran, *Why the Esports Audience is Set to Surge—And How Brands Can Take Advantage of Increased Fans and Viewership*, Business Insider (Nov. 8, 2018), https://www.businessinsider.com/the-esports-audience-report-2018-11.
395. *Id.*
396. AT&T, *AT&T Can Now Reach 22 Million Esports Fans Online Each Month*, https://about.att.com/story/2019/esports_22_million.html (last visited Feb. 5, 2020); See also T.L. Taylor, *Raising the Stakes: E-Sports and the Professionalization of Computer Gaming*, 157 (The MIT Press 2012).
397. Andrew Meola, *The Biggest Companies Sponsoring eSports Teams and Tournaments*, Business Insider (Jan. 12, 2019), https://www.businessinsider.com/top-esports-sponsors-gaming-sponsorships-2018-1; See also Tobias M. Scholz, *eSports is Business: Management in the World of Competitive Gaming*, 82 (Palgrave Macmillan 2019).
398. Tobias M. Scholz, *eSports is Business: Management in the World of Competitive Gaming*, 72 (Palgrave Macmillan 2019).
399. Stephen Boidock, *How Non-Endemic Brands Can Tackle Esports Marketing Opportunities*, AdWeek (May 10, 2018), https://www.adweek.com/brand-marketing/how-non-endemic-brands-can-tackle-esports-marketing-opportunities; See also Kitty Zhao, *Product Placement in Esports: 3 Examples of Brands Getting it Right*, Hollywood Branded (Jul. 14, 2020), https://blog.hollywoodbranded.com/product-placement-in-esports-3-examples-of-brands-getting-it-right.
400. Trent Murray, *T1 Signs Partnership with Hana Bank*, The Esports Observer (Jul. 24, 2020), https://esportsobserver.com/t1-partnership-hana-bank; See also Ben Fischer, *MSG's Counter Logic Gaming Signs Deal with Watch Brand MVMT*, The Esports Observer (Jun. 21, 2018), https://esportsobserver.com/clg-mvmt; Trent Murray, *Australian Org the Chiefs Esports Club Signs L'Oréal Men Expert for 2020*, The Esports Observer (Jul. 6, 2020), https://esportsobserver.com/chiefs-esports-club.
401. Marty Swant, *Miller Lite Sponsors Its First Esports Team as More Big Brands Support Competitive Gaming*, Adweek (May. 15, 2019), https://www.adweek.com/digital/miller-lite-sponsors-its-first-esports-team-as-more-big-brands-support-competitive-gaming; See also Paul 'Redeye' Chaloner, *This is Esports (and How to Spell it)*, 155 (Bloomsbury Sport 2020).
402. Trent Murray, *Team SoloMid Partners with Chipotle as Fortnite House Sponsor*, The Esports Observer (May 31, 2018), https://esportsobserver.com/tsm-fortnite-house-chipotle.
403. TeamSoloMid, *Dr. Pepper & TSM*, https://tsm.gg/news/dr-pepper-and-tsm (last visited Feb. 5, 2020).
404. Adam Fitch, *T1 Finds Exclusive Apparel Partner in Nike*, The Esports Insider (Jan. 16, 2020), https://esportsinsider.com/2020/01/t1-nike-partnership; See also T.L. Taylor, *Raising the Stakes: E-Sports and the Professionalization of Computer Gaming*, 156 (The MIT Press 2012).
405. Graham Ashton, *Misfits Gaming Group and Matrix Keyboards to Build Custom Player Products*, The Esports Observer (Mar. 10, 2020), https://esportsobserver.com/misfits-gaming-matrix-keyboards.

406. Oliver Ring, *Fnatic Sign Exclusive Streaming Partnership with Twitch*, The Esports Insider (Feb. 1, 2019), https://esportsinsider.com/2016/11/twitch-partner-with-tsm-and-cloud9.
407. Oliver Ring, *Twitch to Aid TSM and Cloud9 in Attracting Non-Electric Sponsorship*, The Esports Insider (Nov. 21, 2016), https://esportsinsider.com/2016/11/twitch-partner-with-tsm-and-cloud9.
408. The Esports Observer, *21st Century Fox Invests $100M in Streaming Startup Caffeine*, The Esports Observer (Sep. 5, 2018), https://esportsobserver.com/21st-century-fox-invests-100m-streaming-startup-caffeine.
409. Andrew Hayward, *Dignitas Signs Caffeine as Exclusive Broadcaster, Plots Original Series*, The Esports Observer (May. 28, 2019), https://esportsobserver.com/dignitas-caffeine-broadcaster.
410. *Id.*
411. Graham Ashton, *Team Secret Partners with Chinese Streaming Platform Huya*, The Esports Observer (May 22, 2020), https://esportsobserver.com/team-secret-huya-china.
412. Hongyu Chen, *Huya to Stream Korean League of Legends Matches in Three-Year Exclusive Deal*, The Esports Observer (Oct. 29, 2019), https://esportsobserver.com/riot-huya-lck-deal.
413. James Fudge, *Team Liquid and Huya Streaming Partnership Extended to 2022*, The Esports Observer (Jun. 5, 2020), https://esportsobserver.com/team-liquid-huya-2022.
414. Jacob Wolf, *New Franchised Counter-Strike League B Site Signs Six Teams, to Debut in March in Los Angeles*, ESPN (Jan. 26, 2020), https://www.espn.com/esports/story/_/id/28569076/new-franchised-counter-strike-league-b-site-signs-six-teams-debut-march-los-angeles.
415. Flashpoint, *About Flashpoint*, https://www.flashpoint.live/about (last visited Jul. 26, 2020).
416. David Bloom, *Top Esports Teams Launch Their Own CS:GO League to Counter Franchise Fever*, Forbes (Feb. 6, 2020), https://www.forbes.com/sites/dbloom/2020/02/06/new-esports-league-flashpoint-counter-strike-global-offensive/#1e4d2783961d.
417. *Id.*
418. *Id.*
419. Jeff Drake, *The 10 Most Successful Video Game Publishers of the Decade, Ranked by Revenue*, Game Rant (Nov. 21, 2019), https://gamerant.com/most-successful-game-publishers-2010s-revenue.
420. Alex Gibson, *Top 10 Highest Earning Video Game Publishers in Fiscal 2018*, Twinfinite (Aug. 1, 2018), https://twinfinite.net/2018/08/10-highest-earning-video-game-publishers-2018; See also Kevin Webb, *Video Game Sales Are Down in 2019 as the Industry Prepares for the PlayStation 5 and Xbox Series X, but that Didn't Stop this Year's Best-Sellers from Setting New Records*, Business Insider (Dec. 15, 2019), https://www.businessinsider.com/best-selling-video-games-of-the-year-2019-2019-12.
421. Gabe Gurwin and Jacob Roach, *The Best Free-to-Play Games for 2020*, Digital Trends (Jul. 14, 2020), https://www.digitaltrends.com/gaming/best-free-to-play-games; See also Riot Games, *League of Legends Sign Up*, https://signup.na.leagueoflegends.com/en/signup (last visited Jul. 26, 2020).

422. Melissa Loomis, *The Cost of Nothing: Free-to-Play Games Are Changing the Industry*, Game Rant (Feb. 20, 2015), https://gamerant.com/free-to-play-games-changing-gaming-industry; See also Eddie Makuch, *Microtransactions, Explained: Here's What You Need to Know*, Game Spot (Nov. 20, 2018), https://www.gamespot.com/articles/microtransactions-explained-heres-what-you-need-to/1100-6456995.
423. VideoGames.org.au, *Skins & Skin Betting*, https://www.videogames.org.au/skin-betting/ (last visited Feb. 5, 2020).
424. *Id.*
425. Austen Goslin, *Stranger Things' Upside Down Portals Have Started Appearing in Fortnite*, Polygon (Jul. 3, 2019), https://www.polygon.com/fortnite/2019/7/3/20681067/stranger-things-fortnite-portals.
426. Wasif Ahmed, *Clash Royale Players Have Reportedly Spent Over $3 Billion to Date*, Dot Esports (Jul. 16, 2020), https://dotesports.com/mobile/news/clash-royale-players-have-reportedly-spent-over-3-billion-to-date; See also Eddie Makuch, *Here's How Much Money Take-Two Makes from Microtransactions and Which Games Are the Biggest*, Game Spot (May 20, 2020), https://www.gamespot.com/articles/heres-how-much-money-taketwo-makes-from-microtrans/1100-6477537.
427. Brandon Ridgely, *NBA 2K20: Beginner's Guide to MyTEAM*, Real Sport 101 (Apr. 20, 2020), https://realsport101.com/nba-2k/nba-2k20-beginners-guide-to-myteam-virtual-currency-myteam-tokens-vc-mt; Epic Games, *Fortnite V-Bucks*, https://www.epicgames.com/fortnite/en-US/vbuckscard (last visited Jul. 26, 2020).
428. Eddie Makuch, *Here's How Much Money Take-Two Makes from Microtransactions and Which Games Are the Biggest*, Game Spot (May 20, 2020), https://www.gamespot.com/articles/heres-how-much-money-taketwo-makes-from-microtrans/1100-6477537; See also Chris Jecks, *NBA 2K20: How to Get VC (Money) Fast & Easy*, Twinfinite (Sept. 10, 2019), https://twinfinite.net/2019/09/nba-2k20-how-to-get-vc-money-fast-easy.
429. Paul 'Redeye' Chaloner, *This is Esports (and How to Spell it)*, 110 (Bloomsbury Sport 2020).
430. Eddie Makuch, *EA Made Almost $1 Billion on Microtransactions Last Quarter*, Game Stop (Feb. 3, 2020), https://www.gamespot.com/articles/ea-made-almost-1-billion-on-microtransactions-last/1100-6473240.
431. Ollie Green, *Report: Game Publishers Are Making Billions from Microtransactions*, Game Byte (Feb. 23, 2018), https://www.gamebyte.com/report-game-publishers-making-billions-microtransactions; See also Liz Lanier, *Lawsuit Targets Epic's 'Predatory' Loot Boxes in 'Fortnite,'* Variety (Mar. 1, 2019), https://variety.com/2019/gaming/news/lawsuit-loot-boxes-fortnite-1203152894; Leah Williams, *Apple Hit with Class Action Complaint Over Loot Boxes*, Kotaku (Jun. 19, 2020), https://www.kotaku.com.au/2020/06/apple-app-store-class-action-lawsuit; Ben Gilbert, *The Video Game Industry is Facing Government Scrutiny Over Loot Boxes, and the Most Powerful Leaders in Gaming Are Divided Over What to Do*, Business Insider (Jun. 23, 2019), https://www.businessinsider.com/video-game-industry-loot-box-legislation-2019-6; Makena Kelly, *Game Studios Would Be Banned from Selling Loot Boxes to Minors under New Bill*, The Verge (May 8, 2019), https://www.theverge.com/2019/5/8/18536806/game-studios-banned-loot-boxes-minors-bill-hawley-josh-blizzard-ea.

432. Newzoo, *Top 25 Public Companies by Game Revenues*, https://newzoo.com/insights/rankings/top-25-companies-game-revenues (last visited Jul. 26, 2020); See also Rocket League, *Psyonix is Joining the Epic Family!*, https://www.rocketleague.com/news/psyonix-is-joining-the-epic-family-/ (last visited Feb. 5, 2020).
433. Haydn Taylor, *Top 25 Public Game Companies Grossed Over $100bn Combined Revenue Last Year*, GamesIndustry.biz (Apr. 17, 2019), https://www.gamesindustry.biz/articles/2019-04-17-top-25-public-game-companies-grossed-than-usd100bn-combined-revenue-last-year.
434. Tobias M. Scholz, *eSports is Business: Management in the World of Competitive Gaming*, 51 (Palgrave Macmillan 2019).
435. *Id.*
436. Tobias M. Scholz, *eSports is Business: Management in the World of Competitive Gaming*, 140 (Palgrave Macmillan 2019).
437. *Id.* at 81.
438. Jacob Wolf, *Sources: Overwatch League Expansion Slots Expected to Be $30 Million to $60 Million*, ESPN (May 10, 2018), https://www.espn.com/esports/story/_/id/23464637/overwatch-league-expansion-slots-expected-30-60-million.
439. Mariella Moon, *Owning a 'Call of Duty' eSports Franchise Could Cost $25 Million*, Engadget (Mar. 16, 2019), https://www.engadget.com/2019/03/16/call-of-duty-esports-franchise-25-million; See also Call of Duty League, *Official Site*, https://www.callofdutyleague.com (last visited Jul. 26, 2020).
440. Adam Stern, *Is Franchising the Future for Esports?*, Sports Business Journal (Nov. 11, 2019), https://www.sportsbusinessdaily.com/Journal/Issues/2019/11/11/In-Depth/Franchising.aspx.
441. Truebridge Capital, *Top 4 Reasons Franchises Are the MVP of Esports*, Forbes (Mar. 28, 2019), https://www.forbes.com/sites/truebridge/2019/03/28/top-4-reasons-franchises-are-the-mvp-of-esports/#391d56ec33d2.
442. Morgan Stanley, *The World of Games: eSports from Wild West to Mainstream*, at 15 (Oct. 12, 2018), https://www.goldmansachs.com/insights/pages/infographics/e-sports/report.pdf.
443. ESPN.com, *Overwatch League Comes to ESPN, Disney and ABC*, ESPN (Jul. 11, 2018), https://www.espn.com/esports/story/_/id/24062274/overwatch-league-comes-espn-disney-abc; See also Aaron Mamiit, *Overwatch League, Call of Duty League to Exclusively Stream on YouTube*, Digital Trends (Jan. 27, 2020), https://www.digitaltrends.com/gaming/activision-blizzard-google-youtube-overwatch-call-of-duty.
444. George Geddes, *Call of Duty and Overwatch League Ticket Sales Reported to Be "Largely Positive,"* Dot Esports (Feb. 1, 2020), https://dotesports.com/news/call-of-duty-and-overwatch-league-ticket-sales-reported-to-be-largely-positive.
445. Paul 'Redeye' Chaloner, *This is Esports (and How to Spell it)*, 223 (Bloomsbury Sport 2020); See also *Esports Playbook for Brands 2019* (The Nielsen Company, New York, NY), Mar. 2019, at 8–9.
446. *Esports Playbook for Brands 2019* (The Nielsen Company, New York, NY), Mar. 2019, at 8.
447. Annie Pei, *How Free Games and Streaming Services Sparked a Video Game Boom that Changed Pop Culture*, CNBC (Dec. 25, 2019), https://www.cnbc.com/amp/2019/12/24/how-free-games-and-streaming-services-sparked-a-video-game-boom.html.

448. Hayden Brooks, *Fortnite's Live In-Game Marshmello Concert Was a Massive Success*, iHeartRadio (Feb. 11, 2019), https://www.iheart.com/content/2019-02-11-fortnites-live-in-game-marshmello-concert-was-a-massive-success.
449. Tatiana Cirisano, *Game On: What Travis Scott is Teaching Music Stars about the World's Biggest New (Virtual) Stage*, Billboard (Jul. 25, 2020), https://www.billboard.com/articles/business/9422287/travis-scott-fortnite-billboard-cover-story-interview-2020.
450. Jon Silman, *Fortnite's Movie Nite Will Screen Christopher Nolan Movies*, Digital Trends (Jun. 25, 2020), https://www.digitaltrends.com/gaming/fortnite-movie-nite-christopher-nolan; See also Epic Games, *Fortnite Party Royale*, https://www.epicgames.com/fortnite/en-US/partyroyale (last visited Jul. 26, 2020).
451. Jon Blistein, *100 Gecs Enlist Charli XCX for Digital Charity Festival in 'Minecraft,'* Rolling Stone (Apr. 16, 2020), https://www.rollingstone.com/music/music-news/100-gecs-charli-xcx-minecraft-square-garden-festival-985189.
452. Shaun Prescott, *The Offspring is Playing a Gig in World of Tanks Tomorrow*, P.C. Gamer (Sept. 17, 2019), https://www.pcgamer.com/uk/the-offspring-is-playing-a-gig-in-world-of-tanks-tomorrow; See also World of Tanks, *A New Vehicle Featuring the Offspring, and It's Pretty Fly*!, https://worldoftanks.com/en/news/premium-shop/offspring-pretty-fly (last visited Jul. 26, 2020).
453. T.L. Taylor, *Raising the Stakes: E-Sports and the Professionalization of Computer Gaming*, 63 (The MIT Press 2012).
454. *Id.* at 161.
455. Rich Huggan, *Esports is Hiring—And You Don't Need to Be a Player*, Venture Beat (Aug. 30, 2018), https://venturebeat.com/2018/08/30/esports-is-hiring-and-you-dont-need-to-be-a-player.
456. T.L. Taylor, *Raising the Stakes: E-Sports and the Professionalization of Computer Gaming*, 146 (The MIT Press 2012); Tobias M. Scholz, *eSports is Business: Management in the World of Competitive Gaming*, 132 (Palgrave Macmillan 2019).
457. T.L. Taylor, *Raising the Stakes: E-Sports and the Professionalization of Computer Gaming*, 155 (The MIT Press 2012); Tobias M. Scholz, *eSports is Business: Management in the World of Competitive Gaming*, 59 (Palgrave Macmillan 2019).
458. Graham Ashton, *Esport's Quest for the Average Minute Audience*, The Esports Observer (Sept. 11, 2019), https://esportsobserver.com/nielsen-owl-ama-viewership-intro.
459. *Id.*
460. Id.; See also Sara Fischer, *TV-Like Ratings Are Coming to Esports*, Axios (Mar. 3, 2020), https://www.axios.com/esports-tv-ratings-nielsen-9d59dc2d-3960-48b4-b10c-ea98460d5a32.html.
461. *Esports Playbook for Brands 2019* (The Nielsen Company, New York, NY), Mar. 2019, at 24.
462. Influencer Marketing Hub, *25 Useful Twitch Statistic for Influencer Marketing Managers [Infographic]*, https://influencermarketinghub.com/twitch-statistics (last visited Feb. 5, 2020).
463. Trent Murray, *DreamHack and Twitch Follow 10-Year Partnership Milestone with Multi-Year Deal*, The Esports Observer (Mar. 22, 2018), https://esportsobserver.com/dreamhack-twitch-partnership-renewal.

464. Ben Fischer, *Overwatch League-Twitch Deal Worth at Least $90 Million*, The Esports Observer (Jan. 9, 2018), https://esportsobserver.com/overwatch-league-deal-with-twitch.
465. Adam Stern, *Activision Blizzard Makes Streaming Switch from Twitch to YouTube*, Sports Business Daily (Jan. 27, 2020), https://www.sportsbusinessdaily.com/Daily/Issues/2020/01/27/Media/YouTube-Activision-Blizzard.aspx; See also Adam Stern, *Sources: YouTube's Deal with Activision Blizzard Valued at $160M*, The Esports Observer (Feb. 13, 2020), https://esportsobserver.com/sources-youtube-actiblizzard-160m.
466. Ben Fischer, *Facebook Lands Streaming Rights for Two Major Esports Properties*, The Esports Observer (Jan. 18, 2018), https://esportsobserver.com/facebook-lands-streaming-rights-esports.
467. Trent Murray, *Capcom Pro Tour Adds Facebook and YouTube as Broadcast Partners*, The Esports Observer (Mar. 16, 2018), https://esportsobserver.com/capcom-pro-tour-adds-facebook-and-youtube.
468. Chenglu Zhang, *DouYu Obtains Chinese Streaming Rights for WESG*, Esports Insider (Nov. 26, 2019), https://esportsinsider.com/2019/11/douyu-wesg-streaming-rights.
469. *Id.*
470. Hongyu Chen, *Bilibili to Pay $113M for League of Legends World Championships Media Rights in China*, The Esports Observer (Dec. 3, 2019), https://esportsobserver.com/bilibili-media-rights-china-worlds; See also Reuters, MTG's e-sports firms partner with Chinese streaming platform Huya, Financial Post (Jul. 23, 2020), https://financialpost.com/pmn/business-pmn/mtgs-e-sports-firms-partner-with-chinese-streaming-platform-huya-3.
471. Trent Murray, *ESL Signs One-Year Chinese Streaming Deal with Huya*, The Esports Observer (Jul. 23, 2020), https://esportsobserver.com/esl-one-year-china-huya.
472. Jon Fingas, *NASCAR's Virtual Race Was the Most-Watched Esports TV Show to Date*, Engadget (Mar. 25, 2020), https://www.engadget.com/2020-03-25-nascar-esports-racing-series-sets-tv-record.html.
473. ESPN Staff, *ESPN, Disney, NFL Ink Multiyear Deal for Madden Broadcast Rights*, ESPN (Jan. 26, 2018), https://www.espn.com/esports/story/_/id/22217917/espn-disney-nfl-announce-multi-year-deal-broadcast-madden-nfl-18-championship-series.
474. Chloe Aiello, *Overwatch Hits the Big Time with ESPN Broadcast Deal*, CNBC (Jul. 11, 2018), https://www.cnbc.com/2018/07/11/espn-to-live-broadcast-activision-blizzard-esports-overwatch-league.html.
475. Todd Spangler, *Turner, WME/IMG Form E-Sports League*, With TBS to Air Live Events, Variety (Sept. 23, 2015), https://variety.com/2015/tv/news/turner-wme-img-esports-league-tbs-1201600921.
476. Andrew Hayward, *Psyonix and ELEAGUE Sign Rocket League TV, Ad Sales, and Event Deal*, The Esports Observer (Feb. 11, 2019), https://esportsobserver.com/psyonix-eleague-rocket-league/.
477. Kellen Beck, *NBC Breaks into Esports, Starting with 'Rocket League'*, Mashable (Jun. 21, 2017), https://mashable.com/2017/06/21/rocket-league-nbc-television/.

478. Jack Stewart, *Sport1 Signs Two-Year Deal with ESL for German Esports Channel*, The Esports Observer (Jan. 22, 2019), https://esportsobserver.com/esport1-licensing-deal-esl.
479. Oliver Ring, *Sky and ITV Invest in* Ginx TV, Esports Insider (Sept. 21, 2016), https://esportsinsider.com/2016/09/sky-itv-invest-ginx-tv.
480. Eve Martinello, *TV 2 Denmark Acquires Danish Broadcast Rights for ESL Pro Tour*, Esports Insider (Oct. 21, 2019), https://esportsinsider.com/2019/10/tv-2-denmark-esl-pro-tour.
481. Cody Luongo, *ESL and DreamHack Ink Television Rights Deal with Blake Broadcasting*, Esports Insider (Dec. 18, 2019), https://esportsinsider.com/2019/12/esl-dreamhack-blake-broadcasting.
482. T.L. Taylor, *Raising the Stakes: E-Sports and the Professionalization of Computer Gaming*, 154 (The MIT Press 2012).
483. *Id.* at 155; *Esports Playbook for Brands 2019* (The Nielsen Company, New York, NY), Mar. 2019, at 14.
484. Andrew Hayward, *ELEAGUE Signs AXE as Official Personal Care Partner*, The Esports Observer (Apr. 4, 2019), https://esportsobserver.com/eleague-axe-partner.
485. Andrew Hayward, *DreamHack Summer Adds Doritos as Sponsor*, The Esports Observer (Jun. 13, 2019), https://esportsobserver.com/dreamhack-summer-doritos.
486. Ben Fischer, *Chipotle to Sponsor ESL, DreamHack Events*, The Esports Observer (Apr. 11, 2019), https://esportsobserver.com/chipotle-esl-dreamhack-events.
487. Max Miceli, *Turtle Beach Expands Sponsorship Deal with DreamHack Atlanta*, The Esports Observer (Oct. 30, 2018), https://esportsobserver.com/turtle-beach-dreamhack-atlanta.
488. Graham Ashton, *Samsung Partners with DreamHack for Mobile Gaming Series*, The Esports Observer (May 28, 2019), https://esportsobserver.com/samsung-dreamhack-mobile-series.
489. Jesse Aaron, *How Much Does it Really Cost to Promote Games at Expos and is it Worth it?*, Venture Beat (Oct. 16, 2014), https://venturebeat.com/community/2014/10/16/how-much-does-it-really-cost-to-promote-games-at-expos-and-is-it-worth-it.
490. Andrew Hayward, *DreamHack Summer Adds Doritos as Sponsor*, The Esports Observer (Jun. 13, 2019), https://esportsobserver.com/dreamhack-summer-doritos.
491. Steve Noah, *NBA 2K League Moving to Manhattan Studio for 2020 Season, Complete Schedule Revealed*, Operation Sports (Feb. 28, 2020), https://www.operationsports.com/nba-2k-league-moving-to-manhattan-studio-for-2020-season-complete-schedule-revealed; See also ESL, *ESL One Hamburg – Tickets*, https://www.esl-one.com/dota2/hamburg/tickets (last visited Jul. 31, 2020).
492. Steven Van Sloun, *Esports Franchise Economics*, Loup Ventures (Mar. 9, 2018), https://loupventures.com/esports-franchise-economics.
493. Haley MacLean, *Overwatch League Grand Finals Rickets Cost More than a Bruno Mars, Elton John, or Drake Concert*, Twinfinite (Jul. 12, 2018), https://twinfinite.net/2018/07/overwatch-league-grand-finals-tickets-more-expensive-bruno-mars-elton-john-drake-concert.
494. The Esports Observer, *Overwatch League Finals Sell Out in Two Weeks*, The Esports Observer (Jun. 1, 2018), https://esportsobserver.com/overwatch-league-finals-sold-out.

495. Celia Chen, *League of Legends World Finals Tickets Gone in Seconds, Showing How E-sports Continues to Boom in* China, South China Morning Post (Oct. 26, 2017), https://www.scmp.com/tech/china-tech/article/2117163/league-legends-world-finals-tickets-gone-seconds-showing-how-e.
496. Interview with Cody Luongo, Head of Communications, Ultimate Gaming Championship, *The #EsportsBizShow Episode 2* (Oct. 3, 2019), Available at: https://youtu.be/S-HEzMnEEVo.
497. Twitch, *UGC Twitch* page, *https://www.twitch.tv/ugc/videos* (last visited Feb. 5, 2020).
498. ESL, *ESL Shop*, https://us-shop.eslgaming.com (last visited Feb. 5, 2020).
499. *Id.*
500. Dreamhack, *Dreamhack Store*, https://store.dreamhack.com (last visited Feb. 5, 2020).
501. Graham Ashton, *Overwatch League's Merchandising Strategy Could Make or Break it*, The Esports Observer (Dec. 15, 2017), https://esportsobserver.com/overwatch-leagues-merchandise.
502. NBA 2K League, *NBA 2K League Announces Partnership with Champion Athleticwear Ahead of March 5 Draft*, https://2kleague.nba.com/news/nba-2k-league-announces-partnership-with-champion-athleticwear-ahead-of-march-5-draft (last visited Feb. 5, 2020).
503. Ultimate Gaming Competition, *Custom Gear*, https://ugcstore.gg/product-category/custom-gear (last visited Feb. 5, 2020).
504. Angelo M D'Argenio, *The Ultimate Guide to Running a Local E-sports Tournament*, Game Crate (Nov. 25, 2016), https://gamecrate.com/ultimate-guide-running-local-e-sports-tournament/14967.
505. *Id.*
506. *Id.*
507. Ken Kerschbaumer, *2019 Esports Production Summit: Tips and Considerations for* Venue Design, SVG (Nov. 22, 2019), https://www.sportsvideo.org/2019/11/22/2019-esports-production-summit-tips-and-considerations-for-venue-design.
508. *Guide to Hosting Esports Tournaments & Events* (SportsTravel / MGM Resorts, Secaucus, NJ), Mar. 19, 2019, at 7; See also Adam Fitch, *Sources: PUBG Corp. Responsible for MET Asia Series Controversy*, Esports Insider (Jul. 31, 2019), https://esportsinsider.com/2019/07/met-asia-series-controversy.
509. SteelSeries, *How to Organize a Local Esports Tournament: Part 1*, https://steelseries.com/blog/how-organize-local-esports-tournament-1-151 (last visited Jul. 22, 2020); See also Nigel Zalamea, *5 Esports Tournaments that Ended in Disaster*, One Esports (Feb. 19, 2020), https://www.oneesports.gg/features-and-opinions/5-esports-tournaments-that-ended-in-disaster.
510. *Guide to Hosting Esports Tournaments & Events* (SportsTravel / MGM Resorts, Secaucus, NJ), Mar. 19, 2019, at 7.
511. SteelSeries, *How to Organize a Local Esports Tournament: Part 1*, https://steelseries.com/blog/how-organize-local-esports-tournament-1-151 (last visited Jul. 22, 2020); See also Aron Garst, *The Aggravation of Game-Breaking Bugs in Esports*, Engadget (Mar. 30, 2020), https://www.engadget.com/2020-03-30-esports-game-breaking-bugs.html.

512. Ken Kerschbaumer, 2019 *Esports Production Summit: Tips and Considerations for Venue Design*, SVG (Nov. 22, 2019), https://www.sportsvideo.org/2019/11/22/2019-esports-production-summit-tips-and-considerations-for-venue-design. See also Andrew Webster, *Designing League of Legends' Stunning Holographic Worlds Opening Ceremony*, The Verge (Nov. 11, 2019), https://www.theverge.com/2019/11/11/20959206/league-of-legends-worlds-2019-opening-ceremony-holograms-holonet.
513. Angelo M D'Argenio, *The Ultimate Guide to Running a Local E-sports Tournament*, Game Crate (Nov. 25, 2016), https://gamecrate.com/ultimate-guide-running-local-e-sports-tournament/14967; See also British Esports Association, *How to Host Your Own LAN Party or Small Esports Tournament, https://britishesports.org/news/%E2%80%8Bhow-to-host-your-own-lan-party-or-small-esports-tournament* (last visited Jul. 30, 2020).
514. GEX Esports, *Friday Night Open LAN Bring Your Own Computer*, https://www.gexesports.com/product/friday-night-open-lan-byoc (last visited Jul. 30, 2020).
515. SteelSeries, *How to Organize a Local Esports Tournament: Part 1*, https://steelseries.com/blog/how-organize-local-esports-tournament-1-151 (last visited Jul. 22, 2020).
516. Gillian Linscott, *The Best Venues for Esports Events: Size Isn't Everything*, Esports Edition (Aug. 11, 2017), https://esportsedition.com/general/best-esports-venues.
517. Angelo M D'Argenio, *The Ultimate Guide to Running a Local E-sports Tournament*, Game Crate (Nov. 25, 2016), https://gamecrate.com/ultimate-guide-running-local-e-sports-tournament/14967; See also *Guide to Hosting Esports Tournaments & Events* (SportsTravel / MGM Resorts, Secaucus, NJ), Mar. 19, 2019, at 6.
518. Adam Fitch, *Simplicity Set to Open Five Esports Gaming Centers*, Esports Insider (Mar. 29, 2019), https://esportsinsider.com/2019/03/simplicity-esports-gaming-centers; See also *Guide to Hosting Esports Tournaments & Events* (SportsTravel / MGM Resorts, Secaucus, NJ), Mar. 19, 2019, at 6; HyperX Esports Arena Las Vegas at the Luxor, *Home Page*, https://www.hyperxesportsarenalasvegas.com (last visited Jul. 22, 2020).
519. *Guide to Hosting Esports Tournaments & Events* (SportsTravel / MGM Resorts, Secaucus, NJ), Mar. 19, 2019, at 7.
520. *Id.*
521. *Id*; See also Gillian Linscott, *The First Esports Travel Agency: Another Milestone*, Esports Edition (Jan. 7, 2017), https://esportsedition.com/general/esports-travel-growth.
522. Tobias M. Scholz, *eSports is Business: Management in the World of Competitive Gaming*, 61 (Palgrave Macmillan 2019).
523. T.L. Taylor, *Raising the Stakes: E-Sports and the Professionalization of Computer Gaming*, 63 (The MIT Press 2012); See also Hearthstone, Rules and Policies, https://playhearthstone.com/en-us/esports/programs/rules-and-policies (last visited Jul. 30, 2020); ESL, Rules—Major—CSGO, https://play.eslgaming.com/counterstrike/csgo/csgo/major/rules (last visited Jul. 30, 2020).

524. T.L. Taylor, *Raising the Stakes: E-Sports and the Professionalization of Computer Gaming*, 63 (The MIT Press 2012); See also Josh Raven, *How Riot's Age Restrictions Hurt Its Brightest Talents*, Dot Esports (May 27, 2015), https://dotesports.com/league-of-legends/news/sencux-riot-games-age-restrictions-1895.
525. T.L. Taylor, *Raising the Stakes: E-Sports and the Professionalization of Computer Gaming*, 63 (The MIT Press 2012); See also Rocket League Esports, RLCS Season X *Rules*, https://www.rocketleagueesports.com/rules (last visited Jul. 30, 2020).
526. T.L. Taylor, *Raising the Stakes: E-Sports and the Professionalization of Computer Gaming*, 63 (The MIT Press 2012); See also Classic Tetric World Championship, *Official CTWC Main Event Rules*, https://thectwc.com/rules (last visited Jul. 30, 2020).
527. Angelo M D'Argenio, *The Ultimate Guide to Running a Local E-sports Tournament*, Game Crate (Nov. 25, 2016), https://gamecrate.com/ultimate-guide-running-local-e-sports-tournament/14967 (emphasis added); See also Teddy Amenabar, *Overwatch League Finds a Silver-Lining to Season 3 Turmoil: Tournaments*, Launcher (Jul. 15, 2020), https://www.washingtonpost.com/video-games/esports/2020/07/15/overwatch-contenders-cup-tournament.
528. Nicole Carpenter, *Riot Games Files Lawsuit against Esports Organization Over 'Riot' Trademark*, Polygon (Oct. 10, 2019), https://www.polygon.com/2019/10/10/20908027/riot-games-copyright-trademark-lawsuit-riot-squad.
529. Adam Fitch, *ESL Announces "Simpler, More Powerful" Rebrand*, Esports Insider (Feb. 14, 2019), https://esportsinsider.com/2019/02/esl-rebrands.
530. Phil "DrPhill" Alexander, Esports for Dummies, 13 (Wiley 2020).
531. <DREAMHACK>, U.S. Registration No. 6,079,033.
532. <DREAMHACK LOGO>, U.S. Registration No. 5,320,145; See also <DREAMHACK LOGO>, U.S. Registration No. 5,207,651.
533. Asset Panda, Blog: *Mel Van De Graaf, Hidden Costs of Managing Esports Events*, https://www.assetpanda.com/resource-center/blog/hidden-costs-of-managing-esports-events (last visited Jul. 30, 2020); See also Hamza 'CTZ' Aziz, *So How Much Does it Cost to Host an eSports Competition Anyway?*, Destructoid (Mar. 3, 2014), https://www.destructoid.com/stories/so-how-much-does-it-cost-to-host-an-esports-competition-anyway--271749.phtml.
534. Taylor Soper, *Esports Tournament Operator Matcherino Lands Funding as Question Swirl about Industry's Growth*, GeekWire (Aug. 5, 2019), https://www.geekwire.com/2019/esports-tournament-operator-matcherino-raises-cash-question-swirl-industrys-growth; *Esports Playbook for Brands 2019* (The Nielsen Company, New York, NY), Mar. 2019, at 14.
535. Angelo M D'Argenio, *The Ultimate Guide to Running a Local E-sports Tournament*, Game Crate (Nov. 25, 2016), https://gamecrate.com/ultimate-guide-running-local-e-sports-tournament/14967.
536. Id.; See also David O' Keefe, *Fighting Game Community's Passion Isn't Paying the Bills*, Venture Beat (Dec. 1, 2019), https://venturebeat.com/2019/12/01/fighting-game-communitys-passion-isnt-paying-the-bills.
537. Giulio Coraggio, *eSports Tournaments Limited by Italian Prize Promotion and Gambling Rules?*, Gaming Tech Law (Jan. 22, 2019), https://www.gamingtechlaw.com/2019/01/esports-tournaments-italian-rules.html; See also Imad

Khan, *Japan Grapples with Esports' Harmful Connection to Gambling Laws*, ESPN (Feb. 16, 2019), https://www.espn.com/esports/story/_/id/26011811/japan-grapples-esports-harmful-connection-gambling-laws.
538. Angelo M D'Argenio, *The Ultimate Guide to Running a Local E-sports Tournament*, Game Crate (Nov. 25, 2016), https://gamecrate.com/ultimate-guide-running-local-e-sports-tournament/14967); See also SteelSeries, *How to Organize a Local Esports Tournament: Part 1*, https://steelseries.com/blog/how-organize-local-esports-tournament-1-151 (last visited Jul. 22, 2020).
539. Angelo M D'Argenio, *The Ultimate Guide to Running a Local E-sports Tournament*, Game Crate (Nov. 25, 2016), https://gamecrate.com/ultimate-guide-running-local-e-sports-tournament/14967); See also Adam Fitch, *Allied Esports Partners with Esports Entertainment Group for CS:GO Legend Series*, Esports Insider (Jul. 9, 2020), https://esportsinsider.com/2020/07/allied-esports-partners-with-esports-entertainment-group-for-csgo-legend-series.
540. SteelSeries, *How to Organize a Local Esports Tournament: Part 1*, https://steelseries.com/blog/how-organize-local-esports-tournament-1-151 (last visited Jul. 22, 2020).
541. Tobias M. Scholz, *eSports is Business: Management in the World of Competitive Gaming*, 61 (Palgrave Macmillan 2019).
542. *Force Majeure*, Black's Law Dictionary (10th ed. 2014); See also Poorvi Sanjanwala and Kashmira Bakliwal, *What is Force Majeure? The Legal Term Everyone Should Know during Covid-19 Crisis*, The Economic Times (May 21, 2020), https://economictimes.indiatimes.com/small-biz/legal/what-is-force-majeure-the-legal-term-everyone-should-know-during-covid-19-crisis.
543. Roger Quiles, *Legal Lessons for Event Organizers in the Wake of COVID-19*, Quiles Law (Mar. 24, 2020), http://www.esports.law/blog/legal-lessons-for-event-organizers-in-the-wake-of-covid-19.
544. Nigel Zalamea, *Every Esports Event Disrupted by the COVID-19 Coronavirus Outbreak*, One Esports (Jun. 1, 2020), https://www.oneesports.gg/industry-news/every-esports-event-disrupted-by-the-covid-19-coronavirus-outbreak; See also Nicole Carpenter, *Dota 2's The International Delayed Indefinitely, Likely to 2021*, Polygon (May 1, 2020), https://www.polygon.com/2020/5/1/21243964/dota-2-the-international-2020-delayed-coronavirus-pandemic.
545. Insurance Journal, *K&K Insurance Launches Program for eSports Teams, Events*, https://www.insurancejournal.com/news/national/2018/04/23/487023.htm (last visited Jul. 22, 2020).
546. Adam Malik, *Why E-sports Could Be Insurance's Next Big Opportunity*, Canadian Underwriter (Jul. 14, 2020), https://www.canadianunderwriter.ca/insurance/why-e-sports-could-be-insurances-next-big-opportunity-1004194446.
547. Evan W. Bolla, *COVID-19 and Business Interruption Insurance: Insureds Face Potential Roadblocks to Coverage*, N.Y. Law Journal (Apr. 3, 2020), https://www.law.com/newyorklawjournal/2020/04/03/covid-19-and-business-interruption-insurance-insureds-face-potential-roadblocks-to-coverage.
548. Roger Quiles, *Legal Lessons for Event Organizers in the Wake of COVID-19*, Quiles Law (Mar. 24, 2020), http://www.esports.law/blog/legal-lessons-for-event-organizers-in-the-wake-of-covid-19.

549. See A.S.C.A.P., Why ASCAP Licenses Bars, *Restaurants & Music Venues*, https://www.ascap.com/help/ascap-licensing/why-ascap-licenses-bars-restaurants-music-venues (last visited Jul. 22, 2020).
550. The Esports Observer, *An Introduction to the Esports Ecosystem*, https://esportsobserver.com/the-esports-eco-system (last visited Jul. 22, 2020).
551. *Guide to Hosting Esports Tournaments & Events* (SportsTravel / MGM Resorts, Secaucus, NJ), Mar. 19, 2019, at 8; See also *Esports Playbook for Brands 2019* (The Nielsen Company, New York, NY), Mar. 2019, at 14.
552. *Guide to Hosting Esports Tournaments & Events* (SportsTravel / MGM Resorts, Secaucus, NJ), Mar. 19, 2019, at 8.
553. *Guide to Hosting Esports Tournaments & Events* (SportsTravel / MGM Resorts, Secaucus, NJ), Mar. 19, 2019, at 8.
554. SteelSeries, *How to Organize a Local Esports Tournament: Part 1*, https://steelseries.com/blog/how-organize-local-esports-tournament-1-151 (last visited Jul. 22, 2020).
555. Albert Petrosyan, *Fortnite's Week Three Summer Skirmish Tournament Will Feature a Special Guest Caster*, Dexerto (Jul. 26. 2018), https://www.dexerto.com/fortnite/fortnites-week-three-summer-skirmish-tournament-will-feature-a-special-guest-caster-125339.
556. Tobias M. Scholz, *eSports is Business: Management in the World of Competitive Gaming*, 61 (Palgrave Macmillan 2019).
557. SteelSeries, *How to Organize a Local Esports Tournament: Part 1*, https://steelseries.com/blog/how-organize-local-esports-tournament-1-151 (last visited Jul. 22, 2020).
558. SteelSeries, *How to Organize a Local Esports Tournament: Part 2*, https://steelseries.com/blog/how-organize-local-esports-tournament-2-152 (last visited Jul. 22, 2020).
559. Springfield Area Chamber of Commerce, *Contender eSports*, https://business.springfieldchamber.com/directory/Details/contender-esports-813896 (last visited Jul. 22, 2020); See also Center for Educational Innovation, *Enrichment Programs—CEI Esports*, https://the-cei.org/enrichment-programs/#Esports (last visited Jul. 22, 2020; Chris Burt, *CEI Gives NYC Students Place to Connect, Dream Big through Esports*, District Administration (Nov. 13, 2019), https://districtadministration.com/cei-gives-nyc-students-place-to-connect-dream-big.
560. Austen Goslin, *Startup Company Makes Online Game Events Easier to Organize for Youth Community Groups*, Polygon (Jun. 9, 2020), https://www.polygon.com/2020/6/9/21285783/boom-tv-code-red-online-tournaments-valorant-call-of-duty-warzone.
561. *Myanmar E-sports Players Battle Power Outages*, The Asian Post (Aug. 27, 2019), https://theaseanpost.com/article/myanmar-e-sports-players-battle-power-outages; See also Aron Garst, *The Aggravation of Game-Breaking Bugs in Esports*, Engadget (Mar. 30, 2020), https://www.engadget.com/2020-03-30-esports-game-breaking-bugs.html; Vignesh Raghuram, *Dendi Was DDOS Attacked during the BEYOND EPIC Qualifier Finals Yesterday*, AFK Gaming (Jun. 12, 2020), https://afkgaming.com/articles/dota2/News/4254-dendi-was-ddos-attacked-during-the-beyond-epic-qualifier-finals-yesterday).
562. Patrick J. McKenna, *eSports Practice Becoming a Lucrative Micro-Niche for Law Firms*, Thomas Reuters (Mar. 28, 2019), https://www.legalexecutiveinstitute.com/micro-niche-esports-practice; See also Justin M. Jacobson, *What is*

Esports Law? What is an Esports Lawyer?, The Jacobson Firm, https://www.thejacobsonfirmpc.com/what-is-esports-law-what-is-an-esports-lawyer; Gamma Law, *What is "Esports Law"?*, https://gammalaw.com/esports-law (last visited Jul. 31, 2020).
563. 17 U.S.C. § 102 (1990).
564. *Id.*
565. *Id.*
566. 17 U.S.C. § 102(b) (1990).
567. 17 U.S.C. § 106 (2002).
568. *Id.*
569. United States Copyright Office, *Duration of Copyright*, https://www.copyright.gov/circs/circ15a.pdf (last visited Feb. 9, 2020).
570. W.I.P.O., *Berne Convention for the Protection of Literary and Artistic Works*, https://www.wipo.int/treaties/en/ip/berne/ (last visited Feb. 7, 2020).
571. 17 U.S.C. § 410 (1976); See also U.S. Copyright Office, Copyright in General, https://www.copyright.gov/help/faq/faq-general.html (last visited Feb. 9, 2020).
572. 17 U.S.C. § 411(a) (2008).
573. 17 U.S.C. § 412 (2008).
574. *Id.*
575. U.S. Copyright Office, Registration Portal, https://www.copyright.gov/registration/ (last visited Feb. 7, 2020).
576. 17 U.S.C. § 201(a) (1978).
577. 17 U.S.C. § 101 (2010); See also Stanford University Libraries Copyright and Fair Use, *Copyright Ownership: Who Owns What?*, https://fairuse.stanford.edu/overview/faqs/copyright-ownership/ (last visited Feb. 12, 2020).
578. Nancy Perkins Spyke, *The Joint Work Dilemma: The Separately Copyrightable Contribution Requirement and Co-ownership Principle*, 11 U. Miami Ent. & Sports L. Rev. 31, 31–33 (1993).
579. 17 U.S.C. § 101 (2010); See also 17 U.S.C. § 201(a) (1978).
580. 17 U.S.C. § 201(a) (1978).
581. U.S. Copyright Office, *Circular 15A—Duration of Copyright*, https://www.copyright.gov/circs/circ15a.pdf (last visited Feb. 9, 2020).
582. W.I.P.O., *Video Games*, https://www.wipo.int/copyright/en/activities/video_games.html (last visited Feb. 7, 2020); See also W.I.P.O., *The Legal Status of Video Games: Comparative Analysis in National Approaches*, https://www.wipo.int/export/sites/www/copyright/en/creative_industries/pdf/video_games.pdf (last visited Feb. 7, 2020).
583. Ashley Saunders Lipson and Robert D. Brain, *Computer and Video Game Law—Cases*, Statutes, *Forms, Problems & Materials* (Carolina Academic Press 2009), at 54.
584. Paul 'Redeye' Chaloner, *This is Esports* (*and How to Spell it*), 102 (Bloomsbury Sport 2020).
585. Paul 'Redeye' Chaloner, *This is Esports* (*and How to Spell it*), 105 (Bloomsbury Sport 2020).
586. Tobias M. Scholz, *eSports is Business: Management in the World of Competitive Gaming*, 51 (Palgrave Macmillan 2019).
587. Paul 'Redeye' Chaloner, *This is Esports* (*and How to Spell it*), 109 (Bloomsbury Sport 2020).

588. Sami Kalliokoski, *Why You Should Consider Developing User-Generated Content-Based Mobile Games*, Pocket Gamer (Apr. 7, 2018), https://www.pocketgamer.biz/comment-and-opinion/67934/why-you-should-consider-developing-ugc-mobile-games.
589. Linden Lab, *Second Life Terms and Conditions*, https://www.lindenlab.com/legal/second-life-terms-and-conditions (last visited Feb. 9, 2020).
590. Id.; See also Second Life Wiki, *Linden Lab Official: Snapshot and Machinima Policy*, *http://wiki.secondlife.com/wiki/Linden_Lab_Official:Snapshot_and_machinima_policy* (last visited Feb.12, 2020).
591. Microsoft XBOX, *Game Content Usage Rules*, https://www.xbox.com/en-us/developers/rules (last visited Feb. 12, 2020).
592. *Id.*
593. *Id.*
594. *Id.*; See also Christina Hayes, "Changing the Rules of the Game: How Video Game Publishers Are Embracing User-Generated Derivative Works," 21 *Harv. J.L. & Tech* 567, 571 (2008).
595. Daybreak PlayerStudio, *Design and Create In-Game Items*, https://player-studio.daybreakgames.com (last visited Feb. 12, 2020).
596. Daybreak Planetside 2, *Player Studio*, https://www.planetside2.com/player-studio/faq (last visited Feb. 12, 2020); See also Tom Curtis, *New SOE Program Lets Players Create and Sell Virtual Items*, Gamasutra (Sept. 6, 2012), https://www.gamasutra.com/view/news/177268/New:SOE_program_lets_players_create_and_sell_virtual_items.php.
597. Jenna Pitcher, *Player Studio User Earns More than $100,000 Creating In-Game Items*, Polygon (Apr. 10, 2014), https://www.polygon.com/2014/4/10/5600354/player-studio-user-earns-more-than-100000-creating-in-game-items.
598. Kris Graft, *Team Fortress 2 Introduces Virtual Item Buys*, Gamasutra (Sept. 30, 2010), https://www.gamasutra.com/view/news/30716/Team_Fortress_2_Introduces_Virtual_Item_Buys.php.
599. Tom Curtis, *Team Fortress 2 Community Earns $2M from In-Game Sales*, Gamasutra (Oct. 13, 2011), https://www.gamasutra.com/view/news/127650/Team_Fortress_2_Community_Earns_2M_From_InGame_Sales.php.
600. Paul 'Redeye' Chaloner, *This is Esports* (*and How to Spell it*), 86 (Bloomsbury Sport 2020); See also Phil "DrPhill" Alexander, Esports for Dummies, 52 (Wiley 2020).
601. Blizzard Entertainment, *Warcraft III*, https://www.blizzard.com/en-us/games/war3 (last visited Jul. 26, 2020).
602. B. Wiley, *Warcraft III Shatters Sales Records*, IGN (Jul. 22, 2002), https://www.ign.com/articles/2002/07/22/warcraft-iii-shatters-sales-records.
603. Id.
604. Paul 'Redeye' Chaloner, *This is Esports* (*and How to Spell it*), 88 (Bloomsbury Sport 2020).
605. Notice of Opp'n at 4, *Blizzard Entertainment, Inc. v. Valve Corporation*, ESTTA No. 441431 (Nov. 16, 2011).
606. Id.
607. Id.
608. Id.
609. Id.

610. Depo. of Guinsoo at 17:4-10, *BLIZZARD ENTERTAINMENT, INC. v. LILITH GAMES (SHANGHAI) CO. LTD*, No. 3:15-cv–04084-CRB (N.D. Cal. May 16, 2017); See also Paul 'Redeye' Chaloner, *This is Esports (and How to Spell it)*, 87–88,90 (Bloomsbury Sport 2020).
611. Notice of Opp'n at 4, *Blizzard Entertainment, Inc. v. Valve Corporation*, ESTTA No. 441431 (Nov. 16, 2011).
612. *Id.*
613. *Id.*
614. *Id.*
615. See "EULAs" (Dkts. 120-8 & 120-9), *BLIZZARD ENTERTAINMENT, INC. v. LILITH GAMES (SHANGHAI) CO. LTD*, No. 3:15-cv–04084-CRB (N.D. Cal. May 16, 2017).
616. Notice of Opp'n at 5, *Blizzard Entertainment, Inc. v. Valve Corporation*, ESTTA No. 441431 (Nov. 16, 2011).
617. *Id.*
618. *Id.*
619. Paul 'Redeye' Chaloner, *This is Esports (and How to Spell it)*, 88–89 (Bloomsbury Sport 2020).
620. Eul Decl. 8, *BLIZZARD ENTERTAINMENT, INC. v. LILITH GAMES (SHANGHAI) CO. LTD*, No. 3:15-cv–04084-CRB (N.D. Cal. May 16, 2017); See also Paul 'Redeye' Chaloner, *This is Esports (and How to Spell it)*, 88 (Bloomsbury Sport 2020).
621. Id.
622. *BLIZZARD ENTERTAINMENT, INC. v. LILITH GAMES (SHANGHAI) CO. LTD*, No. 3:15-cv-04084-CRB (N.D. Cal. May 16, 2017); See also Paul 'Redeye' Chaloner, *This is Esports (and How to Spell it)*, 88 (Bloomsbury Sport 2020).
623. Eul Depo. at 46:19-50:7, *BLIZZARD ENTERTAINMENT, INC. v. LILITH GAMES (SHANGHAI) CO. LTD*, No. 3:15-cv–04084-CRB (N.D. Cal. May 16, 2017).
624. Eul Online Post (dkt. 120–17), *BLIZZARD ENTERTAINMENT, INC. v. LILITH GAMES (SHANGHAI) CO. LTD*, No. 3:15-cv–04084-CRB (N.D. Cal. May 16, 2017).
625. Id.
626. Paul 'Redeye' Chaloner, *This is Esports (and How to Spell it)*, 90 (Bloomsbury Sport 2020).
627. Gamepedia, *Dota 2 Wiki - IceFrog*, https://dota2.gamepedia.com/IceFrog (last visited Feb. 12, 2020); See also See also Paul 'Redeye' Chaloner, *This is Esports (and How to Spell it)*, 90 (Bloomsbury Sport 2020).
628. *Id.* at 91.
629. Luke Plunkett, *Blizzard and Valve Go to War Over DOTA Name*, Kotaku (Feb. 10, 2012), https://kotaku.com/blizzard-and-valve-go-to-war-over-dota-name-5883938.
630. Mike Schramm, *Blizzard and Valve Settle DOTA Argument, Blizzard DOTA is Now Blizzard All-Stars*, Engadget (May 11, 2012), https://www.engadget.com/2012/05/11/blizzard-and-valve-settle-dota-argument-blizzard-dota-is-now-bl.

631. Brian Crecente, *'Blizzard All-Stars' is the New Name for "Blizzard DOTA,' Valve Retains 'Dota 2'*, Polygon (May 11, 2012), https://www.polygon.com/gaming/2012/5/11/3014846/dota-trademark-settled; See also Paul 'Redeye' Chaloner, *This is Esports (and How to Spell it)*, 90 (Bloomsbury Sport 2020).
632. Jennifer Lloyd Kelly and Nicholas Plassaras, *Copyright Player-Generated Content in Video Games*, Venture Beat (Jan. 7, 2015), https://venturebeat.com/2015/01/07/copyrighting-player-generated-content-in-video-games.
633. *Id.*
634. *Id.*
635. *Id.*
636. *Id.*
637. *Id.*
638. *Id.*
639. *Id.*
640. Justin M. Jacobson, *What Makes Gamer-Tags and Team Names Such Valuable Trademarks?*, The Esports Observer (Apr. 26, 2017), https://esportsobserver.com/makes-gamer-tags-team-names-valuable-trademarks.
641. U.S.P.T.O., *Trademark Basics*, https://www.uspto.gov/trademarks-getting-started/trademark-basics (last visited Feb. 7, 2020).
642. Justin M. Jacobson, *Trademark Rights in a #HashTag*, Intellectual Property Blawg (Mar. 12, 2016), http://www.intellectualpropertyblawg.com/trademarks/trademark-rights-in-a-hashtag; See also Calum Patteron, *Twitter's New Esport Team Hashtags Emojis Possibly Related to Fortnite—OpTic Gaming, FaZe Clan, Team Envy and More*, Dexerto (Jul. 25, 2018), https://www.dexerto.com/esports/twitter-releases-new-esports-team-hashtag-emojis-optic-gaming-faze-clan-team-envy-and-more-124628; See also Preston Byers, *Twitter Unveils Hashtag Icons for Esports Teams*, Dot Esports (Jul. 25, 2018), https://dotesports.com/business/news/twitter-esports-hashtags-31468.
643. J. Thomas McCarthy, *McCarthy on Trademarks and Unfair Competition*, § 15: 46 (4th Ed. 2009) Stating that secondary meaning does "not need be proven among the general public if a product is targeted at only a specific segment of the general public."
644. 15 U.S.C. § 1052(f) (2006); See also TMEP § 1212.06 (Oct. 2018).
645. Raju Mudhar, *An Esports Battle Erupts in Toronto Over the Use of the City in a Team Name*, The Star (Nov. 16, 2018), https://www.thestar.com/entertainment/2018/11/16/an-esports-battle-erupts-in-toronto-over-the-use-of-the-city-in-a-team-name.html; See also Andy Chalk, *Toronto Esports Club Quits Overwatch after Being Told it Has to Change Its Name*, P.C. Gamer (Nov. 14, 2018), https://www.pcgamer.com/toronto-esports-club-quits-overwatch-after-being-told-it-has-to-change-its-name.
646. U.S.P.T.O., *International Applications/Madrid Protocol FAQS*, https://www.uspto.gov/trademark/laws-regulations/madrid-protocol/international-applicationsmadrid-protocol-faqs (last visited Feb. 7, 2020).
647. Gazala Parveen, *E-sports and Underlying Intellectual Property*, I.P. Leaders (Oct. 30, 2019), https://blog.ipleaders.in/e-sports-underlying-intellectual-property.
648. Twitch.tv, *Trademark Policy*, https://www.twitch.tv/p/legal/trademark-policy/ (last visited Feb. 7, 2020).

649. U.S. Customs and Border Protection, *Intellectual Property Rights*, https://www.cbp.gov/trade/priority-issues/ipr (last visited Feb. 7, 2020).
650. Scott Robertson, *Besiktas Esports Allegedly Hasn't Been Paying League of Legends or CSGO Players*, Dexerto (Aug. 22, 2019), https://www.dexerto.com/csgo/turkish-esports-team-non-payment-league-of-legends-940974.
651. FN Media Group, *Esports Tournaments Look to Digital Payments to Fix Delayed Prize Money Payouts*, Bloomberg News (May 16, 2019), https://www.bloomberg.com/press-releases/2019-05-16/esports-tournaments-look-to-digital-payments-to-fix-delayed-prize-money-payouts; See also Hongyu Chen, *Chinese Organization Newbee Accused of not Paying $100K in Prize Money to Fortnite Players*, The Esports Observer (Jul. 23, 2020), https://esportsobserver.com/newbee-nonpayment-fortnitewc2019.
652. U.S.P.T.O., *Nice Agreement Current Edition Version—General Remarks, Class Headings and Explanatory Notes*, https://www.uspto.gov/trademark/trademark-updates-and-announcements/nice-agreement-current-edition-version-general-remarks (last visited Feb. 7, 2020).
653. <FATAL1TY>, U.S. Registration No. 3,149,347.
654. <NADESHOT>, U.S. Registration No. 5,540,561.
655. <COURAGEJD>, U.S. Registration No. 5,756,419.
656. <NINJA DESIGN LOGO>, U.S. Serial No. 88206559; <NINJA DESIGN LOGO>, U.S. Serial No. 88481530; <NINJA DESIGN LOGO>, U.S. Serial No. 88206555.
657. <DRLUPO>, U.S. Registration No. 5,970,881; <D DESIGN>, U.S. Registration No. 5,970,912.
658. <TFUE>, U.S. Serial No. 88294707.
659. <TIMTHETATMAN>, U.S. Serial No. 88891655.
660. <PEWDIEPIE>, U.S. Registration No. 4,424,201.
661. <TEAM LIQUID>, U.S. Registration No. 5,237,182; <TEAM LIQUID>, U.S. Registration No. 5,299,681; <TEAMLIQUID>, U.S. Registration No. 5,299,682; <TEAM LIQUID>, U.S. Registration No. 5,338,391.
662. <FNATIC>, U.S. Registration No. 4,677,398.
663. <EVIL GENIUSES>, U.S. Registration No. 4,568,877; <EVIL GENIUSES LOGO>, U.S. Registration No. 4,568,877.
664. <SPLYCE>, U.S. Registration No. 5,250,213.
664. <OPTIC GAMING>, U.S. Registration No. 4,870,601.
666. <CLOUD9>, U.S. Registration No. 5,426,731.
667. <COUNTER LOGIC GAMING>, U.S. Serial No. 88877157; <CLG LOGO>, U.S. Registration No. 5,457,919.
668. <COMPLEXITY>, U.S. Registration No. 5,315,085; <COMPLEXITY LOGO>, U.S. Registration No. 6,000,371.
669. <FLYQUEST>, U.S. Registration No. 5,697,874; <FLYQUEST>, U.S. Registration No. 5,280,553; <FLYQUEST>, U.S. Registration No. 5,697,873.
670. <IGC IMMORTALS GAMING CLUB>, U.S. Serial Nos. 88/355,897.
671. <IGC LOGO>, U.S. Serial 88/355,908; See also Immortals, *Immortals Announces Close of Series B Fundraising, Raising $30MM; Rebrands to Immortals Gaming Club*, https://www.immortals.gg/post/immortals-llc-announces-close-of-series-b-fundraising-raising-30mm-rebrands-to-immortals-gaming-c (last visited Feb. 7, 2020).

672. N.Y.L.L.C. Law § 206 (2006); See also N.Y. State Department of State, *Division of Corporations, State Records & Uniform Commercial Code*, https://www.dos.ny.gov/corps/llccorp.html (last visited Feb. 7, 2020).
673. Jonathan R. Macey, *The Three Justifications for Piercing the Corporate Veil*, Harvard Law School Forum on Corporate Governance (Mar. 27, 2014), https://corpgov.law.harvard.edu/2014/03/27/the-three-justifications-for-piercing-the-corporate-veil.
674. Justin M. Jacobson, *Esports Biz 101: Part 1—Business and Legal Considerations for Professional Esports Orgs*, Esports Insider (Jan. 22, 2018), https://esportsinsider.com/2018/01/esports-biz-101-part-1-business-legal-considerations-professional-esports-orgs; See also Justin M. Jacobson, *Esports Biz 101*: Part 2—*Business and Legal Considerations for Professional Esports Orgs*, Esports Insider (Jan. 22, 2018), https://esportsinsider.com/2018/01/esports-biz-101-part-2-business-legal-considerations-professional-esports-orgs.
675. Patrick Shanely, *Immortals Esports Org Sells Overwatch League Franchise to Beasley Media Group*, The Hollywood Reporter (Nov. 14, 2019), https://www.hollywoodreporter.com/news/immortals-esports-org-sells-overwatch-league-franchise-beasley-media-group-1254983.
676. Tobias Seck, *French Esports Organization MCES Secures $2.8M Series A Investment*, The Esports Observer (Jul. 9, 2020), https://esportsobserver.com/mces-series-a-investment.
677. Jacob Wolf, *Evil Geniuses Confirm Acquisition of Echo Fox's LCS Spot*, ESPN (Sept. 29, 2019), https://www.espn.com/esports/story/_/id/27708703/evil-geniuses-confirm-acquisition-echo-fox-lcs-spot.
678. *The Rise of Esports Investments: A Deep Dive with Deloitte Corporate Finance LLC and The Esports Observer* (The Esports Observer / Deloitte Corporate Finance LLC, New York, NY), Apr. 2019, at 4; See also Tobias M. Scholz, *eSports is Business: Management in the World of Competitive Gaming*, 84 (Palgrave Macmillan 2019).
679. *The Rise of Esports Investments: A Deep Dive with Deloitte Corporate Finance LLC and The Esports Observer* (The Esports Observer / Deloitte Corporate Finance LLC, New York, NY), Apr. 2019, at 4.
680. *Id.* at 12.
681. Chris Hana, *The Race to the $1B USD Esports Team – Why Some Investors Believe Esports Franchises Will Get There*, The Esports Observer (Jan. 7, 2020), https://esportsobserver.com/1b-usd-esports-team-valuations.
682. *The Rise of Esports Investments: A Deep Dive with Deloitte Corporate Finance LLC and The Esports Observer* (The Esports Observer / Deloitte Corporate Finance LLC, New York, NY), Apr. 2019, at 11.
683. H.B. Duran, *WISE Ventures' Minnesota Røkkr to Host Call of Duty League 2020 Launch Weekend*, The Esports Observer (Oct. 30, 2019), https://esportsobserver.com/cdl-minnesota-rokkr.
684. Stephen Hays, *Who is Investing in Esports Startups?*, Hacker Noon (Aug. 7, 2017), https://hackernoon.com/who-is-investing-in-esports-startups-by-stephen-hays-of-deep-space-ventures-1efa7a55a60a; Andbox, *NYC Gaming*, https://andbox.com (last visited Jul. 26, 2020).

685. Michael Tan, S *Korean PE Firm ATU Partners Investing in Esports with $17m Fund*, Asia Tech Daily (Jan. 2, 2020), https://www.asiatechdaily.com/atu-partners-esports-fund.
686. Matt Perez, *100 Thieves Investor Raises $100 Million Esports Fund*, Forbes (Nov. 13, 2019), https://www.forbes.com/sites/mattperez/2019/11/13/100-thieves-investor-raises-100-million-esports-fund/#440e94814691.
687. Ben Steverman, *Family Offices Eyeing Minority Stakes in Sports Teams*, Bloomberg (Jul. 15, 2016), https://www.bloomberg.com/professional/blog/family-offices-eyeing-minority-stakes-sports-teams; See also Paul Karger and West Karger, *The Rise of the Family Office Venture Investor*, Tech Crunch (Dec. 21, 2016), https://techcrunch.com/2016/12/21/the-rise-of-the-family-office-venture-investor.
688. Jacob Wolf, Jerry Jones, John Goff Buy *Majority Stake in CompLexity Gaming*, ESPN (Nov. 6, 2017), https://www.espn.com/esports/story/_/id/21309068/dallas-cowboys-owner-jerry-jones-john-goff-buy-majority-stake-complexity-gaming.
689. *The Rise of Esports Investments: A Deep Dive with Deloitte Corporate Finance LLC and The Esports Observer* (The Esports Observer / Deloitte Corporate Finance LLC, New York, NY), Apr. 2019, at 40.
690. Id.; See also Christina Settimi, *'Awful Business' or The New Gold Rush? The Most Valuable Companies in Esports Are Surging*, Forbes (Nov. 5, 2019), https://www.forbes.com/sites/christinasettimi/2019/11/05/awful-business-or-the-new-gold-rush-the-most-valuable-companies-in-esports-are-surging/#5cdca49e324d.
691. *The Rise of Esports Investments: A Deep Dive with Deloitte Corporate Finance LLC and The Esports Observer* (The Esports Observer / Deloitte Corporate Finance LLC, New York, NY), Apr. 2019, at 40.
692. *Id.*
693. *Id.*
694. *Id.*
695. *Id.*
696. *Id.*
697. *Id.* at 12; Imad Khan, *How Training Facilities Can Enhance an Esports Team's Value*, The Esports Observer (Jul. 21, 2019), https://esportsobserver.com/esports-facilities-2019; See also TeamSoloMid, Esports Facility, https://facility.tsm.gg (last visited Jul. 29, 2020).
698. *The Rise of Esports Investments: A Deep Dive with Deloitte Corporate Finance LLC and The Esports Observer* (The Esports Observer / Deloitte Corporate Finance LLC, New York, NY), Apr. 2019 at 40; See also Graham Ashton, *How TSM Expanded from a Single Esports Team to Multi-Vertical Media Company*, The Esports Observer (Jul. 1, 2020), https://esportsobserver.com/how-tsm-expanded-from-esports.
699. *The Rise of Esports Investments: A Deep Dive with Deloitte Corporate Finance LLC and The Esports Observer* (The Esports Observer / Deloitte Corporate Finance LLC, New York, NY), Apr. 2019, at 42.
700. *Id.*
701. *Id.*; See also Roundhill Investments, *How Do Esports Teams Make Money?*, https://www.roundhillinvestments.com/research/esports/how-do-esports-teams-make-money (last visited Jul. 27, 2020).

702. *The Rise of Esports Investments: A Deep Dive with Deloitte Corporate Finance LLC and The Esports Observer* (The Esports Observer / Deloitte Corporate Finance LLC, New York, NY), Apr. 2019, at 41.
703. *Id.* at 46; See also Andrew Meola, *The Biggest Companies Sponsoring eSports Teams and Tournaments*, Business Insider (Jan. 12, 2018), https://www.businessinsider.com/top-esports-sponsors-gaming-sponsorships-2018-1.
704. *The Rise of Esports Investments: A Deep Dive with Deloitte Corporate Finance LLC and The Esports Observer* (The Esports Observer / Deloitte Corporate Finance LLC, New York, NY), Apr. 2019, at 41; See also Thiemo Bräutigam, *FaZe Dominates All Competitors in Esports Social Media Rankings*, Dot esports (Feb. 15, 2017), https://dotesports.com/business/news/most-influential-esports-brands-social-media-followers-4766; Adam Fitch, *GumGum Sports Reveals Esports Social Rankings for Q2 2019*, Esports Insider (Aug. 29, 2019), https://esportsinsider.com/2019/08/gumgum-rankings-q2-2019; Andrew Norton, *Top 10 Biggest Esports Teams by Twitter Followers*, ElecSpo (Jul. 29, 2018), https://www.elecspo.com/games/top-10-biggest-esports-teams-twitter-followers.
705. *The Rise of Esports Investments: A Deep Dive with Deloitte Corporate Finance LLC and The Esports Observer* (The Esports Observer / Deloitte Corporate Finance LLC, New York, NY), Apr. 2019, at 46; See also Influencer Marketing Hub, *Top 41 Esports Influencers You Should Know*, https://influencermarketinghub.com/esports-influencers (last visited Jul. 27, 2020).
706. *The Rise of Esports Investments: A Deep Dive with Deloitte Corporate Finance LLC and The Esports Observer* (The Esports Observer / Deloitte Corporate Finance LLC, New York, NY), Apr. 2019, at 45.
707. *Id.*
708. *Id.*
709. *Id.* at 44.
710. *Id.* at 44–45.
711. Adnan Islam and Ryan Dudley, *US Tax Considerations for eSports & the Online Games Industry*, Thomas Reuters (Apr. 30, 2020), https://tax.thomsonreuters.com/blog/esports-tax-considerations.
712. Ellen Zavian, *For Esports Players, the Tax Man Cometh*, The Washington Post (Jan. 24, 2020), https://www.washingtonpost.com/video-games/esports/2020/01/15/esports-players-tax-man-cometh.
713. *Id.*; See also British Esports Association, Esports Tax Guide: *UK Tax Advice for Streamers, YouTubers and People Working in Esports*, https://britishesports.org/advice/esports-tax-guide-uk-advice-for-streamers-youtubers (last visited Jul. 27, 2020).
714. *Are eSports Profits Taxed?*, MTL Times (Feb. 13, 2020), https://mtltimes.ca/Montreal/social-life/technology/are-esports-profits-taxed.
715. Michael E. Strauss and Jason Feingertz, *As eSports Prizes Get Higher, Pro Gamers May Face 'Jock Taxes'*, Forbes (Feb. 3, 2017), https://www.forbes.com/sites/alexknapp/2017/02/03/state-jock-taxes-may-start-applying-to-esports-players/#4d67c4de4f45.
716. N.Y. Tax Law § 631(c)(2007).
717. 20 N.Y.C.R.R. § 132.22(a)(1)(2006).
718. 20 N.Y.C.R.R. § 132.22(b)(3)(ii)(2006).

719. Justin M. Jacobson, *Business & Legal Tips for NBA 2K League & Pro Esports Players*, NBA2WK (May 10, 2018), https://nba2kw.com/business-legal-tips-for-nba-2k-league-pro-esports-players-by-justin-m-jacobson-esq.
720. Justin M. Jacobson and Jason Feingertz, *Esports Tax Law: A Look at Tax Considerations for Professional Gamers*, Esports Insider (Oct. 17, 2017), https://esportsinsider.com/2017/10/esports-tax-law-considerations-professional-gamers.
721. I.R.S., *Reporting Payments to Independent Contractors*, https://www.irs.gov/businesses/small-businesses-self-employed/reporting-payments-to-independent-contractors (last visited Feb. 19, 2020).
722. Amazon.com, *Tax Information Interview Guide*, https://developer.amazon.com/tax-interview/help?nodeId=201588330&locale=en_USl (last visited Feb. 19, 2020).
723. Google.com, *YouTube Partner Program Overview & Eligibility*, https://support.google.com/youtube/answer/72851?hl=en (last visited Feb. 19, 2020).
724. Galen "Chigginators" Herbst de Cortina, Twitch Affiliated Tax Form Overview, Streamer Square (Jun. 5, 2017), http://streamersquare.com/twitch-affiliate-tax-form.
725. Juan Rodriguez, *Are Donations/Tips Taxable Income for Streamers?*, eFuse Learning (May 30, 2020), https://efuse.gg/learning/skill-development/are-donations-taxable.
726. I.R.S., *Charitable Contribution Deductions*, https://www.irs.gov/charities-non-profits/charitable-organizations/charitable-contribution-deductions (last visited Feb. 19, 2020).
727. Ellen Zavian, *For Esports Players, the Tax Man Cometh*, The Washington Post (Jan. 24, 2020), https://www.washingtonpost.com/video-games/esports/2020/01/15/esports-players-tax-man-cometh.
728. Andrew Hayward, *Esports Essentials: Why is the Prize Pool for Dota 2's The International so Large?*, The Esports Observer (Aug. 21, 2018), https://esportsobserver.com/dota-2-prize-pool-explainer.
729. Allen "Snarkbearkai" Moseley, *T14 Newbee Prize Money to Be Taxed Thirty* Percent, Gosu Gamers (Jul. 24, 2014), https://www.gosugamers.net/dota2/news/28248-ti4-newbee-prize-money-to-be-taxed-thirty-percent.
730. Id.
731. Dreamhack, *Prize Money Policy*—Paragraph II—Payout Policy, https://dreamhack.se/dhs16/esport/prize-money-policy (last visited Feb. 19, 2020).
732. Id.
733. P.G.L., *P.G.L. Esports*, https://www.pglesports.com (last visited Feb. 21, 2020).
734. P.G.L., Prize *Policy—PGL Dota2 Minor*, http://dota2minor.pglesports.com/prize-policy (last visited Feb. 21, 2020); See also P.G.L., Prize *Policy—PGL Legends of the Rift Season 1*, http://lol.pglesports.com/prize-policy (last visited Feb. 21, 2020).
735. P.G.L., Prize *Policy—PGL Dota2 Minor*, http://dota2minor.pglesports.com/prize-policy (last visited Feb. 21, 2020); See also P.G.L., Prize *Policy—PGL Legends of the Rift Season 1*, http://lol.pglesports.com/prize-policy (last visited Feb. 21, 2020).
736. P.G.L., Prize *Policy—PGL Dota2 Minor*, http://dota2minor.pglesports.com/prize-policy (last visited Feb. 21, 2020); See also P.G.L., Prize *Policy—PGL Legends of the Rift Season 1*, http://lol.pglesports.com/prize-policy (last visited Feb. 21, 2020).

737. T.L. Taylor, *Raising the Stakes: E-Sports and the Professionalization of Computer Gaming*, 178 (The MIT Press 2012).
738. Tobias M. Scholz, *eSports is Business: Management in the World of Competitive Gaming*, 72 (Palgrave Macmillan 2019).
739. E.J. Schultz, *Behind the Rise of Esports and What It Means for Brands*, AdAge, https://adage.com/article/news/e-sports/308447 (last visited Feb. 21, 2020).
740. I.R.S., *Deducting Business Expenses*, https://www.irs.gov/businesses/small-businesses-self-employed/deducting-business-expenses (last visited Feb. 21, 2020).
741. Vignesh Raghuram, *OG Dota 2 Player 'Topson' Paid Highest 2018 Taxes Amongst Athletes in Finland*, The Esports Observer (Nov. 15, 2019), https://esportsobserver.com/topson-finland-taxes-2018.
742. *Id.*
743. I.R.S., *Hobby or Business? IRS Offers Tips to Decide*, https://www.irs.gov/newsroom/hobby-or-business-irs-offers-tips-to-decide (last visited Feb. 21, 2020).
744. Intuit Turbotax, *Making Money by Streaming Your Gaming Sessions? Here's What It Means for Your Taxes*, https://blog.turbotax.intuit.com/self-employed/making-money-by-streaming-your-gaming-sessions-heres-what-it-means-for-your-taxes-43269 (last visited Jul. 26, 2020).
745. 26 C.F.R. § 1.183-1(a) (1972); See also I.R.S., IRC §183 Activities Not Engaged In For Profit (ATG), https://www.irs.gov/pub/irs-utl/irc183activitiesnotengagedinforprofit.pdf (last visited Feb. 21, 2020).
746. Andy Smith, *Top 9 Tax Deduction Opportunities for U.S. YouTubers*, Tubular Insights (Feb. 17, 2015), https://tubularinsights.com/tax-deductions-us-youtubers.
747. *Id.*
748. *Id.*
749. Janita, *eSports Pros Can Get Athlete's Tax Treatment in Finland*, Metropolitan.fi (Jul. 29, 2017), http://metropolitan.fi/entry/esports-players-to-get-athletics-tax-treatment-in-finland.
750. E.S.L., *Team Houses and Why They Matter*, https://www.eslgaming.com/article/team-houses-and-why-they-matter-1676 (last visited Jul. 27, 2020).
751. Colton Deck, *Several NiP Players Denied Visas for Rainbow Six Pro League Finals*, Dot Esports (Nov. 4, 2019), https://dotesports.com/rainbow-6/news/several-nip-players-denied-visas-for-rainbow-six-pro-league-finals.
752. Matt Dillon, *An eSports Attorney Reviews the Visa Issues in eSports*, Dot Esports (Jan. 27, 2016), https://dotesports.com/news/an-esports-attorney-reviews-the-visa-issues-in-esports-7606.
753. U.S.C.I.S., *Working in the US*, https://www.uscis.gov/working-us (last visited Feb. 24, 2020).
754. *Id.*
755. Jonathan Soler and Daniel Masakayan, *10 Labor and Employment Considerations in Esports*, Law 360 (Jun. 6, 2019), https://www.law360.com/articles/1164984/10-labor-and-employment-considerations-in-esports.
756. Paresh Dave, *Online Game League of Legends Star Gets U.S. Visa as Pro Athlete*, Los Angeles Times (Aug. 7, 2013), https://www.latimes.com/business/la-xpm-2013-aug-07-la-fi-online-gamers-20130808-story.html.

757. Alan Yu, *U.S. Recognizes a South Korean StarCraft Player as an Athlete*, N.P.R. (Dec. 15, 2013), https://www.npr.org/sections/alltechconsidered/2013/12/15/250793493/u-s-recognizes-a-south-korean-starcraft-player-as-an-athlete.
758. Maryanne Kline, *The Thrill of a Visa, The Agony of Denial: Visa Challenges for the Esports Athlete*, The National Law Review (Feb. 22, 2019), https://www.natlawreview.com/article/thrill-visa-agony-denial-visa-challenges-esports-athlete.
759. Adam Fitch, *Germany Introduces Dedicated Visa for Esports*, Esports Insider (Dec. 22, 2019), https://esportsinsider.com/2019/12/germany-esports-visa/.
760. *Id.*
761. Adam Newell, *CLG's Huhi Becomes a Permanent Resident of the US*, Dot Esports (Jul. 15, 2018), https://dotesports.com/league-of-legends/news/clg-huhi-permanent-resident-us-31021.
762. Xing Li, *New Legislation Could Cause US Green Card Issues for Esports Athletes*, Dot Esports (Aug. 13, 2019), https://dotesports.com/business/news/new-legislation-blocks-esports-green-card.
763. U.S.C.I.S., *P-1A Athlete*, https://www.uscis.gov/working-united-states/temporary-workers/p-1a-athlete (last visited Feb. 24, 2020).
764. U.S.C.I.S., *O-1 Visa: Individuals with Extraordinary Ability or Achievement*, https://www.uscis.gov/working-united-states/temporary-workers/o-1-visa-individuals-extraordinary-ability-or-achievement (last visited Feb. 24, 2020).
765. *Id.*
766. *Id.*
767. *Id.*
768. *Id.*
769. *Id.*
770. *Id.*
771. *Id.*
772. *Id.*
773. *Id.*
774. *Id.*
775. *Id.*
776. *Id.*; See also Brian O' Connell, *How Much Do eSports Players Make?*, The Street (Feb. 12, 2020), https://www.thestreet.com/personal-finance/how-much-do-esports-players-make-15126931.
777. Courtney New, *Immigration in Esports: Do Gamers Count as Athletes?*, Forbes (May 18, 2017), https://www.forbes.com/sites/allabouttherupees/2017/05/18/immigration-in-esports-do-gamers-count-as-athletes/#49ed3fe0468e.
778. U.S.C.I.S., *P-1A Athlete*, https://www.uscis.gov/working-united-states/temporary-workers/p-1a-athlete (last visited Feb. 24, 2020).
779. Jacob Wolf, *Broxah Has Visa Approved, Will Join Team Liquid in NA*, ESPN (Feb. 6, 2020), https://www.espn.com/esports/story/_/id/28648467/broxah-visa-approved-join-team-liquid-na.
780. U.S.C.I.S., *P-1A Athlete*, https://www.uscis.gov/working-united-states/temporary-workers/p-1a-athlete (last visited Feb. 24, 2020); See also Colton Deck, *R6 Pro League Coach Says "A Player's Union is in Talks" Following Visa Issues with ESL for Japan Finals*, Dot Esports (Oct. 31, 2019), https://dotesports.com/rainbow-6/news/r6-pro-league-coach-says-a-players-union-is-in-talks-following-visa-issues-with-esl-for-japan-finals.

781. U.S.C.I.S., *P-1A Athlete*, https://www.uscis.gov/working-united-states/temporary-workers/p-1a-athlete (last visited Feb. 24, 2020).
782. *Id.*
783. *Id.*; See also Barrett Womack, *Athletes and eSports: Why Visas Are Complicated*, Red Bull (Apr. 5, 2016), https://www.redbull.com/us-en/athletes-and-esports-why-visas-are-complicated.
784. U.S.C.I.S., *P-1A Athlete*, https://www.uscis.gov/working-united-states/temporary-workers/p-1a-athlete (last visited Feb. 24, 2020).
785. *Id.*; See also Aron Garst, *Illegal Tournaments and Rejected Visas: Team Vietnam's Long Road to the PUBG Nations Cup*, The Verge (Aug. 20, 2019), https://www.theverge.com/2019/8/20/20812857/pubg-nations-cup-team-vietnam-esports-illegal-tournaments-visa-rejection.
786. U.S.C.I.S., *P-1A Athlete*, https://www.uscis.gov/working-united-states/temporary-workers/p-1a-athlete (last visited Feb. 24, 2020).
787. *Id.*
788. *Id.*; See also Luke Winkie, *When it Comes to Securing Visas, Sherry Nhan is the Matron Saint of Esports*, Launcher (Jan. 22, 2020), https://www.washingtonpost.com/video-games/esports/2020/01/22/when-it-comes-securing-visas-sherry-nhan-is-matron-saint-esports.
789. U.S.C.I.S., *P-1A Athlete*, https://www.uscis.gov/working-united-states/temporary-workers/p-1a-athlete (last visited Feb. 24, 2020).
790. *Id.*
791. Nicole Carpenter, *TyLoo Gaming Team* Members Acquire Multi-Year United States Visas, The Esports Observer (Oct. 13, 2016), https://esportsobserver.com/tyloo-gaming-visas.
792. Reuters, *Charge's Nero Facing Visa Renewal*, Field Level Media (May 3, 2020), https://www.reuters.com/article/esports-overwatch-nero-visa-idUSFLM94qkjt.
793. U.S.C.I.S., *P-1A Athlete*, https://www.uscis.gov/working-united-states/temporary-workers/p-1a-athlete (last visited Feb. 24, 2020); See also Josh Raven, *FNS Gets Visa Renewed Ahead of Key ESL One Cologne Qualifiers*, Dot Esports (Jul. 29, 2015), https://dotesports.com/general/news/mehta-visa-clg-2144.
794. U.S.C.I.S., *P-1A Athlete*, https://www.uscis.gov/working-united-states/temporary-workers/p-1a-athlete (last visited Feb. 24, 2020).
795. Maryanne Kline and Elizabeth C. Egan, *The Thrill of a Visa, the Agony of Denial: Visa Challenges for the Esports Athlete*, Mintz, https://www.mintz.com/insights-center/viewpoints/2806/2019-02-thrill-visa-agony-denial-visa-challenges-esports-athlete (last visited Jul. 26, 2020).
796. U.S.C.I.S., *How Do I Request Premium Processing*, https://www.uscis.gov/forms/how-do-i-request-premium-processing (last visited Feb. 24, 2020).
797. Id.
798. U.S.C.I.S., *Consular Processing*, https://www.uscis.gov/greencard/consular-processing (last visited Feb. 24, 2020).
799. U.S. Dept. of State—Bureau of Consumer Affairs, *Visa Appointment Wait Times*, https://travel.state.gov/content/travel/en/us-visas/visa-information-resources/wait-times.html (last visited Feb. 24, 2020).

800. N.A.F.S.A., COVID-*19 Restrictions on U.S. Visas and Entry, https://www.nafsa.org/regulatory-information/covid-19-restrictions-us-visas-and-entry* (last visited Jul. 26, 2020).
801. Bryce Blum, *The Esports Lawyer Breaks Down the Visa Issue Plaguing the LCS*, ESPN (Jan. 27, 2016), https://www.espn.com/esports/story/_/id/14661486/breaking-league-legends-visa-issue.
802. Ryan Burden, *Super Smash Bros. Player Leffen Denied Visa*, CGM (Apr. 29, 2016), https://www.cgmagonline.com/2016/04/29/super-smash-bros-player-leffen-denied-visa.
803. Nathan Grayson, *Geguri and Other Overwatch League Players Delayed by Visa Issues*, Kotaku (Feb. 15, 2018), https://compete.kotaku.com/geguri-and-other-overwatch-league-players-delayed-by-vi-1823056508.
804. Ferguson Mitchell, *Russian Overwatch Player's U.S. Visa Denied a Week before Contenders in Los Angeles*, The Esports Observer (Oct. 3, 2017), https://esportsobserver.com/russian-overwatch-players-u-s-visa-denied-a-week-before-contenders-in-los-angeles.
805. ELeague, *100Thieves to be Replaced in the ELEAGUE Major: Boston*, https://www.eleague.com/news/100Thieves-to-be-replaced (last visited Feb. 24, 2020).
806. Samuel Lingle, *Visa Issues Keep Gambit Gaming Out of Wembley*, Dot Esports (Jun. 19, 2014), https://dotesports.com/league-of-legends/news/lcs-gambit-gaming-visas-wembley-338.
807. Maddy Myers, *Philly's Overwatch League Team Has Pulled Out of the Entire Preseason*, Kotaku (Dec. 05, 2017), https://compete.kotaku.com/phillys-overwatch-league-team-has-pulled-out-of-the-ent-1821014604; See also Philadelphia Fusion (@Fusion), Twitter (Dec. 4, 2017, 7:35PM), https://twitter.com/Fusion/status/937842944509329408.
808. Ferguson Mitchell, *Esports Primer: Understanding Independent Contractors vs. Employees*, The Esports Observer (Jan. 21, 2016), https://esportsobserver.com/esports-primer-understanding-independent-contractors-vs-employees.
809. Anthony Zaller, *Tfue v. Faze Clan—Esports Lawsuit Raises Many California Employment Legal Issues*, Cali. Employment Law Report (May 24, 2019), https://www.californiaemploymentlawreport.com/2019/05/tfue-v-faze-clan-esports-lawsuit-raises-many-california-employment-legal-issues.
810. Jonathan Soler and Daniel Masakayan, *10 Labor and Employment Considerations in Esports*, Law 360 (Jun. 6, 2019), https://www.law360.com/articles/1164984/10-labor-and-employment-considerations-in-esports.
811. Roger Quiles, *Are Esports Players Actually Independent Contractors?*, Quiles Law (Apr. 17, 2015), http://www.esports.law/blog/are-esports-players-actually-independent-contractors.
812. I.R.S., *Understanding Employment Taxes*, https://www.irs.gov/businesses/small-businesses-self-employed/understanding-employment-taxes (last visited Feb. 24, 2020).
813. Ferguson Mitchell, *Esports Primer: Understanding Independent Contractors vs. Employees*, The Esports Observer (Jan. 21, 2016), https://esportsobserver.com/esports-primer-understanding-independent-contractors-vs -employees.
814. I.R.S., *Understanding Employee vs. Contractor Designation*, https://www.irs.gov/newsroom/understanding-employee-vs-contractor-designation (last visited Feb. 24, 2020); See also New York State Department of Labor, *Independent*

Contractors, https://labor.ny.gov/ui/dande/ic.shtm (last visited Feb. 24, 2020); See also I.R.S., Topic *No. 762 Independent Contractor vs. Employee*, https://www.irs.gov/taxtopics/tc762 (last visited Feb. 24, 2020); See also I.R.S., *Independent Contractor or Employee*, https://www.irs.gov/pub/irs-pdf/p1779.pdf (last visited Feb. 24, 2020).

815. I.R.S., *Independent Contractor (Self-Employed) or Employee?*, https://www.irs.gov/businesses/small-businesses-self-employed/independent-contractor-self-employed-or-employee (last visited Feb. 24, 2020).
816. Margot Roosevelt, *New Labor Laws Are Coming to California. What's Changing in Your Workplace?*, The Los Angeles Times (Dec. 29, 2019), https://www.latimes.com/business/story/2019-12-29/california-employment-laws-2020-ab5-minimum-wage.
817. I.R.S., *Independent Contractor (Self-Employed) or Employee?*, https://www.irs.gov/businesses/small-businesses-self-employed/independent-contractor-self-employed-or-employee (last visited Feb. 24, 2020).
818. *Id.*
819. *Id.*
820. *Id.*
821. *Id.*
822. *Id.*
823. *Id.*
824. *Id.*
825. *Id.*
826. *Id.*
827. *Id.*
828. *Id.*
829. *Id.*
830. *Id.*
831. *Id.*
832. *Id.*
833. *Id.*
834. *Id.*; See also Jacob Wolf, *Sources: Dream Team Fails to Pay ANTi, Dabuz and HugS on Time*, ESPN (Aug. 22, 2016), https://www.espn.com/esports/story/_/id/17369271/dream-team-fails-pay-anti-dabuz-hugs.
835. I.R.S., *Independent Contractor (Self-Employed) or Employee?*, https://www.irs.gov/businesses/small-businesses-self-employed/independent-contractor-self-employed-or-employee (last visited Feb. 24, 2020).
836. *Id.*
837. *Id.*
838. Phil "DrPhill" Alexander, Esports for Dummies, 222 (Wiley 2020).
839. I.R.S., *Independent Contractor (Self-Employed) or Employee?*, https://www.irs.gov/businesses/small-businesses-self-employed/independent-contractor-self-employed-or-employee (last visited Feb. 24, 2020).
840. *Id.*
841. *Id.*
842. *Id.*; See also I.R.S., *Employee Benefits*, https://www.irs.gov/businesses/small-businesses-self-employed/employee-benefits (last visited Feb. 24, 2020).

843. I.R.S., *Independent Contractor (Self-Employed) or Employee?*, https://www.irs.gov/businesses/small-businesses-self-employed/independent-contractor-self-employed-or-employee (last visited Feb. 24, 2020).
844. *Id.*
845. *Id.*
846. Margot Roosevelt, *New Labor Laws Are Coming to California. What's Changing in Your Workplace?*, The Los Angeles Times (Dec. 29, 2019), https://www.latimes.com/business/story/2019-12-29/california-employment-laws-2020-ab5-minimum-wage.
847. Cal. Lab. Codes §§ 3351, 3352 (2005).
848. Cal. Lab. Code § 3357 (2005); See also *Yellow Cab Coop. v. Workers' Comp. Appeals Bd.*, 226 Cal. App. 3d 1288, 277 Cal. Rptr. 434 (1991), stating "a presumption that a service provider is presumed to be an employee unless the principal affirmatively proves otherwise."
849. State of California Department of Industrial Relations, *Independent Contractor versus Employee*, https://www.dir.ca.gov/dlse/FAQ_IndependentContractor.htm (last visited Feb. 24, 2020).
850. *Id.*
851. S. G. Borello & Sons, Inc. v. Dep*'t of Indus. Relations*, 48 Cal. 3d 341, 351 Cal. Rptr. 543 (Cal. Sup. Ct. (1989)).
852. *Id.* at 351; State of California Department of Industrial Relations, *Independent Contractor versus Employee*, https://www.dir.ca.gov/dlse/FAQ_IndependentContractor.htm (last visited Feb. 24, 2020).
853. *Id.*
854. Yellow *Cab Coop. v. Workers' Comp. Appeals Bd.*, 226 Cal. App. 3d 1288, 1295 ((Cal. Sup. Ct. (1991)); See also State of California Department of Industrial Relations, *Independent Contractor versus Employee*, https://www.dir.ca.gov/dlse/FAQ_IndependentContractor.htm (last visited Feb. 24, 2020).
855. Yellow *Cab Coop. v. Workers' Comp. Appeals Bd.*, 226 Cal. App. 3d 1288, 1295 ((Cal. Sup. Ct. (1991)); See also State of California Department of Industrial Relations, *Independent Contractor versus Employee*, https://www.dir.ca.gov/dlse/FAQ_IndependentContractor.htm (last visited Feb. 24, 2020).
856. *Dynamex Operations W., Inc. v. Superior Court*, No. S222732, 2018 Cal. LEXIS 60 (Jan. 10, 2018); See also Tony Marks, *The California Supreme Court Deals a Blow to Independent Contractors*, Forbes (May 29, 2020), https://www.forbes.com/sites/tonymarks/2018/05/29/the-california-supreme-court-deals-a-blow-to-independent-contractors/#123ebfc570a1.
857. *Dynamex Operations W.* at 66–67; See also Michael Arin, *Esports & Employment after Dynamex*, Esports Bar Ass'n J. 1 (2019), https://esportsbar.org/journals/2019/10/esports-and-employment-after-dynamex.
858. *Id.*; See also The Society for Human Resource Management, *California's New Contractor Test Will Impact the Gig Economy*, The San Francisco Business Times (Sept. 4, 2018), https://www.bizjournals.com/sanfrancisco/news/2018/09/04/california-s-new-contractor-test-will-impact-the.html.
859. Arash Markazi, *Team SoloMid to Begin Construction on $13-Million Esports Training Center in Playa Vista*, L.A. Times (Sept. 11, 2019), https://www.latimes.com/sports/story/2019-09-11/largest-esports-training-center-north-america-los-angeles; See also Graham Ashton, *Sandbox Esports Opens Training*

Facility Doors to Pro and Amateur Players, The Esports Observer (May 24, 2017), https://esportsobserver.com/sandbox-esports-facility; Max Rettig, *Alienware*, Team Liquid Unveil First-of-Its-Kind *Esports Training Facility*, Sport Techie (Jan. 12, 2018), https://www.sporttechie.com/alienware-team-liquid-esports-training-facility.

860. State of California Department of Industrial Relations, *Classification of Workers as "Independent Contractors" Rebuffed by the California Court of Appeal*, https://www.dir.ca.gov/dlse/MisclassificationOfWorkers.htm (last visited Feb. 24, 2020).
861. *Id.*
862. Note, Kelsey F. Ridenhour, *Traditional Sports and Esports: The Path to Collective Bargaining*, 105 Iowa L. Rev. 1857 (2020), https://ilr.law.uiowa.edu/print/volume-105-issue-4/traditional-sports-and-esports-the-path-to-collective-bargaining.
863. Paresh Dave, *In E-sports, It's the Bosses Who Are Rallying for a Union*, L.A. Times, May 26, 2017, https://www.latimes.com/business/technology/la-fi-tn-esports-unions-20170526-htmlstory.html.
864. T.L. Taylor, *Raising the Stakes: E-Sports and the Professionalization of Computer Gaming*, 178 (The MIT Press 2012).
865. Maddy Meyers, *Pro Gamers Are Getting Serious about Unionizing*, Kotaku (Mar. 14, 2018), https://compete.kotaku.com/pro-gamers-are-getting-serious-about-unionizing-1823770452.
866. Jonathan Kogel, *State of the Esports Player Union: Drawbacks and Legal Challenges*, The Esports Observer (May 8, 2018), https://esportsobserver.com/state-of-the-esports-union.
867. National Labor Relations Board, *About Us*, https://www.nlrb.gov (last visited Mar. 4, 2020).
868. Harris Peskin, *Unionization in Esports*, Esports Bar Ass'n J. 1 (2019), https://esportsbar.org/journals/2019/9/11/unionization-in-esports; See also Jason Krell, *Esports Players Facing Questions of Whether to Unionize*, Global Sport Matters (Dec. 18, 2019), https://globalsportmatters.com/business/2019/12/18/organizing-esports-unions-requires-education-about-economics-and-history.
869. Liz Mullen, *Two Groups vie to Establish Esports Players Associations*, Sports Business Journal (Mar. 12, 2018), https://www.sportsbusinessdaily.com/Journal/Issues/2018/03/12/Esports/PAs.
870. Anthony 'Skychief' Nel, *Esports Associations & Player Unions: Is it Time for Another Look?*, Red Bull (Apr. 9, 2018), https://www.redbull.com/za-en/esports-associations-and-player-unions; See also Tyler Esguerra, *LCS Players Association Pushing for New West Coast League Server*, Dot Esports (Feb. 5, 2020), https://dotesports.com/league-of-legends/news/lcs-players-association-pushing-for-new-west-coast-league-server.
871. NALCSPA, Home Page, http://www.nalcspa.com (last visited Jul. 31, 2020); See also NALCS Players Association (@NALCS), Twitter (May 2018), https://twitter.com/nalcspa.
872. *Id.*
873. Kieran Darcy, *Riot's Player's Association Lays Groundwork for Unionization*, ESPN (Jun. 12, 2017), https://www.espn.com/esports/story/_/id/19617991/riot-players-association-lays-groundwork-unionization.

874. Graham Ashton, *NALCS Players Association Executive Director Reflects on First Year of Activity*, The Esports Observer (Jan. 9, 2019), https://esportsobserver.com/nalcspa-executive-director-interview.

875. Rachel Samples, *LCS Players Association Establishes Grace Period for Player Signing Window*, AXS (Jan. 15, 2019), https://www.axs.com/lcs-players-association-establishes-grace-period-for-player-signing-wi-136085.

876. *Id.*; Graham Ashton, *NALCS Players Association Executive Director Reflects on First Year of Activity*, The Esports Observer (Jan. 9, 2019), https://esportsobserver.com/nalcspa-executive-director-interview.

877. Counter-Strike Professional Players' Association (@CSPPAgg), Twitter (Sept, 2018), https://twitter.com/ CSPPAgg.

878. Fortnite Professional Players' Association (@FNPPA), Twitter (Oct. 2019), https://twitter.com/FNPPA.

879. Tobias M. Scholz, *eSports is Business: Management in the World of Competitive Gaming*, 76 (Palgrave Macmillan 2019); Counter-Strike Professional Players' Ass'n, *About Us*, https://www.csppa.gg (last visited Mar. 4, 2020).

880. *Id.*; See also Jacob Wolf, *Counter-Strike Pros form the Counter-Strike Professional Players Association*, ESPN (Jun. 29, 2018), https://www.espn.com/esports/story/_/id/23947731/counter-strike-pros-form-counter-strike-professional-players-association.

881. Counter-Strike Professional Players' Ass'n, *CSPPA AoA—Articles of Association*, https://www.csppa.gg/csppaaoa (last visited Mar. 4, 2020); See also Counter-Strike Professional Players' Association (@CSPPAgg), Twitter (Jul. 2, 2020 1:41 p.m.), https://twitter.com/CSPPAgg/status/1278745710498852869; YouTube, *ESPN Esports*: *What's Going on with the Counter-Strike PPA? - The Eco with Jacob Wolf*, https://youtu.be/-662yNNhhNI (last visited Jul. 16, 2020).

882. Andrew Hayward, *Fortnite Pro Players Form Professional Association*, The Esports Observer (Oct. 7, 2019), https://esportsobserver.com/fortnite-pro-players-association; See also Fortnite Professional Player's Association (@FNPPA), Twitter (Oct. 4, 2019 5:00 p.m.), https://twitter.com/FNPPA/status/1180226187630645248.

883. Andrew Hayward, *Fortnite Pro Players Form Professional Association*, The Esports Observer (Oct. 7, 2019), https://esportsobserver.com/fortnite-pro-players-association; See also Fortnite Professional Player's Association (@FNPPA), Twitter (Oct. 4, 2019 5:00 p.m.), https://twitter.com/FNPPA/status/1180226187630645248.

884. Kevin Hitt, ESL, *DreamHack, and CSPPA Create Framework Agreement for CS:GO Competitions*, The Esports Observer (Jan. 18, 2020), https://esportsobserver.com/esl-dreamhack-csppa.

885. Minna Adel Rubio, *CSGO Pro Players' Association Speaks Out on Players' Mental Health*, Daily Esports (May 19, 2020), https://www.dailyesports.gg/csgo-pro-players-association-speaks-out-on-players-mental-health.

886. Jarek Dekay, *Flashpoint Withholds $165,000 Payment to CSPPA Amid Widespread Allegations, Letter Reveals*, DBLTAP (Jul. 1, 2020), https://www.dbltap.com/posts/flashpoint-csppa-payment-withheld-letter-allegations-01ec5e7rg5w4; See also Luis 'Miraa' Mira, *The CSPPA is Acting as an Agent, Raising Conflict-of-Interest Concerns*, HLTV (Jul. 7, 2020), https://www.hltv.org/news/29947/the-csppa-is-acting-as-an-agent-raising-conflict-of-interest-concerns.

887. Liz Mullen, *Professional Overwatch and CS:GO Will Get Esports Players Associations Soon*, The Esports Observer (Mar. 13, 2018), https://esportsobserver.com/pro-overwatch-and-csgo-players-associations; See also Aron Garst, *What Would it Take for There to Be an Overwatch League Players' Union?*, Heroes Never Die (Feb. 28, 2019), https://www.heroesneverdie.com/2019/2/28/18243082/overwatch-league-union-requirements-logistics-planning.
888. Colton Deck, *R6 Pro League Coach Says "A Player's Union is in Talks" Following Visa Issues with ESL for Japan Finals*, Dot Esports (Oct. 31, 2019), https://dotesports.com/rainbow-6/news/r6-pro-league-coach-says-a-players-union-is-in-talks-following-visa-issues-with-esl-for-japan-finals.
889. T.L. Taylor, *Raising the Stakes: E-Sports and the Professionalization of Computer Gaming*, 178 (The MIT Press 2012).
890. Pete Lewin, *Why Every Esports Player Needs a Contract*, The Esports Observer (Nov. 21, 2016), https://esportsobserver.com/every-esports-player-needs-contract.
891. Gary R. Roberts, *Interpreting the NFL Player Contract*, 3 Marq. Sports L. J. 29 (1992), https://scholarship.law.marquette.edu/sportslaw/vol3/iss1/5/.
892. Thiemo Bräutigam, *Riot's New LCS Player Contracts—A Legal Analysis*, The Esports Observer (Nov. 20, 2015), https://esportsobserver.com/riots-new-lcs-player-contracts-a-legal-analysis; See also Noah Smith, *Debate: What Does a Fair Esports Contract Look Like? It's Complicated*, The Washington Post (Jun. 18, 2019), https://www.washingtonpost.com/sports/2019/06/18/debate-what-does-fair-esports-contract-look-like-its-complicated.
893. British Esports Association, Esports Player *Contracts: Basic Info on How They Work*, https://britishesports.org/news/esports-player-contracts-basic-info-on-how-they-work (last visited Jul. 27, 2020); See also Adam Whyte, How to Level-*Up Your Esports Contracts, and Avoid Getting Ganked in a Dispute*, The Esports Observer (Apr. 14, 2017), https://esportsobserver.com/esports-contract-guide-how-to-avoid-getting-ganked-in-a-dispute-and-protecting-your-sponsors.
894. *League of Legends Esports League—Recognized Contract Database*, https://docs.google.com/spreadsheets/d/1Y7k5kQ2AegbuyiGwEPsa62e883FYVtHqr6UVut9RC4o/pubhtml (last visited Jul. 27, 2020).
895. Jacob Wolf, *Overwatch League Announces Standard Player Contract Terms*, ESPN (Jul. 26, 2017), https://www.espn.com/esports/story/_/id/20163254/overwatch-league-owl-announces-details-player-contracts-team-buy-in; See also Nilu Kulasingham, *Team Impulse Banned from the LCS after Repeatedly Failing to Pay Players*, Dot Esports (May 9, 2016), https://dotesports.com/league-of-legends/news/riot-bans-team-impulse-3341.
896. Andrew Hayward, *Call of Duty Global League Player Contract and Salary Details Announced*, The Esports Observer (Aug. 21, 2019), https://esportsobserver.com/cod-global-league-player-contracts.
897. Noah Smith, *Debate: What Does a Fair Esports Contract Look Like? It's Complicated*, The Washington Post (Jun. 18, 2019), https://www.washingtonpost.com/sports/2019/06/18/debate-what-does-fair-esports-contract-look-like-its-complicated.

898. Aabicus Lee, *The Dangers of Esports Contracts: Don't Sign before You Read this*, Daily Esports (Apr. 21, 2019), https://www.dailyesports.gg/the-dangers-of-esports-contracts-dont-sign-before-you-read-this.
899. Jack Stewart, *G2 Esports' Contract Lengths for Their League of Legends Team Revealed*, Daily Mail U.K. (Jan. 10, 2018), https://www.dailymail.co.uk/sport/esports/article-5254385/G2-Esports-contract-lengths-EU-LCS-team-revealed.html.
900. Jamie Hore, *Three G2 Esports Rosters Agree Contract Renewals Until 2022*, The Loadout (Jul. 13, 2020), https://www.theloadout.com/teams/g2-esports/triple-roster-contract-renewal; See also Eren Merdan Gursoy, *Esports G2 Esports Renew the Contract with Hearthstone Player Thijs*, Gaimer (Jun. 8, 2019), https://gaimer.net/g2-esports-renew-the-contract-with-heatstone-player-thijs.
901. David Hollingsworth, *League of Legends: Excel Esports Renew Mickey's Contract for 2020*, ESTNN (Nov. 30, 2019), https://estnn.com/league-of-legends-excel-esports-renew-mickeys-contract-for-2020.
902. Kevin Webb, *A Top 'Fortnite' Player Who Won More than $500,000 is Suing His Team Over an 'Oppressive' Contract. Here's Why Other YouTubers Are Taking Notice*, Business Insider (May 22, 2019), https://www.businessinsider.com.au/tfue-faze-clan-lawsuit-youtube-twitch-2019-5.
903. Schalke 04, *League of Legends: Elias Lipp Leaves Royal Blue*, https://schalke04.de/esports/en/league-of-legends-elias-lipp-leaves-royal-blue (last visited Jul. 28, 2020).
904. L.A. Galaxy, *LA Galaxy Sign eSports Players Kyle Danese, Bobby Park and Martin Oregel*, https://www.lagalaxy.com/post/2019/01/08/la-galaxy-sign-esports-players-kyle-danese-bobby-park-and-martin-oregel (last visited Jul. 28, 2020).
905. Andrew Salazar, *Riot Games Fines Tainted Minds for Contract Violations*, Esports Source (Apr. 13, 2017), https://www.esportssource.org/2017/04/riot-games-fines-tainted-minds-for-contract-violations.html; See also Jacob Wolf, *Sources: Dream Team Fails to Pay ANTi, Dabuz and HugS on Time*, ESPN (Aug. 22,2016), https://www.espn.com/esports/story/_/id/17369271/dream-team-fails-pay-anti-dabuz-hugs; See also Rahul Bhatta, *Iceberg Esports Fail to Pay Their Esports Players*, Esports Junkie (Mar. 2, 2018), https://esportsjunkie.com/2018/03/02/iceberg-esports-fail-pay-esports-players; Jacob Wolf, *Epsilon Allegedly Owes Players Nearly $25K in Outstanding Payments*, ESPN (Nov. 3, 2016), https://www.espn.com/esports/story/_/id/17963730/league-legends-epsilon-esports-players-owed-25000-outstanding-payments.
906. Arda Ocal, *Chicago Huntsmen's Gunless Confirms He's Benched*, ESPN (May 4, 2020), https://www.espn.com/esports/story/_/id/29134431/chicago-huntsmen-gunless-confirms-benched; See also Jacob Wolf, *Misfits Bench Starting Roster, will Start Misfits Premier Players*, ESPN (Jul. 18, 2019), https://www.espn.com/esports/story/_/id/27216124/misfits-bench-starting-roster-start-misfits-premier-players.
907. Preston Byers, *Enable Re-joins Seattle Surge Starting Roster*, Dot Esports (May 12, 2020), https://dotesports.com/call-of-duty/news/enable-re-joins-seattle-surge-starting-roster.

908. Mike Stubbs, *100 Thieves LCS Player Meteos Calls Out Coaches on Twitter after Being Benched*, Forbes (Jun. 29, 2020), https://www.forbes.com/sites/mikestubbs/2020/06/29/100-thieves-lcs-player-meteos-calls-out-coaches-on-twitter-after-being-benched/#203c55cc7233.
909. Samuel O' Dwyer, *CLG's Stixxay Benched in Favor of Academy Player Wind*, Dot Esports (Mar. 7, 2020), https://dotesports.com/league-of-legends/news/clgs-stixxay-benched-in-favor-of-academy-player-wind.
910. Pranjal "pranjal26" Drall, *ACE Fines Iceiceice for not Wearing VG Jacket*, GosuGamer (Jun. 16, 2015), https://www.gosugamers.net/dota2/news/31404-ace-fines-iceiceice-for-not-wearing-vg-jacket.
911. Kevin Hitt, *Golden Guardians Extend Exclusive Streaming Partnership with Twitch*, The Esports Observer (Jun. 11, 2020), https://esportsobserver.com/golden-guardians-twitch-deal.
912. Daniel, *How to Get Your First Stream Sponsor—A Step by Step Guide*, The Stream Setup (Aug. 13, 2017), https://thestreamsetup.com/how-to-get-your-first-stream-sponsor-a-step-by-step-guide; See also Joe Donnelly, *Everspace Dev Reportedly Says They Paid Thousands for a Pro Streamer Who 'Played Like a f**king Moron,'* P.C. Gamer (Apr. 19, 2018), https://www.pcgamer.com/everspace-dev-reportedly-says-they-paid-thousands-for-a-pro-streamer-who-played-like-a-fking-moron.
913. Vincent Plana, *You Can Meet Vancouver's Pro Esports Stars at Rogers Arena June 1*, Listed (May 28, 2019), https://dailyhive.com/vancouver/meet-vancouver-titans-june-1-2019.
914. ONE Esports, *Here's Your Chance to Get Up Close with Your Favorite Players!*, https://www.oneesports.gg/dota2/meet-and-greet-the-best-dota-2-players-at-the-one-esports-dota-2-singapore-world-pro-invitational (last visited Jul. 28, 2020); See also Samsung, *Samsung Teams Up with Global Esports Organization T1 as Official Display Partner*, https://news.samsung.com/us/samsung-esports-t1-official-display-partner-odyssey-gaming-monitors-g7-g9 (last visited Jul. 28, 2020).
915. G FUEL, *Join G FUEL at Walmart's Grand Openings of Esports Arenas in Nashville and Kansas City*, https://blog.gfuel.com/walmart-esports-arenas-nashville-kansas-city-grand-openings (last visited Jul. 28, 2020).
916. Aabicus Lee, *The Dangers of Esports Contracts: Don't Sign before You Read this*, Daily Esports (Apr. 21, 2019), https://www.dailyesports.gg/the-dangers-of-esports-contracts-dont-sign-before-you-read-this.
917. Alan LaFleur, *Sponsorship Activation: How to Get the Most Out of a Partnership*, The Esports Observer (May 28, 2015), https://esportsobserver.com/how-to-get-the-most-out-of-a-sponsorship.
918. Zorine Te, *OpTic Gaming Enters Exclusive Streaming Partnership with Twitch, Joining TSM, Cloud9, Evil Geniuses, Virtus.pro, and More*, Yahoo (Jun. 6, 2017), https://sports.yahoo.com/optic-gaming-enters-exclusive-streaming-partnership-twitch-joining-tsm-cloud9-evil-geniuses-virtus-pro-172820528.html.
919. Phil Hornshaw, *eSports Ain't Easy: Inside the Everyday Grind of Pro Gaming*, Complex (Aug. 6, 2016), https://www.complex.com/sports/2016/08/everyday-grind-of-being-an-esports-athlete.

920. Kevin Webb, *A Pro Call of Duty Player Tracked Exactly How He Spent His Time for a Week, from Over 50 Hours of Esports to After-Hours Twitch Streaming*, Business Insider (Mar. 24, 2020), https://www.businessinsider.com/pro-gamer-weekly-schedule-training-call-of-duty-league-2020-3.
921. Rob Zacny, *The Toll of Travel on eSports Athletes*, Red Bull (Sept. 4, 2014), https://www.redbull.com/us-en/the-toll-of-travel-on-esports-athletes.
922. Eric Van Allen, *Tools of the Trade: The Importance of Quality Esports Equipment*, ESPN (May 19, 2016), https://www.espn.com/esports/story/_/id/15616253/importance-quality-esports-equipment.
923. Joe Craven, *G2 Jankos Explains How He Escaped Fine after Silly Mistake at LEC*, Dexerto (Feb. 2, 2020), https://www.dexerto.com/league-of-legends/g2-jankos-explains-how-he-escaped-fine-after-silly-mistake-at-lec-1322222.
924. Corey Plante, *Why Pro 'Call of Duty' Players All Use this Controller*, Inverse (Dec. 22, 2017), https://www.inverse.com/article/39548-scuf-gaming-controllers-esports-competitive-call-of-duty; See also Mike Stubbs, *Get the Gear that Esports Pros Use to Become the Best in the World*, Forbes (Dec. 25, 2017), https://www.forbes.com/sites/mikestubbs/2017/12/25/get-the-gear-that-esports-pros-use-to-become-the-best-in-the-world/#2db5f0fe5d12.
925. TeamSoloMid, *Esports Facility*, https://facility.tsm.gg (last visited Jul. 29, 2020).
926. Team Liquid, *Alienware Training Facility, The Vision*, https://www.teamliquid.com/AlienwareTF (last visited Feb. 26, 2020); See also Dean Takahashi, *Inside Team Liquid's High-End Esports Training Facility*, Venture Beat (Jan. 28, 2018), https://venturebeat.com/2018/01/28/inside-team-liquids-high-end-esports-training-facility.
927. Adam Kilgore, *Yes, There Are Some Things Pro Athletes Aren't Allowed to Do*, The Washington Post (Jul. 6, 2015), https://www.washingtonpost.com/news/sports/wp/2015/07/06/yes-there-are-some-things-pro-athletes-arent-allowed-to-do; See also Owens S. Good, *Pro Call of Duty Player Phillip Klemenov Killed in Car Wreck*, Polygon (Oct. 3, 2016), https://www.polygon.com/2016/10/3/13147302/phillip-klemenov-phizzurp-killed-dies-car-accident-crash.
928. George Geddes, *Street Fighter Player NuckleDu Reportedly Involved in Car Crash*, Dot Esports (Jul. 2, 2020), https://dotesports.com/fgc/news/street-fighter-player-nuckledu-reportedly-involved-in-car-crash.
929. Tom Gerencer, *How Much Money Do Pro Gamers Make?*, Money Nation (Feb. 7, 2017), https://moneynation.com/pro-gamer-money.
930. Keith Nelson, Jr., *Esports Teams Aren't Cheap and Their Future Revenue Stream Isn't What You'd Expect*, One37pm (Jul. 3, 2019), https://www.one37pm.com/culture/gaming/esports-teams-costs-revenue-psg-rocket-league.
931. Brian O' Connell, *How Much Do eSports Players Make?*, The Street (Feb. 12, 2020), https://www.thestreet.com/personal-finance/how-much-do-esports-players-make-15126931.
932. *Id.*
933. Jared Ramsey, *Highest Paid eSports Players in the World*, Lineups (Jul. 19, 2020), https://www.lineups.com/esports/highest-paid-esports-players-in-the-world.

934. ESPN Staff, *Confidential: Life as a League of Legends Pro*, ESPN (Jan. 12, 2017), https://www.espn.com/esports/story/_/id/18461870/life-league-legends-pro.
935. Xing Li, *NA LCS Salaries Average Over $320K a Year According to OpTic Gaming Manager*, Dot Esports (Feb. 26, 2018), https://dotesports.com/league-of-legends/news/optic-romain-bigeard-na-lcs-player-salaries-21399.
936. Andy Chalk, *Korean e-Sports Association Proposes Minimum Salaries for Pro Gamers*, P.C. Gamer (Oct. 31, 2014), https://www.pcgamer.com/korean-e-sports-association-proposes-minimum-salaries-for-pro-gamers.
937. Activision-Blizzard Entertainment, *Overwatch League—Player Signings, Salaries, and More in the Overwatch League*, https://overwatchleague.com/en-us/news/20937016/player-signings-salaries-and-more-in-the-overwatch-league (last visited Feb. 26, 2020).
938. Preston Byers, *Activision Reveals 2020 Call of Duty League Details, Confirms Path to Pro System*, Dot Esports (Aug. 20, 2019), https://dotesports.com/call-of-duty/news/activision-reveals-2020-call-of-duty-league-details-confirms-path-to-pro-system.
939. Jamie Villanueva, *Fifflaren Alleges NiP Owes Multiple Players Thousands of Dollars*, Dot Esports (Jul. 23, 2019), https://dotesports.com/counter-strike/news/fifflaren-alleges-nip-owes-multiple-players-thousands-of-dollars.
940. Jacob Wolf, *NRG Signs 17-Year-Old Overwatch Pro Sinatraa for $150K*, ESPN (Sept. 3, 2017), https://www.espn.com/esports/story/_/id/20564135/nrg-signs-17-year-old-overwatch-pro-sinatraa-150k.
941. Saqib Shah, *Overwatch's Highest-Paid Pro Lands $150,000 Salary Deal*, Engadget (Sept. 4, 2017), https://www.engadget.com/2017/09/04/overwatch-s-highest-paid-pro-lands-150-000-salary-deal.
942. Peter Cole, *Overwatch League Salary: How Much is an OWL Pro Paid?*, Final Kill (Jul. 14, 2018), https://finalkill.com/overwatch/average-overwatch-league-salary.
943. Preston Byers, *EStar Fines Jungler One Month's Salary for not Taking Smite*, Dot Esports (Jun. 16, 2020), https://dotesports.com/league-of-legends/news/estar-fines-jungler-one-months-salary-for-not-taking-smite.
944. Matt Porter, *All Confirmed Call of Duty League Franchise Teams and Owners*, Dexerto (Aug. 30, 2019), https://www.dexerto.com/call-of-duty/all-confirmed-call-of-duty-league-franchise-teams-and-owners-969321.
945. Jordan Baranowski, *The Truth about the Richest Esports Team Ever*, Looper (May 5, 2020), https://www.looper.com/206999/the-truth-about-the-richest-esports-team-ever.
946. Shannon Liao, *Who is Getting Rich Off of Fortnite*, CNN Business (Aug. 1, 2019), https://www.cnn.com/2019/08/01/tech/fortnite-esports-profit/index.html; See also Tim Maloney, *How Do Esports Teams Make Money?*, Roundhill Investments (Feb. 12, 2020), https://www.roundhillinvestments.com/research/esports/how-do-esports-teams-make-money.
947. Sam Nordmark and Jerome Heath, *The Biggest Prize Money Winners in Esports History*, Dot Esports (Jun. 15, 2020), https://dotesports.com/general/news/top-earning-esports-players-21870.
948. Valve Corp., *Dota 2—The International Dota 2 Champions*, http://www.dota2.com/international/overview/ (last visited Feb. 26, 2020).

949. Andrew Hayward, *Dota 2's International 2019 Prize Pool Surpasses $30M*, The Esports Observer (Jul. 22, 2019), https://esportsobserver.com/dota2-ti19-prize-30m/.
950. Mike Stubbs, *The International 9 'Dota 2' Tournament Prize Pool Breaks $30 Million*, Forbes (Jul. 27, 2019), https://www.forbes.com/sites/mikestubbs/2019/07/27/the-international-9-dota-2-tournament-prize-pool-breaks-30-million/#6bc1e83f2c07; See also Valve Corp., *Dota 2—The International Dota 2 Prize Pool Tracker*, https://dota2.prizetrac.kr/international2019 (last visited Feb. 26, 2020).
951. Valve Corp., *Dota 2—The International Dota 2 Champions*, http://www.dota2.com/international/overview/ (last visited Feb. 26, 2020).
952. Jon Fingas, *'Dota 2' Champions Won More Money than Top Wimbledon Players*, Engadget (Aug. 25, 2019), https://www.engadget.com/2019/08/25/dota-2-the-international-2019-win-sets-records.
953. Gamepedia, *Dota 2 Wiki—The International 2018*, https://dota2.gamepedia.com/The_International_2018 (last visited Feb. 26, 2020).
954. Valve Corp., *Dota 2—The International Dota 2 Prize Pool Tracker*, https://dota2.prizetrac.kr/international2019 (last visited Feb. 26, 2020).
955. Mike Stubbs, *The International 10 'Dota 2' Tournament Prize Pool Breaks $30 Million*, Forbes (Jul. 27, 2020), https://www.forbes.com/sites/mikestubbs/2020/07/27/the-international-10-dota-2-tournament-prize-pool-breaks-30-million/#5d840e562d07.
956. Kevin Webb, *The Fortnite World Cup Finals Start this Friday, and $30 Million is on the Line. Here's What You Need to Know about the Competition*, Business Insider (Jul. 25, 2019), https://www.businessinsider.com/fortnite-world-cup-finals-schedule-players-30-million-prize-money-2019-7#every-player-in-the-fortnite-world-cup-finals-will-win-a-minimum-of-50000-1.
957. *Id.*
958. Theo Salaun, *Overwatch League 2020 Week 25: Chengdu Hunters' Top Plays, Prize Money*, Bleacher Report (Jul. 26, 2020), https://bleacherreport.com/articles/2901248-overwatch-league-2020-week-25-chengdu-hunters-top-plays-prize-money.
959. Michael Domanico, *Overwatch League Announces 2019 Schedule, Including Away Games and Increased Prize Pool*, IGN (Dec. 12, 2018), https://www.ign.com/articles/2018/12/12/overwatch-league-announces-2019-schedule-including-away-games-and-increased-prize-pool.
960. *Id.*; Activision-Blizzard Entertainment, *Overwatch League—2019 Season Playoffs Primer*, https://overwatchleague.com/en-us/news/23053104/2019-season-playoffs-primer (last visited Feb. 26, 2020).
961. Andrew Hayward, *Ubisoft Reveals 14 Teams for Rainbow Six Siege Revenue—Share Pilot Program Phase 2*, The Esports Observer (Aug. 19, 2019), https://esportsobserver.com/r6pl-phase-two-teams.
962. *Id.*
963. Andrew Hayward, *Rocket League to Add Revenue-Sharing Esports Items for 11 Teams*, The Esports Observer (Apr. 10, 2019), https://esportsobserver.com/rocket-league-digital-sales; See also Max Thielmeyer, *Rocket League's Esports Shop to Kick Off RLCS Season* 9 with *Brand New* Items, Forbes (Jan. 28, 2020), https://www.forbes.com/sites/maxthielmeyer/2020/01/28/rocket-leagues-esports-shop-to-kick-off-rlcs-season-9-with-brand-new-items/#771f031d184b.

964. Adam Fitch, *Sources: The Numbers behind PUBG's Esports Revenue Sharing in 2019*, Esports Insider (Jan. 14, 2020), https://esportsinsider.com/2020/01/pubg-esports-revenue-share-numbers.
965. Adam Fitch, *Riot Games to Introduce Revenue-Sharing Passes for League of Legends*, Esports Insider (May 24, 2019), https://esportsinsider.com/2019/05/league-of-legends-revenue-sharing; See also Riots Games, *League of Legends—Team Pass & Fan Hit the Rift on May 31*, https://nexus.leagueoflegends.com/en-us/2019/05/team-pass-fan-pass-hit-the-rift-on-may-31 (last visited Feb. 26, 2020).
966. Nicole Carpenter, *Overwatch League Skins Are Only Available for Real Money—But 50 Percent Goes to the Teams*, Dot Esports (Dec. 5, 2017), https://dotesports.com/overwatch/news/overwatch-league-tokens-revenue-19255.
967. Stefanie Fogel, *New 'Rocket League' Esports Shop Benefits Teams, Players*, Variety (Apr. 10, 2019), https://variety.com/2019/gaming/news/rocket-league-esports-shop-reveal-1203185880.
968. Adam Stern, *Move Allows Esports Teams to Sell More Merchandise*, Sports Business Journal (Sept. 16, 2019), https://www.sportsbusinessdaily.com/Journal/Issues/2019/09/16/Esports/Merch.aspx.
969. Mitch Reames, *How Esports Organizations Make Money*, Hotspawn (Apr. 15, 2019), https://www.hotspawn.com/guides/how-esports-organizations-make-money.
970. WAX, *Immortals Digital Collectibles with WAX*, https://immortals.wax.io (last visited Jul. 29, 2020).
971. Dean Takahashi, *Esports Group Fnatic Teams Up with Blockchain firm WAX on Digital Collectibles*, Venture Beat (Jan. 10, 2019), https://venturebeat.com/2019/01/10/esports-group-fnatic-teams-up-with-blockchain-firm-wax-on-digital-collectibles.
972. Ferguson Mitchell, *New Company Wants to Bring Branded Apparel to the LCS and Esports*, Dot Esports (Jan. 5, 2015), https://dotesports.com/league-of-legends/news/ggculture-branded-apparel-lcs-1975.
973. Michael Gannon-Pitts, *eSports Sponsors: Building Lucrative Brand Partnerships*, Magnetic, https://magneticcreative.com/esports-sponsors; See also Rogue Energy, *Blog: The Ultimate Guide to Gaming Sponsorships*, https://rogueenergy.com/blogs/news/the-ultimate-guide-to-gaming-sponsorships (last visited Jul. 29, 2020).
974. G Fuel, *Censor*, https://gfuel.com/pages/censor (last visited Jul. 29, 2020).
975. Pete Lewin, *Why Every Esports Player Needs a Contract*, The Esports Observer (Nov. 21, 2016), https://esportsobserver.com/every-esports-player-needs-contract.
976. Rick Mele, *The Uprising Are Playing Raptors Basketball, and Winning*, Complex (Jun. 11, 2020), https://www.complex.com/sports/2020/06/meet-raptors-uprising-the-hottest-team-in-the-2k-league; See also Raptors Uprising *GC, FaZe Clan's Offseason Takeover of Bell Fibe House*, https://raptorsuprising.nba.com/news/faze-clans-offseason-takeover-of-bell-fibe-house (last visited Jul. 29, 2020); E.S.L., *Team Houses and Why They Matter*, https://www.eslgaming.com/article/team-houses-and-why-they-matter-1676 (last visited Jul. 29, 2020).

977. Harrison Jacobs, *Here's What Life is Like in the Cramped 'Gaming House' Where 5 Guys Live Together and Earn Amazing Money by Playing Video Games*, Business Insider (May 5, 2015), https://www.businessinsider.com/inside-team-liquids-league-of-legends-gaming-house-2015-4; See also Paul 'Redeye' Chaloner, *This is Esports (and How to Spell it)*, 145 (Bloomsbury Sport 2020).
978. Maddy Myers, *How Pro Gamers Live Now: Curfews, Personal Chefs, and All of it on Camera*, Kotaku (Jun. 21, 2018), https://compete.kotaku.com/how-pro-gamers-live-now-curfews-personal-chefs-and-a-1827017564; See Paul 'Redeye' Chaloner, *This is Esports (and How to Spell it)*, 147 (Bloomsbury Sport 2020); See also Mitch Reames, *Why More and More Brands Are Getting into the Streaming Game on Twitch*, AdWeek (Apr. 1, 2019), https://www.adweek.com/digital/why-more-and-more-brands-are-getting-into-the-streaming-game-on-twitch.
979. Byungho "Haao" Kim and James "Bick" Hong, *Cloud9: A Day in the Life of a Professional Player*, Inven Global (May 27, 2018), https://www.invenglobal.com/articles/5166/cloud9-a-day-in-the-life-of-a-professional-player.
980. Id.; See also HyperX, *Cloud9 CS:GO HyperX Gaming House Tour*, YouTube (Jan. 19, 2017), https://youtu.be/DES6F3XVwMk.
981. Will Beverina, *Where the First Class of NBA 2K League Stars Will Live and Work*, DIMER 2K (Apr. 5, 2018), https://dimer2k.com/2018/04/05/where-the-first-class-of-nba-2k-league-stars-will-live-and-work.
982. Simon Parkin, *Esports: Boot Camps Give Gaming Teams the Vital Edge*, New Scientist (Aug. 13, 2014), https://www.newscientist.com/article/mg22329824-000-esports-boot-camps-give-gaming-teams-the-vital-edge; See also Tyler Erzberger, *An Inside Look at the VALORANT Bootcamp*, ESPN (Apr. 3, 2020), https://www.espn.com/esports/story/_/id/28991386/an-look-valorant-bootcamp.
983. Jeff Parsons, *Inside eSports 'Boot camp' Where Gamers Down Energy Drinks and Stare at Screens for 16 Hours a Day*, Mirror (Sept. 27, 2017), https://www.mirror.co.uk/tech/inside-esports-boot-camp-gamers-11244422.
984. Cision PR Newswire, *G2A to Organize an Esports Bootcamp for Virtus.pro and Natus Vincere*, https://www.prnewswire.com/in/news-releases/g2a-to-organize-an-esports-bootcamp-for-virtuspro-and-natus-vincere-621611093.html (last visited Feb. 27, 2020).
985. Id.; See also Mike Pepe, *NVIDIA to Open GeForce Esports Boot Camps in Munich and Shanghai*, NIVIDIA (Aug. 9, 2018), https://blogs.nvidia.com/blog/2018/08/09/geforce-esports-boot-camps-munich-and-shanghai (last visited Jul. 29, 2020).
986. Simon Parkin, *Esports: Boot Camps Give Gaming Teams the Vital Edge*, New Scientist (Aug. 13, 2014), https://www.newscientist.com/article/mg22329824-000-esports-boot-camps-give-gaming-teams-the-vital-edge.
987. Josh Bury, *Vexed's Ex-CS:GO Roster: Org Did not 'Pay for Our Travel Costs and Salaries for the Past Month,'* The Score (Mar. 10, 2016), https://www.thescoreesports.com/csgo/news/6663.
988. Merriam-Webster Dictionary, *Per Diem*, https://www.merriam-webster.com/dictionary/per%20diem (last visited Feb. 26, 2020).
989. *Doctors Raise the Alarm about Esports Injuries*, CBS News (Mar. 29, 2019), https://www.cbsnews.com/news/esports-video-game-players-injuries-can-be-serious.

990. Jennifer Jolly, *Esports Injuries Real for Pros and At-Home Gamer, from Finger Sprains to Collapsed Lungs*, USA Today (Jul. 29, 2019), https://www.usatoday.com/story/tech/columnist/2019/07/29/video-games-esport-pros-face-serious-injuries-so-can-home-players/1832131001.

991. Lara Jackson, *Family of Pro Gamer Sues Former Teams for Negligence after His Death*, Gamebyte (Apr. 21, 2020), https://www.gamebyte.com/family-of-pro-gamer-sues-former-teams-for-negligence-after-his-death.

992. Rich Stanton, *The Secret to eSports Athletes' Success? Lots—and Lots—of Practice*, ESPN (May 29, 2015), https://www.espn.com/espn/story/_/id/13053116/esports-athletes-put-hours-training-reach-pinnacle.

993. Eric Van Allen, *Physical Therapists Are Helping Esports Pros Play More and Hurt Less*, Kotaku (Mar. 6, 2017), https://compete.kotaku.com/physical-therapists-are-helping-esports-pros-play-more-1793007981.

994. Field Level Media, *TSM's Fortnite Team Fines ZexRow for Profane Rant*, Reuters (May 29, 2020), https://www.reuters.com/article/esports-fortnite-zexrow-fine-idUSFLM7Gl961; See also Emily Rand, *Riot Fines 4 Worlds Participants for In-Game Behavior*, ESPN (Oct. 7, 2018), https://www.espn.com/esports/story/_/id/24926769/riot-games-fines-players-coach-game-behavior-league-legends-world-championship-prep.

995. Aaron Mickunas, *Report Alleges that Perkz and G2 Esports Poached Players in the EU LCS*, Dot Esports (Dec. 3, 2018), https://dotesports.com/league-of-legends/news/report-alleges-that-perkz-and-g2-esports-poached-players-in-the-eu-lcs; See also Xing Li, *Riot Explains: What is Poaching?*, Dot Esports (Dec. 16, 2016), https://dotesports.com/league-of-legends/news/riot-explains-what-is-poaching-2-4117.

996. Andreaa 'Div' Esanu, *CIS Shuffle with a Drama: Virtus.pro Get Na'Vi Zayac after Poaching Him Directly*, VPEsports (Feb. 3, 2020), https://www.vpesports.com/dota2/news/cis-shuffle-with-a-drama-virtus-pro-get-navi-zayac-after-poaching-him-directly; See also Ferguson Mitchell, *Further Poaching Allegations Linked to NA LCS Team Echo Fox*, The Esports Observer (Dec. 1, 2016), https://esportsobserver.com/poaching-allegations-linked-na-lcs-team-echo-fox.

997. Thiemo Bräutigam, *Riot's New LCS Player Contracts—A Legal Analysis*, The Esports Observer (Nov. 20, 2015), https://esportsobserver.com/riots-new-lcs-player-contracts-a-legal-analysis.

998. Caroline Rutledge, *CS:GO: MIBR Fines Fer after Racist Remarks on Twitch Stream*, ESTNN (Jun. 3, 2020), https://estnn.com/csgo-mibr-fines-fer-after-racist-remarks-on-twitch-stream; Vignesh Raghuram, *iLTW Apologises to Xcalibur for His Remarks in the Pub Game*, AFK Gaming (Jun. 6, 2020), https://afkgaming.com/articles/dota2/News/4207-iltw-apologises-to-xcalibur-for-his-remarks-in-the-pub-game.

999. Cristian Lupasco, *2 LPL Teams Reportedly Issue Fines to Players for Inappropriate Remarks on Stream*, Dot Esports (Jul. 14, 2020), https://dotesports.com/league-of-legends/news/2-lpl-teams-reportedly-issue-fines-to-players-for-inappropriate-remarks-on-stream.

1000. Crystal Mills, *Seth 'Scump' Abner Slams 'Call of Duty: Modern Warfare,' Claims 'Warzone' Saved it*, Benzinga (May 16, 2020), https://www.benzinga.com/news/20/05/16049026/seth-scump-abner-slams-call-of-duty

-modern-warfare-claims-warzone-saved-it; See also Jordan Baranowski, *Pro Gamers Who Ruined Their Careers*, SVG (Jul. 27, 2018), https://www.svg.com/129784/pro-gamers-who-ruined-their-careers.

1001. *Liquidated Damages*, Black's Law Dictionary (10th ed. 2014).

1002. N.F.L. Football Operations, *Fines and Appeals*, https://operations.nfl.com/football-ops/nfl-rules-enforcement/fines-appeals (last visited Feb. 26, 2020).

1003. Cale Michael, *Capcom Bans CeroBlast, Low Tier God from All Events*, Dot Esports (Apr. 23, 2020), https://dotesports.com/fgc/news/capcom-bans-ceroblast-low-tier-god-from-all-events; See also Todd Spangler, *Blizzard Bans 'Hearthstone' Player from Esports Tournaments for Pro-Hong Kong Protest Statement*, Variety (Oct. 8, 2019), https://variety.com/2019/gaming/news/blizzard-bans-blitzchung-hearthstone-hong-kong-china-statement-1203363050.

1004. Samuel Lingle, *Mata Fined $8,000 for Troll Pick*, Dot Esports (Mar. 9, 2015), https://dotesports.com/league-of-legends/news/mata-fined-vici-gaming-1584.

1005. Arda Ocal, *San Francisco Shock Suspend and Fine Viol2t*, ESPN (Jul. 28, 2020), https://www.espn.com/esports/story/_/id/29552677/san-francisco-shock-suspend-fine-viol2t.

1006. Wasif Ahmed, *Pittsburgh Knights' Sixless Banned from PUBG Mobile Esports Until 2021*, Dot Esports (Jul. 26, 2020), https://dotesports.com/news/pittsburgh-knights-sixless-banned-from-pubg-mobile-esports-until-2021.

1007. Alistair Jones, *Esports Org Releases CS:GO Team in the Middle of a Competition*, Kotaku (Mar. 9, 2020), https://www.kotaku.co.uk/2020/03/09/esports-org-releases-csgo-team-in-the-middle-of-a-competition; See also Pedro Peres, *Team Envy Drops Out of Overwatch Contenders*, Dot Esports (Apr. 28, 2020), https://dotesports.com/overwatch/news/team-envy-drops-out-of-overwatch-contenders; Tyler Esguerra, *TSM Drops Competitive Rocket League and PUBG Rosters*, Dot Esports (Apr. 11, 2020), https://dotesports.com/news/tsm-drops-competitive-rocket-league-and-pubg-rosters.

1008. Graham Ashton, *How the Esports Player Transfer Market Differs from Soccer or the NBA*, The Esports Observer (Jan. 6. 2020), https://esportsobserver.com/esports-player-transfers-2020.

1009. Jacob Wolf, *Sources: Cloud9 to Pay $1.5 Million Buyout for Dignitas Support Vulcan*, ESPN (Nov. 18, 2019), https://www.espn.com/esports/story/_/id/28109140/sources-cloud9-pay-15-million-buyout-dignitas-support-vulcan; See also Leonardo Biazzi, *Vitality Reportedly Sets $600,000 Buyout for ALEX*, Dot Esports (Jun. 30, 2020), https://dotesports.com/counter-strike/news/vitality-reportedly-sets-600000-buyout-for-alex; Sigma Klim, *How Much Can a CS:GO Player Buyout Be? Shox $450,000 (H3.2 Crore) Coldzera $1 Million (H7.1 Crore)*, Guru Gamer (Sept. 16, 2019), https://gurugamer.com/esports/how-much-can-a-csgo-player-buyout-be-shox-450-000-32-crore-coldzera-1-million-71-crore-6307.

1010. Ross Deason, *G2 Reportedly Sets Staggering Buyout Price for Benches CS:GO Stars*, Dexerto (Jun. 26, 2018), https://www.dexerto.com/csgo/g2-reportedly-sets-staggering-buyout-price-for-benched-csgo-stars-107328.

1011. *Id.*

1012. *Id.*

1013. Nicole Carpenter, *After Landing a Contenders Championship, Eagle Gaming Lifts its Buyout Clause for Players*, Dot Esports (Sept. 25, 2018), https://dotesports.com/overwatch/news/after-landing-a-contenders-championship-eagle-gaming-lifts-its-buyout-clause-for-players.

1014. Activision-Blizzard, *Overwatch Contenders*, https://overwatchcontenders.com/en-us/ (last visited Feb. 26, 2020).

1015. Joe O'Brien, *Team Envy Has Signed an Overwatch Contenders Team*, Dexerto (Jul. 26, 2018), https://www.dexerto.com/overwatch/team-envy-has-signed-an-overwatch-contenders-team-111888.

1016. *Id.*

1017. Scott Gleeson, *eSports Legend Jian 'Uzi' Zihao Retires Citing Stress, Obesity, Diabetes, Hand Injury*, USA Today (Jun. 3, 2020), https://www.usatoday.com/story/sports/2020/06/03/jian-zihao-esports-legend-retires-citing-stress-obesity-diabetes/3133076001; See also Patrick Shanley, *Gamers' Plight: Why So Many Esports Players Retire by 25—And What Comes Next*, The Hollywood Reporter (Sept. 24, 2019), https://www.hollywoodreporter.com/news/gamers-plight-why-e-sports-players-retire-by-25-1242628.

1018. Arijeta Lajka, *Esports Players Burn Out Young as the Grind Takes Mental, Physical Toll*, CBS News (Dec. 21, 2018), https://www.cbsnews.com/news/esports-burnout-in-video-gaming-cbsn-originals.

1019. Alex Andrejev, *Her Son is a Pro Gamer. Here's How She Came to Understand the World of Esports*, The Washington Post (Oct. 21, 2019), https://www.washingtonpost.com/video-games/esports/2019/10/21/her-son-is-pro-gamer-heres-how-she-came-understand-world-esports.

1020. Arjun Kharpal and Saheli Roy Choudhury, *Pro Video Gamers Are Making Millions by Age 30 in the Booming World of 'Esports,'* CNBC (Oct. 5, 2018), https://www.cnbc.com/2018/10/03/esports-pro-video-gamers-are-making-millions-by-age-30-and-retiring.html.

1021. Samuel Lingle, *The Greatest StarCraft Player of All-Time Has Retired*, Dot Esports (Dec. 1, 2015), https://dotesports.com/general/news/flash-retires-starcraft-2721.

1022. Xing Li, *How Trades Should Happen in Esports League*, Dot Esports (Jul. 2, 2028), https://dotesports.com/business/news/how-esports-trades-should-happen-29579.

1023. Jacob Wolf, *Vulcan to Cloud9—Inside the Trade that Defined the 2019 LCS Offseason*, ESPN (Feb. 3, 2020), https://www.espn.com/esports/story/_/id/28614276/vulcan-cloud9-trade-defined-2019-lcs-offseason. See also Patrick Kobek, *Study Shows Just How Much Esports Trades Are Worth*, The Gamer (Mar. 12, 2020), https://www.thegamer.com/study-shows-esports-trades-value.

1024. Liz Richardson, *Overwatch League 2020 Midseason Trade Tracker*, Dot Esports (Jul. 11, 2020), https://dotesports.com/overwatch/news/overwatch-league-2020-midseason-trade-tracker.

1025. Xing Li, *How Trades Should Happen in Esports League*, Dot Esports (Jul. 2, 2028), https://dotesports.com/business/news/how-esports-trades-should-happen-29579.

1026. Preston Byers, *Pacman: I Was Blindsided by OpTic Gaming Los Angeles Release*, Dot Esports (May 14, 2020), https://dotesports.com/call-of-duty/news/pacman-i-was-blindsided-by-optic-gaming-los-angeles-release; See alsoTyler Esguerra, *Invictus Gaming to Reportedly Part Ways with Head Coach Karam*, Dot Esports (Sept. 26, 2019), https://dotesports.com/league-of-legends/news/invictus-gaming-to-reportedly-part-ways-with-head-coach-karam.

1027. Jacob Wolf, *Sources: G2 Nearing Deal to Acquire Jankos*, ESPN (Dec. 5, 2017), https://www.espn.com/esports/story/_/id/21681438/sources-g2-nearing-deal-acquire-jankos.

1028. Right of Publicity, *A Brief History of the Right of Publicity*, https://rightofpublicity.com/brief-history-of-rop (last Feb. 26, 2020).

1029. Frank Ready, *As Esports Take Off, Questions Abound Over Players' Rights of Publicity*, Law.com (Nov. 21, 2019), https://www.law.com/legaltechnews/2019/11/21/as-esports-grow-questions-abound-over-players-rights-of-publicity; See also Aabicus Lee, *The Dangers of Esports Contracts: Don't Sign before You Read this*, Daily Esports (Apr. 21, 2019), https://www.dailyesports.gg/the-dangers-of-esports-contracts-dont-sign-before-you-read-this.

1030. Cristina Fernandez, *The Right of Publicity on the Internet*, 8 Marq. Sports L. J. 289, 306 (1998).

1031. *Id.*

1032. *Haelan Laboratories, Inc. v. Topps Chewing Gum*, Inc., 202 F.2d 866, 868 (2d Cir. 1953); See also Adam Levy, *PWND or Owned? The Right of Publicity and Identity Ownership in League of Legends*, 6 Pace. Intell. Prop. Sports & Ent. L.F. 163 (2016).

1033. Bhernardo Viana, *FaZe Clan Owns the Rights to Every Stream and YouTube Video that Tfue Has Made*, Dot Esports (May 24, 2019), https://dotesports.com/business/news/faze-owns-rights-every-tfue-stream-youtube-video.

1034. 17 U.S.C. § 201(b)(1976); See also Rich Huggan, *Esports is Hiring—And You Don't Need to Be a Player*, Venture Beat (Aug. 30, 2018), https://venturebeat.com/2018/08/30/esports-is-hiring-and-you-dont-need-to-be-a-player.

1035. 17 U.S.C. § 101(1976).

1036. *Id.*

1037. Bhernardo Viana, *FaZe Clan Owns the Rights to Every Stream and YouTube Video that Tfue Has Made*, Dot Esports (May 24, 2019), https://dotesports.com/business/news/faze-owns-rights-every-tfue-stream-youtube-video.

1038. Betsey Rosenblatt, *Harvard Law School—Moral Rights Basics*, https://cyber.harvard.edu/property/library/moralprimer.html (last visited Feb. 26, 2020).

1039. 17 U.S.C. § 101(1976); Betsey Rosenblatt, *Harvard Law School—Moral Rights Basics*, https://cyber.harvard.edu/property/library/moralprimer.html (last visited Feb. 26, 2020).

1040. Andreas Stavropoulos, *Twitch Streamer Neeko Signs with 100 Thieves*, Dot Esports (Jul. 10, 2020), https://dotesports.com/streaming/news/twitch-streamer-neeko-signs-with-100-thieves.

1041. Cale Michael, *T1 Signs fRoD as VALORANT Head Coach*, Dot Esports (May 7, 2020), https://dotesports.com/valorant/news/t1-signs-frod-as-valorant-head-coach; See also Leonardo Biazzi, *100 Thieves Signs CS:GO Head Coach ImAPet*, Dot Esports (May 26, 2020), https://dotesports.com/counter-strike/news/100-thieves-signs-csgo-head-coach-imapet.

1042. Gamer Sensi, *Blog: What Does an Esports Coach Do? A Chat with NRG. Seamoose!* (May 30, 2017), https://blog.gamersensei.com/article/esports-coach-interview-seamoose.

1043. Sports Business Daily, *Bud Light to Sponsor Wizards' Esports Team in NBA 2K League* (May 22, 2018), https://www.sportsbusinessdaily.com/Daily/Closing-Bell/2018/05/22/Wiz-Gaming.aspx; See also Trent Murrary, *NBA 2K League Partnerships: Cavs and the Raynor Group, Wizards and Bud Light*, The Esports Observer (May 24, 2018), https://esportsobserver.com/cavs-legion-bud-light.

1044. Laura Lorenzetti, *You Can Make $50,000 a Year as a Video Game Coach*, Fortune (Jul. 29, 2015), https://fortune.com/2015/07/29/video-game-coach-salary.

1045. Inquirer.net, *P2,000,000 a Year in Salaries as a Videogame Coach*, http://esports.inquirer.net/8812/p2-million-a-year-salaries-as-coach (last visited Jul. 29, 2020).

1046. Adnan Kljajic, *LoL Esports: Wei Loses a Month's Salary for Picking a Wrong Spell*, AltChar (Jun. 17, 2020), https://www.altchar.com/esports/lol-esports-wei-loses-a-months-salary-for-picking-a-wrong-spell-aqRLX7m6LWxC.

1047. Chris Godfrey, *'It's Incredibly Widespread': Why eSports Has a Match-Fixing Problem*, The Guardian (Jul. 31, 2018), https://www.theguardian.com/games/2018/jul/31/its-incredibly-widespread-why-esports-has-a-match-fixing-problem.

1048. Maddy Myers, *Pro Esports Team Analyst Caught Betting on His Own Team's Matches, Which is Somehow Legal*, Kotaku (Mar. 6, 2017), https://compete.kotaku.com/pro-esports-team-analyst-caught-betting-on-his-own-team-1793025674.

1049. Calum Patterson, *League of Legends Pro Player, Coach and Owner Banned for Match-Fixing*, Dexerto (Apr. 25, 2019), https://www.dexerto.com/league-of-legends/league-of-legends-pro-player-coach-and-owner-banned-match-fixing-574043.

1050. Sam Cooke, *X-Bet Terminates Sponsorship of ProDotaCup after 'Betting Irregularities, Collusion and Match Fixing,'* Esports Insider, Dec. 20, 2017, https://esportsinsider.com/2017/12/x-bet-terminates-sponsorship-prodotacup-betting-irregularities-collusion-match-fixing; See also Hongyu Chen, *LGD Gaming Fined for Match-Fixing, Valve Releases Test Version of Dota Underlords*, The Esports Observer (Jun. 19, 2019), https://esportsobserver.com/china-esports-recap-june19-2019.

1051. Emily Rand, *Riot Fines 4 Worlds Participants for In-Game Behavior*, EPSN (Oct. 7, 2018), https://www.espn.com/esports/story/_/id/24926769/riot-games-fines-players-coach-game-behavior-league-legends-world-championship-prep.

1052. Ranjani Ayyar and Aparna Desikan, *Shoutcasters Trend in as Online Gaming Goes Viral*, Gadgets Now (Feb. 22, 2017), https://www.gadgetsnow.com/tech-news/shoutcasters-trend-in-as-online-gaming-goes-viral/articleshow/57286028.cms.

1053. Jason Fanelli, *Esports Arena: Longtime 'Overwatch' Broadcaster Departs; 'League of Legends' Sets 2020 Regional Play Dates*, The Hollywood Reporter (Jan. 15, 2020), https://www.hollywoodreporter.com/news/esports-arena-longtime-overwatch-broadcaster-departs-league-legends-sets-2020-regional-play-dates-1269346.

1054. Saira Mueller, *ELEAGUE Announces Casters and Analysts*, Dot Esports (May 22, 2016), https://dotesports.com/counter-strike/news/eleague-csgo-casters-analysts-3287.

1055. Noah Smith, *The Account of MonteCristo: Why the Caster Won't Return to Overwatch League in 2020*, Launcher (Jan. 7, 2020), https://www.washingtonpost.com/video-games/esports/2020/01/07/account-montecristo-why-caster-wont-be-back-with-overwatch-league-2020.

1056. Pedro Peres, *Why Are so Many Overwatch League Casters Leaving?*, Dot Esports (Jan. 14, 2020), https://dotesports.com/overwatch/news/why-are-so-many-overwatch-league-casters-leaving.

1057. ESL, *Paul Chaloner, The ReDeYe Guide to Being an Esports Broadcaster: Part 5*, https://www.eslgaming.com/article/redeye-guide-being-esports-broadcaster-part-5-1202 (last visited Jul. 30, 2020).

1058. Jessica Conditt, *'League of Legends' Shoutcaster Loves the Game, not the Fame*, Engadget (Oct. 30, 2015), https://www.engadget.com/2015-10-30-league-of-legends-quickshot-interview.html.

1059. E.S.P.N. Staff, *Overwatch League—Everything You Need to Know*, ESPN (Nov. 7, 2017), https://www.espn.com/esports/story/_/id/21331089/everything-need-know-overwatch-league-teams-roster-calendar-news-recaps-overwatch-league-grand-finals.

1060. Jack Stweart, *The Life of an Esports Caster: Uber Explains How Difficult it is for Casters not Only in Perfecting Their Craft but also in Maintaining Their Relationships*, U.K. Mail (Feb. 3, 2018), https://www.dailymail.co.uk/sport/esports/article-5348179/Overwatch-Leagues-Uber-reveals-esports-caster-life.html.

1061. Phoebe Dua, *LPL English Casters Leave China due to Coronavirus Concerns*, Ginx (Jan. 27, 2020), https://www.ginx.tv/en/league-of-legends/lpl-casters-coronavirus.

1062. ESL, *Paul Chaloner, The ReDeYe Guide to Being an Esports Broadcaster: Part 5*, https://www.eslgaming.com/article/redeye-guide-being-esports-broadcaster-part-5-1202 (last visited Jul. 30, 2020).

1063. Vignesh Raghuram, *Interview with Zyori: "It's a Shame that Some of Those People Have to Make the Hard Decision of Do I Go to College or Do I Play Dota 2?*," AFK Gaming (Aug. 13, 2019), https://afkgaming.com/articles/dota2/Interview/2241-Interview-with-Zyori.

1064. Reuters, *Riot Games Instructs Casters, Players not to Discuss 'Sensitive Issues*,' ESPN (Oct. 11, 2019), https://www.espn.com.au/esports/story/_/id/27822502/riot-games-instructs-casters-players-not-discuss-sensitive-issues.

1065. Joe Randall, *Riot Games Curiously Reverse Their Policy and Allow Casters to Earn Stream Revenue*, The Versed (Jan. 25, 2017), https://www.theversed

.com/2480/riot-games-curiously-reverse-their-policy-and-allow-casters-to-earn-stream-revenue/#.zo69HIh3u7.

1066. *Id.*

1067. Xing Li, *Deficio Will Still Be on the LEC Analyst Desk Next Year, but Will He Cast?*, Dot Esports (Jan. 10, 2019), https://dotesports.com/league-of-legends/news/deficio-will-still-be-on-the-lec-analyst-desk-next-year-but-will-he-cast; See also Kyle Wolmarans, *Hi-Rez fires SMITE Shoutcaster DM Brandon after His On-Stream Rant about Suicide*, Critical Hit Gaming (Apr. 21, 2016), https://www.criticalhit.net/gaming/hi-rez-fires-an-employee-after-his-rant-on-stream-about-suicide.

1068. Thiemo Bräutigam, *Editorial: Why Professionalism Doesn't Come along with a Tie*, The Esports Observer (Sept. 9, 2015), https://esportsobserver.com/editorial-why-professionalism-doesnt-come-along-with-a-tie; See also IGN, *We Confront Lol Shoutcaster Phreak about His Terrible Tie*, IGN (Nov. 21, 2015), https://www.ign.com/videos/2015/11/22/we-confront-lol-shoutcaster-phreak-about-his-terrible-tie-esports-weekly-with-coca-cola.

1069. Eriq Gardner, *Viacom Battling the Situation Over Who Owns 'GTL,' 'Twinning,'* The Hollywood Reporter (Aug. 22, 2012), https://www.hollywoodreporter.com/thr-esq/the-situation-jersey-shore-viacom-lawsuit-gtl-363766.

1070. ESPN Esports Staff, *Activision Blizzard Terminates Momo's Contract*, ESPN (Jul. 4, 2020), https://www.espn.com/esports/story/_/id/29410509/activision-blizzard-terminates-momo-contract; See also Preston Byers, *Benson no Longer a Part of Call of Duty League Broadcast Team*, Dot Esports (Jul. 14, 2020), https://dotesports.com/call-of-duty/news/benson-no-longer-a-part-of-call-of-duty-league-broadcast-team.

1071. Vignesh Raghuram, *Dota 2 Caster Zyori Releases Book on Amazon—Surviving Esports: The Zyori Story*, AFK Gaming (Sept. 19, 2019), https://afkgaming.com/articles/dota2/News/2482-Dota-2-Caster-Zyori-Releases-Book-on-Amazon-Surviving-Esports-The-Zyori-Story; See generally Andrew M. Campell, *Surviving Esports: The Zyori Story* (ZyoriTV 2019); Zyori.tv, *Official Site of Andrew 'Zyori' Campbell*, https://zyori.tv.

1072. Tobias Seck, *7 Marketing Strategies to Monetize the Esports Audience*, The Esports Observer (Sept. 18, 2018), https://esportsobserver.com/7-marketing-strategies-to-monetize-the-esports-audience; See also Andrew Hayward, *Pittsburgh Knights Add SmileDirect Club as Sponsor*, The Esports Observer (Apr. 30, 2019), https://esportsobserver.com/pittsburgh-knights-smiledirectclub.

1073. Darren Heitner, *More than 600 Esports Sponsorships Secured Since Start of 2016*, Forbes (Oct. 3, 2017), https://www.forbes.com/sites/darrenheitner/2017/10/03/more-than-600-esports-sponsorships-secured-since-start-of-2016/#6130fcce75e5; See also Andrew Hayward, *Drinks, Tech, Cars, and Fashion: Non-Endemic Sponsor Recap for Q3 2019*, The Esports Observer (Oct. 16, 2019), https://esportsobserver.com/non-endemic-sponsor-q319.

1074. Ben Fischer, *MSG's Counter Logic Gaming Signs Deal with Watch Brand MVMT*, The Esports Observer (Jun. 21, 2018), https://esportsobserver.com/clg-mvmt; See also Trent Murray, *Australian Org the Chiefs Esports Club Signs L'Oréal Men Expert for 2020*, The Esports Observer (Jul. 6, 2020), https://esportsobserver.com/chiefs-esports-club; Hongyu Chen,

Guangzhou Charge Signs Three-Year Non-Endemic Sponsorship Deal with Herbalife Nutrition, The Esports Observer (Jul. 13, 2020), https://esportsobserver.com/guangzhou-charge-herbalife.

1075. E.J. Schultz, *How an Esports League is Changing to Lure Brand Sponsors*, Advertising Age (Jun. 1, 2017), https://adage.com/article/cmo-strategy/esports-league-changing-lure-brand-sponsors/309241.

1076. *Id.*

1077. *Id.*

1078. *Id.*; Adam Stern, *Riot Games Adds In-Game Sponsor Banners to League of Legends Esports*, The Esports Observer (May 26, 2020), https://esportsobserver.com/riot-games-summoners-rift-banners.

1079. E.J. Schultz, *How an Esports League is Changing to Lure Brand Sponsors*, Advertising Age (Jun. 1, 2017), https://adage.com/article/cmo-strategy/esports-league-changing-lure-brand-sponsors/309241; See also Sam Skopp, *Overwatch League Adds Xfinity as 2020 Season Sponsor*, The Gamer (Apr. 18, 2020), https://www.thegamer.com/overwatch-league-xfinity-2020-season-sponsor; Ben Fischer, *HP, Intel Become Overwatch League's First Two League-Wide Sponsors*, Sports Business Daily (Nov. 3, 2017), https://www.sportsbusinessdaily.com/Global/Issues/2017/11/03/Marketing-and-Sponsorship/HP-Intel-Overwatch.aspx.

1080. T.L. Taylor, *Raising the Stakes: E-Sports and the Professionalization of Computer Gaming*, 155 (The MIT Press 2012).

1081. Alejandro Cremades, *How to Create a Pitch Deck*, Forbes (Mar. 2, 2018), https://www.forbes.com/sites/alejandrocremades/2018/03/02/how-to-create-a-pitch-deck/#2fec7dda56c0.

1082. Id.; See also Chris Hana, *Three Things that Will Help You to Improve Your Esports Sales Deck*, The Esports Observer (Aug. 9, 2016), https://esportsobserver.com/three-things-will-help-improve-esports-sales-deck; British Esports Association, *Esports Funding Guide: How to Find Sponsors and Generate Revenues*, https://britishesports.org/advice/esports-funding-guide-how-to-find-sponsors-and-generate-revenues (last visited Jul. 30, 2020); Cosmos Sports & Entertainment, *Blog: Sponsorship Deck: What Information Should You Include*, http://www.cosmossports.com/2017/04/18/sponsorship-deck (last visited Jul. 30, 2020).

1083. Alejandro Cremades, *How to Create a Pitch Deck*, Forbes (Mar. 2, 2018), https://www.forbes.com/sites/alejandrocremades/2018/03/02/how-to-create-a-pitch-deck/#2fec7dda56c0.

1084. Id.; See also Mitch Reames, *How Esports Organizations Make Money*, Hotspawn (Apr. 15, 2019), https://www.hotspawn.com/guides/how-esports-organizations-make-money.

1085. Thiemo Bräutigam, *Sponsor Me: How to Contact a Sponsor*, The Esports Observer (Sept. 10, 2015), https://esportsobserver.com/sponsor-me-the-pitfalls-and-misconception-about-applying-a-sponsorship.

1086. T.L. Taylor, *Raising the Stakes: E-Sports and the Professionalization of Computer Gaming*, 155 (The MIT Press 2012).

1087. Steven Widen, *KPI's: What's Important for Digital?*, Forbes (Aug. 9, 2019), https://www.forbes.com/sites/forbesagencycouncil/2019/08/09/kpis-whats-important-for-digital/#22e6b04481a0.

1088. *Id.*

1089. Newzoo, *Esports Q3 Report: Revenues to Reach $765M in 2018 as Enthusiasts Grow to 165M*, https://newzoo.com/insights/articles/esports-q3-report-revenues-to-reach-765m-in-2018-as-enthusiasts-grow-to-165m (last visited Jul. 30, 2020); See also Greg Paull, *Understanding ROI Behind the Live Streaming of Esports*, AdWeek (May 28, 2019), https://www.adweek.com/brand-marketing/understanding-roi-behind-the-live-streaming-of-esports.

1090. Paul Tassi, *New Report Details How eSports is an Effective Engagement and Marketing Tool*, Forbes (Feb. 25, 2015), https://www.forbes.com/sites/insertcoin/2015/02/25/new-report-details-how-esports-is-an-effective-engagement-and-marketing-tool/#55de24f876e8.

1091. T.L. Taylor, *Raising the Stakes: E-Sports and the Professionalization of Computer Gaming*, 155 (The MIT Press 2012).

1092. Shane Schick, *How Brands Can Score with Esports Marketing*, Marketing Dive (Apr. 8, 2019), https://www.marketingdive.com/news/how-brands-can-score-with-esports-marketing.

1093. *Esports Playbook for Brands 2019* (The Nielsen Company, New York, NY), Mar. 2019, at 18.

1094. Max Miceli, *TimTheTatman Does Sponsored Stream to Promote Gillette Products*, Dot Esports (Jun. 29, 2020), https://dotesports.com/streaming/news/timthetatman-does-sponsored-stream-to-promote-gillette-products; See also *Esports Playbook for Brands 2019* (The Nielsen Company, New York, NY), Mar. 2019, at 21.

1095. Adam Stern, *Popeyes Signs Jersey Sponsorship Deal with Chicago Huntsmen*, The Esports Observer (May 13, 2020), https://esportsobserver.com/popeyes-signs-jersey-sponsorship-deal-with-chicago-huntsmen; See also *Esports Playbook For Brands 2019* (The Nielsen Company, New York, NY), Mar. 2019, at 18.

1096. Will Deller, *Esports Sponsorship Agreements: What to Look Out for*, I.P. Watchdog (Mar. 2, 2018), https://www.ipwatchdog.com/2018/03/02/esports-sponsorship-agreements; See also Daniel Alfreds, *Legal Issues to Consider in Esports Sponsorships: Agreements, Payment Terms and Jurisdiction*, The Esports Observer (Mar. 8, 2016), https://esportsobserver.com/legal-issues-to-consider-in-esports-agreements-payment-terms-and-jurisdiction.

1097. Hongyu Chen, *Nike Signs Endorsement Deal with RNG Player Uzi*, The Esports Observer (Oct. 19, 2018), https://esportsobserver.com/nike-rng-uzi.

1098. Graham Ashton, *Volvic Sponsors BIG League of Legends Team*, The Esports Observer (Jun. 12, 2020), https://esportsobserver.com/volvic-sponsors-big-lol-team.

1099. Hongyu Chen, *Huawei Named Top Sponsor of $420K NetEase Esports X Tournament Summer Season*, The Esports Observer (Jul. 24, 2020), https://esportsobserver.com/huawei-top-sponsor-next; See also Graham Ashton, *KitKat Joins Sponsors for BLAST Dota Tournament*, The Esports Observer (Jun. 8, 2020), https://esportsobserver.com/kitkat-blast-dota-tournament.

1100. Kevin Hitt, *Andbox Extends Partnership* with *T-Mobile, Adds Metro by T-Mobile as Sponsor*, The Esports Observer (Jul. 27, 2020), https://esportsobserver.com/andbox-tmobile-partnerships-2020.

1101. Trent Murray, *HyperX Renews with Pittsburgh Knights*, The Esports Observer (Jul. 8, 2020), https://esportsobserver.com/hyperx-renews-pittsburgh-knights.

1102. Kevin Hiit, *Vancouver Extends and Expands Partnership with Circle K*, The Esports Observer (Jun. 25, 2020), https://esportsobserver.com/vancouver-extends-circle-k.
1103. Michael Gannon-Pitts, *eSports Sponsors: Building Lucrative Brand Partnerships*, Magnetic, https://magneticcreative.com/esports-sponsors.
1104. *Esports Playbook for Brands 2019* (The Nielsen Company, New York, NY), Mar. 2019, at 18.
1105. *Id.*
1106. Jets, *A Look at Social Media in Esports*, Dot Esports (Jan. 26, 2016), https://dotesports.com/news/a-look-at-social-media-in-esports-8176.
1107. Justin M. Jacobson, *OPINION: The Marketing Dilemma of the Esports Influencer*, The Esports Observer (Jul. 25, 2018), https://esportsobserver.com/marketing-esports-influencer; See also GameguideHQ, *Biggest Esports Teams by Social Media Following*, https://gameguidehq.com/biggest-esports-teams-by-social-media-following (last visited Jul. 30, 2020).
1108. Cara Kelly, *Fyre Festival to Fashion Week, How Do Instagram Influencers Make so Much Money?*, USA Today (Feb. 13, 2019), https://www.usatoday.com/story/news/investigations/2019/02/12/instagram-youtube-influencer-rates-fyre-festival-fashion-week-money-rich-branding-ads%20girls/2787560002.
1109. Matt Porter, *Forbes Reveal Surprising List of 13 Most Valuable Esports Orgs*, Dexerto (Nov. 5, 2019), https://www.dexerto.com/esports/forbes-reveal-surprising-list-of-13-most-valuable-esports-orgs-1218128.
1110. Crystal Mills, *FaZe Clan Celebrates 10-Year Anniversary with G FUEL and Apple Beats*, Benzinga (Jun. 5, 2020), https://finance.yahoo.com/news/faze-clan-celebrates-10-anniversary-110251006.html.
1111. *Esports Playbook for Brands 2019* (The Nielsen Company, New York, NY), Mar. 2019, at 18, 21.
1112. Adam Stern, *NRG Esports Shops Naming Rights to Rocket League Team*, The Esports Observer (Jul. 22, 2020), https://esportsobserver.com/nrg-naming-rights-rocket-league.
1113. Tim Dams, *Brands Look to Capitalize on Esports Growth*, IBC (May 28, 2020), https://www.ibc.org/brands-look-to-capitalise-on-esports-growth/6017.article.
1114. *Esports Playbook for Brands 2019* (The Nielsen Company, New York, NY), Mar. 2019, at 18.
1115. Alan LaFleur, *Sponsorship Activation: How to Get the Most Out of a Partnership*, The Esports Observer (May 28, 2015), https://esportsobserver.com/how-to-get-the-most-out-of-a-sponsorship.
1116. Team Liquid, *Sponsors*, https://www.teamliquid.com/partners; See also TeamSoloMid, *Partners*, https://tsm.gg/partners; Cloud9, *Partners*, https://www.cloud9.gg/partners.
1117. *Esports Playbook for Brands 2019* (The Nielsen Company, New York, NY), Mar. 2019, at 18, 21.
1118. Adam Fitch, *Cloud9 Enters Sponsorship Deal with AT&T*, Esports Insider (Mar. 5, 2019), https://esportsinsider.com/2019/03/cloud9-att-sponsorship.
1119. Kevin Hitt, *FaZe Clan Signs Verizon as Exclusive 5G Partner*, The Esport Obsever (Jul. 28, 2020), https://esportsobserver.com/faze-clan-verizon-5g-partner.

1120. The Esports Observer, *Sponsorships & Partnerships*, https://esportsobserver.com/category/market/sponsorships-and-partnerships; See *Esports Playbook for Brands 2019* (The Nielsen Company, New York, NY), Mar. 2019, at 8.

1121. Kevin Hitt, *CS_SUMMIT 6 Adds XPG as Official Gaming Notebook Sponsor*, The Esports Obsever (Jun. 18, 2020), https://esportsobserver.com/cs_summit-6-xpg-notebook-sponsor.

1122. Graham Ashton, *AMD Reunites with SK Gaming as Official Supplier*, The Esports Observer (Jun. 18, 2020), https://esportsobserver.com/amd-reunites-with-sk-gaming.

1123. The Esports Observer, *Mastercard Signs Multi-Year Deal as Global Sponsor of League of Legends Esports*, The Esports Observer (Sept. 19, 2018), https://esportsobserver.com/riot-games-mastercard-global-sponsorship.

1124. Victory Frascarelli, *Simplicity Taps AMC Networks International—Latin America for Flamengo Esports Sponsorships*, The Esports Observer (Jun. 12, 2020), https://esportsobserver.com/riot-games-mastercard-global-sponsorship; See also Graham Ashton, *Kia to Sponsor League of Legends European Championship*, The Esports Observer (Jan. 11, 2019), https://esportsobserver.com/kia-sponsors-lec.

1125. Anirudh Rastogi and Vishakh Ranjit, *E-Sports Player Contracts: Common Clauses and Potential Legal Issues in India*, Mondaq (Jun. 18, 2020), https://www.mondaq.com/india/gaming/955392/e-sports-player-contracts-common-clauses-and-potential-legal-issues-in-india.

1126. Adam Starkey, *NRG Esports Severs Ties with Smash Ultimate pro Nairo after Claims of Sexual Relationship with Underage Player*, GINX (Jul. 2, 2020), https://www.ginx.tv/en/smash-ultimate/nrg-cuts-ties-nairo-claims-sexual-relationship-underage-player.

1127. Schuyler Moore, *Morality Clauses in Hollywood: What You Need to Know*, Forbes (Mar. 12, 2018), https://www.forbes.com/sites/schuylermoore/2018/03/12/morality-clauses-in-hollywood/#3173c90949a5; See also Max Miceli, *Corsair Ends Relationship with Method, More People Leave Org Amid Sexual Assault Allegations*, Dot Esports (Jun. 26, 2020), https://dotesports.com/streaming/news/corsair-ends-relationship-with-method-more-people-leave-org-amid-sexual-assault-allegations.

1128. Trent Murray, *MSI Announces Intent to Terminate Relationship with Method*, The Esports Observer (Jun. 26, 2020), https://esportsobserver.com/method-loses-sponsors.

1129. Huffpost, *Celebrities Who Have Lost Endorsement Deals: Paula Deen, Lance Armstrong, Tiger Woods and More*, The Huffington Post (Jun. 29, 2013), https://www.huffpost.com/entry/celebrities-lost-endorsement-deals-paula-deen_n_3505534; Martin Pengelly, *Aaron Hernandez Dropped by Puma as Police Link Him to Double Homicide*, The Guardian (Jun. 28, 2013), https://www.theguardian.com/world/2013/jun/28/aaron-hernandez-patriots-murder-double-homicide; See also Trent Murray, *MSI Announces Intent to Terminate Relationship with Method*, The Esports Observer (Jun. 26, 2020), https://esportsobserver.com/method-loses-sponsors.

1130. Andrew Webster, *Riot Ends Sponsorship with Controversial Saudi City Neom Following Outcry*, The Verge (Jul. 30, 2020), https://www.theverge.com/2020/7/30/21347858/riot-league-of-legends-lec-sponsorship-neom-canceled.

1131. Cari Grieb, *A 'Sterling' Need for Reverse Morals Clauses in Sports Contracts*, The Sporting News (Mar. 9, 2015), https://www.sportingnews.com/us/nba/news/donald-sterling-and-need-for-reverse-morals-clauses-in-sports-contracts/hehv5zlwbklp11a83iwt0twe0.

1132. Noah Smith, *A Pro 'Fortnite' Player is Suing His Team and the Entire Esports World Could Feel the Fallout*, The Washington Post (May 21, 2019), https://www.washingtonpost.com/sports/2019/05/21/pro-fortnite-player-is-suing-his-team-entire-esports-world-could-feel-fallout.

1133. Michael Martin, *How Claire Fisher Turned YouPorn into a Legitimate Esports Sponsor*, Yahoo! (Aug. 5, 2015), https://sports.yahoo.com/claire-fisher-turned-team-yp-000000412.html.

1134. Trenty Murray, *Gambling, Food, and Mastercard: Non-Endemic Sponsor Recap for Q3 2018*, The Esports Observer (Oct. 3, 2018), https://esportsobserver.com/non-endemic-sponsorship-recap-q3-2018. See also Andrew Hayward, *Unicorns of Love Adds Unikrn as Betting Sponsor*, The Esports Observer (Sept. 20, 2019), https://esportsobserver.com/unicorns-of-love-unikrn-sponsor.

1135. Nicole Pike, *How Valuable Are Sponsorship Deals and Brand Activations When Applying for Esports Franchise League Slots*?, Nielsen (Jul. 12, 2017), https://www.nielsen.com/au/en/insights/article/2017/perspectives-how-valuable-are-sponsorship-deals-andbrand-activations-when-applying-for-esports-franchise-league-slots; See also Xander Torres, *One Year Later: How Franchising Changed the LCS*, Riff Herald (Mar. 28, 2019), https://www.riftherald.com/2019/3/28/18285641/lcs-franchising-changes.

1136. *License*, Black's Law Dictionary (10th ed. 2014); See also U.S. Copyright Office, *Licensing*, https://www.copyright.gov/licensing/ (last visited Feb. 26, 2020).

1137. *License*, Black's Law Dictionary (10th ed. 2014).

1138. Margaret Pardue, Red Bull, *How to Buy Ninja's Headband*, https://www.redbull.com/us-en/ninja-headband-now-available (last visited Feb. 26, 2020).

1139. H.B Duran, *Adidas Originals Reveals Multi-Year Partnership with Tyler "Ninja" Blevins*, The Esports Observer (Aug. 28, 2019), https://esportsobserver.com/adidas-deal-ninja; See also Ninja (@Ninja), Twitter (Dec. 18, 2019, 11:00am), https://twitter.com/ninja/status/1207329881773789185.

1140. Youtooz Collectibles, *Gaming—Valkyrae*, https://youtooz.com/products/valkyrae (last visited Feb. 26, 2020).

1141. Razer Gaming, *Dr. Disrespect Joins Team Razer*, https://www.razer.com/campaigns/dr-disrespect (last visited Feb. 26, 2020).

1142. *Id.*

1143. Patrick Shanley, *Streamer Dr Disrespect Inks TV Development Deal with 'Walking Dead' Creator's Skybound (Exclusive)*, The Hollywood Reporter (Dec. 6, 2019), https://www.hollywoodreporter.com/news/streamer-dr-disrespect-inks-tv-development-deal-walking-dead-creators-skybound-1260034.

1144. Patrick Shanley, *Streamer Dr Disrespect Inks Publishing Deal for In-Character Memoir (Exclusive)*, The Hollywood Reporter (Feb. 20, 2020), https://www.hollywoodreporter.com/news/streamer-dr-disrespect-inks-tv-development-deal-walking-dead-creators-skybound-1260034.

1145. G FUEL, *G FUEL and FaZe Clan Launch New Sour FaZeberry Flavor and #GFUELFaZeX Dream Setup Contest*, https://gfuel.com/blogs/news/sour-fazeberry-gfuelfazex-dream-setup-contest (last visited Jul. 27, 2020); See also G FUEL, *Strawberry Shortcake Tub—Inspired by FaZe Apex*, https://gfuel.com/collections/tubs/products/strawberry-shortcake-tub-40-servings (last visited Jul. 27, 2020); G FUEL *FaZeberry Box*, https://gfuel.com/collections/boxes/products/g-fuel-box-fazeberry (last visited Jul. 27, 2020).

1146. Brent Koepp, *PewDiePie Trolls Fans with Bizarre New "G FUEL" Flavor*, Dexerto (Oct. 9, 2019), https://www.dexerto.com/entertainment/pewdiepie-trolls-fans-with-bizarre-new-g-fuel-flavor-1119119; See also G FUEL, Pewdiepie Flavor, https://gfuel.com/pages/pewdiepie-flavor (last visited Jul. 27, 2020).

1147. Joshalynne Finch, *How to Find Twitch-Approved Music for Streaming*, How-To Geek (Jun. 24, 2020), https://www.howtogeek.com/678148/how-to-find-twitch-approved-music-for-streaming; See also Nicole Carpenter, *Twitch streamers were issued tons of DMCA takedown notices today*, Polygon (Oct. 20, 2020), https://www.polygon.com/2020/10/20/21525587/twitch-dmca-takedown-notice-content.

1148. Twitch.tv, *Music Guidelines*, https://www.twitch.tv/p/legal/community-guidelines/music (last visited Feb. 26, 2020).

1149. *Id.*

1150. B.M.I., *Types of Copyright*, https://www.bmi.com/licensing/entry/types_of_copyrights (last visited Feb. 26, 2020).

1151. Twitch.tv, *Sharing Music on Twitch*, https://www.twitch.tv/p/legal/community-guidelines/music/#sharing-music-on-twitch (last visited Feb. 26, 2020); See also YouTube, *YouTube Help—Usage Restrictions on Claimed Music*, https://support.google.com/youtube/answer/6364458 (last visited Feb. 26, 2020).

1152. Twitch.tv, *Sharing Music on Twitch*, https://www.twitch.tv/p/legal/community-guidelines/music/#sharing-music-on-twitch (last visited Feb. 26, 2020); See also Matt T.M. Kim, *After Twitch's DMCA Music Takedowns, Here's What Streamers Can Do*, IGN (Jul. 31, 2020), https://www.ign.com/articles/twitch-dmca-music-takedowns-what-streamers-can-do.

1153. Twitch.tv, *Sharing Music on Twitch*, https://www.twitch.tv/p/legal/community-guidelines/music/#sharing-music-on-twitch (last visited Feb. 26, 2020).

1154. Twitch.tv, *DMCA Guidelines*, https://www.twitch.tv/p/legal/dmca-guidelines/ (last visited Feb. 26, 2020); See also Cale Michael, *Multiple Twitch Streamers Hit with Wave of DMCA Claims from 2019*, Dot Esports (Jun. 7, 2020), https://dotesports.com/streaming/news/multiple-twitch-streamers-hit-with-wave-of-dmca-claims-from-2019.

1155. YouTube, *YouTube Help—Copyright Strike Basics*, https://support.google.com/youtube/answer/2814000 (last visited Feb. 26, 2020).

1156. *Id.*

1157. YouTube, *YouTube Help—How Content ID Works*, https://support.google.com/youtube/answer/2797370 (last visited Feb. 26, 2020).

1158. Audible Magic, *Home Page, https://www.audiblemagic.com* (last visited Feb. 26, 2020).

1159. Audible Magic, *What's Going on with Twitch and Audible Magic?*, https://www.audiblemagic.com/2014/08/08/whats-going-on-with-twitch-and-audible-magic (last visited Feb. 26, 2020).
1160. Bijan Stephen, *Twitch Streamers Are Getting Blindsided by Years-Old Copyright Notices*, The Verge (Jun. 8, 2020), https://www.theverge.com/21284287/twitch-dmca-copyright-takedowns-clips-controversy-broken-system.
1161. Creative Commons, *Attribution 2.0 Generic (CC BY 2.0)*, https://creativecommons.org/licenses/by/2.0 (last visited Feb. 26, 2020); See also See also Legis Music, *Background Music for Twitch*, https://legismusic.com/background-music-for-twitch (last visited Jul. 31, 2020).
1162. Creative Commons, *Legal Music for Videos*, https://creativecommons.org/about/program-areas/arts-culture/arts-culture-resources/legalmusicforvideos (last visited Feb. 26, 2020).
1163. *Id.*; See also Legis Music, *Background Music for Twitch*, https://legismusic.com/background-music-for-twitch (last visited Jul. 31, 2020).
1164. Legis Music, *What is Music without Copyright or Royalty-Free Music?*, https://legismusic.com/whats-music-copyright-royalty-free (last visited Jul. 31, 2020); See also Streamer Guides, *Music for Streams—Royalty Free and Stream-Friendly Music for Streamers*, https://streamersguides.com/music-for-streams (last visited Jul. 31, 2020).
1165. Legis Music, *What is Music without Copyright or Royalty-Free Music?*, https://legismusic.com/whats-music-copyright-royalty-free (last visited Jul. 31, 2020).
1166. Legis Music, *What is Music without Copyright or Royalty-Free Music?*, https://legismusic.com/whats-music-copyright-royalty-free (last visited Jul. 31, 2020); See also Legis Music, *Background Music for Twitch*, https://legismusic.com/background-music-for-twitch (last visited Jul. 31, 2020).
1167. Legis Music, *What is Music without Copyright or Royalty-Free Music?*, https://legismusic.com/whats-music-copyright-royalty-free (last visited Jul. 31, 2020); See also Daniel Lofaso, *How to Find Non-Copyrighted Music for Your YouTube Videos*, The Digital Elvator, https://thedigitalelevator.com/non-copyrighted-music.
1168. Legis Music, *What is Music without Copyright or Royalty-Free Music?*, https://legismusic.com/whats-music-copyright-royalty-free (last visited Jul. 31, 2020); See also Phil Savage, *Twitch Introduces Royalty Free Music Library*, P.C. Gamer (Jan. 15, 2015), https://www.pcgamer.com/twitch-introduces-royalty-free-music-library.
1169. Legis Music, *What is Music without Copyright or Royalty-Free Music?*, https://legismusic.com/whats-music-copyright-royalty-free (last visited Jul. 31, 2020); See also Soundstripe, *Royalty Free Music and Twitch: Rules and Regulations You Need to Know*, https://www.soundstripe.com/blogs/royalty-free-music-rules-twitch (last visited Jul. 31, 2020).
1170. Justin M. Jacobson, *Legal & Business Tips for Musicians on Twitch*, Tunecore (Apr. 2, 2020), https://www.tunecore.com/blog/2020/04/legal-business-tips-for-musicians-on-twitch.html.
1171. Sandra L. Rodriguez, SoundExchange, *SoundExchange and SourceAudio to Simplify Licensing for Music Creators and Podcasters*, https://www.soundexchange.com/2019/08/16/soundexchange-and-sourceaudio-to-simplify-licensing-for-music-creators-and-podcasters (last visited Feb. 26, 2020).

1172. A.S.C.A.P., *Common Licensing Terms Defined*, https://www.ascap.com/help/ascap-licensing/licensing-terms-defined (last visited Feb. 26, 2020); See also The Emergence, *Playing Music on Twitch: What Are the Rules?*, https://theemergence.co.uk/playing-music-on-twitch-what-are-the-rules (last visited Jul. 31, 2020).

1173. Monstercat, *Licensing Music for YouTube, Twitch and Mixer*, https://www.monstercat.com/licensing/content-creators (last visited Feb. 26, 2020); See also Stevo Jacobs, *Twitch Music: Where to Turn to for Twitch Approved Music*, EDM Sauce (Apr. 8, 2018), https://www.edmsauce.com/2018/04/08/twitch-music.

1174. *Id.*

1175. Emily Gera, *Record Labels Have a New Target: Streamers and Gamers*, The Verge (Jul. 26, 2019), https://www.theverge.com/2019/7/26/8930706/music-labels-twitch-streaming-copyright-strike-monstercat-lost-rings-record-labels.

1176. *Id.*

1177. Pretzel Rocks, *Pretzel for Livestreamers*, https://www.pretzel.rocks/for/livestreamers (last visited Feb. 26, 2020).

1178. *Id.*

1179. Joshalynne Finch, *How to Use Amazon Music on Twitch Live Streams*, How-To Geek (Jul. 19, 2020), https://www.howtogeek.com/678479/how-to-use-amazon-music-on-twitch-streams. See also Twitch, *Amazon Music*, https://help.twitch.tv/s/article/amazon-music?language=en_US (last visited Jul. 31, 2020).

1180. Twitch, *Amazon Music*, https://help.twitch.tv/s/article/amazon-music?language=en_US (last visited Jul. 31, 2020).

1181. Zipchair, *Call of Duty Official Licensed Seating*, https://www.zipchairgaming.com/collections/call-of-duty-officially-licensed-seating; See also Zipchair Gaming, *New York Excelsior*, https://www.zipchairgaming.com/collections/new-york-excelsior.

1182. Ben Fischer and Terry Lefton, *Fanatics Takes a Shot*, Sports Business Journal (Dec. 3, 2018), https://www.sportsbusinessdaily.com/Journal/Issues/2018/12/03/Esports/Overwatch.aspx.

1183. *Id.*

1184. Misfits Gaming, *Misfits Gaming and Outerstuff Launch Esports and Gaming Apparel Joint Venture*, https://misfitsgaming.gg/misfits-gaming-outerstuff-launch-esports-gaming-apparel-joint-venture (last visited Feb. 26, 2020).

1185. *Id.*

1186. *Id.*

1187. Champion Teamwear, *Champion Esports*, https://championteamwear.com/esports (last visited Feb. 26, 2020).

1188. Laura Byrne, *Foot Locker and Champion Athleticwear Team Up for Esports Range*, Esports Insider (May 1, 2019), https://esportsinsider.com/2019/05/foot-locker-and-champion-athleticwear-team-up-for-esports-range.

1189. Puma, *Cloud9 Collection*, https://us.puma.com/en/us/collections/lifestyle/cloud9 (last visited Feb. 26, 2020); See also Frank Holland and Fahiemah Al-Ali, *Puma Teams Up with Cloud9 Becoming the Latest Sports Apparel Brand to Join the Esports Trend*, CNBC (Oct. 10, 2019), https://www.cnbc.com/2019/10/10/puma-teams-up-with-cloud9-esports-in-an-apparel-deal.html.

1190. Adam Fitch, *Kappa Enters Esports with Vexed Gaming Partnership*, Esports Insider (Aug. 7, 2019), https://esportsinsider.com/2019/08/vexed-gaming-kappa-partnership; See also Adam Fitch, *Vexed Gaming Releases Limited-Edition Collection with Kappa*, Esports Insider, https://esportsinsider.com/2019/11/vexed-gaming-kappa-collection (Nov. 4, 2019).
1191. Andrew Hayward, *Team Vitality and Adidas Extend Partnership, Reveal Collaborative Sneakers*, The Esports Observer (Nov. 8, 2019), https://esportsobserver.com/adidas-team-vitality-shoes.
1192. *Id.*
1193. Scuf Gaming International LLC, *SCUF Pro Teams—Scuf Gaming*, https://scufgaming.com/scuf-pro-teams (last visited Feb. 26, 2020).
1194. Andrew Hayward, *Fnatic Unveils Collaboration with Sanrio's Hello Kitty Brand*, The Esports Observer (Nov. 6, 2019), https://esportsobserver.com/fnatic-hello-kitty-partnership.
1195. Graham Ashton, *K-Swiss and Immortals Gaming Club Reveal Esports Shoe Line*, The Esports Observer (Jul. 18, 2019), https://esportsobserver.com/immortals-k-swiss-sneaker-line-2; See also K-Swiss, *Immortals – K-Swiss*, https://kswiss.com/collections/immortals (last visited Feb. 26, 2020).
1196. Kevin Hitt, *Hot Wheels Connects with Spacestation Gaming and TFOX to Produce Limited-Edition Car*, The Esports Observer (Dec. 9, 2019), https://esportsobserver.com/hotwheels-spacestation-partnership.
1197. Adam Fitch, *Spacestation Gaming and Tanner Fox Collaborate with Hot Wheels*, Esports Insider (Dec. 7, 2019), https://esportsinsider.com/2019/12/spacestation-gaming-hot-wheels.
1198. Mother Design, *Mother Design—NYXL*, https://www.motherdesign.com/work/nyxl (last visited Feb. 26, 2020).
1199. Marty Swant, *An Esports Team Created a Fashion Line for Gamers to Feel More Like Traditional Sports Fans*, AdWeek (Jul. 1, 2019), https://www.adweek.com/agencies/an-esports-team-created-a-fashion-line-for-gamers-to-feel-more-like-traditional-sports-fans/.
1200. *Id.*
1201. Adam Fitch, *Astralis to Launch Soft Drinks Line with Royal Unibrew*, Esports Insider (Jan. 28, 2020), https://esportsinsider.com/2020/01/astralis-royal-unibrew.
1202. *Licensor*, Black's Law Dictionary (10th ed. 2014).
1203. *Licensee*, Black's Law Dictionary (10th ed. 2014).
1204. Darren Rovell, *Gaming Apparel Company J!nx Wants to Be the Nike of Esports*, ESPN (Feb. 20, 2017), https://www.espn.com/esports/story/_/id/18725714/esports-jersey-sales-expected-rise-jnx-signs-echo-fox.
1205. Hollie Silverman, *Feds Seize Over $123 Million Worth of Counterfeit Super Bowl Merchandise*, CNN (Feb. 2, 2020), https://edition.cnn.com/2020/02/02/us/cbp-fake-superbowl-merchandise-seized.
1206. U.S.P.T.O., *Basic Facts about Trademarks—Protecting Your Trademark—Enhancing Your Rights Through Federal Federation*, at 3, Feb. 2020 Pg. 3, http://www.uspto.gov/sites/default/files/BasicFacts.pdf; See also PuBG Official Merchandise, *Esports Jersey*, https://pubgglobal.merchandise.game/products/esports-jersey (last visited Jul. 31, 2020).

1207. Natalia Manzocco, *Masks: The Hottest New eSports Merch Item?*, NOW Magazine (Jul. 2, 2020), https://nowtoronto.com/culture/gaming/esports-face-masks.

1208. Patricia Hernandez, *Fortnite's Official John Wick Skin Has Made Things Kinda Awkward*, Polygon (May 17, 2019), https://www.polygon.com/2019/5/17/18629686/fortnite-john-wick-the-reaper-rare-skins.

1209. N.F.L., *NFL Teams Up with Epic Games, Enters World of 'Fortnite'*, http://www.nfl.com/news/story/0ap3000000983715/article/nfl-teams-up-with-epic-games-enters-world-of-fortnite (last visited Feb. 26, 2020); See also Darren Rovell, *Deal between NFL, Epic Games Brings Uniforms to Fortnite*, ESPN (Nov. 5, 2018), https://www.espn.com/nfl/story/_/id/25186295/deal-brings-nfl-outfits-fortnite-shop.

1210. Nick Romano, *Thanos is Coming to Fortnite for Epic Avengers: Infinity War Crossover*, Entertainment Weekly (May 7, 2018), https://ew.com/gaming/2018/05/07/thanos-fortnite-avengers-infinity-war.

1211. Austen Goslin, *Stranger Things' Upside Down Portals Have Started Appearing in Fortnite*, Polygon (Jul. 3, 2019), https://www.polygon.com/fortnite/2019/7/3/20681067/stranger-things-fortnite-portals.

1212. License *Global*, *'Stranger Things Turns 'Fortnite' Upside Down'*, *https://www.licenseglobal.com/video-games/stranger-things-turns-fortnite-upside-down* (last visited Feb. 26, 2020).

1213. *Id.*

1214. Nick Statt, *Fortnite Adds Rey and Finn Skins in Time for Star Wars: The Rise of Skywalker*, The Verge (Dec. 12, 2019), https://www.theverge.com/2019/12/12/21019726/fortnite-star-wars-the-rise-of-skywalker-rey-finn-sith-trooper-skins-buy-now.

1215. *Id.*

1216. Louis Vuitton, *Heritage Presenting Quiyana, League of Legends Champion*, https://us.louisvuitton.com/eng-us/articles/qiyana-league-of-legends-louis-vuitton (last visited Feb. 28, 2020).

1217. Julia Lee, *League of Legends Reveals Its First Louis Vuitton Skin*, Polygon (Oct. 29, 2019), https://www.polygon.com/2019/10/29/20936513/league-of-legends-louis-vuitton-skin-true-damage-qiyana-prestige.

1218. Adam Fitch, *FIFA 19 Announces In-Game Jerseys for Esports Teams*, Esports Insider (Nov. 1, 2018), https://esportsinsider.com/2018/11/fifa-19-esports-jerseys.

1219. *Id.*

1220. Brian Crecente, *Fanatics Signs Major Multi-Year Overwatch League Merch Deal*, Variety (Dec. 3, 2018), https://variety.com/2018/gaming/news/overwatch-league-merchandise-fanatics-1203078174.

1221. Eric Chan, *Overwatch League Trading Cards? Blizzard Enters Multi-Year Deal with Upper Deck*, NBC Sports (May 15, 2019), https://www.nbcsports.com/philadelphia/fusion/overwatch-league-trading-cards-blizzard-enters-multi-year-deal-upper-deck.

1222. The Esports Observer, *NBA 2K League Sponsorship Guide*, The Esports Observer (Jun. 1, 2018), https://esportsobserver.com/nba-2k-league-sponsorship-guide.

1223. NBA 2K League, *Partners*, https://2kleague.nba.com (last visited Feb. 28, 2020); See also Kevin Hitt, *NBA 2K League Signs First Restaurant Partner in Panera Bread*, The Esports Observer (Feb. 6, 2020), https://esportsobserver.com/nba-2k-league-signs-panera-bread.

1224. Andrew Cohen, *Google Buys Streaming Rights to Activision Blizzard's Esports Leagues for $160 Million*, Sport Techie (Feb. 18, 2020), https://www.sporttechie.com/google-exclusive-streaming-rights-activision-blizzards-esports-leagues.

1225. Jason Dachman, *Turner Sports' ELEAGUE Inks Exclusive Domestic-TV-Rights Deal for EA Sports FIFA 20 Events*, Sports Video (Dec. 12, 2019), https://www.sportsvideo.org/2019/12/12/turner-sports-eleague-inks-exclusive-domestic-tv-rights-deal-for-ea-sports-fifa-20-esports-series.

1226. Richard Lawler, *NBA 2K League Comes to Traditional TV on ESPN2*, Engadget (May 5, 2020), https://www.engadget.com/nba-2-k-league-comes-to-broadcast-tv-on-espn-2-021125286.html.

1227. Riot Games, *League of Legends—LCS and Academy Hitting the Skies with Panasonic Avionics*, https://nexus.leagueoflegends.com/en-us/2019/10/lcs-and-academy-hitting-the-skies-with-p (last visited Feb. 28, 2020).

1228. Andrew Hayward, *Riot Games to Bring LCS Matches to Panasonic Avionics In-Flight Systems*, The Esports Observer (Oct. 17, 2019), https://esportsobserver.com/lcs-panasonic-teamup-airlines.

1229. *Id.*

1230. Richard Dai, *The Rise of Video Game Livestreaming in China*, TechNode (Sept. 23, 2019), https://technode.com/2019/09/23/the-rise-of-video-game-livestreaming-in-china; See also Brandon Brathwaite, *Breaking Down the Major Streaming Platforms in Esports*, The Esports Observer (Aug. 31, 2018), https://esportsobserver.com/breakdown-streaming-platforms.

1231. Mohit Kumar, *Fnatic Partners with LOCO for Talent and Content Creation Programs*, Sportskeeda (Jun. 24, 2020), https://www.sportskeeda.com/esports/news-fnatic-partners-loco-take-pubg-mobile-streaming-india-next-level.

1232. Aaron Swerdlow, *The Emerging Legal Battle Over Video Game Streaming Rights*, Venture Beat (May 27, 2017), https://venturebeat.com/2017/05/27/the-emerging-legal-battle-over-video-game-streaming-rights.

1233. Aaron Swerdlow, *The Emerging Legal Battle Over Video Game Streaming Rights*, Venture Beat (May 27, 2017), https://venturebeat.com/2017/05/27/the-emerging-legal-battle-over-video-game-streaming-rights; ATLUS, *A Note on Persona 5 and Streaming*, https://atlus.com/note-persona-5-streaming.

1234. Aaron Swerdlow, *The Emerging Legal Battle Over Video Game Streaming Rights*, Venture Beat (May 27, 2017), https://venturebeat.com/2017/05/27/the-emerging-legal-battle-over-video-game-streaming-rights.

1235. Aaron Swerdlow, *The Emerging Legal Battle Over Video Game Streaming Rights*, Venture Beat (May 27, 2017), https://venturebeat.com/2017/05/27/the-emerging-legal-battle-over-video-game-streaming-rights.

1236. Dave Tach, *Nintendo's New Affiliate Program Will Split YouTube ad Revenue with Proactive Users*, Polygon (May 27, 2014), https://www.polygon.com/2014/5/27/5754560/nintendo-youtube-affiliate-program; See also Jamie Ward, *Nintendo Planning YouTube Affiliate Program*, Nintendo Enthusiast

(May 27, 2014), https://www.nintendoenthusiast.com/nintendo-planning-youtube-affiliate-program.

1237. Charlie Hall, *Overwatch and Other Blizzard Games Can Now Stream Natively to Facebook*, Polygon (Aug. 26, 2016), https://www.polygon.com/2016/8/26/12662160/blizzard-streaming-live-overwatch-hearthstone-twitch; See also Andrew Webster, *You Can Now Stream Any Blizzard Game Live on Facebook*, The Verge (Aug. 26, 2016), https://www.theverge.com/2016/8/26/12661276/blizzard-facebook-live-streaming-launch.

1238. *Id.*; See Andy Chalk, *Facebook Logins and Livestreaming Are Coming to Blizzard Games*, P.C. Gamer (Jun. 6, 2016), https://www.pcgamer.com/facebook-integration-is-coming-to-overwatch-wow-and-other-blizzard-games.

1239. Aaron Swerdlow, *The Emerging Legal Battle Over Video Game Streaming Rights*, Venture Beat (May 27, 2017), https://venturebeat.com/2017/05/27/the-emerging-legal-battle-over-video-game-streaming-rights; See also Seth Northrop and Li Zhu, *Legal Streaming: Build Your Audience without Getting GG'ed*, Tech Crunch (Nov. 28, 2015), https://techcrunch.com/2015/11/28/legal-streaming-build-your-audience-without-getting-gged.

1240. Hongyu Chen, *Douyu Acquires Exclusive Chinese Streaming Rights for WESG*, The Esports Observer (Nov. 20, 2019), https://esportsobserver.com/douyu-wesg-2019-2020.

1241. Martin Ross, *Douyu Secures Blast Premier Streaming Rights in China*, Sport Business (Jun. 2, 2020), https://www.sportbusiness.com/news/douyu-secures-blast-premier-streaming-rights-in-china.

1242. J.P. Morgan, *The Supercharged World of Esports*, https://www.jpmorgan.com/global/research/esports (last visited Jul. 25, 2020); See also Steam, *Valve Corporation—Limited Game Tournament Licenses*, https://store.steampowered.com/tourney/limited_license (last visited Jul. 25, 2020).

1243. Max Miceli, *How the Franchising Model Shook Up North American Esports in 2018*, The Esports Observer (Jan. 28, 2019), https://esportsobserver.com/franchising-north-america-2018.

1244. Alan Bester, *Valve Must Solve Two Dota 2 Pro Circuit Problems*, ESPN (Nov. 30, 2017), https://www.espn.com/esports/story/_/id/21622636/valve-solve-two-dota-2-pro-circuit-problems; See also Steam, *Valve Corporation—Limited Game Tournament Licenses*, https://store.steampowered.com/tourney/limited_license (last visited Jul. 25, 2020); See also Riot Games, *Legal Jibber Jabber*, https://www.riotgames.com/en/legal (last visited Jul. 25, 2020).

1245. Paul 'Redeye' Chaloner, *This is Esports (and How to Spell it)*, 228 (Bloomsbury Sport 2020); See also Jeff Grubb, *Teamfight Tactics Reaches 4.5 Million Installs on Mobile*, Venture Beat (Mar. 31, 2020), https://venturebeat.com/2020/03/31/teamfight-tactics-reaches-4-5-million-installs-on-mobile.

1246. *Evolution of Mobile Esports for the Mass Market* (Niko Partners, China), Aug. 2019, at 4.

1247. Eva Martinello, *PUBG Mobile to Receive Huge Esports Push in 2020*, Esports Insider (Dec. 6, 2019), https://esportsinsider.com/2019/12/pubg-mobile-2020-plans; See also Shounak Sengupta, *PUBG MOBILE Under Scrutiny in India*, The Esports Observer (Jul. 28, 2020), https://esports

observer.com/pubg-mobile-scrutiny-india; See also Dean Takahashi, *How Latin American Esports is Poised for Growth*, Venture Beat (Oct. 6, 2019), https://venturebeat.com/2019/10/06/how-latin-american-esports-is-poised-for-growth.

1248. *Evolution of Mobile Esports for the Mass Market* (Niko Partners, China), Aug. 2019, at 4; See also Eva Martinello, *The Biggest Competitive Mobile Games of 2019*, Dot Esports (Dec. 30, 2019), https://dotesports.com/mobile/news/the-biggest-competitive-mobile-games-of-2019.

1249. *Evolution of Mobile Esports for the Mass Market* (Niko Partners, China), Aug. 2019, at 4; See also Trent Murray, *Editor's Picks: The Top 5 Rising Mobile Esports of 2020*, The Esports Observer (Dec. 27, 2019), https://esportsobserver.com/mobile-esports-picks-2020; See also Wasif Ahmed, *Free Fire Beats PUBG Mobile to Become the Most Downloaded Mobile Game of 2019*, Dot Esports (Dec. 17, 2019), https://dotesports.com/mobile/news/free-fire-beats-pubg-mobile-to-become-the-most-downloaded-mobile-game-of-2019.

1250. Mel Hawthorne, *Mobile Esports Revenue: The Rise of Esports on Mobile*, Esports.net (Aug. 30, 2018), https://www.esports.net/news/industry/mobile-esports-revenue.

1251. Wasif Ahmed, *Clash Royale Players Have Reportedly Spent Over $3 Billion to Date*, Dot Esports (Jul. 16, 2020), https://dotesports.com/mobile/news/clash-royale-players-have-reportedly-spent-over-3-billion-to-date; See also Jon Jordan, *Marvel Contest of Champions is Kabam's Fastest Game to $100 Million Revenue*, Pocket Gamer.biz (Jul. 30, 2015), https://www.pocketgamer.biz/news/61689/marvel-contest-of-champions-100-million; Parkes Ousley, *MARVEL Contest of Champions Summoner Showdown Tournament is Back*, Inven Global (Jul. 27, 2020), https://www.invenglobal.com/articles/11780/marvel-contest-of-champions-summoner-showdown-tournament-is-back.

1252. Wasif Ahmed, *Everything You Need to Know about the PUBG Mobile Club Open Fall Split 2020*, Dot Esports (Jul, 19, 2020), https://dotesports.com/news/everything-you-need-to-know-about-the-pubg-mobile-club-open-fall-split-2020.

1253. Ferguson Mitchell, *Esports Essentials: Mobile Esports Are Here to Stay*, The Esports Observer (Oct. 1, 2018), https://esportsobserver.com/mobile-esports-explainer.

1254. Matthew Forde, *Call of Duty: Mobile Has Best Launch Quarter for a Mobile Game Since Pokemon GO*, PocketGamer.Biz (Jan. 15, 2020), https://www.pocketgamer.biz/asia/news/72357/call-of-duty-mobile-has-best-launch-quarter-since-pokemon-go; See also Wasif Ahmed, *Report*: *PUBG Mobile Passes $1.5 Billion in Lifetime Revenue*, Dot Esports (Dec. 13, 2019), https://dotesports.com/news/report-pubg-mobile-passes-1-5-billion-in-lifetime-revenue.

1255. *Id.*

1256. PUBG (@EsportsPUBGM), Twitter (Jul. 2019), https://twitter.com/EsportsPUBGM; Kevin Hitt, *Tencent Announces $5M in Prize Pool Money for 2020 PUBG Mobile Ecosystem*, The Esports Observer (Dec. 3, 2019), https://esportsobserver.com/pubg-mobile-pro-league-2020.

1257. Wasif Ahmed, *FaZe Clan Signs PUBG Mobile Roster*, Dot Esports (Jan. 11, 2020), https://dotesports.com/news/faze-clan-signs-pubg-mobile-roster.

1258. Adam Fitch, *Spacestation Mobile Launches with Ash and Powerbang*, Esports Insider (Oct. 24, 2019), https://esportsinsider.com/2019/10/spacestation-mobile-launch.

1259. Andrew Hayward, *Fnatic Planning Facility in India after Acquiring PUBG Mobile Team*, The Esports Observer (Oct. 18, 2019), https://esportsobserver.com/fnatic-india-pubg-mobile.

1260. Brawl Stars, *Brawl Stars Championship*, https://esports.brawlstars.com (last visited Mar. 3, 2020).

1261. Clash Royale Esports, *Clash Royale League*, https://esports.clashroyale.com (last visited Mar. 3, 2020); See also Wasif Ahmed, *Clash Royale League World Finals 2020 Will Be Held in Shanghai*, Dot Esports (Jul, 29, 2020), https://dotesports.com/mobile/news/clash-royale-league-world-finals-2020-will-be-held-in-shanghai.

1262. Id.; See also Clash Royale Esports (@ESPORTSROYALEEN), Twitter (Jul. 29, 220, 1:02am), https://twitter.com/EsportsRoyaleEN/status/1288339189008719872.

1263. Shounak Sengupta, *PUBG MOBILE World League Announces Qualcomm Technologies as New Sponsor*, The Esports Observer (Jul. 30, 2020), https://esportsobserver.com/pubg-mobile-world-league-qualcomm.

1264. Shounak Sengupta, *Indian PUBG MOBILE Team Megastars Announce Exclusive Streaming Partnership with Nimo TV*, The Esports Observer (Jul. 7, 2020), https://esportsobserver.com/megastars-signs-exclusive-streaming-deal.

1265. Adam Fitch, *DreamHack Mobile Series Taps Samsung as Presenting Partner*, Esports Insider (May 28, 2019), https://esportsinsider.com/2019/05/dreamhack-mobile-series-samsung.

1266. ELEAGUE, *ELEAGUE to Televise Best Matches from 2019 Clash Royale League World Finals*, https://www.eleague.com/clash-royale-league-2019/news/eleague-supercell-partnership (last visited Mar. 3, 2020).

1267. Adam Stern, *Turner Sports Signs Deal with Supercell for Clash Royale League Ad Inventory, Broadcasting Rights*, The Esports Observer (Dec. 19, 2019), https://esportsobserver.com/turner-supercell-clash-royale; See also Paul 'Redeye' Chaloner, *This is Esports (and How to Spell it)*, 225 (Bloomsbury Sport 2020).

1268. *Id.*

1269. *Evolution of Mobile Esports for the Mass Market* (Niko Partners, China), Aug. 2019, at 40; See also Trent Murray, *Arena of Valor Pro League Returns for Third Season with $200K Prize Pool*, The Esports Observer (Jan. 17, 2019), https://esportsobserver.com/arena-of-valor-pro-league-2019.

1270. Hongyu Chen, *Honor of Kings World Champion Cup Plans, $2.36M Prize Pool Unveiled*, The Esports Observer (May 8, 2019), https://esportsobserver.com/honor-of-kings-world-champion-cup

1271. Hongyu Chen, *Honor of Kings World Champion Cup Plans, $2.36M Prize Pool Unveiled*, The Esports Observer (May 8, 2019), https://esportsobserver.com/honor-of-kings-world-champion-cup.

1272. Hongyu Chen, *Honor of Kings World Champion Cup to Feature $4.6M Prize*, The Esports Observer (Jul. 15, 2020), https://esportsobserver.com/china-esports-recap-july15-2020.

1273. ESL Arena of Valor (@ESLArenaofValor), Twitter (Mar. 2, 2018), https://twitter.com/ESLArenaofValor.

1274. Adam Fitch, *Super Evil Megacorp Steps Back from Vainglory Esports*, Esports Insider (May 23, 2019), https://esportsinsider.com/2019/05/super-evil-megacorp-vainglory-esports.
1275. Trent Murray, *Editor's Picks: The Top 5 Rising Mobile Esports of 2020*, The Esports Observer (Dec. 27, 2019), https://esportsobserver.com/mobile-esports-picks-2020.
1276. *Id.*
1277. *Id.*
1278. Bob Venero, *Why the Rise of Esports is Good for Schools, Students and Even Employers*, Forbes (Feb. 6, 2020), https://www.forbes.com/sites/forbestechcouncil/2020/02/06/why-the-rise-of-esports-is-good-for-schools-students-and-even-employers/#6da159396f50.
1279. Phil "DrPhill" Alexander, *Esports for Dummies*, 177 (Wiley 2020).
1280. Nat'l Fed. of State H.S. Associations, *Esports in High School*, https://www.nfhs.org/sports-resource-content/esports/ (last visited Mar. 3, 2020).
1281. Entertainment Software Association (ESA), *2019 Essential Facts about the Computer and Video Game Industry*, https://www.theesa.com/esa-research/2019-essential-facts-about-the-computer-and-video-game-industry/ (last visited Apr. 23, 2020).
1282. Nat'l Fed. of State H.S. Associations, *Esports in High School*, https://www.nfhs.org/sports-resource-content/esports/ (last visited Mar. 3, 2020).
1283. *Id.*; See also See also William Collis, *The Book of Esports*, 145 (Rosetta Books 2020).
1284. Adam Fitch, *NJCAA Reveals Creation of Esports Association*, Esports Insider (Sept. 13, 2019), https://esportsinsider.com/2019/09/njcaa-esports; See also NJCAA, *NJCAA Announces Creation of NJCAA Esports*, https://www.njcaa.org/general/2019-20/releases/20190909g3cocu (last visited Jul. 31, 2020).
1285. Matt Zalaznick, *Why Esports is Surging into Another School Year*, District Administration (Sept. 19, 2019), https://districtadministration.com/high-school-esports-middle-school-esports-surges.
1286. N.Y.S Ed. Dept., *Rensselaer City School District—Developing an Esports Program*, http://www.nysed.gov/edtech/rensselaer-city-school-district-developing-esports-program (last visited Mar. 3, 2020).
1287. *Id.*
1288. *Id.*
1289. Petula Dvorak, *Coming to a High School Near You: The Brave New World of Esports*, The Washington Post (Jul. 22, 2019), https://www.washingtonpost.com/local/coming-to-a-high-school-near-you-the-brave-new-world-of-esports/2019/07/22/331919d2-aca3-11e9-bc5c-e73b603e7f38_story.html; See also VHSL Athletics (@VHSL_), Twitter (Jul. 9, 2019), https://twitter.com/VHSL_/status/1148599311384682496.
1290. Alyssa Newcomb, *The World's First-Ever Middle School E-sports League Mixes Physical and Virtual Play*, Fortune (Jan. 31, 2019), https://fortune.com/2019/01/31/middle-school-e-sports-league.
1291. N.Y.S Ed. Dept., *Rensselaer City School District—Developing an Esports Program*, http://www.nysed.gov/edtech/rensselaer-city-school-district-developing-esports-program (last visited Mar. 3, 2020).
1292. *Id.*

1293. Video, *New Jersey Middle School Esports Team is 1st of Its Kind*, NBC 10 Philadelphia (Feb. 25, 2019), https://www.nbcphiladelphia.com/news/sports/middle-school-teaches-video-games_philadelphia/4473.
1294. Garden State Esports, *FAQ*, https://gsesports.org/faq (last visited Jul. 31, 2020); See also Garden State Esports (@GSESPORTSORG), Twitter (Nov. 2019), https://twitter.com/GSEsportsorg.
1295. Nat'l Fed. of State H.S. Associations, *Esports in High School*, https://www.nfhs.org/sports-resource-content/esports/ (last visited Mar. 3, 2020).
1296. *Id.*
1297. PlayVS, *How Does PlayVS Work?*, https://www.playvs.com/how-it-works (last visited Mar. 3, 2020).
1298. High School Esports League, *Our Mission*, https://www.highschoolesportsleague.com (last visited Mar. 3, 2020).
1299. North American Scholastic Esports Federation (N.A.S.E.F.), *Mission*, https://www.esportsfed.org (last visited Mar. 3, 2020).
1300. N.A.S.E.F., *Club Eligibility*, https://www.esportsfed.org/clubs/season-2/ (last visited Mar. 3, 2020).
1301. *Id.*
1302. Kevin Hitt, *PlayVS and Epic Games to Offer Fortnite Leagues to High Schools and Colleges*, The Esports Observer (Jan. 22, 2020), https://esportsobserver.com/playvs-epic-fortnite-leagues; See also Annie Pei, *20-Something Delane Parnell's PlayVS Expands by Locking in Deal with Tencent-Owned Riot Games*, CNBC (Feb. 13, 2020), https://www.cnbc.com/2020/02/13/playvs-expands-by-locking-in-deal-with-tencent-owned-riot-games.html.
1303. PlayVS, *League of Legends*, https://www.playvs.com/league-of-legends (last visited Mar. 3, 2020).
1304. Trent Murray, *PlayVS Adds Overwatch, Varsity/Rec League System to High School Esports Offering*, The Esports Observer (Jul. 28, 2020), https://esportsobserver.com/playvs-overwatch-varsity-league.
1305. Valerie Honeycutt Spears, *Fortnite Banned in KY High School E-sports: 'No Place for Shooter Games in Our School'*, Lexington Herald Leader (Jan. 27, 2020), https://www.kentucky.com/news/local/education/article239675978.html.
1306. Matt Zalaznick, *How Soft Skills Drive Virgina's High School Esports League*, District Administration (Nov. 4, 2019), https://districtadministration.com/high-school-esports-league-games-launched-virginia.
1307. Ben Hill, *Inaugural Indiana High School Esports Season Kicks Off this Fall*, NBC 13 WTHR (Oct. 14, 2019), https://www.wthr.com/article/inaugural-indiana-high-school-esports-season-kicks-fall.
1308. Colorado High School Esports League, *CHSAA—Esports, https://chsaanow.com/activities/esports/* (last visited Mar. 3, 2020).
1309. Wisconsin High School Esports Association, *WIHSEA—Esports, https://chsaanow.com/activities/esports/* (last visited Mar. 3, 2020).
1310. Kellen Beck, *Connecticut is the First State to Officially Welcome Esports into High Schools*, Mashable (Oct. 5, 2017), https://mashable.com/2017/10/05/connecticut-high-school-esports.
1311. Esports Ohio, *What is Esports Ohio?*, https://www.esportsohio.org (last visited Mar. 3, 2020).

1312. John Keilman, *Video Gaming: The Next High School Sport? Competitive Esports Gain Traction*, The Chicago Tribune (May 12, 2017), https://www.chicagotribune.com/sports/high-school/ct-esports-high-school-met-20170511-story.html.
1313. Blair Merson, *North Dakota High Schools to Form Esports League*, The Bismarck Tribune (Jul. 8, 2019), https://bismarcktribune.com/news/state-and-regional/north-dakota-high-schools-to-form-esports-league/article_58a26a79-650f-5f8a-8891-4a06143e1078.html.
1314. Jordan Rodenberger, *Over 60 Alaskan High Schools Register for Varsity eSports Program*, NBC 11 (Sept. 18, 2019), https://www.webcenter11.com/content/news/Over-60-Alaskan-High-Schools-register-for-varsity-eSports-program-560733881.html.
1315. California Interscholastic Federation, *CIF Esports Initiative*, https://www.cifstate.org/esports/index (last visited Mar. 4, 2020).
1316. *Id.*
1317. *Id.*
1318. David Hollingsworth, *HyperX partners with California Interscholastic Federation*, Esports Insider (Dec. 29, 2019), https://esportsinsider.com/2019/12/hyperx-california-interscholastic-federation.
1319. *Id.*
1320. Phil "DrPhill" Alexander, *Esports for Dummies*, 182–194 (Wiley 2020).
1321. University Interscholastic League, *Home Page*, https://www.uiltexas.org (last visited Jul. 31, 2020); See also Jason Parker, *Generation Esports Becomes Exclusive Sponsor of University Interscholastic League in Texas*, Esports Talk (Jul. 8, 2020), https://www.esportstalk.com/news/generation-esports-becomes-exclusive-sponsor-of-university-interscholastic-league-texas.
1322. Tobias M. Scholz, *eSports is Business: Management in the World of Competitive Gaming*, 70 (Palgrave Macmillan 2019).
1323. Oklahoma City University, *eSports OCU*, https://www.okcu.edu/artsci/enrichment/esports (last visited Mar. 4, 2020).
1324. University of Arizona, *Esports and Gaming at the University of Arizona*, https://arizona.campuslabs.com/engage/organization/arizonaesports (last visited Mar. 4, 2020).
1325. Lenore Sobota, *Illinois State University to Add Varsity Esports in Fall 2020*, The Pantagraph (Oct. 29, 2019), https://www.pantagraph.com/news/local/education/isu-to-add-varsity-esports-in-fall/article_c4b80aca-f210-53ee-888d-693bf90e8d14.html.
1326. Northwood University, *Esports at Northwood University*, https://www.northwood.edu/esports (last visited Jul. 31, 2020); See also Northwood University, *Northwood University to Offer Degree in Esports Management*, https://www.northwood.edu/news/northwood-university-to-offer-degree-in-esports-management (last visited Jul. 31, 2020).
1327. Lenore Sobota, *Illinois Wesleyan Adding More Esports; Lincoln College Competing, Too*, The Pantagraph (Oct. 21, 2019), https://www.pantagraph.com/news/local/education/illinois-wesleyan-adding-more-esports-lincoln-college-competing-too/article_feaa318e-91c4-532b-b827-f48b06339850.html.
1328. Jason Krell, *ASU Esports Seeks Official Program Status with More Institutional Support*, Cronkite News (Dec. 17, 2019), https://cronkitenews.azpbs.org/2019/12/17/asu-esports-program-seeks-support.

1329. Next College Student Athlete, *List of Colleges with Varsity Esports Programs*, https://www.ncsasports.org/college-esports-scholarships/varsity-esports (last visited Mar. 4, 2020); See also Phil "DrPhill" Alexander, *Esports for Dummies*, 182–194 (Wiley 2020).
1330. Full Sail University, *Full Sail Armada Collegiate Sports*, https://www.fullsail.edu/about/esports (last visited Apr. 23, 2020); Shenandoah University, *Esports*, https://www.su.edu/esports/ (last visited Oct. 22, 2020).
1331. Alex Andrejev, *This Small Pennsylvania School Wants to Be the Notre Dame of Esports*, The Washington Post (Oct. 16, 2019), https://www.washingtonpost.com/video-games/esports/2019/10/16/this-small-pennsylvania-school-wants-be-notre-dame-esports.
1332. Next College Student Athlete, *List of Colleges with Varsity Esports Programs*, https://www.ncsasports.org/college-esports-scholarships/varsity-esports (last visited Mar. 4, 2020); See also Frank Witsil, *Oakland University Adds Varsity Esports Team, Celebrates Value of Video Games*, Detroit Free Press (Dec. 6, 2019), https://www.freep.com/story/news/local/michigan/oakland/2019/12/06/esports-oakland-university-varsity/4352295002.
1333. ECAC Esports, *ECAC Esports Mission*, http://www.ecacesports.com/about (last visited Mar. 4, 2020).
1334. National Association of Collegiate Esports (N.A.C.E.), *Home Page*, https://nacesports.org (last visited Mar. 4, 2020).
1335. National Association of Collegiate Esports (N.A.C.E.), *About NACE*, https://nacesports.org/about (last visited Mar. 4, 2020).
1336. *Id.*
1337. N.A.C.E., *Esports*, https://nacesports.org/what-is-e-sports/games (last visited Mar. 4, 2020).
1338. Tespa, *What is Tespa?*, https://tespa.org/about,(last visited Mar. 4, 2020); See also Phil "DrPhill" Alexander, *Esports for Dummies*, 180 (Wiley 2020).
1339. Tespa, *Compete—Tespa*, https://tespa.org/compete (last visited Mar. 4, 2020).
1340. Collegiate Starleague, *CSL*, https://cstarleague.com (last visited Mar. 4, 2020).
1341. Collegiate Starleague, *What is CSL?*, https://cstarleague.com/about (last visited Mar. 4, 2020).
1342. Collegiate Starleague, *CSL Announces Official Partnership with Dreamhack*, https://cstarleague.com/lol/news_articles/1106 (last visited Mar. 4, 2020).
1343. Gamepress, *Collegiate StarLeague's 2020 Grand Finals Winners Announced*, Gamasutra (Jun. 4, 2020), https://www.gamasutra.com/view/pressreleases/364203/Collegiate_StarLeagues_2020_Grand_Finals_Winners_Announced.php.
1344. Riot Games, *University League of Legends*, https://ulol.na.leagueoflegends.com (last visited Mar. 4, 2020).
1345. Riot Games, *2019 League of Legends College Championship*, https://nexus.leagueoflegends.com/en-us/2019/05/2019-league-of-legends-college-championship (last visited Mar. 4, 2020); See also Riot Games, *University League of Legends*, https://ulol.na.leagueoflegends.com (last visited Mar. 4, 2020).
1346. Riot Games, *What is College LOL*, https://ulol.na.leagueoflegends.com/what-is-college-lol (last visited Mar. 4, 2020).

1347. ESPN, *Riot Outlines Changes for College League of Legends 2020 Season*, ESPN (Oct. 3, 2019), https://www.espn.com/esports/story/_/id/27761433/riot-outlines-changes-college-league-legends-2020-season.
1348. SVG Staff, *First-Ever ESPN Collegiate Esports Championship Finalizes Participating Schools*, SVG (May 1, 2019), https://www.sportsvideo.org/2019/05/01/first-ever-espn-collegiate-esports-championship-finalizes-participating-schools.
1349. Associated Press, *Colleges Are Starting Degrees in Esports, with $36,000 Programs*, CBS News (Oct. 1, 2019), https://www.cbsnews.com/news/college-esports-universities-launch-degrees-in-esports.
1350. Twitch.tv, *Students*, https://www.twitch.tv/p/students (last visited Mar. 4, 2020).
1351. *Id.*
1352. *Id.*
1353. *Id.*
1354. Collegiate Starleague, *Prime Examples: Twitch Student and Collegiate Progress*, https://cstarleague.com/ow/news_articles/672 (last visited Mar. 4, 2020); See also Twitch.tv, *Students*, https://www.twitch.tv/p/students (last visited Mar. 4, 2020).
1355. Collegiate Starleague, *Prime Examples: Twitch Student and Collegiate Progress*, https://cstarleague.com/ow/news_articles/672 (last visited Mar. 4, 2020); See also Twitch Student (@TwitchStudent), Twitter (Jul. 30, 2017), https://twitter.com/twitchstudent.
1356. Ann Smajstrla, *Twitch is Helping to Create an Esports League for HBCUs*, Engadget (Jul. 30, 2020), https://www.engadget.com/twitch-nonprofit-hbcu-esports-league-140016892.html.
1357. TUES, *Torneio Universitário de e-Sports*, https://tuesport.com.br (last visited Mar. 4, 2020).
1358. S.G.N., *Student Gaming Network*, https://sgnw.fr (last visited Mar. 4, 2020).
1359. Amazon University Esports, *La Liga Interuniversitaria Esports*, https://universityesports.es (last visited Mar. 4, 2020).
1360. Amazon University Esports, *The NUEL—Home of UK University Esports*, https://thenuel.com (last visited Mar. 4, 2020).
1361. Irish Collegiate Esports, *Irish Collegiate Esports*, https://collegeesports.ie (last visited Mar. 4, 2020).
1362. Uniliga.gg, *University eSports Germany*, https://www.uniliga.gg (last visited Mar. 4, 2020).
1363. Uniliga.gg, *Uber uns—University eSports Germany*, https://www.uniliga.gg/about (last visited Mar. 4, 2020).
1364. Amazon University Esports, *Nace Amazon University Esports*, https://universityesports.es/noticias/nace-amazon-university-esports (last visited Mar. 4, 2020).
1365. Andrew Hayward, *Amazon University Esports Launches with GGTech and the Nuel*, Esports Insider (Feb. 3, 2020), https://esportsinsider.com/2020/02/amazon-university-esports-launches.
1366. National Student Esports (NSE), *Home Page*, https://www.nse.gg (last visited Jul. 31, 2020); See also GamesPress, *National Student Esports and Nintendo UK Announce the Launch of the Super Smash Bros. Ultimate*

University Championship, Gamasutra (Sept. 23, 2019), https://www.gamasutra.com/view/pressreleases/350954/National_Student_Esports_and_Nintendo_UK_Announc e_the_launch_of_the_Super_Smash_Bros_Ultimate_University_Championship.php.

1367. Jonno Nicholson, *Barclays Bolsters Esports Presence with NSE Sponsorship*, Esports Insider (Jun. 1, 2020), https://www.esportsinsider.com/2020/06/nse-barclays-partnership; See also Jonno Nicholson, *ESL, Intel, and NSE Launch FutureGen Development Programme*, Esports Insider (Sept. 20, 2019), https://esportsinsider.com/2019/09/esl-nsl-intel-futuregen.

1368. Jonno Nicholson, *NSE Partners with Nintendo UK for Super Smash Bros. Events*, Esports Insider (Sept. 24, 2019), https://esportsinsider.com/2019/09/super-smash-bros-ultimate-university-championship.

1369. Graham Ashton, *Governing the Wild West—An Introduction to Esports Federations and Associations*, The Esports Observer (Jan. 3, 2019), https://esportsobserver.com/esports-federations-intro.

1370. Christopher Fam, *Represent Malaysia in eSports for the 2019 SEA Games*, The Star (Mar. 15, 2019), https://www.thestar.com.my/tech/tech-news/2019/03/15/esports-qualifying.

1371. Tobias M. Scholz, *eSports is Business: Management in the World of Competitive Gaming*, 74 (Palgrave Macmillan 2019); See also 2019 World Esports Ass'n, *Home Page*, http://www.wesa.gg (last visited Mar. 4, 2020).

1372. World Esports Ass'n, *WESA Members*, http://www.wesa.gg (last visited Mar. 4, 2020).

1373. World Esports Ass'n, *Rules and Regulations—WESA Code of Conduct Teams and Players*, http://www.wesa.gg/rr/rules-and-regulations (last visited Mar. 4, 2020).

1374. World Esports Ass'n, *Code of Conduct and Compliance for Teams and Players—Section 1.1*, at 1 (Dec. 2017), http://www.wesa.gg/wp-content/uploads/2019/05/WESA-Code-of-Conduct-Teams-and-Players-Final-03052019-1.pdf.

1375. World Esports Ass'n, *WESA to Approve Pro League License Transfer between Optic and MIBR*, http://www.wesa.gg/2018/09/17/wesa-to-approve-pro-league-license-transfer-between-optic-and-mibr (last visited Mar. 4, 2020).

1376. World Esports Consortium, *Global Esports—What IS WESCO?*, https://wescoesport.com/portal/who-we-are/what-is-wesco (last visited Mar. 4, 2020).

1377. Tobias M. Scholz, *eSports is Business: Management in the World of Competitive Gaming*, 74 (Palgrave Macmillan 2019); See also International e-Sports Federation, *About IESF*, https://www.ie-sf.org/iesf (last visited Mar. 4, 2020).

1378. T.L. Taylor, *Raising the Stakes: E-Sports and the Professionalization of Computer Gaming*, 174 (The MIT Press 2012); See also International e-Sports Federation, *Member Nations*, https://www.ie-sf.org/about/#member-nations (last visited Mar. 4, 2020).

1379. International e-Sports Federation, *IESF Grows to a Record-Breaking 72-Nation Count as Five New Countries Join as Members*, https://ie-sf.org/news/4629 (last visited Jul. 31, 2020).

1380. Andy Chalk, *Esports Integrity Coalition Launches in the UK*, P.C. Gamer (Jul. 5, 2016), https://www.pcgamer.com/esports-integrity-coalition-launc

hes-in-the-uk; See also Thiemo Bräutigam, *Esports Watchdog Group ESIC Launches*, Dot Esports (Feb. 7, 2017), https://dotesports.com/business/new s/esports-integrity-coalition-4694.

1381. ESIC, *ESIC Announces Introduction of Talent Agent Regulations*, https://es ic.gg/esic-announces-introduction-of-talent-agent-regulations (last visited Jul. 31, 2020); See also Brandon Brathwaite, *Esports Integrity Coalition Regulations Go into Effect for Superliga Orange*, The Esports Observer (Jul. 16, 2018), https://esportsobserver.com/esic-superliga-orange; Kevin Hitt, *Esports Integrity Commission Sanctions 37 CS:GO Coaches in Cheating Scandal*, The Esports Observer (Sept. 28, 2020), https://esportsobserver.c om/esic-sanctions-csgo-coaches/ .

1382. Asian Electronic Sports Federation, *Recognised Members*, https://www.aesf .com/en/Members/Recognised-Members.html (last visited Mar. 4, 2020).

1383. Asian Electronic Sports Federation, *Who is AESF*?, https://www.aesf.com/ en/About-Us/Who-Is-Aesf.html (last visited Mar. 4, 2020).

1384. Graham Ashton, *European Esports Federation to Form with 12 National Members*, The Esports Observer (Apr. 18, 2019), https://esportsobserver.c om/european-esports-federation-formed.

1385. *Id.*; See also Esports Europe, *Esports Europe—An Esports Vision for Europe*, https://esportseurope.org/ (last visited Mar. 4, 2020).

1386. Esports Europe, *The Berlin Declaration—An Esports Vision for Europe*, at 1 (Apr. 10, 2019), https://esportseurope.org/wp-content/uploads/sites/3/20 19/04/The-Berlin-Declaration-An-Esports-Vision-for-Europe.pdf.

1387. *Id.*

1388. Esports Europe, *Esports Europe—An Esports Vision for Europe*, https:// esportseurope.org/ (last visited Mar. 4, 2020).

1389. Japanese Esports Union, *JESU—About Us*, https://jesu.or.jp/contents/un ion_summary (last visited Mar. 4, 2020).

1390. Cody Luongo, *ESI Gambling Report: Pro-Gaming Licenses and Esports in Japan*, Esports Insider (Mar. 2, 2018), https://esportsinsider.com/2018/03/ esi-gambling-report-pro-gaming-licenses-esports-japan.

1391. United States eSports Federation, *About Us*, http://www.esportsfederation .org/pages/about (last visited Mar. 4, 2020).

1392. United States eSports Federation, *Welcome*, http://www.esportsfederation .org (last visited Mar. 4, 2020).

1393. Claire Wanja, *Kenya Set to Launch E-Sports League by July 2019*, KBC Channel 1 (May 15, 2019), https://www.kbc.co.ke/kenya-set-to-launch-e-s ports-league-by-july-2019.

1394. Federación Nacional de Deportes Electrónicos México, *Welcome*, http:// www.fndem.mx (last visited Mar. 4, 2020).

1395. Graham Ashton, *Thailand Esports Federation Looks to dentsu x for Marketing Solutions*, The Esports Observer (Dec. 1, 2018), https://esportsobserver.c om/thailand-esports-dentsu.

1396. Adam Fitch, *Germany Introduces Dedicated Visa for Esports*, Esports Insider (Dec. 22, 2019), https://esportsinsider.com/2019/12/germany-esports-visa ; See also German Esports Federation (ESBD), *German Esports Federation ESBD Welcomes Gov't Plans to Grant Full Esports Visa to Pro Players*, https://es portbund.de/blog/2019/09/30/german-esports-federation-esbd-welcomes-go vt-plans-to-grant-full-esports-visa-to-pro-players (last visited Mar. 4, 2020).

1397. Medium.com, *Nico Besombes—National Esports Associations*, https://medium.com/@nicolas.besombes/national-esports-associations-e63862840f2a (last visited Mar. 4, 2020).
1398. Jeremy Ainsworth, *Sri Lanka Recognizes Esports as an Official Sport*, Esports Insider (Oct. 8, 2019), https://esportsinsider.com/2019/10/sri-lanka-recognises-esports.
1399. Chenglu Zhang, *The Chinese Government Recognizes Esports as a Profession*, Esports Insider (Feb. 13, 2019), https://esportsinsider.com/2019/02/the-chinese-government-recognises-esports-as-a-profession.
1400. International e-Sports Federation, *E-Sports Now a Full Member of Finnish Olympic Committee*, https://www.ie-sf.org/news/e-sports-now-a-full-member-of-finnish-olympic-committee (last visited Mar. 4, 2020).
1401. Adam Fitch, *Esports Integrity Coalition Rebrands to Esports Integrity Commission*, Esports Insider (Sept. 17, 2019), https://esportsinsider.com/2019/09/esports-integrity-commission-rebrand.
1402. World Anti-Doping Agency (WADA), *Welcome*, https://www.wada-ama.org/ (last visited Mar. 4, 2020).
1403. International Olympic Committee, *IOC—Who We Are*, https://www.olympic.org/the-ioc (last visited Mar. 4, 2020).
1404. International Olympic Committee, *Fight against Doping*, https://www.olympic.org/the-ioc (last visited Mar. 4, 2020).
1405. Phil "DrPhill" Alexander, *Esports for Dummies*, 222 (Wiley 2020).
1406. Noah Smith, *Debate: What Does a Fair Esports Contract Look Like? It's Complicated.*, The Washington Post (Jun. 18, 2019), https://www.washingtonpost.com/sports/2019/06/18/debate-what-does-fair-esports-contract-look-like-its-complicated.
1407. Nathan Grayson, *Popular Twitch Streamer Tfue's Contract with FaZe Leaks as Public Dispute Rages On*, Kotaku (May 23, 2019), https://kotaku.com/popular-twitch-streamer-tfues-contract-with-faze-leaks-1834987080.
1408. Jordan Crook, *Pro gamer Tfue Files Lawsuit against Esports Org Over 'Grossly Oppressive' Contract*, Tech Crunch (May 21, 2019), https://techcrunch.com/2019/05/21/pro-gamer-tfue-files-lawsuit-against-esports-org-over-grossly-oppressive-contract; Jessica Conditt, *FaZe and Tfue have settled their lawsuit and said goodbye*, Engadget (Aug. 26, 2020), https://www.engadget.com/tfue-faze-lawsuit-settled-224753030.html.
1409. Nicole Carpenter, *Heroes of the Storm Players File Lawsuit against Naventic Owner for $50,000 in Missed Payments*, Dot Esports (Jan. 18, 2019), https://dotesports.com/general/news/heroes-of-the-storm-players-file-lawsuit-against-naventic-owner-for-50000-in-missed-payments.
1410. THR Staff and Alison Brower, *The Hollywood Reporter 100: The Most Powerful People in Entertainment 2018*, The Hollywood Reporter (Sept. 20, 2018), https://www.hollywoodreporter.com/lists/thr-100-hollywood-reporters-powerful-people-entertainment-1142979.
1411. Justin M. Jacobson, *OPINION: Why Every Professional Gamer Needs a Team (of Professionals)*, The Esports Observer (May 15, 2018), https://esportsobserver.com/gamers-need-a-team.
1412. Tobias M. Scholz, *eSports is Business: Management in the World of Competitive Gaming*, 71 (Palgrave Macmillan 2019).

1413. Kimberly Buffington, *As Investment in Esports Grows, Insurance Coverage Must Keep Up*, Pillsbury (Aug. 12, 2019, https://www.policyholderpulse.com/esports-insurance-coverage; See also Hamza Ali, *Game On: Why Wealth Firms Are Targeting Esports Clients*, Citywire (May 24, 2018), https://citywire.co.uk/wealth-manager/news/game-on-why-wealth-firms-are-targeting-esports-clients/a1122631.

1414. Sarah Leboeuf, *Why a Major Hollywood Talent Agency is Betting Big on Gaming Influencers*, Variety (May 22, 2019), https://variety.com/2019/gaming/features/uta-esports-influencers-1203223400; See also Jason Fanelli, *Former 'Call of Duty' E-sports Coach Launches Talent Agency*, The Hollywood Reporter (Sept. 4, 2019), https://www.hollywoodreporter.com/news/call-duty-esports-coach-launches-talent-agency-1236509.

1415. H.B. Duran, *From Trick Shots to Talk Shows: The Rise of Talent Agencies in Esports*, The Esports Observer (Nov. 28, 2019), https://esportsobserver.com/talent-agencies-interview.

1416. Thiemo Bräutigam, *NiKo's Buyout Was around $500,000*, Dot Esports (Feb. 13, 2017), https://dotesports.com/business/news/niko-buyout-faze-clan-mousesports-breaks-csgo-record-4744.

1417. Jacob Wolf, *Sources: Cloud9 to Pay $1.5 Million Buyout for Dignitas Support Vulcan*, ESPN (Nov. 18, 2019), https://www.espn.com/esports/story/_/id/28109140/sources-cloud9-pay-15-million-buyout-dignitas-support-vulcan.

1418. Ross Deason, *G2 Reportedly Sets Staggering Buyout Price for Benches CS:GO Stars*, Dexerto (Jun. 26, 2018), https://www.dexerto.com/csgo/g2-reportedly-sets-staggering-buyout-price-for-benched-csgo-stars-107328.

1419. James B. Cutchin, *How to Be a Pro Gamer: A Glimpse Down the Esports Talent Pipeline*, L.A. Times (Oct. 25, 2019), https://www.latimes.com/business/story/2019-08-22/esports-how-to-go-pro.

1420. Jacob Wolf, *Dallas Fuel Suspend xQc for Anti-gay Slurs; Overwatch League Fines Player*, ESPN (Jan. 19, 2018), https://www.espn.com/esports/story/_/id/22156350/dallas-fuel-suspends-felix-xqc-lengyel-following-use-anti-gay-slurs-stream.

1421. Jacob Wolf, *No Response from Overwatch League to Taimou's Use of Gay Slurs on Stream*, ESPN (Mar. 4, 2018), https://www.espn.com/esports/story/_/id/22626466/despite-anti-gay-slurs-made-stream-timo-taimou-kettunen-faces-no-punishment-overwatch-league.

1422. Jacob Wolf, *xQc Released from Dallas Fuel after Receiving Second Overwatch League Suspension*, ESPN (Mar. 11, 2018), https://www.espn.com/esports/story/_/id/22727221/xqc-released-dallas-fuel-receiving-second-overwatch-league-suspension.

1423. Preston Byers, *Evolved Talent Agency Places CEO Ryan Morrison on Unpaid Leave*, investigates accusations of sexual harassment and other conduct, Dot Esports (Jun. 23, 2020), https://dotesports.com/general/news/evolved-talent-agency-places-ceo-ryan-morrison-on-unpaid-leave-investigates-accusations-of-sexual-harassment-and-other-conduct; See also Evolved Talent Agency (@EVOLVEDTALENT), Twitter (Jun. 23, 2020, 9:25pm), https://twitter.com/EvolvedTalent/status/1275601003249676288; See also Jacob Wolf and Ashley Kang, *Riot Korea Fines Griffin, Bans Team's Former Director and Coach from LCK*, ESPN (Nov. 20, 2019), https://www.espn.com/esports/story/_/id/28123613/riot-korea-fines-griffin-bans-team-former-director-coach-lck.

1424. Tobias Seck, *FINRA Fines Renegades CEO for Unauthorized Soliciting of Investments*, The Esports Observer, May 26, 2020, https://esportsobserver.com/finra-fines-renegades-ceo.

1425. Jason Fanelli, *Former 'Call of Duty' E-sports Coach Launches Talent Agency*, The Hollywood Reporter (Sept. 4, 2019), https://www.hollywoodreporter.com/news/call-duty-esports-coach-launches-talent-agency-1236509; See also Graham Ashton, *Former MAMMOTH Team Director Joins AZYT Global Talent*, The Esports Observer (May 18, 2020), https://esportsobserver.com/ahilleas-papantos-azyt-talent; Kevin Hitt, *Ford Models Enters Esports, Expands Global Talent Management Platform*, The Esports Observer (Aug. 11, 2020), https://esportsobserver.com/ford-models-enters-esports.

1426. Merriam Webster, *Influencer*, https://www.merriam-webster.com/dictionary/influencer (last visited Mar. 4, 2020).

1427. Dan Rys, *Inside the Gaming Collective that's Drawing Big-Time Music Investors—And Star Players*, Billboard (Jul. 24, 2020), https://www.billboard.com/articles/deep-dive/gaming-musics-next-big-play/9423526/inside-the-gaming-collective-thats-drawing-bigtime-music-investors-and-star-players; See also Kelly Cohen, *NBA 2K MVP Nidal Nasser Becomes First to Get Solo Endorsement*, ESPN (May 23, 2020), https://www.espn.com/esports/story/_/id/29213666/nba-2k-mvp-nidal-nasser-becomes-first-get-solo-endorsement.

1428. Everything after Z by Dictionary.com, *The Meteoric Rise of the Word "Influencer," https://www.dictionary.com/e/influencer* (last visited Mar. 4, 2020); See also Bloomberg News, *Instagram to Make it Clearer When Influencer Posts Are Paid Ads*, AdAge (Jun. 14, 2017), https://adage.com/article/digital/instagram-make-clearer-influencer-posts-paid-ads.

1429. Justin M. Jacobson, *OPINION: The Marketing Dilemma of the Esports Influencer*, The Esports Observer (Jul. 25, 2018), https://esportsobserver.com/marketing-esports-influencer.

1430. Adam Levy, *Facebook is Going after TikTok's Top Creative Talent*, The Motley Fool (Jul. 29. 2020), https://www.fool.com/investing/2020/07/29/facebook-going-after-tiktok-top-talent-reels.aspx; See also Matt Perez, *Top-Earning Video Gamers: The Ten Highest-Paid Players Pocketed More than $120 Million in 2019*, Forbes (Jan. 29, 2020), https://www.forbes.com/sites/mattperez/2020/01/29/top-earning-video-gamers-the-ten-highest-paid-players-pocketed-more-than-120-million-in-2019/#1dc713b4880b.

1431. Everything after Z by Dictionary.com, *The Meteoric Rise of the Word "Influencer," https://www.dictionary.com/e/influencer* (last visited Mar. 4, 2020).

1432. Federal Trade Commission (FTC), *What We Do*, https://www.ftc.gov/about-ftc/what-we-do (last visited Mar. 4, 2020).

1433. 15 U.S.C. § 45 (1914); 16 C. F. Part § 225.0(a)(2010); See also Federal Trade Commission (FTC), *Disclosures 101 for Social Media Influencers* (Nov. 2019), https://www.ftc.gov/sites/default/files/attachments/press-releases/ftc-publishes-final-guides-governing-endorsements-testimonials/091005revisedendorsementguides.pdf.

1434. 16 C. F. Part § 225.0(a)(2010); See also Federal Trade Commission (FTC), *Disclosures 101 for Social Media Influencers* (Nov. 2019), https://www.ftc.gov/sites/default/files/attachments/press-releases/ftc-publishes-final-guides-governing-endorsements-testimonials/091005revisedendorsementguides

.pdf; See also Ted Knutson, *Video Games Can Be a Gateway to Problem Gambling, FTC Warned*, Forbes (Aug. 8, 2019), https://www.forbes.com/sites/tedknutson/2019/08/08/video-games-can-be-a-gateway-to-problem-gambling-ftc-warned/#33c8011a978a.

1435. Federal Trade Commission (FTC), *FTC Releases Advertising Disclosures Guidance for Online Influencers*, https://www.ftc.gov/news-events/press-releases/2019/11/ftc-releases-advertising-disclosures-guidance-online-influencers (last visited Mar. 4, 2020).

1436. Id.; See also Brian Bell, *Top CS: GO Streamer Sues Twitch Two Years after Being Suspended*, Paste (Feb. 20, 2018), https://www.pastemagazine.com/games/twitch/top-csgo-streamer-sues-twitch-two-years-after-bein.

1437. 16 C. F. Part § 225.0(a) & (d) (2010); See also Federal Trade Commission (FTC), *Disclosures 101 for Social Media Influencers* (Nov. 2019), https://www.ftc.gov/sites/default/files/attachments/press-releases/ftc-publishes-final-guides-governing-endorsements-testimonials/091005revisedendorsementguides.pdf.

1438. 16 C. F. Part § 225.0(a) & (d) (2010); See also Federal Trade Commission (FTC), *Disclosures 101 for Social Media Influencers* (Nov. 2019), https://www.ftc.gov/sites/default/files/attachments/press-releases/ftc-publishes-final-guides-governing-endorsements-testimonials/091005revisedendorsementguides.pdf.

1439. Federal Trade Commission (FTC), *FTC Releases Advertising Disclosures Guidance for Online Influencers*, at 2, https://www.ftc.gov/news-events/press-releases/2019/11/ftc-releases-advertising-disclosures-guidance-online-influencers (last visited Mar. 4, 2020); See also Charlie Hall, *FTC Panel Reveals Troubling Relationship between Streamers and Loot Box Creators*, Polygon (Aug. 7, 2019), https://www.polygon.com/2019/8/7/20758974/ftc-loot-box-panel-streamer-publisher-sponsorships.

1440. Federal Trade Commission (FTC), *FTC Releases Advertising Disclosures Guidance for Online Influencers*, at 2, https://www.ftc.gov/news-events/press-releases/2019/11/ftc-releases-advertising-disclosures-guidance-online-influencers (last visited Mar. 4, 2020); See also Andy Smith, *YouTubers in Breach of FTC if They Fail to Disclose Sponsorships*, Tubular Insights (Oct. 16, 2014), https://tubularinsights.com/youtube-ftc-sponsorships.

1441. Federal Trade Commission (FTC), *FTC Releases Advertising Disclosures Guidance for Online Influencers*, at 2, https://www.ftc.gov/news-events/press-releases/2019/11/ftc-releases-advertising-disclosures-guidance-online-influencers (last visited Mar. 4, 2020).

1442. *Id.*

1443. Federal Trade Commission (FTC), *The FTC's Endorsement Guides: What People Are Asking*, https://www.ftc.gov/tips-advice/business-center/guidance/ftcs-endorsement-guides-what-people-are-asking (last visited Mar. 4, 2020).

1444. *Id.*; See also Sara Hawkins, *Are You Disclosing? What You Need to Know about FTC Rules and Social Media*, Social Media Examiner (Oct. 4, 2011), https://www.socialmediaexaminer.com/are-you-disclosing-what-you-need-to-know-about-ftc-rules-and-social-media.

1445. Federal Trade Commission (FTC), *Disclosures 101 for Social Media Influencers*, at 4 (Nov. 2019), https://www.ftc.gov/sites/default/files/attachments/press-releases/ftc-publishes-final-guides-governing-endorsements-testimonials/091005revisedendorsementguides.pdf.
1446. *Id.*; See also Robert Williams, *Study: Just 25% of Instagram Influencers Are Compliant with FTC Rules*, Mobile Marketer (Mar. 14, 2018), https://www.mobilemarketer.com/news/study-just-25-of-instagram-influencers-are-compliant-with-ftc-rules.
1447. *Id.*
1448. *Id.*
1449. *Id.*
1450. *Id.*
1451. Federal Trade Commission (FTC), *FTC and FDA Send Warning Letters to Companies Selling Flavored E-liquids about Social Media Endorsements without Health Warnings*, https://www.ftc.gov/news-events/press-releases/2019/06/ftc-fda-send-warning-letters-companies-selling-flavored-e-liquids (last visited Mar. 4, 2020); See also T.L. Stanley, *The First CBD Pro Sports Sponsorship Was a Huge Gamble*, AdWeek (Ju. 4, 2019), https://www.adweek.com/brand-marketing/the-first-cbd-pro-sports-sponsorship-was-a-huge-gamble.
1452. Brandoan A. Dorfman, *How Esports Gamers Are Using CBD to Increase Cognitive Responses*, Venture Beat (Dec. 7, 2018), https://venturebeat.com/2018/12/07/how-esports-gamers-are-using-cbd-to-increase-cognitive-responses.
1453. Federal Trade Commission (FTC), *Disclosures 101 for Social Media Influencers*, at 5 (Nov. 2019), https://www.ftc.gov/sites/default/files/attachments/press-releases/ftc-publishes-final-guides-governing-endorsements-testimonials/091005revisedendorsementguides.pdf.
1454. *Id.*
1455. *Id.*; See also Ari Lazarus, *Is that Post #Sponsored?*, FTC Consumer Information (Apr. 19, 2017), https://www.consumer.ftc.gov/blog/2017/04/post-sponsored.
1456. Federal Trade Commission (FTC), *Disclosures 101 for Social Media Influencers*, at 6 (Nov. 2019), https://www.ftc.gov/sites/default/files/attachments/press-releases/ftc-publishes-final-guides-governing-endorsements-testimonials/091005revisedendorsementguides.pdf.
1457. Federal Trade Commission (FTC), *The FTC's Endorsement Guides: What People Are Asking*, https://www.ftc.gov/tips-advice/business-center/guidance/ftcs-endorsement-guides-what-people-are-asking (last visited Mar. 4, 2020).
1458. Jessica Lindsay, *How to Find Out if People Have Paid for Twitter and Instagram Followers*, Metro UK (Jan. 29, 2018), https://metro.co.uk/2018/01/29/find-people-paid-twitter-instagram-followers-7270364.
1459. Nicholas Confessore, Gabriel J.X. Dance, Richard Harris, and Mark Hansen, *The Follower Factory*, New York Times (Jan. 27, 2018), https://www.nytimes.com/interactive/2018/01/27/technology/social-media-bots.html.
1460. Federal Trade Commission (FTC), *Fake Followers: A Social Media Hoax*, https://www.consumer.ftc.gov/blog/2019/10/fake-followers-social-media-hoax (last visited Mar. 4, 2020).

1461. Andrew Hutchinson, *FTC Rules that Selling Followers and Likes is Illegal, Along with Posting Fake Reviews*, Social Media Today (Oct. 23, 2019), https://www.socialmediatoday.com/news/ftc-rules-that-selling-followers-and-likes-is-illegal-along-with-posting-f.

1462. Nicholas Confessore, Gabriel J.X. Dance, Richard Harris, and Mark Hansen, *The Follower Factory*, New York Times (Jan. 27, 2018), https://www.nytimes.com/interactive/2018/01/27/technology/social-media-bots.html.

1463. Federal Trade Commission (FTC), *Devumi, Owner and CEO Settle FTC Charges They Sold Fake Indicators of Social Media Influence; Cosmetics Firm Sunday Riley, CEO Settle FTC Charges that Employees Posted Fake Online Reviews at CEO's Direction*, https://www.ftc.gov/news-events/press-releases/2019/10/devumi-owner-ceo-settle-ftc-charges-they-sold-fake-indicators (last visited Mar. 4, 2020); See also Federal Trade Commission (FTC), *Federal Trade Commission v. Devumi, LLC,* et. Al., Case No. 9:19-cv-81419-RKA, https://www.ftc.gov/system/files/documents/cases/devumi_settlement.pdf (Oct. 18, 2019).

1464. Federal Trade Commission (FTC), *Devumi, Owner and CEO Settle FTC Charges They Sold Fake Indicators of Social Media Influence; Cosmetics Firm Sunday Riley, CEO Settle FTC Charges that Employees Posted Fake Online Reviews at CEO's Direction*, https://www.ftc.gov/news-events/press-releases/2019/10/devumi-owner-ceo-settle-ftc-charges-they-sold-fake-indicators (last visited Mar. 4, 2020); See also Federal Trade Commission (FTC), *Federal Trade Commission v. Devumi, LLC,* et. Al., Case No. 9:19-cv-81419-RKA, https://www.ftc.gov/system/files/documents/cases/devumi_settlement.pdf (Oct. 18, 2019).

1465. Federal Trade Commission (FTC), *Devumi, Owner and CEO Settle FTC Charges They Sold Fake Indicators of Social Media Influence; Cosmetics Firm Sunday Riley, CEO Settle FTC Charges that Employees Posted Fake Online Reviews at CEO's Direction*, https://www.ftc.gov/news-events/press-releases/2019/10/devumi-owner-ceo-settle-ftc-charges-they-sold-fake-indicators (last visited Mar. 4, 2020); See also Federal Trade Commission (FTC), *Federal Trade Commission v. Devumi, LLC,* et. Al., Case No. 9:19-cv-81419-RKA, https://www.ftc.gov/system/files/documents/cases/devumi_settlement.pdf (Oct. 18, 2019).

1466. David Lazarus, *Column: Video Games Are Thriving Amid COVID-19—And Experts Say that's a Good Thing*, L.A. Times (Jun. 16, 2020), https://www.latimes.com/business/story/2020-06-16/column-coronavirus-video-games; See also Billboard Staff, *Here's How Celebs Are Helping Out During the Coronavirus Pandemic*, Billboard (Jun. 30, 2020), https://www.billboard.com/articles/news/9337427/stars-giving-back-coronavirus-pandemic.

1467. Cherie Hu, *Why the Intersection of Music and Esports is Bigger Business than Ever*, Forbes (Oct. 25, 2018), https://www.forbes.com/sites/cheriehu/2018/10/25/why-the-intersection-of-music-and-esports-is-bigger-business-than-ever; See also Shawn Krest, *Duke NBA Alumni Beats UNC, Kentucky in Call of Duty Tournament*, Sports Illustrated (Apr. 28, 2020), https://www.si.com/college/duke/basketball/duke-nba-alumni-beats-unc-call-of-duty; Charu Sinha, *AOC Plays Among Us in One of Twitch's Most Watched Streams Ever*, Vulture (Oct. 21, 2020), https://www.vulture.com/2020/10/aoc-plays-among-us-in-one-of-twitchs-most-watched-streams.html.

1468. Nicole Carpenter, *15 Celebrities and Sports Pros that Stream on Twitch*, Dot Esports (Jan. 23, 2017), https://dotesports.com/culture/news/15-celebrities-and-sports-pros-that-stream-on-twitch-4506; Steve McCaskill, *Twitch Continues Push into Traditional Sports with Dedicated Channel Launch*, Forbes (Jul. 23, 2020), https://www.forbes.com/sites/stevemccaskill/2020/07/23/twitch-continues-push-into-traditional-sports-with-dedicated-channel-launch; See also Mike D. Sykes, II, *Karl-Anthony Towns is Participating in the Call of Duty League's Celebrity Tournament*, For The Win (Jan. 16, 2020),https://ftw.usatoday.com/2020/01/karl-anthony-towns-is-participating-in-the-call-of-duty-leagues-celebrity-tournament; Jamie Cooper, *Aerial Powers Is Hosting An All-Female 'NBA 2K' Tournament Called 'Powerz Up,'* Uproxx (Jul. 8, 2020) https://uproxx.com/dimemag/aerial-powers-all-female-nba-2k-tournament-powerz-up.

1469. The Esports Observer, *Luminosity Gaming Signs Exclusive Partnership with Universal Music Canada*, The Esports Observer (Jul. 13, 2018), https://esportsobserver.com/luminosity-gaming-universal-music-canada; See also Adam Fitch, *ESL Launching Record Label with Universal Music Group Europe*, Esports Insider (Aug. 22, 2018), https://esportsinsider.com/2018/08/esl-universal-music-group-europe; Melany Moncav, *ESL Introduced New Label Enter Records*, Esports Insider (Oct. 5, 2018), https://esportsinsider.com/2018/10/esl-introduced-new-label-enter-records; Adam Fitch, *Riot Games Adds Warner Music and Tchibo as LEC Sponsors*, Esports Insider (Jun. 7, 2019), https://esportsinsider.com/2019/06/riot-games-warner-music-tchibo-lec.

1470. Business Wire, *NBA 2K21 Sets the Gold Standard for Music with Its Definitive In-Game Soundtrack Developed in Partnership with UnitedMasters*, The Daily Times (Jul. 27, 2020), https://www.thedailytimes.com/business/nba-2k21-sets-the-gold-standard-for-music-with-its-definitive-in-game-soundtrack-developed/article_3be36776-ce5b-50ec-8286-8bd2ba2f9951.html.

1471. David Greenwald, *Jay-Z Scores U2, Kanye West for 'NBA 2K13' Soundtrack*, Billboard (Jul. 13, 2012), https://www.billboard.com/articles/news/480678/jay-z-scores-u2-kanye-west-for-nba-2k13-soundtrack.

1472. Associated Press, *Pharrell Does Music for 'NBA 2K15,'* Billboard (Aug. 12, 2014), https://www.espn.com/nba/story/_/id/11342592/pharrell-curates-soundtrack-nba-2k15-game.

1473. Slam Staff, *DJ Khaled, DJ Mustard and DJ Premier to Collaborate on NBA 2K16 Soundtrack*, Slam (Jul. 9, 2015), https://www.slamonline.com/archives/dj-khaled-dj-mustard-and-dj-premier-to-collaborate-on-nba-2k16-soundtrack.

1474. Brian Mazique, *'NBA 2K20' Soundtrack Announced along with New Talent Search Initiative for New Artists*, Forbes (Jul. 20, 2019), https://www.forbes.com/sites/brianmazique/2019/07/20/nba-2k20-soundtrack-announced-along-with-new-talent-search-initiative-for-new-artists.

1475. Elton Jones, *NBA 2K20: Full Soundtrack and Artists List*, Heavy (Jan. 28, 2020), https://heavy.com/games/2019/07/nba-2k20-full-soundtrack-list-lineup; See also Tatian Cirisano, *UnitedMasters Inks Deal to Help Curate NBA 2K20 Soundtrack*, Billboard (Jul. 20, 2019), https://www.billboard.com/articles/business/8520405/unitedmasters-curate-nba-2k20-soundtrack.

1476. Brian Mazique, *NBA 2K21 Soundtrack Revealed with Heavy Damian Lillard Influence*, Forbes (Jul. 27, 2020), https://www.forbes.com/sites/brianmazique/2020/07/27/nba-2k21-soundtrack-revealed-with-heavy-damian-lillard-influence; See also James Wright, *NBA 2K21 Music Revealed Including Two New Tracks from Cover Star Damian Lillard*, Daily Star (Jul. 27, 2020), https://www.dailystar.co.uk/tech/gaming/nba-2k21-music-revealed-including-22424474.

1477. Melinda Newman, *ESports Collective FaZe Clan Partners with Culture Platform NTWRK*, Billboard (Apr. 9, 2020), https://www.billboard.com/articles/business/9355615/faze-clan-ntwrk-partners-jimmy-iovine.

1478. Trilby Beresford, *FaZe Clan Execs Form New Gaming Organization with Focus on Inclusion*, The Hollywood Reporter (Jul. 16, 2020), https://www.hollywoodreporter.com/news/faze-clan-execs-form-new-gaming-organization-1303488.

1479. Annie Pei, *Gaming Industry Veterans Raise $17 Million to Launch VENN, an Esports Network*, CNBC (Sept. 17, 2019), https://www.cnbc.com/2019/09/17/venn-raises-17-million-to-launch-an-esports-network.html; See also VENN, *About*, https://www.venn.tv/#about-index (last visited Jul. 31, 2020); Mike Stubbs, *Gaming Network VENN Secures $26M Series A Funding, Hires MTV Exec*, Forbes (Oct. 20, 2020), https://www.forbes.com/sites/mikestubbs/2020/10/20/gaming-network-venn-secures-26m-series-a-funding-hires-mtv-exec/#58c634b8559e; Ian Walker, *G4 Is Coming Back, Apparently*, Kotaku (Jul. 24, 2020), https://kotaku.com/g4-is-coming-back-apparently-1844499971.

1480. Seamus Byrne, *Melbourne Esports Open Reflects Growth and Current State of Australia's Esports Market*, The Esports Observer (Sept. 5, 2019), https://esportsobserver.com/melbourne-esports-open-recap; See also Rebekah Valentine, *Newzoo: Global Esports Market Will Exceed $1 Billion in 2019*, GamesIndustry.biz (Feb. 12, 2019), https://www.gamesindustry.biz/articles/2019-02-12-newzoo-global-esports-market-will-exceed-USD1-billion-in-2019; Dean Takahashi, *How Latin American Esports is Poised for Growth*, Venture Beat (Oct. 6, 2019), https://venturebeat.com/2019/10/06/how-latin-american-esports-is-poised-for-growth.

Index

D

H

I

Q

R

S

Taylor & Francis eBooks

www.taylorfrancis.com

A single destination for eBooks from Taylor & Francis with increased functionality and an improved user experience to meet the needs of our customers.

90,000+ eBooks of award-winning academic content in Humanities, Social Science, Science, Technology, Engineering, and Medical written by a global network of editors and authors.

TAYLOR & FRANCIS EBOOKS OFFERS:

A streamlined experience for our library customers

A single point of discovery for all of our eBook content

Improved search and discovery of content at both book and chapter level

REQUEST A FREE TRIAL

support@taylorfrancis.com